BLOOD TALK

BLOOD TALK

AMERICAN RACE MELODRAMA

AND THE

CULTURE OF THE OCCULT

⎯⎯◆⎯⎯

SUSAN GILLMAN

⎯⎯◆⎯⎯

THE UNIVERSITY OF CHICAGO PRESS

CHICAGO & LONDON

SUSAN GILLMAN is professor of literature and American studies at the
University of California, Santa Cruz. She is the author of *Dark Twins:
Imposture and Identity in Mark Twain's America,* also published by the
University of Chicago Press.

The University of Chicago Press, Chicago 60637
The University of Chicago Press, Ltd., London
© 2003 by The University of Chicago
All rights reserved. Published 2003
Printed in the United States of America
12 11 10 09 08 07 06 05 04 03   1 2 3 4 5

ISBN : 0-226-29389-0 (cloth)
ISBN : 0-226-29390-4 (paper)

Library of Congress Cataloging-in-Publication Data

Gillman, Susan Kay.
  Blood talk : American race melodrama and the culture of the occult /
Susan Gillman.
    p. cm.
  Includes bibliographical references (p.) and index.
  ISBN 0-226-29389-0 (cloth : alk. paper) — ISBN 0-226-29390-4 (pbk. :
alk. paper)
      1. American Literature—20th century—History and criticism.
  2. Race in literature. 3. Du Bois, W. E. B. (William Edward Burghardt),
  1868–1963—Political and social views. 4. Hopkins, Pauline E.
  (Pauline Elizabeth)—Political and social views. 5. Griggs, Sutton
  Elbert, 1872– —Political and social views. 6. American literature—
  19th century—History and criticism. 7. Dixon, Thomas, 1864–
  1946—Political and social views. 8. Twain, Mark, 1835–1910—
  Political and social views. 9. African Americans in literature. 10. Occultism in literature. I. Title.
  PS228.R32 G55 2003
  810.9'355—dc21

                                                                 2003005007

CONTENTS

ACKNOWLEDGMENTS

THE DEBTS that I have incurred in writing this book trace a history that looks, like Benjamin's angel of time, both backward and forward—back to my first book, *Dark Twins*, and forward, I hope, to the horizons of the Americas that so many of my colleagues have illuminated for me. Most memorable are the locations—the conferences, lectures, and colloquia—that mark the moment when conversations started that have stood me in great stead ever since. These are, for me, points of origin for a set of intellectual friendships without which my book would not have been possible. At Berkeley, never all at the same moment but together in my memory: Eric Sundquist, José David Saldívar, and Linda Williams, with a special place for Mike Rogin, whose presence we deeply miss and will never forget. At Cornell, on the occasion in the late 1980s of Shirley Samuels's conference on sentimentality: Lauren Berlant and Hortense Spillers. At the Stanford Humanities Center (1993–94): Harry Elam, Ariela Gross, George Fredrickson, and all the members of my reading group on race in American culture. At various meetings of the American Studies Association: Sandra Gunning, Priscilla Wald, and Alys Weinbaum. At a 1995 conference on José Martí at the University of California, Irvine: Doris Sommer, who had earlier, in 1989, co-organized a conference at Harvard on nationalisms and sexualities where I first encountered Benedict Anderson. At my own home institution, the University of California, Santa Cruz: all my colleagues in world literature and cultural studies (whose work in French, classics, Latin America, and the Asian Pacific was the single, greatest force toward internationalizing my study of the United States), plus those, from Santa Cruz and beyond, associated over the years with events held by the Center for Cultural Studies (Jonathan Arac and Jane Gaines, Jim Clifford and Gail Hershatter).

Finally, spanning many of these places and moments: Amy Kaplan, whose work has intersected for so long and so deeply with my own, from the moment we bonded over Mark Twain to our mutual challenge in reading Du Bois; and Kirsten Silva Gruesz, who provides daily inspiration as my closest colleague and coconspirator in so many intellectual projects, most memorably the Inter-Americas Research Cluster.

A portion of chapter 2 appeared in an earlier incarnation in "Pauline Hopkins and the Occult: African-American Revisions of Nineteenth-Century Science," *American Literary History* 8, no. 1 (winter 1996): 57–82; reprinted with permission of Oxford University Press. A shorter version of chapter 3 was published as "Mark Twain's Travels in the Racial Occult: *Following the Equator* and the Dream Tales," in *The Cambridge Companion to Mark Twain*, ed. Forrest G. Robinson (Cambridge: Cambridge University Press, 1995), 193–219; reprinted with permission of Cambridge University Press.

I owe the most to the best and most rigorous of critics: my family, Daniel, Elena, and John, to whom this book is dedicated.

ABBREVIATIONS

GEORGE WASHINGTON CABLE

G   *The Grandissimes: A Story of Creole Life* (1880; reprint, New York: Penguin, 1988)

CHARLES W. CHESNUTT

MT   *The Marrow of Tradition*, ed., and with an introduction by, Eric J. Sundquist (New York: Penguin, 1993)

THOMAS DIXON JR.

C   *The Clansman: An Historical Romance of the Ku Klux Klan* (Lexington: University Press of Kentucky, 1970)

LS   *The Leopard's Spots: A Romance of the White Man's Burden, 1865–1900* (New York: Doubleday, Page, 1903)

W. E. B. DU BOIS

A   *The Autobiography of W. E. B. Du Bois: A Soliloquy on Viewing My Life from the Last Decade of Its First Century*, ed. Herbert Aptheker (New York: International, 1968)

BF   *Black Folk Then and Now: An Essay in the History and Sociology of the Negro Race* (New York: Henry Holt, 1939)

BRA   *Black Reconstruction in America* (1935; reprint, with an introduction by David Levering Lewis, New York: Touchstone, 1995)

D   *Darkwater: Voices from within the Veil* (1920; reprint, with an introduction by Herbert Aptheker, Millwood, N.Y.: Kraus-Thomson, 1975)

"DBF" "The Drama among Black Folk," *The Crisis*, August 1916, 169–73

DD   *Dusk of Dawn: An Essay toward an Autobiography of a Race Concept* (1940; reprint, New York: Schocken, 1968)

"MG"   "Marcus Garvey," in *The Oxford W. E. B. Du Bois Reader*, ed. Eric J.
            Sundquist (New York: Oxford University Press, 1996), 265–76

N   *The Negro* (1915; reprint, Millwood, N.Y.: Kraus-Thomson, 1975)

PN   *The Philadelphia Negro* (1899; reprint, with an introduction by Herbert
            Aptheker, Millwood, N.Y.: Kraus-Thomson, 1973)

SBF   *The Souls of Black Folk*, in *The Oxford W. E. B. Du Bois Reader*, ed. Eric J.
            Sundquist (New York: Oxford University Press, 1996), 99–240

"SE[1]"   "The Star of Ethiopia," in *The Oxford W. E. B. Du Bois Reader*, ed. Eric J.
            Sundquist (New York: Oxford University Press, 1996), 305–10 (i.e., the
            pageant itself)

"SE[2]"   "The Star of Ethiopia," *The Crisis*, December 1915, 89–94 (i.e., Du Bois's
            review of the pageant)

"SNP"   "The Study of the Negro Problems," in *W. E. B. Du Bois on Sociology and
            the Black Community*, ed. Dan S. Green and Edwin D. Driver (Chicago:
            University of Chicago Press, 1978), 70–84

Sutton Griggs

HH   *The Hindered Hand; or, The Reign of the Repressionist* (1905; reprint, Miami:
            Mnemosyne, 1969)

II   *Imperium in Imperio* (1899; reprint, New York: AMS, 1975)

U   *Unfettered* (Nashville: Orion, 1902)

Frances Harper

IL   *Iola Leroy; or, Shadows Uplifted* (1892; reprint, with an introduction by
            Hazel V. Carby, Boston: Beacon, 1987)

Pauline Hopkins

CF   *Contending Forces: A Romance Illustrative of Negro Life North and South*
            (1900; reprint, with an afterword by Gwendolyn Brooks, Carbondale:
            Southern Illinois University Press, 1978)

OOB   *Of One Blood; or, The Hidden Self*, in *The Magazine Novels of Pauline
            Hopkins*, with an introduction by Hazel Carby (New York: Oxford Univer-
            sity Press, 1988), 439–621

William James

"HS"   "The Hidden Self," in *Essays in Psychology* (Cambridge, Mass.: Harvard
            University Press, 1983), 247–68

Mark Twain

"PAF"   "Papers of the Adam Family," in *Letters from the Earth*, ed. Bernard

DeVoto, with a preface by Henry Nash Smith (Greenwich, Conn.: Fawcett, 1962), 56–102

"CJ"   "Concerning the Jews," in *The Complete Essays of Mark Twain*, ed. Charles
Neider (Garden City, N.Y.: Doubleday, 1963), 235–50

FE   *Following the Equator: A Journal around the World* (Hartford, Conn.: American, 1897)

MMS   "Morgan Manuscript" of *Pudd'nhead Wilson*, J. Pierpont Morgan Library,
New York

MS   *The Mysterious Stranger*, ed., and with introduction by, William M. Gibson
(Berkeley and Los Angeles: University of California Press, 1969)

PW   *Pudd'nhead Wilson and Those Extraordinary Twins*, ed. Sydney E. Berger
(New York: Norton, 1980)

"TTYM"   "Three Thousand Years among the Microbes," in *Which Was the Dream?
and Other Symbolic Writings of the Later Years*, ed. John S. Tuckey (Berkeley
and Los Angeles: University of California Press, 1968), 433–553

"WWI"   "Which Was It?" in *Which Was the Dream? and Other Symbolic Writings of
the Later Years*, ed. John S. Tuckey (Berkeley and Los Angeles: University
of California Press, 1968), 179–429

CHAPTER ONE

AMERICAN RACE MELODRAMAS IN THE CULTURE OF THE OCCULT

AN INTRODUCTION

KEYWORDS

W. E. B. DU BOIS is known for a lifetime of speaking out on, and against, what was known as *the Negro Problem*. (The term, capitalized and in singular form, makes visible the derogatory grammars of nineteenth-century racial science and social policy: "the Negro" is a "problem" to be studied, managed, disciplined.) In doing so, he employed various formulations, ranging from the neutral and scientific (titling his influential 1897 address to the American Academy of Political and Social Sciences "The Study of the Negro Problems"), to the disturbingly personal (posing the rhetorical question, "How does it feel to be a problem?" in his 1903, multigenre *The Souls of Black Folk*), to the aphoristic (asserting at the 1900 Pan African Conference, "The problem of the twentieth century is the problem of the color-line," a statement repeated so often it became almost a signature incantation).[1] All three formulations ring changes on the term/concept *the Negro Problem*.

Du Bois invoked the famous color-line aphorism most famously in *The Souls of Black Folk*, where it is repeated three times by the end of only the second chapter. (The repetition is internal as well: twice in the line the term *the problem* is used.) Formulated in this fashion, the problem gestures both back to the grounds of its own solution, in the form of the thesis statement of "The Forethought" (as the preface is titled), and forward to its restatements in chapter 2 of *The Souls of Black Folk*, those framing the opening and closing.[2] If the lines all echo one another in a kind of call-and-response, they also amplify their own sound, for chapter 2 begins with a revised and expanded version of the refrain: "The problem of the twentieth century is the problem of the color-line,—the relation of the darker to the lighter races of men in Asia and Africa, in America and the islands of the sea" (*SBF*, 107). From these generative moments, Du Bois went on to numerous other reformulations, restatements, and replayings of the Negro Problem in other texts and venues throughout his career.

The point of all the citations is, invariably, to make plural the stubbornly singular formulation *the Negro Problem*. The social, political, and intellectual challenge of such redefinition—from the singular *Problem* to the plural *problems*, from the Negro *being* the problem to the Negro *having* problems—is viscerally present in the sheer number of times that Du Bois repeats the term. The multiple formulations refuse the concept of a single problem or question, adding up, rather, to "a plexus of social problems, some old, some new, some simple, some complex," as he insists in his 1940 autobiography, *Dusk of Dawn*. "Perhaps it is wrong," he concludes at the climactic end of a climactic chapter, "to speak of it at all as 'a concept' rather than as a group of contradictory forces, facts, and tendencies," correcting the grammar of the book's subtitle (*An Essay toward an Autobiography of a Race Concept*) as well as that of the chapter title ("The Concept of Race").[3] To pluralize the "race concept" as a set of contradictions is to historicize the notion of race itself: "Because of a firm belief in a changing racial group," Du Bois notes in *Dusk of Dawn* and repeats in his last, 1968 autobiography, "I easily grasped the idea of a changing, developing society rather than a fixed social structure."[4] The "I" that does the grasping here is constitutive rather than coincidental. Meditating in *Dusk of Dawn* on the generic challenges of writing "an autobiography of a race concept," Du Bois argues, "My life had its significance and its only deep significance because it was part of a Problem; but that problem was, as I continue to think, the central problem of the greatest of the world's democracies and so the Problem of the future world" (*DD*, vii–viii). "Elucidated, magnified, and doubtless distorted" through the autobiography, repeated "in the thoughts and deeds which were mine" (*DD*, viii), the singular racial terminology of Du Bois's moment—*the Negro Problem*, alternatively upper- and lowercase—both masks and indicates the excesses, the contradictions, and the ambiguities of race relations in the *longue durée* of the global "American 1890s."[5]

Making plural the singular *Negro Question* is a fundamental aim, his and mine. The history of race in America, long told as a master narrative, the Manichaean drama of black and white, appears finally to be coming to an end. We hear so many announcements, invocations, and prophetic calls willing a postmodern "beyond" race, spoken by academics, activists, and politicians alike on both the Left and the Right. Such institutional changes as the category *mixed race* on the 2000 U.S. census are another index of the rising call against the continued use of *race* as an analytic, social, or legal category. Yet so many of these pronouncements continue, willfully or willy-nilly, to depend on the old, supposedly outmoded racialisms for their political and ethical utopian force. The American race melodrama of black and white, at once so familiar as to breed contempt and so strange in its ability to assume uncanny new guises, has had an exceptionally long shelf life. *Promiscuous* is the historian Barbara Fields's word for the boundless facility of racialist ideologies to adapt to new experience while continuing to draw on apparently fixed attitudes. The results for how Americans think about their history have been both a misconception of the historical continuity of racism (reflected in the view that racial attitudes "have a life of their own") and the enduring narrative of race as the "tragically recurring central theme" of American, and not just Southern, history. The persistence, both in mainstream U.S. historiography and in popular culture generally, of according race "a transhistorical, almost metaphysical status," of assuming that race is a phenomenon outside history, accounts for the extraordinary burden and challenge of the effort to historicize race that drives the race melodramas that I explore in this book.[6]

Du Bois establishes how the project of making plural the Negro Problem was coextensive with demonstrating that the race concept has, and is, a historical development. To recognize race as a product of history, not of nature or metaphysics, rejects both the dominant arguments from biology and the notion of the "tragic flaw"; most critically, "the history of the development of the race concept" (*DD*, 97), such as that on which Du Bois embarked, insists on "the idea of a changing, developing society rather than a fixed social structure." If the race concept changes over time, then racial groups have both a past and a future. One could say that American race relations at the turn of the century were forged and fought for on the terrain of history, both U.S. and world. Foundational events (the American Revolution) and locations (Africa) provided the grounds (battle- and epistemological) of debate over how to narrate "race history." If only not to exaggerate the rumors of its death (to invoke the spirit of Mark Twain, another central figure in the nineteenth-century culture of the color line), we need to revisit yet again the *longue durée* of the master-race narrative's greatest cultural authority.

I define that turn-of-the-century moment formally and historically through two keywords: *race melodrama* and *the occult*. Turning first to the former, my point of departure in *Blood Talk* is a pattern of derogatory references, made by cultural commentators then and now, to a wide variety of turn-of-the-century race representations as "melodramatic," simultaneously heightened and hyperbolic, flat and wooden. Such objections mirror the misconceptions about race and history that Du Bois and so many others have fought. Just one example should suffice. Oscar Micheaux's 1925 silent classic *Body and Soul* is, according to a *New York Times* review of a screening of the film at the 2000 New York Film Festival, "an old-fashioned melodrama," the screening redeemed only by the original score composed for the occasion, which lent "the melodrama the resonance of a historical fable." The assumption here that melodrama is at once dated and ahistorical deepens as the review continues, the reviewer commenting scornfully on the good twin–bad twin plot, "'Body and Soul' is a silent film after all, and the movie employs the melodramatic formulas of the period."[7] Old-fashioned and a period piece, yet lacking historical resonance: melodrama is, like the "beyond-race" talk today, dismissed as archaic yet without and outside history.

Invariably a term of opprobrium, even when used simply descriptively, *melodrama* provides for that very reason the key to my subject. In noun form, it encompasses both a worldview of race crisis and conflict, in a period that Rayford Logan called the "nadir," and a protean narrative mode embracing a variety of forms, including sentimental, regional, and historical fiction, fantasy and science fiction, and scientific and social-scientific discourses derived from race law, racial science, and allied discourses of family, ethnos, and nation.[8] Temporally, race melodrama is an equally mobile cultural mode, cutting across histories and ideologies and producing a wide-ranging textual history that we can trace from pre-Emancipation semiobscurity (William Wells Brown's *Clotel*) and fame (Harriet Beecher Stowe's *Uncle Tom's Cabin*) to the mass-cultural filmic and legal texts of the twentieth century (*Birth of a Nation, Gone with the Wind*, and the televised cases of Anita Hill, O. J. Simpson, and others). Finally, the term *race melodrama* points to the irreducible historical identity of race itself as melodrama in the United States.

The material subject of *Blood Talk* is the voluminous "race literature" produced in the late-nineteenth-century United States, interpreted against a period of crisis and transformation in global race relations. If 1877, the end of Reconstruction, marks the start of this seemingly amorphous era, the close might be placed in 1920, when Du Bois published *Darkwater*, the second of his multigenred autobiographies, in which lyric race history and global anticolonialism produced a classic race melodrama in the shadow of

World War I.[9] The work's sweeping critique of race relations on the home front also points to another watershed, the year 1915, when D. W. Griffith's *The Birth of a Nation* completed the post-Reconstruction project of rewriting American history, with the ex-slave as scapegoat, in order to heal sectional divisions and reunite the nation. In response to this volatile phase of American social history and historiography, new narrative modes, derived from earlier forms and adapted in the context of emerging racial discourses, surfaced to narrate the history of the race concept. The mode of race melodrama, associated earlier with such abolitionist classics as *Uncle Tom's Cabin*, reemerged, encompassing a set of otherwise aesthetically and politically heterogeneous texts, including the historical romances of George Washington Cable, Charles Chesnutt, Sutton Griggs, and Thomas Dixon, the sentimental novels of Frances Harper and Pauline Hopkins, the travel and regional writings of Mark Twain and Kate Chopin, and, perhaps subsuming them all, the mixed-genre work of W. E. B. Du Bois. Not only do these race melodramas reflect widely variant politics, from the one extreme of white supremacy to the other of black nationalism (with a range of civilizational and uplift positions in between), but, crossing the boundaries of literature, law, history, and science, they also represent widely variant formal locations, from the high-canonical (Du Bois, Twain), to the noncanonical (Griggs, Dixon), the recently canonized (Harper, Hopkins, Chopin), and the emergent recanonized (Chesnutt, Cable). These multiple political and formal locations offer one indication of just how fundamentally protean race melodramas of the period were.

The writers on my shortlist—Hopkins, Griggs, Dixon, Twain, and Du Bois figure here most prominently, with supporting roles played by Chesnutt, Cable, Arthur Schomburg, John Bruce, and Marcus Garvey—are also all activists, notable for careers in a variety of institutional and public spheres, from the pulpit, to the periodical press, to the lecture circuit. They can often be found speaking to and against one another, across a range of geographic, intellectual, and political locations: both Griggs and Du Bois respond publicly to Dixon's Klan trilogy; both Hopkins and Du Bois work within the emergent historical study of Africa and blacks; both Twain and Du Bois address black-Jewish questions. They also all share a range of references to the same unruly set of nominally mainstream and fringe elements: ancient Egyptian and African history; secret societies and mystic symbologies (such those of the Ku Klux Klan and the Masons); racial sciences old (craniometry, ethnology) and new (archaeology, anthropology, psychology); empires and imperialism. Such crosscutting dialogues establish the cultural milieu, local and international, and the far-flung venues for racial discourses that shape and are corroborated by the protean quality of race melodramas in the *longue durée*.

At the same time, the work of my race melodramatists defines the contextual limits of the race melodrama. One way to place the figures on my shortlist is to see them as exceptional, even brilliant practitioners of a degraded mode, as much symptom of as strategic response to the contradictions of the race concept. In that sense, the Manichaean logic and affective intensity of the melodramatic mode are perfectly attuned to the heightened polarities, the sheer violence, of U.S. race relations and race representations at the turn of the century. But, in the hands of Hopkins, Griggs, Dixon, Twain, et al., the binary structures of melodrama are, as we will see, exploded by the barely hidden excess of race that they make visible (the regional, socioeconomic, political, and gender divisions that exceed racial categories) while formally and narratively containing—ostentatiously but nevertheless only imperfectly—the occluded plurals that are Du Bois's subject. When racialized, the melodramatic mode becomes relational rather than divided and divisive, imagining a range of crosscutting, contradictory alliances and conflicts across groups variously defined, not only by race, gender, and nation, but also by competing political, economic, and sociocultural identities and differences. The results outline, as I hope to show, the limits and possibilities of melodrama as an aesthetic and cultural form.

Turning now to my second keyword, *the occult*, I was struck by the persistent entangling of familiar U.S. racial discourses with another, more shadowy zone, less well-known but equally disreputable, defined by a range of transnational cultural phenomena that we might colloquially, and loosely, call *occultist*. In the late nineteenth century, thinking through race as a mode of historical consciousness, and not simply as a category of biology or identity, meant engaging with a variety of emerging disciplines and belief systems in which consciousness was the explicit object even if it was not always explicitly racialized. Examples of such systems range from the New Psychology of Jean-Martin Charcot, Sigmund Freud, William James, and the Society for Psychical Research to the mystical symbologies and rituals that characterized not only such explicitly race-based groups as the Ku Klux Klan (or, as the Klan officially called itself, "The Invisible Empire of the South") and the Garveyites, but also such fraternal and cultic organizations, less overtly racially defined, as Freemasonry and Theosophy. The cultural appeal of these social movements stemmed from their protean functioning both as threat and as promise. Invisible empires imagined in the same breath racial fraternity and race war in their search for the "hidden transcript" of political affiliation among subaltern groups, of the mainstream Right and Left both.[10] Many of these groups are linked by the roots that, drawing on quasi-mystical, quasi-scientific sources, they trace to imagined racial pasts: Anglo-Saxon Scotland and black Egypt (with the race of the ancient Egyptians hotly contested) are most frequently claimed. There is also a connection to be made between the uses of specific occult iconography, such as the Egyptological sphinx and pyramid, in the many varieties of street theater, political performance, and historical pageantry staged in U.S. cities during and immediately following World War I. These would include openly racial spectacles, such as Marcus Garvey's Universal Negro Improvement Association (UNIA) parades, Du Bois's pageant "The Star of Ethiopia," and the public celebrations of Carter Woodson's Negro History Week, as well as the apparently racially unmarked cultural production of the left-wing culture critics and activists known as *the Lyrical Left*.[11] Their "racial occults" are all also, again to varying degrees, projects with valences of the political, the performative, and the historiographic.

The paradigmatic literary example of such a racial occult may be found in Thomas Dixon's *The Clansman*, in which the guilt of the black rapist is revealed under hypnosis by the white Southern doctor, "like an ancient alchemist ready to conduct some daring experiment in the problem of life." Dr. Cameron's "powers of hypnosis," gained during medical study abroad in Edinburgh and Paris ("Southern doctors are always pioneers in the science of medicine"), allow him to prove, by a combination of the "mystic" and the "scientific," the identity of the criminal, a local ex-slave, now captain of the "African Guards" under the occupying federal troops. However clear the racial forces that make necessary such self-appointed counter-terrorism, when he is asked to account for his experimental powers, the doctor explains that he cannot: "They belong to the world of spiritual phenomena of which we know so little and yet which touch our material lives at a thousand points every day. How do we account for sleep and dreams, or second-sight, or the day-dreams which we call visions?"[12] The particular cluster of occult terms here is echoed by Sutton Griggs's theory of "racial hypnotism," by Pauline Hopkins's vocabulary of the "supernatural phenomena or *mysticism*" associated with the "great field of new discoveries in psychology," by Mark Twain's fascination with dream states and waking visions, and, finally, by Du Bois's well-known language of the veil, messianic second sight, and double consciousness.[13] As a racialized formation, the occult was both capacious and mobile.

A figure for other worlds beneath the "veil" (to use the spiritualist language appropriated as a defining racial image throughout Du Bois's work), the occult provided a means to express both racial problems and solutions to those problems.[14] *Racial hypnotism* is Sutton Griggs's term for the practice of engendering in both races a psychic sense of black inferiority and white superiority, a subtle form of social control far more effective than overt racial violence. Theories of double and multiple personalities spoke to the internal psychic state of Du Bois's racial double consciousness, while mystical notions of past lives and reincarnation, in concert with archaeological evidence of ancient civilizations, were transmogrified into racial mysticism. To unearth a glorious racial past, as in the theory of the African origins of Western civilization, was also to signal a prophetic future, as in Ethiopianism's signature biblical refrain ("Princes shall come out of Egypt, and Ethiopia shall soon stretch forth her hands unto God" [Ps. 68:31]). Finally, the occult vision of an infinite universe, unbounded by space or time, provided a medium of transracial contact and the promise of transracial consciousness. In conjuring such a racial occult, my race melodramatists seek to historicize race consciousness itself and, thus, to reveal the ideological and geopolitical contours of racial thinking.

In casting about for a term to give habitation and a name to this nexus of disparate cultural phenomena, I ultimately settled on *occult*. Meant only minimally as a provocation (although it turned out to be just that, a problem of which more later), *occult* is an umbrella term, intended primarily to summon forth a specific historical context, the confluence in the early twentieth century of popular occultisms encompassing such varied movements as Theosophy, Rosicrucianism, and the "Jung cult." These occultisms represent the Western esoteric tradition, broadly conceived, and derived, according to conventional historical accounts, from Gnosticism, hermetic writings on alchemy and magic, and the cabala. More important, however, Western occultism produced a long and protean history of revivals across time and widely distributed localities. Historians trace the surfacings of occultisms, for example, from a series of Greek texts, composed in Egypt amid the breakdown of the agricultural order of the late Roman Empire, to the Renaissance, when prominent humanists edited the classical texts and created a modern corpus of occult speculations, and then to late-eighteenth-century Europe, where occultism took the form of a by-product of and reaction to the Enlightenment, along with allied interests in the Middle Ages, medieval mysticism, and secret brotherhoods devoted to Rosicrucianism, Masonry, and alchemy. In this latter phase, occultism in the age of revolution, a qualified radicalism or quasi-progressive politics emerged in such visible figures as E. J. Hobsbawm's "primitive rebels," among whom were Masons prominent in the French and American Revolutions as well as in revolutionary movements in Ireland and Italy.[15] The *occult*, then, as I use the term, in part as an homage to the Renaissance occult sciences, points more broadly to the long, and strange, career of that protean phenomenon.[16]

The occult revival most germane to my race melodramatists, however, is the international circuit of popular occultisms at the turn of the century, most influential in the United States and Europe, but extending as far as India, including Theosophy, probably the best known of the occult movements, allied with modern Rosicrucianism and Freemasonry as well as other "secret," fraternal orders. The late-nineteenth-century culture of the occult belongs to a widespread mode of racial thinking that explicitly crossed geographic and national boundaries to invoke, paradoxically, either an intensely nationalist spirit of the *Volk* or a transnational and pan-racial consciousness. The resulting racial occult displaced what Du Bois calls *the race concept* onto paranormal phenomena and structures of consciousness that formed core bodies of research for, to take two examples, the emerging fields of Jamesian philosophy and Continental psychology (from Charcot to Freud). Paradigmatic of the transnational cross-fertilization and the paradoxical politics among these groups was, for example, the modern German occult revival, a synthesis of pseudo-Hinduism and Oriental mysticism with a mongrel politics of *Volk*-like nationalism and vague reformism. This heady brew, associated with the Ariosophists of Austria and Germany from 1890 to 1935, secret Aryan cults that the historian Nicholas Goodrick-Clarke links to the occult roots of Nazism, was based, according to Goodrick-Clarke, on the widespread popularity of Theosophy throughout the "Anglo-Saxon world" of the 1890s: the "international sectarian movement . . . of the Russian adventuress and occultist Madame Helena Petrovna Blavatsky," who drew on—many said plagiarized—the texts and ideas of the Rosicrucians, Freemasons, and other secret societies as well as the occult lore of ancient Egypt and contemporary works on Hinduism and modern science to produce the hybrid that she called *Theosophy*. The "occult synthesis" at the turn of the century, a veritable "global boom," thus worked a heterogeneous territory that combined overlapping mystical ritual and symbology with a variety of racial, national, and international politics.[17]

Today, *occult* generally conjures up images of New Age claptrap, a fraudulent and commercialized consumer spiritualism, but, a hundred years ago, it stood for a far more malleable and flexible field. As a cultural formation specific to the turn of the century, the occult was not exclusively the province of what Howard Kerr calls the "mediums, spirit-rappers, and roaring radicals" that held sway earlier in the century,[18] nor was the divide between believer and skeptic the only available epistemological and political stance to be taken. Put another way, for every Arthur Conan Doyle and Mark Twain (both of whom used and lampooned the problems and possibilities of the séance), there was also an F. W. H. Myers, the president of the British Society for Psychical Research (SPR), and a William James, a member of the American branch of the SPR and the president of the Anti-Imperialist League, for both of whom the occult constituted an investigative field *for* the will to believe. For both Du Bois and Pauline Hopkins, an occult syncretism of New World and Africanist epistemologies, religious and scientific, ancient and modern, fostered the intellectual concept of African "survivals" throughout the diaspora and enabled the narrating of a global history of race consciousness. Finally, as all these figures demonstrate, the racial occult represented the point at which an international matrix of psychic researchers, academic investigators, artists, and activists—along with the usual assortment of frauds and poseurs—coalesced. The question of belief or skepticism is not the issue; rather, the confluence of American race melodramas with the culture of the occult stakes out one of those contentious and paradoxical conversations on race in the United States and beyond. The "twilight zone" of "hidden and partially concealed causes of race hate" (*DD*, 282, 284) provided Du Bois and others with a means of accounting for the occulted forces, social and psychological, reasoned and irrational, of race relations and race consciousness that Barbara Fields sums up, in hauntingly similar terms, as "the twilight world of racial ideology."[19]

My goal in this book is to emphasize both the historical specificity and the variability of that twilight world and to explore more precisely, at the moment of the culture of the racial occult, the flexibility of the overlapping rhetorical and political nexus of race, family, nation, and transnation. Even the nominal separation of the most commonly used racial tropes—*race, family,* and *nation*—from their own multipliers—*the transnational* and *the pan-racial*—is a historical oversimplification, for these terms were regularly, and at times contradictorily, used almost as synonyms.[20] Just so, a variety of turn-of-the-century nationalisms, black and white, relied on and even transmuted into pan-racial visions of transnational unities: Pan-Africanism and Anglo-Saxonism are only the most obvious examples. Exposing such contradictions from within the rigid logic of racial binaries is the province of all the race melodramas that I explore, but each does so by engaging, in different occult contexts, different variants of the so-called Negro Question. The results are, as I will outline in a brief sketch of the chapters to follow, plural sets of "questions" and of occultisms, narratively linked by a common, if protean, devotion to what Du Bois calls "the history of the development of the race concept in the world and particularly in America" (*DD*, 96).

I start with what many would consider a paradigmatic melodramatic form, the maternal melodramas recognized by feminist literary and film theorists as *social texts*, works of cultural critique based in a maternal and familial locus. In the nineteenth-century sphere, the pre-Emancipation literature of the slave family is already well-known, as is the later, postbellum cultural production of the "women's era." The definitive figure of that era, Pauline Hopkins provides the essential texts and contexts. Her 1900 novel *Contending Forces* formulates the basic equations for my project as a whole: black versus white is enmeshed in and multiplied by a tangle of socioeconomic, sexual, and political forces, summed up by the conflict between the overdetermined Negro Question and what Hopkins calls *the Woman Question*, a racial and gender conflict that divides black communities from within as much as it unifies the black community from without. Working within the historical opposition between Washingtonian and Du Boisean positions on the Negro Question, Hopkins supplements that division with the Woman Question, a third term that reveals one of the set pieces of African American history, so often narrated as a struggle between diametrically opposed leaders, to be a stabilizing opposition, working to contain deeper, gendered rifts. Chapter 2 constructs an alternative chronology for the maternal melodramas, taking Reconstruction, rather than slavery and Emancipation, as the watershed and Hopkins as the definitive melodramatist of the "contending forces" that simultaneously undergird and overflow the divisions of racial conflict. Hopkins's moment is framed by the novelists George Washington Cable, marking the beginning of the end of Reconstruction, and Charles Chesnutt, foreshadowing the open end of what, following the historian Eric Foner, can be called the "unfinished revolution."[21]

Hopkins establishes how race melodramas—whether maternal or, as are those discussed in chapter 3, predominantly paternal—are a literature of gender conflict and revenge, both inter- and intraracial. In the texts that I discuss, by Cable and Chesnutt as well as Hopkins, the fictional figure of the mixed-race mother, the locus of threat and desire for both blacks and whites, locates one point of origin for the notorious "black-matriarchy" thesis, thus revealing its imaginative as well as its politically charged significance. Finally, Hopkins's magazine writing covering Africa, both ancient and modern, invents a composite Egypt-Ethiopia that provides a space of imaginary resolution, bringing together the knowledge fields of ancient African magic, mysticism, and modern science as well as the paradoxes of biblical one-bloodedness and Ethiopianism. Hopkins's occult is topicalized by her research on the race of the ancient Egyptians as well as in several scientific fields, including ethnology, psychology, and archaeology, disciplines that at the time were neither explicitly racially determined nor clearly bounded but rather fluid, sites where emergent and competing theories could often be found. These are only some of the deeply contradictory contending forces crowding the structurally and morally polarized race melodrama.

In chapter 3, on those "procrustean bedfellows" (to borrow from C. Vann Woodward) Sutton Griggs and Thomas Dixon, the paternal melodrama reinterprets U.S. history as a drama of race war, both visible and occulted.[22] Whether conjuring the threat of a mulatto "nation inside a nation," as Dixon does,[23] or the desire for the *imperium in imperio* of a secret, black empire in Texas, as Griggs does, their race melodramas foreground what I (not they) call *the Conspiracy Question*. The one question for which I've had to invent a name, drawing on classic scholarship on conspiracy theory and the paranoid style, the Conspiracy Question points to the prevalence during the post-Reconstruction period in local, state, and national U.S. politics of a rhetoric of hidden alliances that are said to account for, to exceed, or to threaten visible unities. Phenomena as diverse as the 1898 Wilmington "race riot" and the extension of the Fourteenth Amendment to corporations as persons were interpreted as the products of broad-ranging conspiracies of white elites, just as the accusation of underground black organizing often justified intimidation of and violence toward blacks at the polls, in the military, and in their homes. Providing the raw materials for this chapter, Sutton Griggs's novels and manifestos (on what he calls a racial "science of collective efficiency") as well as Thomas Dixon's Klan trilogy demonstrate how two key events, the American Revolution and the Spanish-American War, anchor the reframing of U.S. history in racial terms, with the focus of both novelists as much on politics, class, and economics as on race and nation, as much on intraracial divisions and collectivities as on interracial conflict.

For both Griggs and Dixon, the visible racial violence of the post-Reconstruction United States masks, yet points to, the occulted reality of total race war embodied in the paradoxical form of a racial underworld populated by secret societies conspiring either to rescue or to destroy the nation. The conspiratorial imagination taps threats to national (read: racial) unity that come as much from within as from without the group; in the romance plots common to both Griggs and Dixon, miscegenation becomes the hidden betrayal of blood purity and the secret, internal threat to the unity of racial identity. For both writers, the occult, defined through a hyperinvisible realm of secret brotherhoods known for and by public spectacle and the performance of supposed mystic ritual, dictates an erosion of boundaries between inside and outside. As those borders become porous and *the nation* a less stable entity, the race-nation equation rigidifies in compensation.

In chapter 4, we see how, in a series of science-fiction and fantasy narratives linking blacks and Jews in Dreyfusard France to the antebellum South and the equatorial Black Belt, Mark Twain works the Griggs-Dixon conspiratorial vein of unstable bodies and borders between insides and outsides, with its vision of aliens within and traitors without. He wrote most of these texts, including the little-known "Three Thousand Years among the Microbes" and his best-known late work, *The Mysterious Stranger,* while living and traveling in Europe during the time of the Dreyfus case in France, when anti-Semitism was reaching new extremes on the Continent and Euro-American imperialism was extending its reach from Africa to the Asian Pacific. Both Twain and Du Bois, also living in Europe at the time, were personally and intellectually affected by the Dreyfus case and the associated political and intellectual climate: each was, at different times, mistaken for a Jew, an odd conjunction that I examine in this chapter. Twain's writing from this period, largely unfinished variants of travel narratives, engages a variety of spiritualist and occult notions—time travel, thought transference, spirit communication, out-of- and inside-body travel—as the medium for revisiting the old terrain of U.S. race slavery, the basis of his greatest fiction, and linking it to the newer global imperialisms of the 1890s. Twain's mysterious stranger, a prototype of so many of his protagonists, occupies a threefold identity as Satan, master of occult powers, as Jew, and as blackface trickster in a ghostly minstrel show. The most striking result of Twain's "occult travel" is such a twinning of the Negro Question of his Southern past with the "Jewish Question" of his global present.

Chapter 5 on Du Bois as an intellectual systematizer whose capacious, analytic imagination reveals a synergy among the varieties of racial occults, and whose influence can, therefore, be seen in some form in all the works discussed in the previous chapters, represents the culmination of my study. Du Bois provides a comprehensive measure of how a single nexus of figures, locations, events, and issues—the Ku Klux Klan and other secret fraternal, or conspiratorial, organizations; the Spanish-American War and other episodes of global imperialism; racial science; and romantic racial-ism—is common to but differently constellated in all the race melodramas under discussion here. Du Bois adapts the mode of maternal melodrama to suit his own historical pageantry of black history. He untangles, and ex-plains, the terms of the ongoing procrustean relations between white-supremacist and black-nationalist groups as well as linking both to "the propaganda of history," the production of a misconceived and misleading historiography of the United States and the Negro.[24] A fellow traveler of Twain's, he extends the black-Jewish analogy to meditate on the historical links between diaspora and Zionism, racism and anti-Semitism. Finally, as a philosopher of what I call *occult history,* Du Bois identifies the common his-toriographic thread running through the disparate phenomena constituting the racial occult and exposes the pressures—social, political, and histori-cal—faced by Du Bois and his contemporaries, and by us, when thinking race through the occult.

THEORIES: MELODRAMA AS EXCESS

In taking the *melodramatic*—still a persistently derogatory adjective—as a key to reading turn-of-the-century race literature, I am drawing on the rich rehabilitations of melodrama as a genre that have emerged over the past twenty years in film studies and feminist film theory. The most important contribution of this influential work, generally based on "women's films" and "family melodramas" from the 1920s to the 1950s, has been to highlight the protean nature of melodrama, its transformations across media, histo-ries, and national cultures. Simultaneously, an awareness of historical con-text, in part shaped by Marxist theories of culture, helped formulate how the inheritance of nineteenth-century melodrama shaped modern mass cinema. And, perhaps most influential, from a combined theoretical interest in his-tory and the Freudian language of the body, new conceptions emerged of the relation between melodrama and politics. Not the quietist, bourgeois form that it has usually been assumed to be, melodrama in fact mediated so-cial and political change through the interpersonal domain of the body, this role becoming particularly apparent in the maternal melodramas and women's films produced by American filmmakers between the wars. Open-ing up the politics of melodrama also reopened the question of the form's treatment of race, a question long dominated by discussions of Griffith's *Birth of a Nation.* The result was not simply to challenge the assumption of the racist origins of popular cinema but also to encourage archival and recovery work on early black cinema. It is not going too far to say that an alternative critical theory reconstituted melodrama as a form, not against, but of modernity, both engaging with and processing the politics of sociocultural change.[25]

Closest to my own work on race melodramas is that of Jane Gaines on "mixed-race movies" in the silent era and Linda Williams on the "race card" in "American melodramas of black and white."[26] Whereas Gaines concentrates on racial themes in American silent cinema of the 1910s and 1920s, Williams's "racial melodramas" have the "leaping" quality that Henry James once ascribed to Harriet Beecher Stowe's *Uncle Tom's Cabin:* mass-cultural blockbusters, they leap from medium to medium and across time, always functioning, whether on the page, on the stage, on the screen, or in the courtroom, as what James calls a "state of vision, of feeling and consciousness."[27] My race melodramas combine elements of both Gaines's and Williams's approaches, incorporating (rather than leaping across) different modes of racialized discourses and knowledges, including those not generally recognized as racially marked but located in the historically specific moment of what I call *the culture of the occult.* Like Gaines, Williams, and so many other cultural critics writing well after the establishment of black studies, I explore the interraciality—the intersections and interdependence—of black and white culture, an exploration codified by Toni Morrison as a search for the "ghost in the machine," the "unspeakable thing" that is "race."[28] My texts, however, represent a popular form and a model of *melos* that differ both from the well-defined, even self-defined, but little-known genre of early race movies and from the hyperselling blockbusters, leaping over modes and times, but always adhering to the model of moral polarities incarnate in the "Tom or anti-Tom story of racial victims and villains."[29] The American race melodramas that I explore cross the bestseller (Dixon and Griffith's collaborative work) with popular fiction that reached specific, targeted audiences (Griggs, Hopkins, and even Twain, whose protean persona had always spoken to different groups without necessarily bringing them together) as well as with highbrow, multigenre work written for a national public (Du Bois). All of them work within the Manichaean model of race in America, but each bends the binary formulas of melodrama, at once inhabiting and overflowing them, to expose the "group of contradictory forces, facts, and tendencies" that, for Du Bois, constitutes, by exceeding, the singular race concept.

Virtually all the work that has been done to rehabilitate melodrama as a mode for our times is indebted to Peter Brooks's foundational *The Melo-*

dramatic Imagination.[30] Superimposing "classic" French theatrical melodrama on the nineteenth-century novel and reading both through the
Freudian narrative of the psyche, Brooks demonstrates the modernity of
nineteenth-century melodrama, long assumed to be an archaic form, and
links it to mainstream cinema. The melodramatic imagination is, Brooks
shows, structured by moral polarities, the struggle between readily iden-
tifiable, or personalized, virtues and vices, and by narratives of victimization and rescue—all of which have correspondences in the antinomies of
the American race melodramas. Thanks to Brooks, we can view the *melodramatic*—not pejoratively, but descriptively—as a "mode of excess"
(rather than as a definite dramatic genre) that cuts across periods, cultures,
and art forms, as an "imagination" dominated by a Manichaean worldview.

For me, as for Brooks, *excess* is, like *Manichaeism*, a key descriptive
term for a "literary aesthetic," both "coherent" and "necessary" to the
melodramatic mode. Brooks defines the excess of melodrama as the effect
of the mode's fundamental drive toward "expressivity": the "desire to express all," to "utter the unspeakable," produces an excess of meaning in
defiance of social and psychic repression. The melodramatic excess goes
beyond simply achieving "plenitude of meaning," however, to total
"legibility." If "making the world morally legible" constitutes the ruling
force of melodrama, it depends on the ultimate visibility of what Brooks
calls the "moral occult," a sphere of spiritual values and latent moral meanings "both indicated within and masked by the surface of reality." Brooks insists, in fact, that the melodramatic mode and all its key features—moral
Manichaeism and structural polarity as well as spectacle and excess—exist
in large measure to locate and to articulate the moral occult. The moral occult, too, enacts the drive toward expressivity, referencing a psychoanalytic
dynamic in the domain of the unconscious, with the analogy to melodrama
in the will to speak the unspeakable, the melodramatic aesthetic as a form of
embodied, talking cure. Melodramatic utterance represents a victory over
repression, "social, psychological, historical and conventional." The dynamics of repression and the return of the repressed, of "expressive liberation from the 'primal scene,'" thus figure the plot of Brooksean melodrama.
The promise of a morally legible universe is the key dynamic of melodrama
and psychoanalysis, both of which are driven by a "Promethean sense-
making system."[31]

As I have indicated, racializing this account initially requires only some
shifting and rearranging; the consequences, however, are wide-ranging.
Race melodramas are narratively organized through the structural polari-

ties dear to the melodramatic imagination, but the doubling of plots, characters, and events in these texts—formal expressions of polarity—fails notably to provide the sense of order associated with the moral Manichaeism
of melodrama. The melodramatic will to revelation drives the race melodramas, as it does Brooks's examples: hidden marks, proofs of identity on
body or paper, are repeatedly unveiled in the many recognition scenes in
these novels (the lotus-lily birthmark on the breast of ancient Ethiopian
royalty in Hopkins's *Of One Blood,* the fragment of a slave song in Harper's
Iola Leroy, the fingerprints in Twain's *Pudd'nhead Wilson*). But, in all race
cases, the exposure of occluded identities and relations fails to produce the
requisite reconciliation of racial, national, and gender conflict, even from
within a nominally happy ending. Symptomatically underscoring the failure of narrative resolution, despite the marks of recognition and identification, are the many prefaces and afterwords, manifestos and commentaries,
that are such a striking characteristic of the race melodramas. Appended to
and exceeding the bounds of the novels proper, these documentary materials—usually written directly in the author's own voice—compensate for
what the fiction fails to say or to contain.

If, as Brooks says, after Henry James, "the melodramatic imagination
needs both document and vision," then moral legibility is further compromised by the discrepant interplay of fact and fiction in the race melodramas.[32] The melodramatic conventions of mistaken, disguised, double, or
multiple identities and the related plots of hidden incest and secret miscegenation are at odds with our knowledge of the transparency of actual or
thinly disguised historical figures (Thomas Dixon's Lincoln and Austin
Stoneman/Thaddeus Stevens, Pauline Hopkins's Will Smith/W. E. B. Du
Bois and Dr. Arthur Lewis/Booker T. Washington). In their dual identities
as fictional characters and historical referents, Pauline Hopkins's protagonists may be allowed to pair off in a conventional melodramatic resolution,
but the marriages leave unresolved, and uncommented on, the contending
forces of *Contending Forces:* the repressed conflicts, the gender and political
affiliations and divisions that exceed, and often contradict, the binary reality of the black-white racial divide. Unlike the "extrapolation" from document to vision in the James example, the hard facts of race are textually excessive: endlessly repeated yet unassimilable, defying all plot and thematic
devices of containment, resolution, or closure. The incommensurability of
document and vision, of the factual and the fictional, points to the mode of
excess as both central problem and solution in the epistemology of race
melodramas.

One might say, therefore, that race melodramas work by exposing the excess of American race relations. This excess is not, like Brooks's moral occult, a domain of the unseen and unspeakable that must be made legible and expressible; it is, instead, paradoxically, hyperinvisible, as in the paradigmatic case of the Invisible Empire of the Klan. A different conception of legibility, one more qualified and contradictory than Brooks's, is required to make visible the relations among what appear to be counterdiscourses of race at the turn of the century: the discourses of Negrophobia hyperbolically inflate the presence of the Negro on, and the discourses of racial science and race law accomplish the disappearance of the Negro from, the evolutionary, cultural, and national stage. Nor is the spectacular excess of race tamed through the total expressivity that, for Brooks, defines the melodramatic imagination, in which the visual—the pictorial tableau—exemplifies a primordial concern to see meanings represented and moral states rendered in "clear, visible signs."[33] Instead, the spectacle of race is explosive and conflicted, embodied in the hyperinvisibility of racial terror at the specific moment of the turn of the century, when extralegal violence against African Americans was magnified in the stagings of lynchings and race riots but disavowed in U.S. legal practice. Finally, while Brooks's moral occult, the raison d'être of melodramatic legibility, is a metaphoric realm of operative spiritual values, the racial occult as I have defined it is itself a historically specific phenomenon, both a form and a sociohistorical content, both text and context.

Race melodramas thus propose several alternative models of legibility. The promise of a morally legible universe in Brooks's melodramas is complicated, often compromised, by the sociopolitical project in turn-of-the-century racial science and race law of reading race on the body. For the logic of racial visibility, for every bodily mark of racial identification "discovered" by eugenicists and others, there was a counterconsciousness, the fear of race operating in unseen ways beneath the surface of society. Twain's *Pudd'nhead Wilson* ends, both reluctantly and jubilantly, with the failed promise of Francis Galton's hypothesis that fingerprints would reveal the mark of race on the criminal body. Dixon's *The Clansman* defines the paradox of the Invisible Empire in a prayer that precedes the ritual burning of the hypervisible Fiery Cross: "As we wrestle with powers of darkness . . . , give to our souls to endure as seeing the invisible" (*C*, 319). *Seeing the invisible*—a construct both figurative and literal, fantasy and reality—sums up the threat and the promise of racial legibility in the melodramas. The ostentatious invisibility of racial forces barely hidden beneath the social surface is revealed through two different models of legibility that organize the race melodramas, the invisible "one drop" revealed by the narratives of passing and the invisible empires that dominate the narratives of race conspiracy and race riots. The Invisible Empire replaces the invisible drop of blood. In exposing the hyperinvisibility of race, not in individual identity (the blood narratives), but as a collectivity (the empire/conspiracy narratives), however, the effect is to explode the organizing polarities. In effect, race oversaturates the melodramas in both occulting and occulted modes: the frustrated visibility of "blackness," in which racial science seeks to detect race on the body—in fingerprints, in facial characteristics, or, at the very least, in the one drop of black blood—must be paired with a compensatory invisibility of "whiteness," which allows the unity of whites in the nation to be represented *as* invisible, unseen and largely unspeakable, deeper than the equally unspoken, surface differences of politics, region, and class that threaten the united front of white supremacy.

The threat, actuality, or sheer imagining of such invisible racial collectivities in the post-Reconstruction era produced a dizzying excess of possibilities. Describing the "shape of fear" inspired by the underground method of the new Klan of the 1920s, Du Bois notes that anyone unsure of "the sinister meaning of its existence should go to the nearest movie and see that Washington parade, that tremendous outpouring of hosts, white-gowned and hooded if not masked."[34] Hooded if not masked: the methods of night and mask, so ostentatiously displayed, produce what Du Bois diagnoses as a psychology of unknown ill and unanswerable innuendo. On the other hand, for white supremacists in the South, the imagined threat of organized black violence always just below the surface, only rarely erupting in the symptomatic race riot, countered the unmistakably visible evidence of the interracial, political coalitions that lasted, especially on the state and local levels, well beyond the onset of Jim Crow. The imagined communities of international black empires and Pan-Africas compensated for the divisive presence of intraracial divisions within the U.S. black "community"—the latter itself a singular construct serving varied, often-competing needs. By the same token, the heightened reality of the invisible empires of the Klan and the mob served simultaneously to visualize an imagined "white unity" masking divisions of region, economics, and politics within the white community and to hyperrepresent the lawlessness that in practice supported but in theory contradicted legal segregation in the states and the nation. The asymmetries of these relations underscore how the hyperinvisibility of race melodramas works, in protean, often imperfect ways, to distract attention away from the unspeakable, not beneath (as in Brooks's model), but on the very surface of race relations.

If "'race'" is, as Toni Morrison says in "Unspeakable Things Unspoken," underscoring the paradoxical "deference" of her own quotation marks, "still a virtually unspeakable thing," it is also the "ghost in the machine," just barely unseen. Invisible things have a virtual presence, defined by double negation, the "not necessarily 'not-there.'" Writing *race* as *"race"* (as in *"Race," "Writing, and Difference,* the title of the groundbreaking issue of *Critical Inquiry* that came out in 1985, just three years before Morrison's essay), we make its name "elaborately, painstakingly masked."[35] A century earlier, the race melodramatists work within and on the open secret—elaborately masked—of race by making a spectacle of what everyone knows but does not speak and what only later were historians able to document. Belying the increasing rigidity of the racial divide in the United States at the turn of the century is a ghost in the machine, the hyperinvisible marks unspoken but not unseen, both threatening and promising, of intraracial conflict and interracial cooperation. These are the class, regional, and political differences that fissure the unity of white supremacy in the South; the economic, social, and gender divisions that undercut the unity, and the singularity, of both the black and the white communities; the provisional and unstable alliances across racial lines in state politics well beyond the end of Reconstruction and the equally unstable, procrustean alliances between white-supremacist and black-nationalist groups that intermittently reappear to this day; the various pan-racial movements based on transnational histories of global dispersal. This is the excess of American race relations, the occult domain revealed by the race melodramas. Through the racial polarities with which we are so familiar, the melodramatic Manichaeism exposes much of what is unsettling, and unsettled, about race relations in the post-Reconstruction period.

Yet one condition of making legible through the melodramatic mode the open secrets of race is keeping the unspeakable things unspoken, that is, saying the name of race, itself always elaborately masked, and then, structurally, canceling out the saying. It is not just that the race melodramas must appear formally to sew up all the loose ends. How many late-nineteenth-century U.S. spokesmen—for that matter, how many of the writers on my shortlist known as racial ideologues—are known for their expressive breakthroughs? Here is where the excess of melodrama comes in, and this is why we still need the cultural work that it does in relation to race. First, not only do historical outcomes always remain provisional, but also, in specific terms, the work of the race melodramatists remains, like Reconstruction itself, America's "unfinished revolution," as noted above.[36] The race melodramas challenge the fatalism—the determinism of the tragic flaw—of the master narrative, dating to the *Birth of a Nation* school of historiography, which, in defiance of so much evidence to the contrary, still speaks as though black and white form the nation's primary, if not only, racial divide and as though *race* itself is a transhistorical, transcendent category.[37] Moreover, we create and re-create race, ritually repeating, reenacting, and, thus, reinventing its vocabularies to fit our own terrain.[38] So adaptable to change is the language of racial ideology that it can even tolerate its own demise—and apparently not just once, either. "Suddenly," Toni Morrison wrote in the late 1980s ("for our purposes, suddenly," she notes parenthetically), "'race' does not exist," and, now, in the early twenty-first century, we hear that "race" is dead, again.[39] Both the repetition and the exaggeration of the rumors of its death point to the particular excess of the language of racial ideology. To track in our everyday language the nineteenth-century vocabularies of race, most of them now attached to new things and usages, is to open up "a vast realm of complications," and "complications within complications," that constitute the history of the ideological ensemble of race.[40]

Precisely such an explicitly linguistic excess provides the motor of the race melodramas. Unlike the clarifying effects of melodramatic excess, achieved, more conventionally, through spectacle or affect, the varieties of rhetorical and formal excess characteristic of race melodramas prove explosive; the power of their verbal representations enacts linguistic uncertainty and anxiety. In formal terms, the happy endings, like their more overtly pessimistic counterparts, provide, at best and often ostentatiously, only imperfect closure. When families divided by slavery are reunited—as in Hopkins's *Contending Forces* or George Washington Cable's *The Grandissimes*, where the protagonists, in pairs, are last seen sailing off to Europe—or permanently fractured by that legacy—as in Hopkins's later *Of One Blood* and Charles Chesnutt's *The Marrow of Tradition*—the revelation of occluded relations clarifies only the past, leaving a future imperfect. Similarly, the linguistic repetitions that define melodramatic style produce a plethora of terms, slogans, and refrains—from *nation within the nation* to *Negro Problem*—circulated repeatedly among competing communities and resisting their own logic of orderly summary and encapsulation of meaning. Mapping the varieties of linguistic excess that drive the race melodramas and tracing that excess to the (plural) conceptions of history that dominate the texts will be my final task before bringing this introductory chapter to a conclusion.

First, excess and forms of closure: If Brooks's extended assessment of the end point of melodramatic ritual favors struggles over reconciliation— "it can offer no terminal reconciliation, for there is no longer a clear transcendent value to be reconciled to"—the race melodramas conclude even more inconclusively, more like film melodramas (of Oscar Micheaux, Douglas Sirk, and others) known for their imperfect happy ending.[41] Focusing on the maternal melodrama in American films of the 1930s, Christian Viviani notes that happy endings in this genre are as common as unhappy ones but that the former often have "a false or tacked-on quality" that does not really affect the "basic pessimism of the maternal melo."[42] Extending this reading to the ideological function of melodrama, broadly construed, with Sirk as the example, Laura Mulvey argues that "the strength of the melodramatic form lies in the amount of dust the story raises along the road, a cloud of over-determined irreconcilables which put up a resistance to being settled in the last five minutes."[43] A simple difference between these imperfect happy endings and the open-endedness of the race question represented in the melodramatic mode derives from the difference in audience and standpoint: both the maternal melodrama and the Sirk-style family melodrama are made with a female audience in mind, and the dominating, sometimes initiating point of view is most often the female protagonist's. The race melodramas, on the other hand, act out contradictions between racial and sexual dilemmas that end, not in impossible resolutions and probable defeats, but with the markedly incomplete containment of an open-ended future: the provisional outcome of the history of race relations itself.

To take only one example of just such an imperfect ending: many of the race melodramas work within an erotics of politics (characteristic of the nineteenth-century historical romance from Cooper to Melville as well as of the "foundational fictions" of Latin America that the critic Doris Sommer has identified), in which lovers representing different races, regions, or class interests are united in marriage as a figure for national unity.[44] But the marital unions and, more to the point, familial reunions that conclude many of the late-nineteenth-century U.S. race melodramas are, notably often, too little, too late, accentuating, within the formal closure, the absence of social resolution or political reconciliation. From within a nominally allegorical relation between fiction and history, the U.S. race melodramas force us to rethink the grounds of that relation. What the novels leave unresolved or unreconciled are historical forces generated by, but not limited to, race.

These include gender conflict, the ongoing debate over the positive or negative role (not to mention the very existence) of the matriarchal black family,
and new national and transnational conflicts and collectivities emerging in
this era of global empire. Put another way, the imperfect happy ending of the
race melodramas enacts in formal terms the unfinished revolution in race relations that, as noted earlier, Eric Foner sees as the legacy of Reconstruction.

Second, excess and melodramatic style: The lack of formal resolution
in the melodrama produces, in turn, the compensatory structures of melodramatic excess. The excess becomes explicitly discursive, taking the form
of a cultivated rhetorical doubling or repetition of dominant racial tropes
and discourses. A variety of stylistic and formal elements refuse to be textually incorporated, from the repetition of key terms and lines, seemingly
taking on a life of their own within the texts, to the packaging of prefaces
and afterwords, notes and manifestos, appended to the text and written in
the author's own voice—as though to reiterate what has not actually been
said, despite the repeated refrains, in the text proper. "Can you build, in a
Democracy," Thomas Dixon asks repeatedly in *The Leopard's Spots,* the
first volume of his Klan trilogy, "a nation inside a nation of two hostile
races?" For Dixon, there is no definitive answer; instead, the central question of *The Leopard's Spots*— *"Shall the future American be an Anglo-Saxon
or a Mulatto?"*—remains a kind of anxious refrain, posed repeatedly
throughout the novel (e.g., *LS,* 159, 438).[45] The repetition enacts melodrama's incessant struggle against enemies without and within, enemies
who must be confronted and expunged, Brooks says, "over and over." But,
rather than assure the triumph of virtue in "clear language," the race melodramas are left with the imperative to rehearse and reenact, "over and over,"
the conflicts in confronting the provisional historical outcome of race in the
United States.[46] The clear language of melodrama is entangled with, and
compromised by, the fraught and unstable terminology of race, so often derived from legal and scientific usage that exceeds its own bounds. The
rhetorical doublings, repetitions in different registers, of such key terms as
blood and *mulatto* in Twain, Hopkins, Dixon, et al. are echoed in the larger
doubling structures—of character and plot, factual and fictional realms—
that organize the novels. It is an organization by excess. Like exploding allegories, the doublings either fail to dovetail, as in the asymmetry of Hopkins's Negro and Woman Questions, or multiply excessively, as in Griggs's
ornate and torturous interlocked plottings in *Love and Politics* as well as
Twain's dizzying twinning of racial and sexual masquerade in *Pudd'nhead
Wilson.*

The race melodramas exceed the binary of black and white by extending it into a different logic of supplementarity that constitutes the reiterative
excess of the melodramatic mode. The binary structures are, in effect, required in order to be exceeded. In Judith Butler's account of such discursive
excess, it is the "reiterative" or "citational" power of discourse that produces or performs both the regulatory norms of race and sex and the possibility of a counterreiteration that "mimes and renders hyperbolic the discursive convention that it also reverses."[47] Homi Bhabha similarly describes
mimicry in the colonial context as at once resemblance and menace.[48] The
ambivalence of mimicry is fundamental to the discursive excess of the race
melodramas, in which reiteration of racial formulas and discourses can be a
strategy both of simple repetition and of historical resignification. In all
cases, the doubling structures enact, not simply binary division (of black vs.
white or North vs. South), but the reiteration with a difference that could be
said to characterize the tangle of contradictory and overlapping identifica-
tions and divisions in American race relations of the late nineteenth century.

Thus we have a history of excess or, put another way, excess in and as
history. The historical narratives that define the post-Reconstruction era
through binaries, whether the Old South–New South divisions of traditional Southern historiography or the Washington–Du Bois, Du Bois–
Garvey splits of African American history, have proved so resilient, with-
standing repeated, revisionist pressures, in large part because they establish
the black-white parameters that must be continually redefined in order to be
broken. Since W. E. B. Du Bois's *Black Reconstruction in America* (1935),
followed later by C. Vann Woodward's work on the strange careers of Jim
Crow and Tom Watson, several generations of Southern historians have
revised the master themes—black incapacity, white supremacy—of the
Birth of a Nation, or Dunning, school of Southern history.[49] Disputing the
narratives of politically and morally polarized racial opposites that Dixon,
Griffith, et al. purveyed, revisionist historians focus on the post-
Emancipation era's shifting alliances and antagonisms—interracial, cross-
class—that exceeded the enshrined divisions of Republican versus Democrat, New versus Old South, white versus black.[50] To acknowledge this
historical excess from within the long-standing polarities of American race
relations is the challenge taken on by the race melodramas explored in this
book.

In the wake of the Civil War, as U.S. nationalism was reconsolidated
through and against the pressures of new imperialist and internationalist
ventures, struggles over the meaning of the nation's history were waged,

most obviously in *Birth of a Nation*, but also in other, less visible venues. From the Dunning school of academic historians, which revised sectional conflict through a focus on post-Emancipation Southern history as "the tragic era" (G. Claude Bowers, William A. Dunning), to the black-history movement of Carter Woodson, Arthur Schomburg, and others, the racialization of modern U.S. historiography in the early twentieth century is as unmistakable as the ideological rifts that it embodies. In the 1930s, Du Bois's *Black Reconstruction in America* indicted "the propaganda of history" and showed "how the facts of American history have in the last half century been falsified because the nation was ashamed." In such a heated context, Du Bois notes at the end of *Black Reconstruction*, what would ordinarily be a straightforward survey of bibliographic sources becomes "an arraignment of American historians and an indictment of their ideals" (*BRA*, 725).[51] As the discipline of American history was, thus, institutionalized and politicized, a variety of counterhistoricisms and alternative kinds of historical consciousness simultaneously sprang up, including, most notably, the practice of black history in both academic and popular-cultural spheres. Woodson not only founded a scholarly quarterly, the *Journal of Negro History*, but also established Negro History Week, the "crowning achievement," according to Du Bois, of "one man who in a lifetime has, unaided, built up such a national celebration." Woodson "literally made this country, which has only the slightest respect for people of color, recognize and celebrate each year . . . the effect which the American Negro has upon life, thought, and action in the United States."[52] Woodson and his journal—the aim of which was "to popularize the movement to save and make available the scattered historical materials bearing on the Negro"—embody the twin scholarly and popular imperatives that characterize so much of the historiography, emanating from all political perspectives, of the period.[53]

At virtually the same moment, the race melodramas are engaged in their own avowedly historiographic projects. Concepts of time in the melodramas reflect their different historicist visions and positions: from the relational histories of the maternal melodrama, which pair and compare the black mother in slavery and in freedom; to the twinned repetition of evolutionary and, its opposite, atavistic "nation-time" of the paternal melodramas; to the messianic modes of Du Boisean occult history.[54] The maternal melodrama represents both the reconciliation of the nation through the reunion of dispersed families and the invisible dispersal of "black blood" into the national mainstream via the maternal-passing plot (Chesnutt, Cable, Twain, Harper, Hopkins). The national-conspiratorial mode of

Griggs and Dixon retraces the history of the nation from the American Revolution to the Spanish-American War, with Reconstruction as the contested midpoint, almost an excluded middle, simultaneously vilified and forgotten. Twain's time-travel narratives discover the presence of empire within and without the democratic American body. Finally, subsuming and overarching all these modes is what I call *occult history*, a prophetic form and futurist imagining of a transhistorical racial consciousness that crosses boundaries of blood and nation. As a philosopher of occult history, Du Bois most explicitly systematizes the variety of historicisms in the race melodramas. His conception of the veil as both the material line historically dividing white from black America and the spiritual source of the American Negro's prophetic future outlines the practice of occult history, which resists divisions between the rational and the mystical, between art and science.

This is the moment of the racial occult—not a Brooksean metaphor for a hidden moral legibility, but a specific historical formation. The popular occult synthesis of the early twentieth century provided an unlikely outlet for the convergence of both racial and historicist thinking. If we take only the example of Freemasonry as one of the occult fraternities that flourished at the turn of the century, the Masonic commitment to tracing an implicitly racialized past through a variety of occult forms and discourses is striking. Not only did most Masonic lodges include a "grand historian," responsible for recording local members and activities and reflecting the portrayal of modern fraternalism as the embodiment of ancient traditions, but Masonic chroniclers also traced the origins of Freemasonry back to the building of King Solomon's temple and, simultaneously, emphasized the foundational status of ancient Egypt as the source of all knowledge and the Egyptian mysteries as a specific source of Masonic ritual and symbology. The longstanding debate over the race of the ancient Egyptians was only one way in which racial history entered the picture.[55] If we follow the lead of the black Prince Hall Masons, we will see how Masonic historicism joined with the larger project of race history, resulting, for example, in internationalist histories like Du Bois's *The Negro*, his 1915 study intended for the general reader.[56] In tandem with this larger project (and advertised in *The Crisis* alongside *The Negro*), a study of Negro Masonry, George W. Crawford's *Prince Hall and His Followers*, argued for the legitimacy of the black fraternity through its historical origins in the Revolutionary War and its founding father, the Barbadian immigrant and war hero Prince Hall.[57] As the grand secretary of a New York lodge populated largely by African Americans and West Indians, Arthur Schomburg cultivated public awareness of

Masonry's historic events and figures, including Prince Hall, even as, as a bibliophile and the founder of the Negro Society for Historical Research, he collected books on the Negro from all over the world and, by his own assessment, "brought together for the first time co-operatively in a single society African, West Indian and Afro-American scholars," all part of the effort to promote "race scholarship."[58]

In addition, what historians variously characterize as the theatricality and public display of fraternal ritual points to the broad uses made during this period of pageantry, processional, parade, and spectacle—to educate, for example, or to intimidate, or to advance a political cause. The Klan paraded, hooded if not masked, as Du Bois comments, and lynchings were orchestrated, organized spectacles of racial violence, both phenomena on the rise, we know, during the early decades of the twentieth century.[59] Fraternal drill teams and parade units, along with various women's auxiliaries, were on the march, growing in popularity with the increasingly visible militarism of the culture of U.S. imperialism. This is no Brooksean spectacle, no transhistorical aesthetic of the melodramatic imagination. Rather, all the pageantry, parades, and mass meetings, as well as the street theater and oratory, that one finds in the early decades of the twentieth century represent the historically specific use of spectacle to promote fraternal and race-based, national and internationalist, social and political movements.

One geographic focal point was New York City during the period of Southern migration and Caribbean immigration. Here, Schomburg was photographed in his Mason's fez; here, he also presided over the 1921 opening ceremonies of the New York State Prince Hall Grand Lodge, which included a service at the Mother Zion African Methodist Episcopal Church on West 136th Street in Harlem, followed by two parades through the neighborhood. Downtown, in Greenwich Village, socialists and others of the Lyrical Left staged plays and pageants to dramatize class struggle, the most famous being the 1913 Paterson Pageant at Madison Square Garden. Marcus Garvey's spectacular UNIA rallies adapted the "West Indian parade complex" to produce a tremendously effective, transculturated performance that represented the Caribbean, immigrant ethos of the New York Garvey movement.[60] Du Bois reluctantly recognized Garvey as a fellow master of propaganda, one who staged his own "comic opera" in the form of the parades of uniformed troops and "Black Cross" nurses in Harlem and rallies at Madison Square Garden.[61] Although Du Bois may have been neither a "stepladder radical"—like Garvey, who spoke from a specially built platform at the speaker's corner at Lenox Avenue and 135th Street—nor a "street historian"—like John E. Bruce (who wrote under the name "Bruce Grit"), a militant black journalist, Garveyite, and close friend (and fellow Mason) of Arthur Schomburg—he, too, ventured into political theater. He staged his own pageant of race history, "The Star of Ethiopia," at a New York armory in 1913, during the celebrations marking the fiftieth anniversary of Emancipation, and the Pan-African Congresses that he organized and attended are often criticized as primarily symbolic spectacles. Not only do all these events and figures share a penchant for dramatic form, but they also underscore the intertwined historicism, internationalism, and activism that characterized the spectacle as a form.[62]

If this is the moment of the racial occult, then where it leads, to what historical and political ends, is perhaps the most vexed question that I address in this book. Compounding the prevalence of fraud and victimization in so many occult movements, the political associations of occultism with conspiratorial and right-wing groups confront modern commentators with perhaps the most intractable ethical problem. Paul Gilroy distills these objections into a compelling, overarching critique of *occultism*, a term that he associates with the mystical, irrational sources of fascism and its reliance on "raciology." Pondering the recurrent appeal of fascism, Gilroy argues that, whereas the language of belonging—essential notions of the unity and purity of race—undergirding fascist authoritarianism once relied on the "rational wisdom of racial science," it has now been updated, articulated through other, "less respectable, varieties of race-thinking that derive from occult, mystical, and assertively irrational sources." Although Gilroy sees the noxious mix of modern occultism in part as a return to and a revival of the biological codes of the eighteenth century, "leavened with New Age themes," he also stresses how race stabilizes the interconnection between these different and potentially incompatible systems.[63] My racial occult, located in the temporal, middle ground, as it were, of the turn of the century, foregrounds the moment when science and the occult converged around the central fact of racial difference, demonstrating their fundamental affinities as modes of racial thinking—and militating against the division between the rational and the irrational, the intellectual and the anti-intellectual.

So, too, is this a moment marked by the emergence of the intersection between fraternalism and militarism that Gilroy sees as central to the recurrent appeal of fascism. For Gilroy, fraternalism coalesces the pathology of raciology, particularly its principles of irrational authoritarianism and its ideology based on an archaic form of kinship, intolerant, masculinist, and militaristic. Some of his most pointed questions briefly touch on the specific, political meanings of Prince Hall Freemasonry, from his invocation of Martin Delany's critique of Freemasonry's "weak and glittering follies" to the pernicious uses by the Nation of Islam of the Prince Hall tradition.[64] For me, black Freemasonry must, instead, be situated squarely within the culture of the racial occult, where the extraordinary range of both occultism's limits and its possibilities come into view. For example, within that larger context, the masculinism of Masonry, in particular, and the gendering of fraternalism, in general, constitute a zone of debate rather than an assumption. Historians have long conjectured about the striking conjunctions between the vogue for spiritualism, dating to the 1840s, and the flowering of reform movements, especially women's rights; although many feminists were interested in both spiritualism and Theosophy, it is not clear whether or how such occult movements provided a coherent framework for feminism. The point is that the politics of occultism range all over the map and resist being reduced either to the conservative or to the radical.[65]

Finally, an assessment of the social and political meaning of the racial occult must take into account what Gilroy calls "the racial politics of temporality." As *Modernity and Double Consciousness,* the subtitle of *The Black Atlantic,* indicates, Gilroy focuses on the interrelations between modernity (with its implied opposite, tradition) and double consciousness, and, in *Against Race,* he explores fascism's fascination with racialized origins and apocalyptic futures.[66] Even more capaciously than these temporal possibilities, the varying concepts of time noted above, in relation to the historiographic imperative of the race melodramas, point to the often implicit but nonetheless foundational role of temporality in producing race consciousness. The hyperinvisibility of race, which Toni Morrison names *the unspeakable,* is located temporally in an occult zone in which past, present, and future coexist in unstable and shifting relations. Time travel, whether to the space and time of slavery, the Revolutionary War, or Africa, is only the most conventional way in which to describe the disjunctive temporality of the race melodramas. Just such a sense of disoriented and disorienting time is conjured in the prologue to *Invisible Man:* "Invisibility, let me explain, gives one a slightly different sense of time, you're never quite on the beat. Sometimes you're ahead and sometimes behind. Instead of the swift and imperceptible flowing of time, you are aware of its nodes, those points where time stands still or from which it leaps ahead. And you slip into the breaks and look around."[67] How does what we might call this *sense of occult time* open up and redefine the telling of racial history that is fundamental to the race melodramas?

Ishmael Reed's novel *Mumbo Jumbo* limns some of the limits and pos-sibilities of the racial occult. What Reed does is to invent an alternative, se-cret black history—carefully "documented"—supposedly revealing the underground existence of a movement dubbed "Jus' Grew." This history is based on a lost "Book," a work traced back to the ancient Egyptian triangle of Osiris-Isis-Set, and grounded in the self-mocking and subversive but still scholarly apparatus of footnotes and a "Partial Bibliography." The bibliog-raphy, equally divided among classics of the Western occult, studies of voodoo, and scholarly books on psychoanalysis, ancient Egypt, and jazz, in-cludes Blavatsky's *Isis Unveiled*, Zora Neal Hurston's *Mules and Men*, and Montague Summers's *The History of Witchcraft and Demonology* as well as several histories of Freemasonry. *Mumbo Jumbo* pretends to reveal the se-crets or hidden word of black history (of "The Work," as the lost book is slyly called), but its genuinely controversial move is to attribute the prove-nance of that historical knowledge to an improvisational, syncretic oc-cultism recorded, even flaunted, in the bibliographic sources.

Attempting to solve the mystery of Jus' Grew by recovering its lost text, *Mumbo Jumbo* reaches its climax with the final revelation of PaPa LaBas, the "Neo-Hoodoo" detective figure, who tells a story that begins with Osiris discovering or inventing Jus' Grew and passing "The Work" down through Isis to Moses and ends, provisionally, with the modern legacy of the holy wars of the Knights Templar, the struggles of black Freemasonry becoming a symbol for black struggle worldwide. The voo-doo tradition instructs, the novel tells us, and "H. P. Blavatsky concurs: 'The fraternity of Free Masons was founded in Egypt and Moses communi-cated the secret teaching to Israelites, Jesus to the apostles and thence it found its way to the Knights Templar.'" The result: "We learned what we had always suspected, that the Masonic mysteries were of a blacker origin than we thought . . . and the reason they wanted us out of the mysteries was because they were our mysteries!"[68] Not only does *Mumbo Jumbo* thus fill in some of the spaces on the map of the racial occult outlined by the race melo-dramas, but also, much more surprisingly, the misogynist Reed, target of so much well-deserved feminist critique, gestures toward a potentially radical, female gendering of ancient Egypt, similarly centered in the figure of Isis, which (as we will see in the last chapter) flowers in Du Bois's work during the war decade.

Where does this leave us? Certainly, the question of the political and social efficacy of such occultisms—whether the racial occult can shape politics or even have a meaningful politics of any kind—remains unan-

swered. (It stands beside the related question of the credentials of melodrama as a revolutionary genre or mode: the historical convergence of theatrical melodrama with the French Revolution has inspired, and con-
founded, critics from Peter Brooks to Marxist theorists of popular and mass
culture, all of whom debate the possible cause-and-effect relation between
the form and the political context.)[69] One finds as many answers as one finds
critics. Acknowledging this uncertainty, Stuart Hall holds that, given the
"'*problem*' of ideology," all systems of representation, including popular-
cultural forms such as melodrama, offer no guarantees, only articulations
both to the Left and to the Right.[70] The culture of the occult is rife with evidence of such shifting, and shifty, politics. Du Bois considers Garvey and
the Ku Klux Klan to be "birds of a feather, believing in titles, flummery and
mumbo-jumbo" ("MG," 274). The historian T. Jackson Lears finds in the
turn-of-the-century vogue for "popular occultism," as in other antimod-
ernist tendencies, "a dual significance": "It promoted accommodation to
new modes of cultural hegemony while it preserved an eloquent edge of
protest."[71] Historians generally continue to argue about the role of Theosophy in such political causes as Indian independence.[72] And Paul Gilroy attacks black political culture on the grounds that it is occultist, irrational,
and authoritarian.[73] Ultimately, the rest of my book attempts to answer such
questions, which could follow only after beginning first by establishing
that the move to the culture of the occult always takes phenomena not out
of but into the realm of the social and political and, thus, deep into the realm
of social intervention.

CHAPTER TWO

PAULINE HOPKINS AND BLOOD TALK

———

REVISING RACIAL SCIENCE, TELLING
RACE HISTORY IN MATERNAL MELODRAMAS

IN HER by now almost canonical magazine novel of 1902–3 *Of One Blood; or, The Hidden Self,* Pauline Hopkins combines the science of the occult—meaning what the opening pages describe as theories of "supernatural phenomena or *mysticism*" associated with "the great field of new discoveries in psychology" (*OOB,* 442)—with a science that can be considered occult as well, that of archaeology, and specifically Egyptology, to reveal in both sciences the overt and implicit racializing that shaped so many late-nineteenth-century Euro-American discourses.[1] Hopkins's novel, a melodrama of tangled kinship relations originating during the time of slavery, is divided into two parts—one American, one African—that together solve the mystery of identity—unveiling the hidden self—utilizing "supernatural phenomena," such as mediumistic trance and spirit communication, as well as the long-lost "wisdom and science" (*OOB,* 572) of ancient Africa, recovered during an archaeological expedition to the ruins of the Ethiopian city of Meroë, the site of an important nineteenth-century dig. As does Hopkins's ethnological companion text, *A Primer of Facts Pertaining to the Early Greatness of the African Race* (1905), the novel combines two different sciences—one psychological, the other archaeological, but both based on notions of excavation, mysticism, and occulted wisdom, and both contributing significantly to scholarly and popular discourse on mind and race—in order to identify and engage a striking range of positions and debates, inter- and intraracial, within the nineteenth century's "ubiquitous race question" (*OOB,* 584): political issues of black leadership, black nationalism, Pan-Africanism, and the African-origins-of-Western-civilization thesis, including its implications for theories of species origins, identity, and race purity.[2]

Of One Blood was serialized in the *Colored American Magazine* during 1902–3. By that time, Hopkins had already produced a wealth of "race literature" in this "monthly magazine, distinctly devoted to the development of Afro-American art and literature," as an editorial statement announced in the first issue of 1900. For Hopkins, this meant writing that aspires above all to develop "the bonds of racial brotherhood" and that does so, not only in fiction and poetry, but also in "the arena of historical, social, and economic literature."[3] To that end, Hopkins's own writing for the journal included, in addition to four novels and several short stories, two long-running biographical series ("Famous Men of the Negro Race" and "Famous Women of the Negro Race") and numerous essays offering political and social commentary on such topics as Roosevelt's black political appointments, the Philippine War and the subsequent U.S. occupation, and the role of blacks in the suffrage and labor movements. In the context of this varied literary production, *Of One Blood* incorporates many of the factual issues covered by Hopkins in her nonfiction. At the same time, the novel represents the turn in her thinking, as well as in that of the *Colored American Magazine* and the community of black activist-intellectuals in general, elevating the status of the Negro Problem from that of primarily a domestic issue to that of a global issue. The novel's African setting and its Pan-Africanism take an international perspective on race relations that is also summarized in the series of documentary articles, running concurrently with *Of One Blood*, entitled "Ethiopians of the Twentieth Century," written by A. Kirkland Soga, a South African journalist, and described in an editorial announcement as reflecting the magazine's mission "to do whatever we have the power to do to advance the best interests of the race everywhere."[4]

Equally, although less obviously, central to Hopkins's project of inspiring "race progress" is the investment of *Of One Blood* in several Euro-American scientific rhetorics and debates of the day. Some of them, notably those dealing with ethnology and theories of blood, were notorious, then and now, for their association with racist social projects and goals, while others, particularly both the long-standing occult sciences and the modern science of psychology, were not generally perceived as shaped by the "Negro Question," local, global, or otherwise. In Hopkins's rendering, none of these sciences is race neutral. The question at stake for reading Hopkins's engagement with racial science—as she so broadly construes it—is whether and how she, like so many African American intellectuals throughout the nineteenth century, stereotyped as different and inferior by those sciences, not only responds to those dominant discourses, but also converts them to her own use. A preliminary answer: given the particular volatility at this time of the sciences of Egyptology and psychology, not yet clearly bounded disciplines, but still fluid sites of sometimes competing orthodox and emergent theories, it is no coincidence that, as we will see, it is specifically the latter, minority traditions within these sciences that Hopkins selects and adapts to her racial project.[5]

It takes only a brief plot summary to indicate how saturated *Of One Blood* is in the occult sciences of its day. Drawing on the formulas and strategies of nineteenth-century popular fiction—disguised, doubled, and multiple identities, babies exchanged in the cradle, magical signs and birthmarks as proofs of identity, incest and miscegenation—the novel does not conclude with the tidy, order-restoring resolution associated with such fiction. The opening, American half of the novel narrates the relations among three mixed-race protagonists: Reuel Briggs, a medical doctor and an expert in "animal" or "volatile magnetism" whose "olive" skin marks and masks his ancestry (he is rumored to be either Italian or Japanese) (*OOB,* 468, 444); his only friend, Aubrey Livingston, a Southern aristocrat; and Dianthe Lusk, the beautiful ex-slave whom they both love. Dianthe temporarily loses her memory after a train accident in which she is taken for dead but revived by Reuel's magnetizing powers, which are themselves emblems of barely conscious and potentially illicit sexual control. Subsequently, both men conspire to hide Dianthe's identity as a "Negress," allowing her to maintain her "incognito" and to pass as white (*OOB,* 479, 474). In this guise, Reuel marries her but is forced by the machinations of Aubrey, who uses his knowledge of Briggs's black heritage to undermine his applications for medical positions, to take the post of medical adviser on the Meroë archaeological expedition and to entrust Dianthe to the care of his "false friend," as, he says with unknowing accuracy and the portentous foreshadowing of popular fiction, "I would intrust her to my brother, had I one" (*OOB,* 504, 497). This first section of the novel closes with Aubrey's seduction of Dianthe; in a postbellum recapitulation of the sexual violence done to her female forebears, Dianthe succumbs, "against her will," to the "invisible influences" of Aubrey, himself the son of the slaveholding white father and doctor who mesmerized and took as his concubine his slave Mira, the mother of all three protagonists (*OOB,* 505).

The rest of the novel unfolds this tangled American past within the future history of "Afro-Americans" as what A. Kirkland Soga called "Ethiopians of the Twentieth Century"—or, as Hopkins puts it in the novel, "the modern Ethiopian," "a branch of the wonderful and mysterious Ethiopians who had a prehistoric existence of magnificence, the full record of which is lost in obscurity" (*OOB*, 532, 560). (The term *Ethiopian*—regularly used to refer to all Africans, just as *Ethiopia* meant all sub-Saharan Africa—was sometimes used, especially by New World black nationalists, including Hopkins, to refer to all blacks in the diaspora.) Reuel Briggs is acknowledged by the inhabitants of the hidden city of Telassar—once part of the Ethiopian civilization of Meroë, "the very metropolis where science and art had their origin," now "a magnificent Necropolis"—as their long-awaited king, Ergamenes, who will restore the Ethiopian (African, Negro) "race" to its ancient glory (*OOB*, 538, 556). He is also united with the Ethiopian virgin queen Candace, who, according to evidence presented in Hopkins's *Primer of Facts*, is one of the historical line of great Ethiopian queens who periodically ruled Meroë and, in the novel, is a reincarnation of Dianthe, pointedly cast as a "Venus worked in bronze" (*OOB*, 567).[6] Meanwhile, back in America, Dianthe herself learns—through a story told her by her maternal grandmother, a "noted 'voodoo' doctor or witch"—of her incestuous relationships with Reuel and Aubrey both and is forced by Aubrey to take the poison that she intended for him (*OOB*, 603). Aubrey then takes his own life, in the tradition of the royal Ethiopian line. Having been forewarned of these events through a series of occult visions, in which "the hand of mysticism," in the "fine, female" script of their mother, Mira, is visible, Reuel returns to America, but too late to do anything more than to allow Dianthe to die in his arms (*OOB*, 506). After this history of the destructive social relations of slavery, the novel concludes that, for the protagonists, there is no possibility of a happy ending, or of any conclusive ending, in America, Africa, or elsewhere. The last scene takes place in Africa, where Reuel and Queen Candace rule over an imagined Pan-African community that is already threatened: "He views, with serious apprehension, the advance of mighty nations penetrating the dark, mysterious forests of his native land. . . . Where will it stop? he sadly questions. What will the end be?" (*OOB*, 621).

Even such a brief summary suggests how thoroughly Hopkins's occult is topicalized by her research in the history of ancient African arts and languages as well as in the modern, scientific fields of ethnology, psychology, and archaeology. Drawing on both complementary and conflicting relations among these knowledges, *Of One Blood* demonstrates the complexities, cultural and historical, that beset the putatively objective use of "blood" as a marker of racialized identity/identities. The novel also emplots the discursive excess of blood through its melodramatic formulas, unfolding a hidden set of kinship relations structured by the overdetermined history of slavery in the United States. In so doing, the novel enacts the fundamental project of the maternal melodrama: to historicize the black family in slavery and freedom. As in so many antebellum novels, not to mention the slave codes themselves, the slave mother provides the locus of identity, the agent both of the passing down of slavery and, in cases of mixed-race families, of the possibility of passing out of that condition. But, in contrast to pre-Emancipation race melodramas (by, e.g., Harriet Beecher Stowe and William Wells Brown), which are driven by the urgency of the issue of abolition, the post-Reconstruction texts focus more on constructing comparative histories of slavery and freedom that analyze and assess present race relations in the context of the past, condensing those temporal relations in the locus of the family.

More specifically, Hopkins's matrilineal genealogies should be placed in the context of other, contemporary maternal melodramas that foreground the constitutive relations between slave history and what Du Bois exposes in *Black Reconstruction* as the move "back toward slavery" (*BRA*, 670) of post-Reconstruction socioeconomics.[7] Tracing the often-occluded presence of the past in post-Emancipation race relations, the maternal melodramas offer two basic, relational plots: the maternal-familial plot of reuniting the dispersed family and, alternatively, the maternal-passing plot of the invisible dispersal of "black blood" into the national mainstream. Each of these plots takes a different approach to constructing the relation of the past to the present. Frances Harper's *Iola Leroy* (1892) and Charles Chesnutt's *The Marrow of Tradition* (1901), as well as Hopkins's fiction, represent the possible outcomes of the first alternative. Structured via flashbacks to the slavery past that are incorporated into the narrative setting of the post-Reconstruction present, these novels reveal unexpected histories and new collectivities embedded in the aftereffects of slavery. The second alternative, most familiar in the so-called local-color tradition of George Washington Cable and Kate Chopin as well as the "realism" of Mark Twain, all of whom use settings in the antebellum South to exploit, and challenge, the vogue for plantation novels in the post-Reconstruction era, works differently. The maternal-passing plots in texts such as Cable's "Madame Delphine" (1881), Chopin's "Desirée's Baby" and "La Belle Zoraïde" (late 1880s), and Twain's *Pudd'nhead Wilson* (1894) are set entirely in a pre-Emancipation time and place, displacing the present by collapsing onto the antebellum past anxieties over the instability of racial and sexual identities produced in the aftermath of slavery and Reconstruction. In contrast to the maternal-familial plot of reunion, the historical tragedies of broken matrilinearity dramatized in these plots—the denial of kinship by and to the many mixed-race mothers (Cable's Madame Delphine, Twain's Roxy, Chopin's Desirée as well as her husband's, and, possibly, her own, unknown biological mother), who provide motor and motive for the plot, and the ensuing loss, to the worlds of whiteness or blackness, of their sons and daughters—bear only the most oblique relation to the present, available mostly indirectly through the layering or superimposition of temporalities.

Together, Twain and Cable best convey the limited temporal consciousness of the maternal-passing plot. As Eric Sundquist has shown, *Pudd'nhead Wilson*, Twain's detective novel of exchanged babies, fingerprinting, and murder, superimposes onto the 1840s, the time in which the novel is set, the legal issues surrounding the concept of separate but equal that, with *Plessy v. Ferguson* (1896), came to a climax during the decade when the novel was published.[8] The layering of periods veils even as it gestures toward the constitutive relations between past and present. Allegory provides a related mode of indirectly linking past and present in Cable's *The Grandissimes* (1880), set during the 1803 Louisiana "Cession," widely perceived by post-Reconstruction readers as a metaphor for the South during Secession. (In a telling conversation rendered in the novel's Creole dialect, a painting of "Louisiana rif-using to hanter de h-Union" is praised by the young Creole artist as a "Gran' subjec'!" to which the novel's German outsider figure replies with a cryptic "'Allegorical.'")[9] Here, the story of a racially divided New Orleans family—in which one brother, the white Honoré Grandissime, seeks restitution for his wronged half brother, known as "Honoré f.m.c." (free man of color)—extends beyond the recognizable terrain of the literature of national reconciliation to posit a genuinely alternative maternal genealogy for another of the novel's Creole aristocrats, the rival Fusilier clan. For "the proudest old turkey," Agricola Fusilier, Cable invents a royal ancestry, complete with "Indian-Queen" Lufki-humma, born of "the blood of the royal caste of the great Toltec mother-race, which before it yielded its Mexican splendors to the conquering Aztec, throned the jeweled and gold-laden Inca in the South and sent the sacred fire of its temples into the North" (*G*, 101, 18). The inset tale—another maternal melodrama—of "Agricola's most boasted ancestor" ("it appears the darkness of her cheek had no effect to make him less white" [*G*, 18]) brings in the long New World history of colonization and empire, just as a series of interpolated tales of *marronnage* centered on the runaway slave Bras Coupé, once an African king, brings in the companion histories of slave rebellion and black resistance. But the potential link between the Bras Coupé story and that of Honoré f.m.c. is never made, just as the gap between past and present remains unbridged. Like all the texts driven by varieties of the maternal-passing plot, the relation of slavery past to the post-Reconstruction present is, thus, disrupted, always only implied or at best allegorized, with no direct access route between temporalities, whereas the maternal-familial plots of Harper, Chesnutt, and especially Hopkins explicitly bring the slavery past into notably disjunctive alignment with the present.

Enacting the circuit of past, present, and deferred future relations, the maternal-familial plot foregrounds the function of storytelling in the many interpolated narratives and flashbacks through which matrilineal histories, typically hidden or otherwise inaccessible, are reconstructed. For both Harper and Chesnutt, the past extends into the narrative present specifically through the revelation of the aftereffects of a conundrum of slave law, which recognized the female slave as mother but not as wife. Even, or especially, in cases of white men marrying their manumitted slaves, "the marriage certificate is not worth the paper it is written on," as one of the characters of Harper's *Iola Leroy* puts it.[10] That legal contradiction accounts, we learn in an extended flashback near the beginning of *Iola Leroy,* for the ignorance of their mixed identity in which the Leroy children are initially kept, for the "remanding to slavery" of the whole Leroy family after the death of their white father, and, finally, for the subsequent choice of both Iola and her brother not to "slip out from the race and pass into the white basis" (*IL,* 95, 263). However, rather than laying to rest these issues of identity, the flashback ends abruptly back in the novel's present, with the still-pressing need "to bind anew the ties which slavery had broken" (*IL,* 148). Although the rest of the novel does, indeed, "gather together the remnants of the scattered family" (*IL,* 148), the shadows of the history of slavery continue to obscure the future, if not the novel's own narrative present.

In *The Marrow of Tradition,* Chesnutt offers the same legal conundrum with a post-Emancipation twist: interracial marriages that date from the period of "military occupation of the state just after the civil war" are "legally valid, though morally and socially outrageous," according to the view of Major Carteret, an unreconstructed Southerner and the owner of one of the state's most prominent newspapers.[11] Unbeknownst to Carteret, a marriage of precisely this kind has created the "distressing family secret" that both divides and unites the novel's half sisters, his own wife, the white Olivia Carteret, and the black Janet Miller, the wife of a prosperous black doctor, all of whom live together in the intersecting but segregated worlds of Wellington, North Carolina (the fictional Wilmington) (*MT*, 129). Although the wealthy Millers have bought and now live in the old Carteret mansion and the Carterets and the Millers occasionally cross paths (sometimes casually, sometimes not, as when the Carteret baby becomes ill and needs medical attention from Dr. Miller), the tie between the sisters is not recognized until old Aunt Polly Ochiltree tells Olivia, her niece, "the whole story" of how the family estate had been saved from her father's mulatta housekeeper (*MT*, 133). The family relations—of a type "all too common in the old slavery days" and "projected into the new era" as well—have already been hinted at, but only when Aunt Polly takes over the narration and tells her niece "what I did for you and yours" are we provided proof, in the form of a missing marriage certificate and will, that identifies the two "lawful sisters" as legitimate daughters and heirs of a wealthy, slaveowning father, Olivia the child of his "beloved first wife," Janet the unacknowledged child of his secret second marriage to his mulatta housekeeper (*MT*, 7, 133–34, 327, 258). Aunt Polly's maternal melodrama brings us back directly to the night of the father's death, when Aunt Polly, "a second mother" to Olivia, stole the marriage certificate that would have legitimated the claim of the mulatta wife and daughter and "turned the hussy and her child out into the street" (*MT*, 133–34). The scene is replayed in its entirety, complete with extensive dialogue, thanks to the transparent mediation of the storyteller, whose "story, as it advanced, became as keenly dramatic as though memory had thrown aside the veil of intervening years" (*MT*, 7).

Yet the knowledge of kinship produced by this intrusion of the past on the present—the legality of the interracial marriage confirms the legitimacy of both sisters—results, not in the "sisterly recognition for which all her life Janet had longed in secret," but rather in further maternal efforts to hide the evidence (*MT*, 329). Olivia Carteret burns her father's will and destroys what she had initially seen as a "pretended" marriage certificate, "but its ghost still haunt[s] her," leaving her in "what might be called, vulgarly, a moral 'pocket'" (*MT*, 263–64, 267). She can neither make personal restitution nor "atone" for the "crime" of slavery without disclosing the marriage and admitting that she destroyed the will (*MT*, 266). So, like the flashback to slavery in *Iola Leroy*, the interpolated tale of the past acts in *Marrow of Tradition* as a disruptive presence in the narrative present, narrating what amounts to an unredeemed claim of the past on the present. Both Harper and Chesnutt underscore the open-ended and uncertain sense of future time that results from such a narrative encounter with an unpaid, perhaps unpayable, debt to the past. "There's time enough, but none to spare," reads the last line of the novel (*MT*, 329).

Pauline Hopkins's fiction works the whole terrain of the maternal melo-drama, incorporating moves from both plot types discussed so far: the maternal passing and the maternal familial. The history of rape, illegitimacy, and disrupted motherhood in her first novel, *Contending Forces: A Romance Illustrative of Negro Life North and South* (1900), revises and redeems the domestic tragedy of mixed-race mothers and children à la Twain and Chopin; *Of One Blood* crosses Cable's internationalist history of empire and resistance with the nationalist histories of blood relations in the story-telling and narrative flashbacks of Harper and Chesnutt. Hopkins, however, rearranges these elements into a fictional ensemble that foregrounds her own conception of historical time as relational, an often-unstable inter-twining of past and present summed up in the series title "Ethiopians of the Twentieth Century" or, as she puts it, "modern Ethiopians." Neither ex-pression makes sense without the implied past referent, yet both formula-tions work from the present (that of the modern, the twentieth century) backward rather than starting with the postulate of an origin. And the fu-ture is notably absent, except insofar as the term *Ethiopian* inevitably brings in, at this historical conjuncture, the prophetic mood of Ethiopianism, de-rived from the central text, "Princes shall come out of Egypt, [and] Ethiopia shall soon stretch forth her hands to God" (Ps. 68:31). The biblical prophecy, written in the future imperative *shall*, rests on an implied past (princes have come forth out of ancient Egypt, and so they shall in the fu-ture). This temporal configuration enters both Hopkins's novels through the already-familiar methods of flashback and storytelling, but, as we will see, unlike Harper and Chesnutt, Hopkins intensifies the sense of the inter-polated tales as intrusions, erupting from the past into the present and in-terrupting or even preventing the forward movement of the narrative. Like Ellison's *Invisible Man* and its disjunctive tempo, Hopkins's stories give "a slightly different sense of time," making us aware of those "nodes" when time "stands still" or "leaps ahead."[12]

The effect is to underscore what will emerge as Hopkins's conception of history: as, first and foremost, the uncompleted narrative of, in Walter Benjamin's terms, "a secret agreement between past generations and the present one." The agreement—in the nature of a contract or claim—is never to allow the images of the past to go unrecognized, and, therefore, be-come irretrievably lost, as concerns of the present. Hopkins's "modern Ethiopians," represented fictionally by her King Ergamenes (né Reuel

Briggs), speak to the present from a frozen moment in the past, secretly preserved in the present for the sake of the future. They are also endowed with Benjamin's *"weak* Messianic power," a redemptive and futurist power lodged in the present to which the past has an as-yet-unredeemed claim. Benjamin's terms sum up the tensions between past and future, between genealogical and messianic modes of thinking, that constitute Hopkins's historical consciousness.[13]

Both Hopkins's novels work through the full disclosure in the present of broken matrilineal ties from the past, but with no sense of closure for the future. In addition, there turn out to be, not one, but multiple pasts corresponding to the different geographies of the novels. The revelation of blood relations in *Of One Blood* recapitulates in a transnational location the history of rape and incest exposed in the more local setting established by the subtitle of *Contending Forces* (*A Romance Illustrative of Negro Life North and South*). Chronologically, too, *Contending Forces*, the earlier novel, set mostly during the late 1890s, exhibits traces of the longer race history articulated more fully in *Of One Blood*. It opens with "A Retrospect of the Past," set in the 1790s, just after the abolition of slavery in the British Empire, as the wealthy, slaveowning Montfort family takes their slaves and leaves the island of Bermuda for the North Carolina coast, where they meet with tragedy: thanks to the twin rumors—spread by the villain of the piece, Anson Pollock—that Charles Montfort intends to free his slaves and that his wife, Grace, is of mixed blood, the family plantation is attacked, their property confiscated, Charles and Grace murdered, and their two sons enslaved and subsequently separated, Charles rescued and taken to England, Jesse escaping as a fugitive slave to a free black community in New England. The rest of the novel, set several generations later (1896) in Boston, traces the conflicts of the past in relation to the present, with all the principals, including the main perpetrator, John Pollock Langley, clearly marked by their given names as representatives of the Montfort and Pollock heirs. The Smith family acknowledges the descent of Ma Smith in the names of their children, William Jesse Montfort Smith and Dora Grace Montfort Smith. Will Smith plays the novel's Du Boisean figure to its representation of Booker T. Washington, Dr. Arthur Lewis, head of "a large industrial school in Louisiana" and Dora's fiancée (*CF,* 123). The novel concludes with the newly reconstituted extended black family on board a ship bound for Europe and a reunion with their English kinfolk.

The focal point of the novel's many interpolated historical tales is the narrative of the past of an unrelated character, the beautiful and mysterious

Sappho Clark, a lodger in the boardinghouse run by the Smith family. It is Sappho's violent history as a black victim of sexual abuse in New Orleans that erupts, without warning, even to her, into the Boston present as her story is recounted, without her prior knowledge or consent, by one of the speakers at the American Colored League, a black political organization dedicated to "agitation and eternal vigilance in the formation of public opinion."[14] The delegate from Williamstown, Luke Sawyer, a "gaunt man of very black complexion," introduces himself as a thirty-year-old who looks fifty as a consequence of the histories that he is about to reveal, two tales of post-Reconstruction Louisiana that together illustrate what he calls "the contending forces that are dooming this race to despair!" (*CF*, 256). One story is of the lynching and murder of Sawyer's own family, sparked by his father's commercial success as a shopowner; the other is of the ruin of Mabelle Beaubean, the young daughter of a "colored planter" (of the planter, it is said, "His father had been his owner") and quadroon mother (of whom it is said, "Louisiany abounds in handsome women of color") from a nearby township who is kidnapped and held in a house of prostitution by her father's half brother, a wealthy white man and state senator (*CF*, 258). When she is finally rescued and the uncle confronted with his crime, his reaction typifies the specter of concubinage that the novel pairs with lynching as the twin forces undergirding the racial violence that duplicates, in these days of mob violence, the atrocities of slavery: "'What does a woman of mixed blood, or any Negress for that matter, know of virtue? It is my belief that they were a direct creation by God to be the pleasant companions of men of my race'" (*CF*, 261). The story ends abruptly, the specific relevance of its revelations to the present moment still unknown, with the narrator's report that Mabelle died in the "colored convent" at New Orleans after her child was born (*CF*, 261).

Although, as readers, we are privy to the (admittedly thinly veiled) secret that the supposedly dead Mabelle is our heroine, Sappho, who is in the audience and carried out, having fainted when she heard the end of the tale, we have no sense of how her past will work itself out or even of why Luke Sawyer chose to tell her story to the assembled American Colored League. His motivation, as far as it has been revealed, reflects the presentist expropriation of the past, the pressing need in the present moment to identify "the contending forces that *are* dooming this race to despair" (emphasis added). Even Will Smith, one of the speakers at the league, who has by now fallen in love with Sappho, fails to see the personal significance of the Mabelle Beaubean story to his speech, in passionate "defense of his race," attacking white men for the twin crimes of rape and lynching. It is not until three years later that the claim of the past, in Walter Benjamin's terms, even begins to be redeemed in and by the present. During the intervening years, Sappho is propositioned by a descendant of the villain who had violated the Montforts. She subsequently disappears from Boston, fleeing to New Orleans, where she reclaims her child and her identity as a mother. In the meantime, her true love, Will Smith, completes his degree at Harvard and a course of study at Heidelberg. Only after the progressively intertwining paths of the novel have been thus forced apart do they finally come together to redeem the past in the reactivating, and living out, of social interrelations that had first been established and then disrupted under slavery. Even then, it is no accident that the redemptive moment of Will and Sappho's marriage arrives—tellingly, ambivalently marked—on Easter Sunday as this "fairy tale of love and chivalry" closes with "a love sanctified and purified by suffering" (*CF*, 398). If the redemption of past suffering is partially undercut by the skepticism of the term *fairy tale*, the corollary of a redeemed future is equally in doubt as the novel concludes with the departure of the extended black family for Europe.

The inset tales in *Of One Blood*—again, flashbacks to the past—are, if anything, even more disruptive and irresolute than their counterparts in *Contending Forces*. The most striking tale-teller in the later novel, another frame narrator in the vernacular tradition of Huck Finn, is "old Aunt Hannah," the "noted 'voodoo' doctor or witch," who tells the "old story of sowing the wind and reaping the whirlwind," reiterating near the end of the novel the whole history of incest and miscegenation that has clouded the narrative present and threatened to disrupt even the promise held out by the "of one blood" passage that is now repeated so often as we approach the end (*OOB*, 603–4). At this moment, we have returned from Africa to the ancestral Livingston plantation in Maryland, where Dianthe has learned through spirit communication—the ghostly visitations of the slave woman Mira that have punctuated the novel since we first hear of her "tricks of mind-reading" performed under the hypnotic influence of Livingston *père*—of the villainous doings of Dianthe's husband Aubrey, who has himself subjected her to "hypnotic experiments," induced her to marry him, and turned her into a bigamist ("a wife yet not a wife") (*OOB*, 593, 486). Wandering to a nearby "typical Southern Negro cabin," Dianthe meets Aunt Hannah and learns in a chapter-long tale what we have known for so long, that she and both her husbands are all Mira's offspring (*OOB*, 603). The ghostly presence of the spirit mother Mira, who hovers over the novel, has repeatedly warned, in clairvoyant messages imprinted in "the hand of mysticism," of the secret of the sibling identities that bound the protagonists in the past but now irretrievably divide them, not despite but because of the lotus-lily birthmark that they all share (*OOB*, 506). The long narrative thus seems almost a digression, for it reveals little more than the one secret that we have not yet penetrated (old Aunt Hannah, none other than Dianthe's maternal grandmother, had switched her daughter's and her mistress's babies in the cradle) and, further, obsessively reiterates the incantation "of one blood," as though the taleteller, her interlocutor, and the novel itself cannot get beyond the image: "'So, honey, Aubrey is your own blood brother'"; Dianthe has "a look of utter horror that froze her blood"; "'Yes, honey; all of one blood!'" (*OOB*, 606–7). Even the narrative voice of the novel gets into the act, stepping into the scene to comment directly: "The slogan of the hour is 'Keep the Negro down!' but who is clear enough in vision to decide who hath black blood and who hath it not? . . . 'Of one blood have I made all nations of men to dwell upon the whole face of the earth,' is as true today as when given to the inspired writers to be recorded. No man can draw the dividing line between the two races, for they are both of one blood!" (*OOB*, 607).

The unexpected effect of the interpolated tale, so full of repetition and return to the same phrase, is, thus, to stop time, exposing, in a single instant, the image in and by which the past lives on in the present. As a mode of historical consciousness, this verges on Walter Benjamin's historical materialism, in which the time of the present is divided between the claims of the past and those of the future. For Benjamin, "to articulate the past historically" means, first, to seize it as an "image" that "flashes up at a moment of danger" and, second, to recognize "the sign of a Messianic cessation of happening" that "blasts a specific era out of the homogeneous course of history" and allows the historian to "grasp the constellation which his own era has formed with a definite earlier one."[15] The interpolated narrative of one blood seizes that image of the past at what Hopkins emphasizes as a long moment of danger, for all that remains to happen after Aunt Hannah tells her story is for Dianthe and Aubrey to die, both deaths extending over the subsequent three chapters that conclude the novel. Further, the inset tale, in which time both repeats itself and stands still, echoing the temporal disjunction that Ellison associates with the invisibility of race, not only stops narrative time but also disrupts the telos of the Ethiopianist prophecy so as, in Benjamin's terms, to "blast open the continuum of history." Finally, we will see that, with the qualified representation of the rule of Reuel as King Ergamenes, united with Queen Candace, Hopkins offers a Benjaminian "conception of the 'present' as the 'time of the now' which is shot through with chips of Messianic time."[16] That the present is endowed only with a *"weak"* messianic time is confirmed by the conclusion of the novel, which stresses the "shadows" and "memory" (*OOB*, 621) of the past that darken Reuel-Ergamenes' rule as well as the apprehension with which he views the "advance of mighty nations penetrating the dark, mysterious forests of his native land." The present is still in thrall both to the past and to the future.

Both Hopkins's novels, then, end irresolutely, in the ambivalent temporality of the present, caught between the still imperfectly redeemed claims of the past and the future imperative. Yet, in their engagement with the occult and its temporal multidimensionality, both novels also propose a counterconception of time that can accommodate the disjunctions and eruptions of the race history—a history of invisibility, according to Ellison—that Hopkins traces. In *Contending Forces,* Hopkins makes only limited forays into the occult through such scattered moments as Will Smith's "acute clairvoyant sight" (*CF*, 329), produced by Luke Sawyer's story ("written before his eyes in letters of fire" [*CF*, 400]) of Sappho's past agonies, and the dire predictions of the death of the novel's villain, produced by the "mediumistic powers" of the old fortune-teller Madame Frances (*CF*, 286). What *Contending Forces* only touches on, however, is developed full-blown in *Of One Blood,* where the meaning of race history emerges much more explicitly, through the novel's global settings, temporalities, and occultisms, encompassing simultaneously a lost Ethiopian past, a hidden U.S. present, and an African future clouded by the European imperial presence. Finally, the novel remains balanced between a transformative, intercultural appropriation of the occult sciences and a determinist reading of the intractability of the material forces of racism and imperialism.

BLOOD, INTRODUCED

Most readers are struck, for better or worse, by Hopkins's incorporation within the melodramatic formulas of nineteenth-century popular fiction utilized in *Of One Blood* of a wide range of factual discourses and debates. For worse: Houston Baker derides Hopkins's fiction, in all its topical comprehensiveness, as a curiosity cabinet of its era.[17] For better: I would describe Hopkins's work as culturally omnivorous, her strategic, and felt, response to "the ubiquitous race question," as one of her naive but sympathetic white characters says, shocked at the possibility, raised by the Ethiopians' awareness of modern racism, that the Meroë expedition may be "up against" the race question (*OOB*, 584). Hopkins's particular combination of fictional and factual discourses is not idiosyncratic; rather, it characterizes much race literature of the time, from the historical romances of Cable and Chesnutt to the domestic, "women's" novels of Harper and Hopkins herself.[18] One way in which to think of this literature is to see the referential excess, the often-discrepant allusions to contemporary discourses and debates that appear to have nothing in common, in the context of melodramatic excess, a means of making legible a wide range of racial polemics.[19] The very capaciousness of Hopkins's work should be seen as a challenge to the late-nineteenth-century rhetorics of race, at once so rigid and so flexible that they seemed to have taken over all available cultural space.

A figure speaking both for the novel's melodrama and for its occult sciences, *blood* is, as we have already seen, the central trope of *Of One Blood*. It was also probably the most commonly used term in racist and racialist discourses of the nineteenth century. Blood appears as a legal concept in the United States through the one-drop rule of racial identity; as an allied scientific term in the movement to measure and classify racial differences; as a medicoreligious concept justifying anti-Semitism through medicalized notions of the disease/disorder of the Jew and his "cure" through the ritual use of Christian blood; as a basis for scientific and social-scientific theories of the heredity (and degeneracy) of racial characteristics; and as a quasi-mystical figure for nation and race purity ("Anglo-Saxon blood," e.g.).[20] As such a ubiquitous rhetorical figure, *blood* reappears over and again throughout the novel, virtually constituting a textual refrain in different cultural registers. Further, reiteration of this key regulatory term of racial difference becomes one of the novel's fundamental narrative strategies: by proliferating an excess of meanings within the terms of racial discourse, Hopkins demonstrates their internal contradictions, their volatility, and, ultimately, their unexpected potential for oppositional uses.[21]

Hopkins's project to unmake and remake the term *blood* starts most explicitly with the title drawn from the novel's repeated biblical refrain, "Of one blood have I made all nations of men to dwell upon the whole face of the earth" (Acts 17:26). As a common nineteenth-century term for origins, *blood* also brings into the text a set of cultural contexts, centering on theories of heredity, that are at odds with the title's biblical vision of one-blooded unity. Hopkins organizes the novel around these competing discourses, using blood to mediate the conflicting contexts of biblical and scientific discourses on human origins. On one side is science: both the racially divisive science of ethnology, with its debates over monogenesis and polygenesis (the former theorizing human descent from a single source, the latter insisting on separate, and unequal, origins), and the science of Egyptology, with its debate over the Ethiopian (or African) origins of western civilization (centering on whether *African* means "black" or "white"). On the other side is the Bible: the prophecy that "Ethiopia shall soon stretch forth her hands to God" repeated as yet another refrain throughout the novel, giving it Ethiopianism's focus on the glorious past and future greatness of the "race." The novel's archaeological knowledge provides a reading of Scripture that foregrounds the occluded greatness of the past but leaves uncertain the future redemption of Africa. Finally, inserted, as we will see, within the plot's melodrama of identity disguised and revealed, the term *blood* is, over the course of the novel, ultimately transformed into a mystical vision of (black) racial distinctiveness and interracial harmony while remaining a biologism, rooted in racial and social inequities.[22]

The source of Hopkins's racial mysticism is located in the novel's paired scientific discourses of archaeology and psychology. They first make the novel into a late-nineteenth-century, African American woman's "psycho-archaeological quest." Hopkins's interest in ancient Egypt and the New Psychology functioned much as did Freud's parallel quests in the ancient world and the unconscious: as a mode of negotiating her relation as a black (his as a Jew) to the racist (anti-Semitic) culture of the West.[23] At the same time, Hopkins draws on the context of scientific racism to assimilate archaeology and psychology where they most typically would *not* be placed by historians of science, under the rubric *ethnology*. Ethnology is the science of race differences that had its heyday in the 1840s and 1850s as part of the nineteenth-century search for methods of determining and classifying races. By the late 1890s, the director of the Smithsonian's Bureau of Ethnology flatly asserted the failure of these efforts—"there is no science of ethnology"—but, as Thomas Gossett notes, many anthropologists still hoped for a testable method of race classification, and racists in general were hardly daunted by the failures of the ethnologists.[24] Precisely this transitional moment for racial science, when the eugenics movement was just establishing the basis for a new post-Darwinian, Euro-American science of heredity, provided the setting for Hopkins's psychoarchaeological quest.

This setting is also appropriately considered as part of the science of the occult. Although we may now think of these as fundamentally opposed fields of knowledge—an anachronistic view often expressed through the modifier *pseudoscientific*—the phrase *occult science* was regularly, and variously, used at the time.[25] Theosophists, for example, used *occult science* as a marker to distinguish their nonmaterialist methodology from the empiricism of the spiritualists, while anthropologists (among them James George Frazer in *The Golden Bough*) investigating magical practices in ancient India, Babylon, and Egypt, Greece, and Rome as well as in Australia, Africa, and the Americas analyzed the "principles of thought" (Frazer) or the "ideational logic" (Evans-Pritchard) of these "Occult Science[s]" (Tylor).[26] What is common among the different uses of *occult science* is the willingness to work within the canons of accepted scientific theory and methodology in the study of mystical, magical, or supernatural traditions. The serious students of the occult in the late nineteenth century, from Hopkins herself to William James and Freud, resisted the modern distinction between science and mysticism. The Society for Psychical Research (SPR), which came to have well-known chapters in both Great Britain and the United States, was founded in 1882 with the express intent, according to a statement printed at the front of every issue of its *Journal*, of examining, "without prejudice or prepossession and in a scientific spirit, those faculties of man, real or supposed, which appear to be inexplicable on any generally recognized hypothesis."[27] Similarly, Madame Blavatsky, characterized by one historian as an "occult evolutionist," claimed to have founded Theosophy, not to reject, but to counter and extend Darwinian science on its own turf with her evolutionary conception of consciousness.[28] And Frazer's intellectual predecessor, E. B. Tylor, says that "the principal key to understanding Occult Science is to consider it as based on the Association of Ideas, a faculty which lies at the very foundation of human reason."[29] Seeing science and spiritualism as allies rather than antagonists, forms of knowledge specifically wedded in a syncretizing of Western and African worldviews, is also, we will see, central to Hopkins's racial vision in *Of One Blood*.

Both archaeology and psychology took up, as orthodox scientific topics, the contemporary interest in modes of alternative consciousness that is now often identified with the "merely" popular, the marginal, or the outright outré, such as Anglo-American spiritualism, for example, or Blavatskian occultism. Reflecting the fluid boundaries of science, the interdisciplinary "discovery of the unconscious" entailed a crossing of professional interests (those of neurology, psychiatry, and academic psychology) with popular interests, much as did the broad venue for racial theorizing in the late nineteenth century.[30] These multiple cultural levels of "the ubiquitous race question," as Hopkins broadly construes it, account for the curio-cabinet effect of her fiction: if she throws in (as Mark Twain would say) Egyptology and ethnology, the New Psychology, U.S. slavery and racism,

Pan-Africanism, and occultism, it is because she wants to demonstrate, not her own topicalness (as Houston Baker would say), but the racial continuities among these topics. Yoked together as occult sciences, Hopkins's archaeological and psychological discourses exhibit their participation in the racializing of late-nineteenth-century Euro-American culture that extended, as she demonstrates, well beyond the purview of what is now called *scientific racism*. Turning first, via the novel's different uses of *blood*, to the more explicitly race-conscious fields of ethnology and Egyptology will finally allow us to see the array of racial uses and abuses that Hopkins attributes to the apparently race-neutral psychological sciences.

BLOOD, ETHNOLOGY, EGYPTOLOGY: TOOLS OF TRANSCULTURATION

A gloss of the title *Of One Blood* identifies several locations of Hopkins's engagement with the multiple nineteenth-century blood discourses. *One blood* refers textually both to a horror and to a promise: to the horror of the incestuous, sibling relations among the three protagonists, exposed as literal blood brothers and sisters ("Yes, honey; all of one blood!" their maternal grandmother says), and to the promise of racial unity in the biblical refrain, "Of one blood have I made all nations of men." Invoking this scriptural passage at a culminating moment near the end of the novel, just after the grandmother reveals the protagonists' consanguinity, Hopkins tries to come to terms with the horror of that history. She moves, via the figure of blood, from the present race crisis in the United States—"The slogan of the hour is 'Keep the Negro down!'"—to a potential solution, via her own monogenetic conclusion: "But who is clear enough in vision to decide who hath black blood and who hath it not? . . . No man can draw the dividing line between the two races, for they are both of one blood!" Finally, the very last paragraph of the novel implicitly conflates this multivalent one-bloodedness with the prophetic vision of the novel's other major biblical reference point, the coming redemption of Ethiopia's outstretched hand: "To our human intelligence these truths depicted in this feeble work may seem terrible,—even horrible. . . . Caste prejudice, race pride, . . . are but puppets in His hand, for His promises stand, and he will prove His words, 'Of one blood have I made all races of men'" (*OOB*, 621). Here, paradoxically opposed, are the novel's promises of both racial distinctiveness, for the Ethiopian "race," and racial unity, for "all races."[31]

More paradoxically, Hopkins adapts the scientific language of blood, as articulated by both Egyptology and ethnology, in the service of her Ethiopianism. It is difficult to pin down the meaning of *Ethiopianism*, a "notoriously protean term," says Eric Sundquist, one of the phenomena, says Paul Gilroy, that "we struggle to name as Pan-Africanism, Ethiopianism, Emigrationism. . . ."[32] Adding yet a third term, Wilson J. Moses characterizes Ethiopianism as a variant form of black nationalism, itself "often indistinguishable from the idea of Pan-Africanism."[33] Broadly, Ethiopianism is the religious, literary, and political philosophy derived from the biblical passage picturing Ethiopia stretching forth her hands to God (i.e., Ps. 68:31). The passage was cited repeatedly by African and African American intellectuals and leaders from the early nineteenth century forward and widely interpreted as forecasting the rise of Pan-African unity. In narrower historical terms, Ethiopianism also played a crucial role in the rise of African independence movements and of black independent churches in Africa.[34] In that sense, the historical heyday of this long-standing doctrine could be said to have arrived in 1896, six years before the serialization of *Of One Blood*, with the military defeat of Italy by the armies of Menelik II, the emperor of Christian Ethiopia, the only African state to retain independence during the European colonization of Africa. This modern victory was so exhilarating for the Ethiopians that, as Hopkins's novel demonstrates, it buttressed Ethiopianism's claims of ancient African greatness—and so humiliating for the Italians that Mussolini would later avenge the defeat by invading Ethiopia at the beginning of World War II.[35] At the same time, modern Africa was considered by blacks and whites alike as a primitive and backward continent, whereas ancient Africa served as a more-distanced, less-ambivalent focus for pride in a black racial heritage. The charge of "assimilationist" impulses in the African civilizationist rhetoric of black distinctiveness points to only one of the many problems, and possibilities, posed by the protean phenomenon of Ethiopianism.[36]

In particular, Hopkins's Ethiopianism engages with the "American science of ethnology," which emerged in the 1840s and 1850s to address the long-standing debate over racial origins (and differences) through the doctrine of polygenesis.[37] Hopkins interweaves Africanist and Euro-American symbologies in a process of "transculturation," adapting and transforming the dominant discourses of the contemporary sciences of heredity—the sciences of "blood" that were so deeply and so variously racialized that both black and white proponents could use them in support of virtually any racial cause.[38] The end product of the transculturation process necessarily reflects both compromise and contradiction: Hopkins's American Africanism, for example, reveals what Wilson Moses sees as the classic split in nineteenth-century black nationalism between political separatism and cultural assimilation.[39] More broadly, however, Hopkins's goal was to demonstrate an equivalence between scientific theories of the physiological "passing down," or inheritance, of "blood" and occult or spiritualist theories of a psychic and cultural identity that endures over time and space: both, in Hopkins's vision, are equally mysterious and mystified, deterministic and liberatory.

Hopkins's transcultural dynamics raise a problem consistently associated with all her work, that of reading her texts reductively either as "authentic" self-expression or as "inauthentic" assimilation. Is Hopkins reclaiming African cultural traditions by Westernizing them, in the "bourgeois" tradition that Kevin Gaines indicts of reconstructing "backward" Africa as a Christianized, and, therefore, "uplifted," continent?[40] She may likewise be counted as one of Anthony Appiah's Egyptianists, who value Africa's modern identity for its roots in an imaginary past of wholeness and unity.[41] Or she may be presenting, in Wilson Moses's terms, the classic black nationalist's "dream of a renascent Africa," which, like the "dream of a reconstructed black America," "always implied making blacks more like whites."[42] She would, then, simply be promulgating a vision of Africa that is compatible with integrationist and assimilationist ideals. Even more broadly and more damningly, she would be—like other African American "bourgeois" women novelists of the period, who wrote predominantly in the sentimental genre, for a mixed-race audience, with mostly near-white mulatto heroes and heroines—doing little more than producing a "mulatto aesthetics," a "Victorian morality in whiteface."[43] All these readings, superficially plausible but false, indicate how much is at stake, politically, in Hopkins's transcultural project.

Another symptom of the problem emerges in the contradictory efforts made in *Of One Blood* to confront dominant Western ideologies of beauty. Hopkins may praise black skin and hair in the novel, Hazel Carby (one of Hopkins's best, most sensitive readers) argues, "but profiles and bone structure remain Athenian," just as the novel's "idealization of black beauty . . . retains classically European pretensions."[44] For Hopkins, anxious to demonstrate the line of influence from Ethiopia to Egypt and then to classical civilization, as did most contemporary black historians and some white Egyptologists drawing on Greco-Roman as well as biblical sources, it is culturally significant to describe her African heroine, Candace, as a "Venus in bronze" (*OOB*, 567). Given the controversy within Egyptology over whether, as the creators of the Nilotic "cradle of civilization," the ancient Egyptians were black or white and particularly the marked decline by the late nineteenth century in the belief that they *were* black, to assert the blackness of Venus was simultaneously to take a minority position and to make a dissenting intervention within a powerful racial-political debate.

In working out a solution to these problems, Hopkins uses a reclamation strategy common among African American intellectuals from Du Bois onward: she cites the "Negroid" facial evidence of Greek sculpture. For example, in her *Colored American Magazine* article "Venus and the Apollo Modelled from Ethiopians," she argues that "scientific authority" verifies that the "most famous examples of classic beauty in sculpture . . . were chiseled from Ethiopian slave models," while Sterling Stuckey describes how, in 1972, "a walk through the British Museum reveals, so routinely as to be shocking, a black presence in the features of those depicted in statues that line the corridors of the Egyptian section."[45] Professor Stone, the British expedition leader of *Of One Blood*, suggests the value of such strategies when he argues that, "in connecting Egypt with Ethiopia, one meets with most bitter denunciation from most modern scholars": "Science has done its best to separate the race from Northern Africa, but the evidence is with the Ethiopians" (*OOB*, 532). He concludes that the ruins at Meroë will prove modern science wrong. Professor Stone alludes to the historical necessity, emerging within Western thought only after the rise of black slavery and the concomitant racism, of distancing black Africans as far as possible from the centers of European civilization. His quest and the "Venus in bronze" disrupt that demarcation, even as they incorporate the racist logic that values blackness, and Africanity, for its close ties to Western civilization. It was hardly just "modern science" in Hopkins's day that struggled with these issues, for what better demonstration could there be of the still-potent debate over the African origins of classical civilization than Martin Bernal's highly controversial *Black Athena*?[46]

Even more than her modern counterpart, "Black Athena," the "Venus in bronze" marks a paradigmatic moment of transculturation. In the service of her own multivalenced Ethiopianism, Hopkins enlists the polygenetic affirmation of separate racial origins but counters its assumption of black inferiority. In so doing, she also indirectly uses, for her own purposes, polygeny's Egyptological data, in the form of craniological and archaeological evidence derived from Egypt, while answering, in the affirmative, Egyptology's particular Negro Question, that of the blackness of ancient Egyptian civilization. We are all of one blood, the novel insists, yet, like its mulatto hero who discovers that he is the direct descendant of ancient Ethiopian royalty, African Americans are "Ethiopians of the Twentieth Century." We are all of one blood, the novel further insists, yet God decrees that some races rule others, a state of affairs that is at once repudiated as the present ascendancy of the white race and recuperated as a utopian elevation of African peoples.

Hopkins's Ethiopianism is, then, not simply an elite black intellectual tradition combining the doctrine of uplift (of the "degraded" African American masses and the "backward" modern continent of Africa) with the theme of ancient African cultural retentions and return. Neither does Hopkins's Egyptianist vision enshrine an imaginary African past at the expense of present problems and future solutions.[47] As indicated by the extensive coverage in the *Colored American Magazine* of political, social, and economic developments in Africa and throughout the diaspora, including the series of articles entitled "Ethiopians of the Twentieth Century," ancient Egypt was, for the magazine's editor, the means to a modern end. As a novelist, Hopkins constructs a transculturated Africa, a fictional representation derived largely from factual sources and black history, not all of it glorious, and inclusive of both the contemporary United States and the colonial world as well as of a diasporic, Pan-African future, itself contingent on colonial incursions in present-day Africa.

The Meroë section of the novel brings us to the heart of Hopkins's Africa and the center of her strategy of using archaeological data to refute the claims of ethnological science. She uses the master's tools, not to dismantle his house, but rather to expose, and perhaps undermine, its deeply racialized foundations. Thus, to support the theory, which Professor Stone sees as anathema to contemporary science, of "the primal existence of the Negro as the most ancient source of all that you value in modern life, even antedating Egypt," Hopkins mobilizes what is hardly a friendly witness for her case, the science of Egyptology (*OOB,* 520). "It is especially significant," wrote Du Bois in *The World and Africa* (1946), "that the science of Egyptology arose and flourished at the very time that the cotton kingdom reached its greatest power on the foundations of American Negro Slavery."[48] This historical conjunction between Egyptology and the race question was later intensified by a set of ongoing archaeological debates, buttressed in the 1880s and 1890s with increasing material evidence from numerous digs in Egypt and the Sudan, over how Herodotus and other classical writers defined the "race" or "ethnicity" of the ancient Ethiopians and Egyptians and exactly what African peoples the term *Ethiopian* included for the ancients. Ironically, for the ancients, there was no Negro Question.[49] The Greek historian Diodorus provided, as Hopkins acknowledges repeatedly in *Of One Blood*, the classical source both for her chronology and her vision of ancient Ethiopian occult wisdom: not only did he see (black) Ethiopians as pioneers in religion, but he was also an early advocate of an often-challenged tradition that regarded most Egyptian institutions as derivative of Ethiopian civilization.

The scholarly Egyptological debates also provided, in all their racial volatility, the ethnological context for Hopkins's *Primer of Facts*, "compiled and arranged," according to the book's title page, "from the works of the best known ethnologists and historians." The twin burden of this work is to convince us that ancient African civilizations were black and that modern blacks are their descendants. Opening in the most hostile, racial-origins territory by titling chapter 1 "Original Man," Hopkins invokes in the *Primer of Facts* physiological theories about African skin color and structure, often cited by racial environmentalists to argue for permanent, environmentally produced rather than innate racial differences, in order to answer, in the positive registers of Ethiopianism, the question of the hour: "Can all races have sprung from the same parent stock?" Hopkins's answer in the *Primer of Facts:*

> The color of the Blackest African is then simply concentrated red, . . . really purple and nothing else. Purple involves a mixture of red and blue, and implies the existence of blue in the blood. This is true, or whence come the blue veins of the white race and its blue eyes? Blue is an element of the blood; hence the purple color of the African. It is a significant fact that purple as a dress color originated in Africa; the Ethiopians and the Egyptians, who had the most delicate perception of color, adopted purple as a royal shade, and it was probably emblematic of the complexion of their kings and queens. . . . In human races, running through all shades of complexion, there is but one color, modified and intensified from the purest white to the purest black.[50]

Moving virtually without skipping a beat from color (black, purple, red, and blue), to blood, to culture (purple as a royal Ethiopian shade), and then to race, Hopkins grafts biological and ethnological assumptions onto an Ethiopianist worldview. Her strategy relies simply on the profusion, the sheer excess, of colors. The result is the monogenetic conclusion that, "in human races, . . . there is but one color," resting on the color-coded sensitivity to gradations of blood characteristic of racist ethnology.

The *blood* pattern is repeated with *Egypt*, also a key term in nineteenth-century racial thinking, whether conservative, romantic, assimilationist, or radical. Most striking, perhaps, is the biblical Egypt of antislavery and black-liberation discourse from the eighteenth century to the present. The Egypt of pharaonic bondage and deliverance is invoked as a parallel to U.S. slavery throughout African American expressive culture as well as by Hopkins, in the latter case through the spiritual "Go down, Moses," sung by Dianthe at a Boston performance of the Fisk Jubilee singers. The popular-cultural venue is appropriate given the ubiquity of nineteenth-century American Egyptomania, as expressed in the tremendously popular exhibition of Egyptian relics in P. T. Barnum's American Museum, the century-long vogue for Egyptian travel among the wealthy and for travel books among a mass audience, the "Egyptian Revival" in public art and architecture (particularly influential in cemetery and prison design), and the opening of American diplomatic relations with Egypt in 1832. Hopkins herself twice comments on Egyptology's deep popular-cultural resonance through Charlie Vance, among the expedition members the naive American par excellence, who conveys his satisfaction at the first sight of Meroë and its pyramids through a Barnum analogy: "It promises to be better than anything Barnum has ever given us even at a dollar extra reserved seat . . . a sort of Barnum and Kiralfy" (*OOB*, 510, 514).

In science, a major date for American Egyptology was 1844, which marked the publication of *Crania Aegyptiaca*, the influential treatise on polygeny and the black race by Dr. Samuel Morton, the leading proponent of the American doctrine of polygenesis. (Morton was considered polygeny's "data analyst," Louis Agassiz its "theorist.") Morton's earlier *Crania Americana* (1839) had ranked the mental capacities of different races according to skull size and, thereby, provided new, empirical evidence of separate and unequal human racial origins. The equally influential *Crania Aegyptiaca* reported and analyzed data gleaned from a collection of mummy heads and tomb inscriptions provided by George R. Gliddon, vice-consul at Cairo and an Egyptologist. The doctrine of polygeny became one of the first internally recognized theories of the American school of anthropology.[51]

Thus did Egyptology meet up with and buttress ethnology. Morton further cemented the Egytological connection when he continued his "empirical" work in *Crania Aegyptiaca* using data derived from Gliddon's skull collection. Gliddon was a highly successful self-promoter, characterized as "one-half serious student and one-half P. T. Barnum," who had lectured (from 1842 to 1844, as far west as St. Louis) on Egyptian ethnology and chronology against the backdrop of a "Grand Moving Transparency" of the

Nile.[52] Gliddon's Barnumesque lectures had been so well received that they had been published as *Ancient Egypt: Her Monuments, Hieroglyphics, History, and Archaeology* (1843), a scholarly book that sold a remarkable twenty-four thousand copies, suggesting again how voracious was the American appetite for things Egyptological. No less than Barnum's American Museum (which included two mummies among its curiosities), polygeny, the American school of ethnology, also sought to trade in the currency of race and Egyptology. Following Morton's death, Gliddon collaborated with Dr. Josiah Nott—another leading polygenist and an apologist for slavery—on the now-infamous ethnological work *Types of Mankind* (1854), a massive compilation of the opinions of the American school. On his use of Egyptology in his lectures on what he called "niggerology," Nott commented, perhaps disingenuously, "The Negro question was the one I wished to bring out and [I] embalmed it in Egyptian ethnography, etc., to excite a little more interest."[53]

Egyptology, then, developed as a mobile field in which the popular and the scholarly were virtually indistinguishable, a field marked from the beginning by a range of racialisms and racisms and mobilized to competing political purposes and programs. Although the earliest Egyptologists, working in the wake of the Napoleonic Egyptian expeditions of 1798, had asserted that the ancient Egyptians were both black and part of the great development of Western civilization (from Ethiopia and Egypt to Greece and Rome), by the mid-1800s, as we have seen, the field of Egyptology had been largely taken over by the "new ethnology" and enlisted in the service of polygenist arguments for slavery. And, while the archaeology of ancient Egypt provided turn-of-the-century black historians with accounts of ancient Africa that counterbalanced white historiography and Darwinist racial thought, modern Egyptologists consistently provided the scholarly data used to buttress arguments for black inferiority. It is further striking that these early black historians, such as George Washington Williams, the author of the two-volume *History of the Negro Race in America* (1883), drew freely—or "eclectically"—on the available modern scholarship, incorporating those who argued against as well as those who defended the black ethnicity of the Ethiopians, even in Williams's case citing the work of Nott and Gliddon.[54]

So mobile, indeed, are the positions in, and the sociopolitical uses of, the whole debate over racial origins that historians of science now argue over exactly how racially enlightened the early French Egyptologists were. One such early Egyptologist was the well-known traveler the comte de Volney,

who, with Herodotus and other classical writers, was so often cited in late-
nineteenth-century black-history writing for his positive views of ancient
Africa. When Hopkins herself cites "the great French writer Volney" in *Of
One Blood*, it is to suggest how equivocal is the enthusiasm of this son of the
Revolution for black Egyptian civilization. "How we are astonished," begins the Volney excerpt quoted in *Of One Blood*, "when we reflect that to
the race of Negroes, the object of our extreme contempt, we owe our arts,
sciences, and even the use of speech!" (*OOB*, 536). This particular passage
displays the cultural assumption of black inferiority coexisting with Volney's racial "liberalism." And thus Hopkins underscores the inconsistencies
in Volney's position while quoting him as an authority to affirm the "Negro" origins of civilization. In this, she does more than many general histories of Egyptology, which simply do not acknowledge the racial question at
stake from the field's beginnings.[55]

Historians today similarly question, or even deny, the precise relation
between the science of ethnology and the arguments justifying the system
of American slavery and racial subordination—notwithstanding Du Bois's
assumption of the conjunction of Egyptology and ethnology with slavery.
Some historians (e.g., Fredrickson and Gould) are with Du Bois in asserting that the American school was developed to provide a scientific rationale
for American racial policies, but others (e.g., Stanton and, again, Gould) argue that the polygenist doctrine did not ultimately occupy a primary place
in the ideology of slavery because its assertion of a plurality of creations
contradicted orthodox religious belief in a single Adam.[56] Finally, polygeny
itself proved to be a highly flexible doctrine, adapting well to (rather than
being challenged by) Darwinism, which explained physical differences as
the permanent results of natural selection.[57] In the context of establishing
the field's mobile nature, it is important to remember that, although both
monogenists and polygenists assumed racial ranking, and although leading
American polygenists differed in their attitudes toward slavery, it was the
theory of separate origins, so tied to the Egyptological evidence, that paved
the way for a proslavery use of ethnology—however that use is ultimately
assessed. As Stephen Jay Gould remarks trenchantly in *The Mismeasure of
Man*, "It is obviously not accidental that a nation still practicing slavery and
expelling its aboriginal inhabitants from their homelands should have provided a base for theories that blacks and Indians are separate species, inferior to whites."[58]

What does this volatile antebellum debate have to do, finally, with Hopkins's early-twentieth-century novel? In part, the long shelf life of the

innatist-environmentalist debate accounts for the ongoing insistence on the apparently outmoded monogenetic discourse of one-bloodedness in African American writing through the late nineteenth century. More important, in Hopkins's hands, as in those of early black historians, the mobile site of Egyptology accomplished a tremendous amount of African American cultural work. First, the consuming passion for things Egyptological, broadly conceived, provided the conditions of possibility, not only for the novel's setting in a North African dig, but also for the shift in its center of value from a purely Western to a syncretic, pan-racial perspective. Second, Hopkins's command of the archaeological data enabled her explicitly to connect the study of Egypt with the Negro Question (a connection that very few in the field have been willing to acknowledge, then or now) and, further, to refute Egyptology's racist theories with its own evidence. Looking at the history of the discipline from an explicitly racialized perspective, Hopkins reveals what the traditional historiography effaces. Finally, the surprising marriage of Egyptology and Ethiopianism produced Hopkins's racial mysticism, the cultural inheritance of an ancient African race soul that she held out to all diasporic blacks. That messianic vision is critical as well as utopian, a consciousness sharpened by the long tradition of ethnological research and attuned to imperialism as the new global development of the color line.

BLOOD AND THE NEW PSYCHOLOGY

Equally central to Hopkins's mysticism was the science of psychology, particularly "the great field of new discoveries in psychology" mentioned at the opening of *Of One Blood*. This alternative tradition was identified with William James and other Anglo-American psychical researchers as well as with such Continental practitioners and theorists of hypnosis as Jean-Martin Charcot, Hippolyte Bernheim, Pierre Janet, and Alfred Binet—the latter said to be the author of *The Unclassified Residuum*, the book on new psychological discoveries that Reuel Briggs is reading at the outset of the novel. The excerpts that Briggs reads are actually quoted from William James's "The Hidden Self" (hence Hopkins's subtitle). James's essay, which opens with the assertion, adapted by Hopkins for her novel's own opening (and mined as well for the title of Briggs's book), that "the great field for new discoveries . . . is always the Unclassified Residuum," summarized for popular and scholarly audiences the theories of double and multiple consciousness developed independently by Binet (in *On Double Consciousness*) and Janet (in *L'Automatisme psychologique*).[59] Within the novel proper, this opening text by the onetime president of the American Society for Psychical Research identifies one pole of the broad psycho-occult complex informing the novel: what James calls, in the passage that Hopkins quotes, the "occult powers" (ranging from "divinations" to "demoniacal possessions") that, he laments, are dismissed by "the ordinary medical man . . . with the cut-and-dried remark that they are 'only effects of the imagination.'" This dismissive remark, invoked not once but twice in both the James ("HS," 248, 267) and the Hopkins (*OOB*, 442, 443) texts, underscores the same skeptical institutional context of ordinary medicine and psychology confronting the serious student of the occult in turn-of-the-century Europe and America. The other pole emerges only when the novel moves to Africa, where, according to popular (Western) mythology, such occult powers are not dismissed, relegated to the realm of the imaginary, but rather acknowledged within the spiritual traditions of ancient Ethiopia.

But these "poles" of the occult are not ultimately presented by Hopkins as antagonistic opposites. She is not, in the Du Boisean tradition of *Souls of Black Folk*, decrying the materialism of the United States and advocating an infusion of the spirituality of African culture. Rather, locating the two occult realms, as the novel does, in the differing racial and cultural contexts of the United States and Africa tends to underscore their affinities. The hidden self of the title, simultaneously an African spiritualist, orthodox psychological, and emergent occult construction, turns out to be racialized in overlapping ways in both the American and the African halves of the novel. And both civilizations—but most notably the ancient Ethiopian world, supposedly perfectly preserved in the hidden city of Telassar (which is, in fact, represented by Hopkins as being in constant contact with the outside world)—emerge as transculturated, the products of an ongoing cultural syncretism.

Not the least of the markers of this continuity is the hostility toward any and all theories of the occult, Western or African, attributed to the novel's "Harvard professors" (*OOB*, 576). Both Hopkins and James, as well as other psychical researchers, represented the marginal status of the new occult science as a main force motivating its development, not, however, as an oppositional field, but *as a science*. James documents, and lauds, the efforts (in data collection and experimental methodology) of psychical research to normalize itself by aspiring to "the ideal of every science . . . , that of a closed and completed system of truth" ("HS," 247). His argument *for* the scientific basis of psychical research—that "in its essence science stands only for a method and for no fixed belief"—is also an argument *against* the current state of normal science, which has so identified itself with "a certain set of results," the "fixed belief" in a mechanical explanation of nature, as to "degrade the scientific body to the status of a sect."[60] Hopkins goes farther in her novel, raising the intellectual stock of Reuel's Western scientific mysticism by grounding it in the even more suspect (by the lights of the Harvard professors) supernatural traditions of African origin. Dianthe, we recall, is supposed first to be "reanimated" ("the secret of life lies in what we call volatile magnetism," explains Dr. Briggs to his skeptical colleagues) in the American half of the novel (*OOB*, 468). She is finally "reincarnated," as Queen Candace, in the Ethiopian half (*OOB*, 562), suggesting that what, in the face of their orthodox colleagues' skepticism, contemporary psychical researchers were calling *reanimation* the ancient Ethiopians recognized as *reincarnation*. In "knowledge of Infinity," Reuel learns from his Ethiopian teacher, Ai, in the hidden city of Telassar, the ancient Africans definitely surpassed modern science; "I am told," says Ai, "with a gentle smile of ridicule," that the modern world has not yet solved the "simple process" of preserving the natural appearance of plants and human bodies, "handed down from the earliest days of Ethiopian greatness" (*OOB*, 561–62).

Hopkins is not simply challenging the mythology of European superiority and its concomitant theories of black inferiority. Nor is she merely creating her own Africanist counternarrative of the primitive, reversing the traditional hierarchy of higher and lower races. Rather, she joins together the two mystical traditions, the Western and the African, locating both under the rubric of "the abstract science of occultism" (*OOB*, 574). For Ai, "a technical conversation" with Reuel on the science of occultism reveals the Western-trained medical doctor already to be "well-versed" (*OOB*, 574) in ancient Ethiopian "knowledge of Infinity" and confirms his identity as, and fitness to be, the king Ergamenes. Linking his American and African heritages, Reuel's mysticism—inherited, the novel establishes by the lotus-lily birthmark on his breast, from his American slave mother as well as from his white mesmerist father, who exploits her mediumistic powers, and honed by his Harvard medical training as well as by his studies in animal magnetism and psychical research—meets up with its African counterpart in Telassar.[61] The novel thus twins rather than opposes Euro-American science (both ordinary psychology and the emerging field of psychical research) and African spiritualism, offering different traditions or systems of the occult as the syncretic meeting ground between the two civilizations.

If the *one blood* of the novel's title simultaneously invokes a series of paradoxical meanings and uses of *blood*, the subtitle synthesizes yet another set of apparently conflicting meanings. The *hidden self* is simultaneously the Jamesian "cosmic consciousness" dear to psychical research,[62] the blackness that Hopkins's history of interracial rape shows to be a permeating but un-acknowledged presence behind the veil of American identity, and, finally, what the novel explicitly calls, in spiritualist language, "the undiscovered country within ourselves—the hidden self lying quiescent in every human soul," a region that comprises both the unconscious and Africa itself (*OOB*, 448). All these meanings converge in what may be called Hopkins's (and Du Bois's) theory of *diasporic consciousness*, which brought together psycholog-ical and occult conceptions of an unconscious personality with conceptions of race nationalism from black-nationalist thinking.[63]

In developing this theory of diasporic consciousness, Hopkins imag-ines a mystic idea of "personality" as a means of recovering the hidden self and history of the race, that is, both the kinship relations obscured by Amer-ican slavery and an African ancestral spirit or race soul. To do so, she inter-weaves occult symbologies: the ancient Ethiopian theory of the "ever-living faculty"—called, in a transculturating move, the "Soul" or "Ego"—and defined "as a Personality that continues to live after the body per-ishes"—is linked to a specific Euro-American tradition within the New Psychology itself and primarily to James (*OOB*, 562, 573). Discussing the "splitting up of the mind into separate consciousnesses," James argues for the positive value of "sub-conscious states" in opposition to the more criti-cal theory of "M. Janet and his confreres" ("HS," 264–65). While James, like Hopkins, clearly admires the clinical results of this pioneering work—results that Reuel Briggs duplicates with his revival of Dianthe from a mes-meric trance—he concludes that Janet's theory assumes erroneously that "the secondary self is always a symptom of hysteria, and that the essential fact about hysteria is the lack of synthesizing power and consequent disin-tegration of the field of consciousness" ("HS," 268). Rather, James himself, again like Hopkins, takes a far more positive view of secondary or alterna-tive consciousness as an "immensely complex and fluctuating thing," whose investigation holds out a "possible application to the relief of human misery . . . nothing less than the cure of insanity" ("HS," 268, 265).

In so doing, James and his cadre of psychical researchers took an im-portant theoretical step away from the orthodoxy of Janet, Binet, and oth-ers, for whom the phenomena of the unconscious, including hysteria, dreams, hypnotic trances, and somnambulism, were rare and pathological, an essentially "degenerative" part of the human personality.[64] In this intel-lectual schism, Hopkins is aligned with psychical researchers, interested in the "supernormal," and against psychotherapists, interested in the "abnormal."[65] She even draws Reuel Briggs, with his dual paternal (Western scientific) and maternal (African mystical) heritages, in the tradition of James's ideal researcher, "who will pay attention to facts of the sort dear to the feminine-mystical mind, while reflecting upon them in academic-scientific ways" ("HS," 249). Both the broadly positive view of the unconscious promoted by Anglo-American psychical researchers and James's specifically androgynous sense of the unconscious as a combined academic-scientific and feminine-mystical phenomenon are constitutive elements for Hopkins's racial theory of the unconscious.

To borrow from the language of psychical research, Hopkins clearly considers Briggs's mysticism and occult powers as what James would call "evolutive" rather than "degenerative."[66] Summing up the scientific impact of Briggs's reanimation of the seemingly dead Dianthe, the novel depicts it as the result of a fertile alliance, à la James, between spiritualism and science: "The world scarcely estimates the service rendered by those who have unlocked the gates of sensation by the revelations of science; . . . then came a stampede for all scientific matter bearing upon animal magnetism" (*OOB*, 472). The combined realization of Briggs's maternal, slave inheritance ("the shadow of Ethiopia's power") and the despised legacy of his father-master (his medicoscientific training) always within him (*OOB*, 558), Briggs's occult powers not only signify his ultimate reintegration of personality at the novel's end and the possible fulfillment of Ethiopianism's teleology but also provide the narrative means for solving the novel's larger mysteries of identity.

It is not coincidental that the metaphors of evolution—the evolutive versus the degenerative—should, thus, work so well to characterize Hopkins's position on the unconscious. For, in presenting Briggs's mystical powers as the key to his racial unconscious, Hopkins refashions what she stresses in the novel's Cambridge section was then a minority position within medicopsychiatric theory and practice into an implicit stance against some fundamental evolutionary assumptions. The novel represents the unconscious—operating through both Briggs's "blood" inheritance and the occult sciences that he studies in Meroë and Cambridge—as *racially* evolutive, that is, as the means of the restoration of the formerly great Ethiopian "race." As such a tool of evolutionary progress for the race, Hopkins's unconscious may be read as a response to the debate within evolutionary theory over so-called black degeneracy, the view that, having inherited inferior physical and mental traits, and lacking white influences and control, postbellum blacks and especially mulattoes would not survive the Darwinian social struggle but revert to African savagery, suffer species degeneration, and eventually die out as a race. Hopkins's Ethiopianist vision explicitly rewrites the evolutionary narrative of reversion to savagery by predicating the prophetic future of the black race directly on its early greatness.

Even closer to home for Hopkins than the racial Darwinists, who succeeded in reconstituting the proslavery racial argument into turn-of-the-century evolutionary terminology, was a less well-known participant in scientific racism: none other than Reuel Briggs's nemesis, the orthodox science of psychology. The influence of evolutionary theory on American psychology resulted in a number of racially charged developments. In the work of such American psychologists as G. Stanley Hall (a specialist in child psychology known for his theory of biogenetic recapitulation, applied to explain the characteristics of both child and racial development) and James Mark Baldwin (whose important *Mental Development in the Child and the Race* [1894] popularized a version of heredity, adapted from Jean-Baptiste Lamarck, called *organic selection*), evolutionary terminology was both racialized and adapted to psychic development. If, according to the recapitulationist logic of both Hall and Baldwin, the child represents a primitive adult ancestor, then the adults of "inferior" groups—races, sexes, and classes—must be like the children of "superior" groups, the more "highly developed" white males. Recapitulation—a general theory of biological determinism linking blacks and women as savages of the race—also stands behind Hopkins's narrative of the ancient Ethiopian as "the primal race," the advanced ancestor of "the modern world . . . yet in its infancy" (*OOB*, 521, 551). Adapting the developmental association of children and races, Hopkins fashions a complicated inversion of "ontogeny recapitulating phylogeny," in which the phylogenetically primal is more advanced than the "infant" civilization that it precedes.

Most proximate to Hopkins's novel was a powerful contribution by psychologists to the racial Darwinist effort through the development of intelligence testing, which occurred, not, as we tend to think, much later than, but virtually coextensively with Hopkins's own moment. The "hereditarian theory of IQ"—an American invention, according to Stephen J. Gould, that perverted the intentions of Alfred Binet's tests, first published in 1905— supported the views of eugenicists that mental and emotional qualities are largely a matter of heredity.[67] While all the earlier, nineteenth-century efforts to measure the physical differences among races had failed, the notion of hereditary intellectual inferiority gave racist theorizing, in Thomas Gossett's words, a "new lease on life." When mental tests were introduced in the

United States in the 1890s, one of the first experiments compared the sensory perception of blacks, Indians, and whites. "By 1900," Gossett concludes, "the idea was widely accepted that both intelligence and traits of character tend to be inherited, and one of the proofs of this contention was believed to be found in racial differences."[68]

In the midst of this pervasive racialization of the sciences of the mind, Hopkins, like so many American psychologists, embraces the notion that mental capacity is hereditary. In the African American case that she presents, however, the mental (read: occult) powers are inherited through the maternal line, traced from American slavery back to Africa. Moreover, Hopkins's theory of diasporic consciousness racializes the mind's occult powers and gives them a positive, evolutionary spin. The racial occult thus makes possible a series of alternative temporalities grafting Christian time onto an ancient Egyptian cosmology. The immense sphinx at the entrance to the city of Telassar is engraved with the words, "'That which hath been, is now; and that which is to be, hath already been; and God requireth that which is past'" (*OOB*, 552). Through the racial unconscious Hopkins unveils the Africanist future, prophesied by Ethiopianism, as always already present within the American slave past. Indeed, Hopkins even presents Ethiopianism's biblical prophecy of Ethiopia stretching forth her hand unto God as itself belonging to the racial occult, yet another manifestation, Ai instructs Reuel, of the "sense of the supernatural always near us": "all the prophecies of the Trinity shall in time be fulfilled. They are working out today by the forces of air, light, wind,—the common things of daily life that pass unnoticed. Ethiopia, too, is stretching forth her hand unto God, and He will fulfill her destiny" (*OOB*, 573). As Dianthe is dying, a "pageant" of her "royal ancestors"—"Candace, Semiramis, Dido, Solomon, David"— seems to pass before her eyes, seemingly accompanied by the music of Beethoven and Mozart ("sons of song") in "so vast a rush" that "the unseen mass must have been the disembodied souls of every age since Time began" (*OOB*, 615). In this mystical version of the historical pageantry that I discussed in chapter 1, Hopkins foregrounds a sense of disjunctive temporalities as Old Testament figures are wedded, to the strains of classical music, to the royal line of ancient Ethiopia. Hopkins's syncretism of Euro-American biblical and ancient African occult traditions, then, articulates a racially liberatory position, an African American adaptation of a minority position within the discipline of psychology. It is not coincidental that Hopkins's archaeological argument for the blackness of the ancient Ethiopians was also itself a minority view shared by few Egyptologists at the turn of the century. For those, like Hopkins, seeking to contest racial science by using its tools and techniques to create a scientific counterdiscourse, it could hardly be otherwise.[69]

In a suggestive assessment of the limits and possibilities of such a position within his own field of psychology, William James argues in his 1909 essay "The Last Report: The Final Impressions of a Psychical Researcher" that, despite "how often 'Science' has killed off all spook philosophy and laid ghosts and raps and 'telepathy' away underground as so much popular delusion," still, in the rigorous language of logic, from his ("limited enough") experience, "one fixed conclusion" emerges: "There is a continuum of cosmic consciousness, against which our individuality builds but accidental fences, and into which our several minds plunge as into a mother-sea or reservoir. . . . Not only psychic research, but metaphysical philosophy and speculative biology are led in their own ways to look with favor on some such 'panpsychic' view of the universe as this."[70] It is not going too far, perhaps, to say that Hopkins was led through the sciences of the occult to develop her own pan-psychic view of the universe. Her syncretic adaptation of these various symbologies produced in *Of One Blood* the complex theory of the Africanist "hidden self" or mystic, racial personality, a theory not so much of (Du Boisean) double consciousness as of (Jamesian, or, to be precise, psychical-researchian) cosmic, pan-racial consciousness.

Blood, Concluded

The essential tension that many readers sense in Hopkins's theory of racial consciousness may be summarized by the unstable unity of opposites conveyed in the title *Of One Blood; or, The Hidden Self.* The universal humanism of *one blood* vies with the racial exceptionalism of the *hidden self,* paradoxically made visible in the lotus-lily birthmark that "proves race and descent" of the ancient Ethiopian royal line (*OOB,* 555).[71] The differentiating mark on the body belies the unifying "brotherhood" of the blood within (*OOB,* 590). Moreover, the language of blood is itself internally contradictory, speaking both to and from the racialized contexts of religion and science. Here, and elsewhere in Hopkins's writing—notably a controversial passage in her *Contending Forces* linking evolution and the Negro Question to the discourse of blood—she draws on the instability of the terminology to transform *blood* from a biologized term, the staple of nineteenth-century scientific racism, into a multivalent figure of speech capable of generating new meanings from within old terms and narratives. Among those uses of *blood* are meanings drawn directly from, rather than countering, contemporary scientific discourses. Hopkins not only draws on these multiple meanings of *blood* but also generates some of her own. If, as we have seen, Hopkins's *blood* refers to the literal passing down of inheritance theorized by the biological sciences as well as to the biblical inheritance of spirit or culture, it also produces, in the novel's occult context proper, a metaphysics of psychic identity that endures over time and space.

No simple process of reversal and reassemblage of the idioms of science, then, Hopkins's strategy placed her—as the strategies of other late-nineteenth-century African American writers placed them—in a more ambiguous position: that of challenging the claims and terms of science from within, of being, that is, occupied by such terms yet occupying them oneself. Charting the range of responses to scientific racism by degrees of distance from the dominant discourses, the historians of science Nancy Leys Stepan and Sander L. Gilman might place Hopkins somewhere just short of the pole of greatest distance. It remains to be seen whether she succeeds in creating the "alternative ideology" that, for Stepan and Gilman, represents the most effective strategy with which to counter the elements of existing racial science.[72] Whether Hopkins's racial occult posits such a radically different worldview, with different perceptions of reality, the repeated invocations of *blood* throughout her writings clearly make her vulnerable to charges of complicity with scientific racism itself while adding up to something more: in Judith Butler's words, "a repetition of the law into hyperbole" produces a set of meanings that creates more than it ever meant to, signifying in excess of any intended referent.[73] The proliferating meanings, particularly Hopkins's dizzying shifts from literal to figurative *blood* and back again, destabilize—but do not dismantle—the rigidities of the term and of the racist vision that it articulates.

The challenge in presenting Hopkins as an early race theorist may best be appreciated by quoting in full the controversial passage from *Contending Forces* on the discourse of blood and the Negro Question. This passage comes as something of an interruption, inserted in the middle of a descriptive catalog of the characters in Ma Smith's lodging house. Taking off suddenly from a discussion of how such middle-class "families of color manage to live as well as they do," the narrator steps entirely outside the world of the novel:

> Why should we wonder or question, then, when we see the steady advance of a race overriding the barriers set by prejudice and injustice? Man has said that

from lack of means and social caste the Negro shall remain in a position of serfdom all his days, but the mighty working of cause and effect, the mighty unexpected results of the law of evolution, seem to point to a different solution of the Negro question than any worked out by the most fertile brain of the highly cultured Caucasian. Then again, we do not allow for the infusion of white blood, which became pretty generally distributed in the inferior black race during the existence of slavery. Some of this blood, too, was the best in the country. Combinations of plants, or trees, or of any productive living thing, sometimes generate rare specimens of the plant or tree; why not, then, of the genus homo? Surely the Negro race must be productive of some valuable specimens, if only from the infusion which amalgamation with a superior race must eventually bring. This is a mighty question. Today, with all the heated discussions of tariff reform, the parity of gold and silver, the hoarding of giant sums of money by trusts and combinations, still the Negro question will not "down"; it is the most important, the mightiest in the land. (*CF*, 87–88)

Steeped in repetition, both compromising and strategic, this passage poses "a mighty question," whether "the mighty unexpected results of the law of evolution, seem to point to a different solution of the Negro question than any worked out by the most fertile brain of the highly cultured Caucasian." The language here brands Hopkins as, as Gwendolyn Brooks puts it, "the brainwashed slave revering the modes and idolatries of the master."[74] And, indeed, the narrator answers her own already-conflicted question by using, one after another, a profusion of all the most conventional racialized, biological terms. Alluding to long-standing debates about racial mixture (debates over whether it occurred at all and, if so, which "blood" will triumph)—or what the narrator calls "the infusion of white blood, which became pretty generally distributed in the inferior black race during the existence of slavery" ("some of this blood, too, was the best in the country")—and then to the crossbreeding of plants and trees that generates "rare specimens," she asserts, "Why not, then, of the genus homo? Surely the Negro race must be productive of some valuable specimens, if only from the infusion which amalgamation with a superior race must eventually bring." Is there any mitigating irony to be detected here? most readers wonder, or, more precisely, worry.

To argue that Hopkins offers these questions as a rhetorical gambit to persuade the novel's intended, mixed-race audience is a necessary but insufficient explanation, one with which readers should begin rather than end.[75] For the narrator's own position, as well as the coordinate means and ends of her persuasive effort, is notoriously difficult to pin down. She uses *blood* simultaneously as a biological marker of race, specifically of black inferiority, and as a marker of culture, specifically of white superiority ("the highly cultured Caucasian" of the "best" blood). Combining and disrupting these two meanings, Hopkins takes the assumption of black inferiority as the starting point of her series of questions, which ends unexpectedly, but not contradictorily, asserting positively the might, not the superiority, of both the Negro race and the Negro Question. To do so, she draws on a biological vision of the "valuable specimens" of the Negro race—which must exist, according to racist logic, "if only" through intermixture with whites—and a cultural vision of the Negro Question as "the most important, the mightiest in the land." The repetition of two key terms here provides a further clue to Hopkins's strategic blood talk. "This is a mighty question," she concludes—her referent initially and significantly unclear—one that, in the context of "all the heated discussions" (of tariffs, silver, and trusts), "will not 'down'": it is, she repeats, "the Negro question."

Speaking dangerously from within the language of evolution, Hopkins enumerates the contradictions inherent in that racial discourse: although many denied the fact of widespread racial intermixture at all and others argued either for the bestial (sexual) aggressiveness or for the sterility (not to say impotence) of the mulatto as a racial hybrid, still others insisted that the "best" blood will outweigh (or "outvote," in Twain's ironic term in *Pudd'nhead Wilson*) the rest. Countering the one-drop ideology of miscegenation law, the narrator now implicitly poses another rhetorical question: How could the infusion of blood from the "superior race" result in anything other than superior "specimens" that would demonstrate and affirm the scientific law of evolution? Extending the logic of the post-Darwinian, "bloodmixture" arguments to their logical extreme, she pushes them into an unanticipated and unwelcome corner: the possible production of an evolved Negro race. Yet still perplexing is the apparent assertion that the Negro race may or may not have produced superior beings ("valuable specimens") because of racial intermingling.

Thus, we end with the "mighty question" of the day, "the Negro question," advanced as nothing less than one of "the mighty unexpected results of the law of evolution." Through the excess of reiterative citation, the one-dimensional and demeaning Negro Question—reminding us, in its relegation of the "Negro" to an abstract, depersonalized "question," of the Negro Problem and Du Bois's famous response, "How does it feel to be a problem?" (*SBF*, 625)—is transformed, paradoxically, without being changed. The one question multiplies into the many hidden, sometimes contradictory, constitutive questions that are reduced, oversimplified, and denied by a racist culture. Miming the suffocating reiteration and proliferation within the master's culture of the terms of racial difference, Hopkins both harnesses and exposes the excess that makes racism possible. We have seen how, in a strikingly similar move, Du Bois's 1897 speech to the American Academy of Political and Social Sciences, "The Study of the Negro Problems," explicitly redefined the Negro Problem as, not one problem, but "rather a plexus of social problems, some new, some old, some simple, some complex."[76] In Hopkins's complementary strategy, a singular and literal question becomes at once multiple and figurative, in a move to destabilize, and perhaps to open up, what yet remains a closed and fixed racial system. The Negro Question—still a racist code, but now identified with and simultaneously outstripping a multitude of other nonracial social, political, and economic questions—becomes *the* mighty question, incorporating within itself all the rest.

To make *blood* thus speak out of school, as Hopkins does, to underscore its excessive meanings, revealing how many of them are at odds with both one another and themselves, is to expose the competing contexts, and conflicting narratives, in which the term was regularly used. The term is dislodged from its conventional representational status as a seamless, unitary abstraction and recontextualized, returned to the multiple cultural contexts (the late-nineteenth-century curio cabinet) in which it had meaning(s). Such radical contextualizing makes *blood* mean differently, including Hopkins's own use of *blood* in all its complexities. For one, this idiom of science is equally at home in the world of Hopkins's melodrama, where the referential excess of *blood*, an excess of meaning, joins with the emotional and structural excess of the melodramatic imagination. Further, the *one blood* of the novel advances, on the one hand, a positive, monogenetic argument for global racial origins and the possibility of future pan-racial harmony and, on the other, a pessimistic vision of how the blood history of the United States and contemporary developments on the worldwide color line will conclude. Hopkins's commitment to an understanding of intelligence as part of blood inheritance (not unlike the theories of hereditary intelligence of U.S. psychology) makes mental (occult) powers inherited, traceable through slavery back to Africa. Thus, mental capacity becomes powerful, reconceived as positive. Finally, and more broadly, when Hopkins invokes in *Of One Blood* the sciences of the occult, ethnology, and archaeology as well as psychology, she foregrounds the mobility of nineteenth-century racialized sciences as interracial, transcultural meeting grounds.

Yet the point is that the uses of *blood* do not add up: both literal and figurative, *blood* remains both a stubborn biologism and a vision of interracial harmony. The contradictoriness of the blood talk is related to historical contradictions figured in the realm of the popular occultism to which Hopkins was so attracted. Like most popular cultural forms, it is not that the occult is identified, in any one-to-one relation, with a particular class; rather, class cultures tend, in Stuart Hall's terms, to "overlap and intersect in the same field of struggle." The resulting cultural relations, "the class struggle in and over culture," are in Hopkins's case, perhaps, even more pronounced than usual.[77] Once associated with the revolutionary politics of Hobsbawm's primitive rebels (so many of whom were members of the Freemasons and other occultist societies),[78] the culture of the occult was, at this historical conjuncture, produced and consumed by antagonistic elements, both markedly middle class and elite. On the one hand, the séances and mediumistic trances of *Of One Blood*, in which female figures (the slave mother Mira and her daughter Dianthe) predominate, belong to the realm of popular occultism in the United States, often associated with reform movements, including a relatively privileged, middlebrow feminism (Mary Baker Eddy's Christian Science, Katherine Tingley's Theosophy, Point Loma, California, style). On the other hand, the theories of duality and hidden selves and the studies of "the Unclassified Residuum" that buttress the "supernatural phenomena or *mysticism*" of the novel are drawn either from the elite sphere of academic and professional sciences or the equally rarified world of psychological and psychical research presided over by a cast of international figures. The culture of the occult is, thus, a battleground of what Raymond Williams would call *emergent, residual, and incorporated moments*, especially if we take into account the historical process by which the radical political possibilities of such occultist movements as the early-modern Freemasons have been recuperated in the late nineteenth century in support of dominant cultural values. Hopkins's intervention in such a battleground not only means that she must speak to multiple audiences at once, with the result that her blood talk makes the term *blood* mean in so many different ways that it can never be counted on to mean one thing, but also accounts for the failure of the occult as a popular discourse to comprehend rapidly changing developments around both class and race in the historical and economic realm.

Finally, the battleground of popular occultism is also organized around the contradictory place of tradition in so much popular culture. Hopkins's focus on the past puts her at risk of seemingly courting the conservative impulse that has so often been (over)ascribed to the traditionalism of popular culture.[79] Yet, far from advocating a single originary moment in a monumental great culture of the past, Hopkins proposes, as we have seen, not one but two pasts with constitutive relations to *the Negro*, defined diasporically, of the present. Moreover, these historical relations, occulted and occulting, summed up in the enigmatic words engraved on the sphinx, do not appear as a linear narrative but must be demystified if, as Walter Benjamin says, "a redeemed mankind" is to "receive the fullness of its past"—which is to say, a past "citable in all its moments."[80] The possibility and shape of the future, that is, rest on the redemption of the claim of the past on the present. Hopkins's pasts are apparently at odds: one a narrative of slavery and racial terror in the New World, the other a "song of the past of Ethiopia," the ancient African glory days (*OOB*, 559). Both pasts, however, erupt into the present through a hidden matrilineal line (the legacy of occult powers, "the shadow of Ethiopia's power," inherited from the slave mother Mira, the science and art of ancient Ethiopia, governed by the virgin queen Candace [*OOB*, 558]). Both pasts are also transmitted in the form of arcane texts that must be recognized, rendered legible by the present (Mira's "hand of mysticism," the ancient texts of Meroë, written in what was once the common ancestral language, known now as the "language of prophecy" [*OOB*, 572]). "For there is nothing covered that shall not be revealed, neither hid that shall not be known," reads the passage from Luke (12:2) that twice appears as a kind of automatic writing signed in the "female" spirit hand of Mira (*OOB*, 506, 598). Intervening in the present through a maternal foresight enabled by the perspective of the past, the African and American histories in the novel embody the kind of "weak Messianic power" to which, Benjamin argues, the past has a claim. "The past carries with it a temporal index by which it is referred to redemption."[81] Such a futurist conception of multiple pasts constitutes Hopkins's historical consciousness, both genealogical and messianic, enacting both a contract and a covenant between past and present.

But the limits of what we might call Hopkins's alternative mode of *maternal messianism*, embedded in the presentist promise both of expropriation and of redemption of the past, emerge in the more conventional messianism of her future imaginary, dominated by male leaders and paternal structures of leadership. Not only was the historical Candace, the female monarch of the ancient Ethiopians, constrained to await the coming of Ergamenes to inaugurate a "dynasty of kings," but also Reuel-Ergamenes himself is left at the end of the novel, having returned to the hidden city with his "faithful subjects," in a passive posture of waiting and wondering, "What will the end be?" (*OOB*, 561, 621). If Hopkins wants this moment of messianic time to presage the race-free promise of the one-blood passage that she quotes, once more, as the novel's last line, it is less a Benjaminian "chip of Messianic time," blasting into the "'time of the now'" and taking "a revolutionary chance in the fight for the oppressed past," than what Toni Morrison would decry as the illusion of a race-free world posited as "ideal, millennial, a condition possible only if accompanied by the Messiah."[82] Such are the limits of the black radicalism made possible by popular Ethiopianism. Or, as Stuart Hall would put it, any theory of history or politics that acknowledges, as Hopkins does, the provisionality of the historical—the necessary openness and relative indeterminacy of historical struggle, the impossibility of foreordained political outcomes—must be a theory "without final guarantees."[83]

CHAPTER THREE

PROCRUSTEAN BEDFELLOWS?

BLACK NATIONALISM AND WHITE SUPREMACY AT THE TURN OF THE CENTURY

WHILE, DURING THE heyday of global imperialism and superna-
tionalism at the turn of the century, the United States pursued the
domestic project of national reunification abroad by intervening in Cuba
and the Philippines—a bout of foreign wars that helped lay to rest divisive
memories of the Civil War—at home the Americas witnessed the consolidation of several, strikingly different race-based nationalist movements.
Among the most prominent are the various black nationalisms of Sutton
Griggs, Marcus Garvey, and W. E. B. Du Bois, some of which shade into
Pan-Africanism, all of which developed in reaction to the domestic context
of the increasing dominance of white supremacy in the law and in American
culture at large. Internationally, the impact of empire on these burgeoning
nationalisms stems from a new global self-consciousness of racial identity that
created conflicting collectivities across national boundaries: the "white"
versus the "darker" or "colored" "races." As interpreted by Thomas Dixon's Klan trilogy, and culminating in D. W. Griffith's film *The Birth of a
Nation*, white supremacy came to define the U.S. national imaginary in
racial terms. "Can you build, in a Democracy," Dixon asks repeatedly in
The Leopard's Spots, the first volume of the trilogy, "a nation inside a nation
of two hostile races?" (*LS*, 159). Increasingly, the response was that a nation divided by the rigors of the Civil War and Reconstruction could put itself securely on the road to reunion only through "the nationalization of
race": a contradictory process of inflating and effacing, demonizing and, ultimately, excluding the black.[1] To be American was to be white.[2] So went the
logic of white supremacy, itself one of the protean discourses of empire as
well as nation and of sexuality as well as race.

If Dixon is seen as one of white supremacy's main spokesmen, Griggs is a relatively minor literary figure even in histories of black nationalism. Griggs's nationalism is not easily defined, running the gamut of positions usually associated with opposed programs: at various points he advocated both vocational and higher education for blacks and espoused both interracial cooperation at home and African emigration as solutions to the U.S. "race problem." Although he participated in the Niagara movement, Griggs, a Baptist minister in Memphis, was supported, and funded, as an acceptable race leader by local whites. Critical of both Booker T. Washington and W. E. B. Du Bois, Griggs also expressed admiration for Washington in the specific context of his treatise on the "laws of collective action for racial success," *Life's Demands; or, According to Law* (1916).[3] Finally, while he wrote five monographs setting forth what he called, in Spencerian terms, a racial "science of collective efficiency," works in which he drew on theories in the social and biological sciences to argue for racial cooperation in the confines of an organized black community, Griggs's novels anatomize various approaches to black leadership, all variants of authoritarianism. Thus we have, on the one hand, Griggs the bundle of paradoxes and, on the other, Dixon the apparently seamless ideologue.[4]

Griggs and Dixon are an odd couple in more ways than this one. Simply to speak in the same breath of Griggs's black nationalism and Dixon's white supremacy runs the risk of perversely equating two opposed ideologies. It was, for example, common practice at the turn of the century to condemn black political organizations—from the Union (or Loyal) League of Reconstruction to the Garvey movement of the 1920s—for their supposed resemblance to, or traffic with, white terrorist groups, the Ku Klux Klan in particular.[5] Similarly, the "procrustean politics," in C. Vann Woodward's terms, of the post-Reconstruction South were marked by forced conformity among warring factions, black and white, that frequently made political bedfellows of otherwise deeply divided groups.[6] Most recently, Paul Gilroy has characterized the well-known association between Garvey and the Klan as symptomatic of a "profound kinship"—a "fraternalist mirroring" and "transracial symmetry"—between Garvey's Universal Negro Improvement Association (UNIA) and the fascist political movements of the period in which it grew.[7] But, even if we resist turning the two novelists into such procrustean bedfellows, why, and how, pair them at all? Both are known primarily as ("sub")literary figures associated with writing so-called bad fiction—criticized most frequently for being melodramatic and didactic or polemical—to advance supposedly militant or extremist ideological projects.[8] Yet the obvious asymmetries in their relative positions as public fig-

ures, then and now, remind us that bad reputations, both aesthetic and political, are not always equal.

However problematic, the link between bad art and bad politics is my
starting point. As far as the politics is concerned, both black nationalism and
white nationalism have—the charge of political extremism notwithstanding—long, well-documented histories within mainstream American culture. Griggs and Dixon, therefore, speak, not from the periphery, but from
different centers of late-nineteenth-century U.S. culture. As for the aesthetics, the question "But is it any good?" is more complicated to answer. At
this point, a reformulation of the question, and some preliminary responses,
will have to suffice. How do the forms and formulas of popular fiction en-
able the political projects of Griggs and Dixon, not simply as vehicles or
covers or distractions, but as representations bound up with the meaning of
their politics? Their racial ideologies will emerge as procrustean in that a
shared bed of formal and structural elements articulates almost diametrically opposed racial and political views. Among the shared elements we find
the following: For both Griggs and Dixon, seeking to historicize race relations of the 1890s, the melodramatic provides a historiographic mode that
reframes U.S. history in racial terms. As historiographers, they focus as
much on politics, class, and economics as on race and nation and as much on
intraracial divisions and collectivities as on interracial conflict. As melodramatists, they make fertile use of what I call the American *conspiratorial
imagination* in anatomizing the sources and tracing the contradictions of the
domestic racial scene. And, finally, the focus in both on the local and domestic is continually counterbalanced by a burgeoning international awareness, grounded in the worldwide imperialisms emerging at the turn of the
century.

For both Griggs and Dixon, fiction writing was a natural extension of
their lifelong, proselytizing work in the pulpit and on the speaker's platform. Both were Baptist ministers whose views on racial and political questions of the day ultimately reached audiences beyond their congregations,
although their relations to those audiences are by no means comparable.
Griggs, based in Memphis and Nashville, and involved both with the Niagara movement and the National Baptist Convention, received some financial support for his publishing ventures from white Baptists, who saw him
as a credible black spokesman. He wrote prolifically, as we have seen, in a
range of genres. But he himself railed against his poor sales among black
readers and the neglect of his fiction by the predominantly black audience
that he wanted to reach. Later, Du Bois would contrast Griggs, who "spoke

primarily to the Negro," to Charles Chesnutt and Paul Dunbar, who "spoke to the whole nation."[9] In contrast, Dixon preached and lectured widely throughout the country from 1889 to 1903, even before publishing his first novel, the overnight success *The Leopard's Spots: A Romance of the White Man's Burden* (1903), which connected Dixon's enthusiasm for the Spanish-American War, expressed in such lecture titles as "The Victory of Manila" and "The Anglo-Saxon Alliance," with his burgeoning Negrophobia. The notoriety of *The Leopard's Spots*, both praised and condemned in the national media, largely over the question of historical accuracy, was cemented by the second volume in Dixon's Klan trilogy, the best-selling *The Clansman: An Historical Romance of the Ku Klux Klan* (1905), which (along with Woodrow Wilson's scholarly *History of the American People*) provided the basis for Griffith's *The Birth of a Nation* (1915).[10] Despite the fundamental differences in their commercial success as authors, both Griggs and Dixon viewed the novel as a means of historical revision and social intervention; incorporated into their fiction was factual material drawn from newspapers, histories of the Civil War and Reconstruction, and social-scientific theory as well as from their own nonfictional writing. Finally, in a series of prefaces to their novels, both developed a literary philosophy in which fiction is the nationalist expression of a people and their history. In all these ways, then, in their lives and in their writing, art and politics were one for Griggs and Dixon.

But there is also a specific place where Griggs directly addresses Dixon, in a lengthy response to *The Leopard's Spots* incorporated into his fourth novel, *The Hindered Hand* (1905), in the guise of a thinly veiled, conversational debate on "the book of a rather conspicuous Southern man, who had set for himself the task of turning the entire Negro population out of America."[11] In the third revised edition of the novel, Griggs expanded his response into an essay, "A Hindering Hand, Supplementary to *The Hindered Hand: A Review of the Anti-Negro Crusade of Mr. Thomas Dixon, Jr.*," appended at the end of the book, a place where he frequently included polemical material in the form of various "plans" or manifestos.[12] Griggs argues that the success of Dixon's book was clearly due to "the moment of its publication," characterized through the nexus of race, nation, and empire:

> The coming together of the English speaking races at the bier of Queen Victoria, . . . ; the treacherous blowing up of Anglo-Saxon lads in the harbor of a Latin nation and the war that followed; the assuming of an unaccepted relation to another race by the white people of the North, which thereby provided the one outstanding section of the Anglo-Saxon race with some form of a race problem—these things brought the English speaking people wondrously

close together and bridged the chasms made by internecine wars and conflicting ideas of government. This moment of Anglo-Saxon rapprochement was seized upon by this Southerner to assault the stranger within his gates.[13]

Griggs here formulates the densely textured cultural context that produced both himself and Dixon, a context in which race, nation, and empire informed, collaborated with, and conflicted with one another in different ways on both the domestic and the international scenes. Mapped out are virtually all the major historical events, figures, and tropes shaped in and by their fiction: race as defined by common language (the English-speaking people); race as common heritage (Anglo-Saxonism); race as conflict (the Spanish-American War); race as a regionalized problem in the United States, a nation divided into North and South; the social and legal assault on the black "stranger within"; and, finally, the paramount question of Anglo-Saxon unity, globally considered.

The moment of international Anglo-Saxon rapprochement turns out to be, for both writers, the crux of the nation's ongoing, unsolved race problem. Lest we run the risk of simplifying Griggs and Dixon, we need to locate them in the history of the post-Reconstruction context that they themselves characterize, not as a clearly defined period, but as a long process of transition and experimentation, contradiction, conflict, and ambiguity. Griggs calls into question, even as he asserts, the stability of this "moment" of white unity ("the English speaking people" being brought "wondrously close together"), pointedly born of the divisions of war and politics as well as a shared "race problem" at home and abroad. Rather than retreating to a fanatical nationalism, as he is most often read as doing, Griggs forces with his global moment a recognition of the international dimensions of the American racial conflict. The Spanish-American War figures prominently in several of his novels as a crisis point for domestic racial politics. For Dixon, white supremacy is neither simply an assertion nor simply an assumption; rather, the central question of *The Leopard's Spots*—"*Shall the future American be an Anglo-Saxon or a Mulatto?*"—remains a kind of anxious refrain, repeatedly posed throughout the novel (*LS*, 159). "The future of the American people," Dixon concludes, is shadowed by "two great questions, the conflict between Labor and Capital" and the "unsolved Negro problem" (*LS*, 331). Despite their reputations as racial dogmatists, both Griggs and Dixon can be understood as making the race question the dominant theme of American history only insofar as "race" exceeds its own bounds, intersecting, often in unexpected and even contradictory ways, other political, economic, and social issues, conflicts, and affiliations. Politics—the various uses of the "cult of racism" by Republicans, Democrats, and Populists, ranging paradoxically from courting the black vote to charging "Negro domination"—and economics—the uneven development of the New South, Western, and national economies—complicate or supplant the focus on race and nation that we commonly associate with late-nineteenth-century nationalisms, just as the emergence of intraracial collectivities and divisions disrupts the supposed focus of these writers on interracial conflict.[14]

Individually, Griggs and Dixon repeatedly return to sources of conflict: politics and class and regional and national differences as much as race. In their accounts of both intraracial collectivities and divisions and interracial conflict, both novelists focus particularly on the contradictions of racial politics, especially how the continuing presence of an independent black vote—which, through enticement and intimidation, could be and was mobilized by all parties—invariably sparked, but was just as often neutralized by, appeals to what Charles Chesnutt calls in *The Marrow of Tradition* (1901), his novel about the 1898 Wilmington race riot, the "race question," the "all-powerful race argument" (*MT*, 238–39). Like Griggs's *Hindered Hand*, *The Marrow of Tradition* was seen as a possible response to Dixon's *Leopard's Spots*, but Chesnutt's letters reveal that, at best, his novel was taken—by members of the House of Representatives, to whom he had sent copies—as an alternative to rather than a refutation of Dixonian Negrophobia.[15] *The Marrow of Tradition* identifies the arbitrary brutality of the color line itself with its procrustean nature: "It was a veritable bed of Procrustes, this standard which the whites had set for the negroes. Those who grew above it must have their heads cut off, figuratively speaking,—must be forced back to the level assigned to their race; those who fell beneath the standard set had their necks stretched, literally enough, as the ghastly record in the daily papers gave conclusive evidence" (*MT*, 61). The forced conformity of interracial relations, which subjects all blacks to versions of the same ghastly treatment, also intensifies the divisions inherent in the differences between figurative and literal punishments.

Thus, Chesnutt and Griggs demonstrate how the race question often divided groups otherwise allied by social and economic interests, particularly middle-class professionals, but also the working class (as W. E. B. Du Bois would confirm in his social studies of black and white folk). In stark contrast, Dixon repeatedly insists that white supremacy transcends class difference, bringing together in *The Leopard's Spots* the yeoman farmer

Tom Camp, the landless ex-Confederate aristocrat Charles Gaston, and the mill-owning successful entrepreneur General Worth. Such mosaics of contradiction in the fiction point to the many fissures, the shifting political, class, and sectional alignments, and the multiple cross- and countercurrents that underlie, and to an extent give the lie to, the deeply polarized racial realities of the turn of the century.

This is the deeply confusing and ambiguous sphere that Woodward later called the *procrustean politics* of the New South. Like Chesnutt's bed of Procrustes, Woodward's procrustean politics was fundamentally characterized by an ironic racial contradiction: the manipulation of black votes by or the collaboration of black voters with white-supremacist Democrats, meant simultaneously to diminish the threat of local white Republican leadership and to allow the charge of race treason to be leveled against the Republican Party. Not satisfied with white supremacy, Democrats also co-opted Populist issues and rhetoric. The Republican Party—the party of hard money, big business, and black rights—allied itself with agrarian antimonopolists and a proimperialist position. Southern Progressivists championed both white supremacy and imperialism. Machine politicians, Democrat and Republican, commonly endorsed a ticket and repudiated the platform on which it ran. And all this, remarks Woodward, "with no apparent sense of inconsistency, certainly none of duplicity."[16]

Sharing the procrustean bed are not only black voters and white Democrats but also other conspiring forces, those of culture, such as the forms of melodrama and historiography. The procrustean contexts revealed by Griggs and Dixon extend beyond the politics of the South to the more ambiguous sphere of the cultural, where conspiratorial imaginaries meet up with hypernationalism and international imperialism. The paradoxical, racial discourse of invisible empires, secret societies, nations within the nation, and other open secrets was one result. The threat of race war at home—sometimes fabricated, always exaggerated—complemented the ambiguous promise of imperial expansion abroad. Together, these forces produced the procrustean version of the American race melodramas.

THE STRANGE CAREER OF RECONSTRUCTION

As interpreters of slavery's aftermath, Griggs and Dixon take part in the popular-cultural project of the postbellum "romance of reunion," associated with such varied literary modes as George Washington Cable's New Orleans local color, Thomas Nelson Page's plantation novels, Mark Twain's

Southwestern humor, and W. E. B. Du Bois's multigenred works. While their fiction shares many of the generic, melodramatic features of the literatures of familial and national reconciliation, Griggs and Dixon locate the body of their work in more specific geographic, chronological, and political contexts. Set in Texas (Griggs's 1899 *Imperium in Imperio*), the cities of the Deep South (Griggs's 1902 *Unfettered* and 1905 *Hindered Hand*), and the Carolinas (Dixon's Klan trilogy), these novels take as their predominant historical referents, not slavery (as do most maternal melodramas), but rather the American Revolution, Reconstruction, and the Spanish-American War, represented both as events of and as tropes for revolutionary overturning—for better or worse—of the established order.

Two central sets of events/issues of the 1890s frame the locations of all the Griggs and Dixon novels on which I have chosen to focus. The first set of events is the state and national elections held during the period 1890–1900. In this decade of an emerging third party—that emergence signaling multiple alliances and fragmentation—the actuality or the threat of an independent black vote could be and was mobilized by Democrats, Republicans, and Populists alike, raising issues of the interrelations among race and racial violence, on the one hand, and politics and elections, on the other. Griggs's two explicitly political novels, *Unfettered* and *The Hindered Hand*, explore the connections during the 1890s between the prevalence of lynching and the renewed visibility of the black vote, between black voters' historic ties with the Republican Party and their prospects of breaking with the (white) Republicans and forging new, interracial alliances. Dixon's Klan trilogy, especially *The Leopard's Spots*, is also informed by the continuing success of local black candidates in such areas as the famous black Second Congressional District of North Carolina and the South Carolina Piedmont, both, not coincidentally, the locale of the trilogy. Klan activity itself was concentrated in the Piedmont counties (*Clansman*) and the North Carolina foothills (*Leopard's Spots*), where blacks constituted a minority or small majority of the population and support among voters for the two major parties was evenly divided.[17] The historical narrative of disfranchisement in *The Leopard's Spots* is steeped in the minutiae of electoral politics in these areas, from the volatile summer of 1867, when the Klan was "born," to the 1898 Wilmington race riot.

Second is the Spanish-American War. Almost instantaneously interpreted as an apotheosis of national healing and unity—"Populists, Democrats, Republicans are we, but we are all Americans to make Cuba free," in the words of the white supremacist Ben Tillman, a senator from South Carolina—the war masked but barely contained both interracial divisions and intraracial differences of class, politics, section, and gender.[18] For Dixon, the war serves the same role as black rape, providing in the last extreme a reliable basis for white solidarity when almost any other issue runs the risk of dividing whites. The opposite is true for Griggs, in part because the war unravels the national identity of black soldiers and citizens, who identify both with Cubans as latter-day American revolutionaries fighting a colonial power and with the Filipino struggle against America, the ascendant military-imperial power. The Griggs-Dixon focus on conflict, domestic and international, inter- and intraracial, constitutes a counterpoint to the exaggerated nationalism of the reigning romance of reunion.

As the obverse face of literature's celebratory role in the forging of national reunion, Griggs and Dixon together bring into focus the charged cultural context in which literature played the roles of both political battleground and site of reconciliation. In their particular contribution to the popular interpretation of the nation's history of slavery and the Civil War, the melodramatic functions as a specifically historiographic mode and Reconstruction, so often twinned with the American Revolution, as the pivotal, revolutionary event through which race relations of the 1890s are interpreted. As such, Griggs and Dixon join with other "Reconstruction" novelists to produce, during this era of sectional reunion, national reconciliation, and imperial ventures, almost a second wave of national romances. These "foundational fictions" narrate the rebirth of the nation, culminating in its new imperial identity.[19] Like the first-wave U.S. nationalist novels (by, e.g., Cooper and Melville), the romance plots common to all are no mere subplots but rather modes of mediating national conflict through loves that transgress some of the nation's most threatening inner divisions but stay firmly within its territorial borders. The paradigm of "Love and Politics," the title of one of the chapters in Griggs's first novel, *Imperium in Imperio*, is elaborated in Dixon's preface to *The Clansman*. Introducing this second book of the Klan trilogy, "a series of historical novels on the Race Conflict . . . from the enfranchisement of the Negro to his disfranchisement," Dixon writes, "I have sought to preserve in this romance both the letter and the spirit of this remarkable period. The men who enact the drama of fierce revenge into which I have woven a double love-story are historical figures" (*C*, 1–2). The love plots of the race melodrama are, like those of national allegory, supposed to parallel, and resolve, the racial, regional, and socioeconomic fissures of the politics plots, with couples divided, for example, between North and South (*The Clansman*), or New South and Old South

(*The Leopard's Spots*), or mulatto and pure black (*Imperium in Imperio*), or pro- and antiexpansionism (*Unfettered*), or American militancy and African mysticism (*The Hindered Hand*).[20]

In the new national romances, however, the conventional allegorical relation of love to politics is destabilized, doubled in Dixon's work, but multiplied and fragmented in Griggs's. Not only does *The Clansman* (as Dixon notes) unite two North-South pairs (each including a child of the Radical Republican Austin Stoneman, the novel's Thaddeus Stevens figure), but *The Leopard's Spots* features a main-plot romance between an Old South son and a New South daughter as well as an adulterous subplot romance between the scalawag Allan McLeod and the wife of the Reverend Durham, the novel's premier white-supremacist spokesman. Even more dizzyingly, Griggs explodes the conventional pairings into multiples. The lovely mulatta of *Unfettered,* the "Ardent Expansionist" and "unyielding Republican" Morlene, is twice married, first unhappily to the opportunistic Republican tool and ex-plantation Negro Harry Dalton, then to the well-educated, independent-minded political visionary Dorlan Warthell (*U,* 121, 126). *The Hindered Hand* counterposes three romances: the positive pair (the dark-skinned preacher Ensal and the feminist Tiara, advocates of racial pride, political agitation, and the "dream of Africa" [*HH,* 144]) against the destructive pair (the self-hating mulatta Eunice and the militant radical Earl) and, finally, both these couples against the tragic fate of the lower-class innocents Bud and Foresta, twin victims of a gruesome lynching. As these various representative couples suggest, both writers also rely for their narrative structure on the melodramatic polarities of rival, intraracial leaders, procrustean spokesmen for the community who are shown to espouse opposing political, social, and economic visions and programs.

Yet, as we will see, rather than dividing and simplifying, the highly ordered structure of melodrama paradoxically makes legible the turn-of-the-century nexus of race, nation, and empire that generated conflicting racial, regional, and political loyalties. Even the brief list of couples just given demonstrates how affiliations often crossed established party lines demarcating interest groups defined by class and gender, race and politics. Attempting in response—like the rallying cries of white supremacy and Anglo-Saxon unity—to bring "order out of chaos" (Dixon's words [*LS,* 150]), the polarizing modes of melodrama dramatize instead the complexities of post-Reconstruction history. Adapted by Griggs and Dixon as a mode of Reconstruction historiography, melodrama generates many of the messy stresses and strains of that long national crisis, finally refusing to resolve or contain them.

Together, Griggs and Dixon offer an interpretation of the aftermath of slavery as an extended moment of crisis and contradiction. Not a linear model of historical progress, like that which undergirds the texts of national reconciliation, theirs is an unstable history combining continuity and rupture, pairing the 1890s with Reconstruction through what is alternately characterized as a process of reversion and as one of repetition. Rather than adhering to the Southern Redemption model of an unbroken racial retrenchment from the end of Reconstruction (1877) to legalized Jim Crow segregation (marked by the 1896 *Plessy v. Ferguson* decision), Griggs and Dixon characterize the aftermath of Reconstruction through chronological asymmetries, displacements, and repetitions. Among the major historical ironies revealed by their chronology is the fact that, even as legalized segregation in federal and state law defined the place of blacks in the new social and economic order and extralegal violence against them escalated locally, spiraling in apparently paradoxical relation to a decreasing black presence on the national scene, politics—both state and local—was in some places in the South marked by the continuing or revived power of the black vote. Southern Populists secured the black vote through deals with dissident Republicans, an arrangement that came to be called *fusion* and that was decried by those Democrats who were competing for the same black vote. Such contradictions, emerging especially prominently in the 1890s, were interpreted by Griggs and Dixon, among others, as repetitions of an earlier, hotly debated Reconstruction moment, itself layered through the still-earlier, foundational symbology of the American Revolution.

In the complex historicity of the post-Emancipation moment, both the antebellum and the Reconstruction eras were remembered and reimagined in multiple, competing modes, from the national nostalgia of plantation mythology, to the imagery, both threatening and promising, of a repeat of Reconstruction so common in Southern political discourse of the 1890s. Bourbon Democrats warned against a "New Negro" domination, keeping alive memories of black political power in the dark days before Redemption, while the invention of a New South, with economic ties to the industrialized North, depended on the myth of Old South paternalism with its generations of loyal black "uncles" and "aunts." Different pasts were invoked both to avert and to ensure the future.

In explicit contrast to the "fawning, sniffling, cowardly Negro" of slavery, Griggs's "New Negro" confronts white violence as a recurrence of the

intimidation and lynching of the Reconstruction Klan, but with a difference:[21] rather than a localized phenomenon, this is a radicalizing violence so
widespread as to "contain the germs of a race war" (*U*, 29). The New Negro will meet the threat through returning to the revolutionary legacy of
Valley Forge and Patrick Henry's "Give me liberty or give me death," a line
quoted in the Imperium documents to claim the national heritage of independence that underwrites the separate black nation to be established in
Texas if the "peaceful revolution" of the vote continues to be denied to
blacks (*II*, 220, 245). For Dixon, "the chaos" of Radical Reconstruction
produced "a Revolution in our Government and the bold attempt of Thaddeus Stevens to Africanise ten states of the American Union" (*C*, 1); "the
new revolution destroyed the Union a second time" and, therefore, had to
be thwarted repeatedly, first by the Klan's rescue and redemption of the
South from the Northern carpetbagger, the native scalawag, and the Negro
demagogue, then by a "second Declaration of Independence from the in-
famy of corrupt and degraded government" in the face of a Republican-
Populist-Negro alliance in the late 1890s (*LS*, 83, 411). Justifications of
campaigns to disfranchise black voters, especially in regions roughly
equally divided between races and parties—such as the Piedmont counties
of South Carolina (the setting of *The Clansman*) and the Blue Ridge Mountains of North Carolina (*The Leopard's Spots* is set in and around Ham-
bright, home of "the men who had first declared their independence
of Great Britain in America" [*LS*, 5])—often relied on the repeat-of-
Reconstruction theme and the need to revert to violent, revolutionary tactics, paradoxically to avoid a full-scale repetition of those days. Keeping
alive the memory of Reconstruction, Dixon has Charles Gaston, the hero of
The Leopard's Spots, ask rhetorically in his climactic political speech, "Shall
we repeat the farce of '67?" The answer has been clear all along: "The day
of Negro domination over the Anglo-Saxon race shall close, now, once and
forever" (*LS*, 435, 412).[22] The comparison was also drawn by Populists
themselves and the appeal to violence advocated, and to some extent practiced, by both sides.[23] The theme of revolutionary violence was, thus, mobile and explosive, traveling in both positive and negative trajectories between black and white nationalisms. There was no simple cause-and-effect
relation to be found in the responses of blacks to white racism, textual and
actual, or of whites to black power, real and imagined.

    In foregrounding what the historian Joel Williamson terms the largely
unnoticed phenomenon of the *echo Reconstruction*, Griggs's and Dixon's
melodramas put them, in the 1890s, squarely where modern historians

would, only much later, finally end up.[24] If Woodward's "strange career of Jim Crow" postulated a long period of transition and experimentation preceding the solidification of segregation in the late 1890s, Williamson's echo Reconstruction demonstrates the striking persistence of black activism in politics, the locus both of Griggs's ambivalence and Dixon's animus.[25] This is part of what historians today call Reconstruction's *chaotic chronology* when they argue that, like nearly every other aspect of the period, its chronological boundaries remain open to dispute. Reconstruction had, on this view, no definitive beginning. Was it as early as the 1863 Emancipation Proclamation, or did it start in 1865? Neither, and more important, did it have a definitive end. Was the conclusion in 1877, with the withdrawal of federal troops, the advent of "Redemption," and the return to home rule? Did it last until 1954 and *Brown v. Board of Education*? Or, to take the most radical position, as Du Bois did in 1935 (in *Black Reconstruction in America*), was it an unfinished effort to construct a democratic, interracial order as well as a phase in the ongoing struggle of labor and capital?[26] As historiographers, Griggs and Dixon together formulate their own chaotic chronology, constructing a complex history of race relations that extends the 1890s both backward, to earlier "revolutionary" moments of the Reconstruction period and the Revolution, and forward, in an ongoing process of transition, contradiction, class and race conflict, and unfulfilled possibility. The modern historians Woodward, Williamson, and company may even be said to document, in their evidence of Reconstruction's chaotic chronology, the strange temporality that Ellison recognized in racial invisibility, itself such a striking feature of the political movements, both black and white, of the post-Reconstruction era of Griggs and Dixon.

The Griggs-Dixon historiography articulates a multiplicity of positions and alternatives that was in the early twentieth century homogenized by "consensus historians," who constructed a narrative of Southern history dominated by the tragic theme of race. With the exception of Du Bois's dissenting voice in *Black Reconstruction in America* (1935), which argues that Reconstruction was a "splendid failure" initiating a "second slavery" (*BRA*, 708), the standard modern histories of the post-Reconstruction South were dominated by the tradition of the Dunning school, with its views of the homogeneous "solid South" as a region entirely determined by the central theme of race and of Reconstruction as a "tragic era" of corruption presided over by Northern carpetbaggers, Southern scalawags, and ignorant freedmen.[27] Du Bois's refutation of this "frontal attack on Reconstruction" as the "propaganda of history" coming out of major universities

(*BRA*, 711, 718)—particularly Columbia (where William Dunning trained an influential generation of graduate students) and Johns Hopkins (where Woodrow Wilson taught and wrote his two-volume *History of the American People*, a source for Griffith's *Birth of a Nation*)—was largely ignored at the time. Not until the revisionist histories of the 1950s and after—for example, Woodward's thesis of "the strange career of Jim Crow," an "unstable interlude" marked by "experiment, testing, uncertainty" and "forgotten alternatives," and Eric Foner's "America's unfinished revolution"—did the Griggs-Dixon vision of Reconstruction as an open-ended, conflicted process of social and economic change in race relations reshape the predominant historiographic accounts.[28]

Literary critics, even those whose project is to rewrite an interracial literary history of the late-nineteenth-century United States, tend to operate within the older, historical model, focusing on a few literary and cultural figures of the period who are still generally isolated in the confines of this racial history, as either exceptions (Du Bois) or extremists (Dixon). But, when we turn to the very different, conflict-oriented views of the Griggs-Dixon melodramas of crisscrossing racial, political, and class tensions, a series of discrepant couplings of strange ideologies emerges as an alternative to the narrowly conceived, race-dominated conception of turn-of-the-century American culture.[29] Not only does thus opening up the context to contradiction and anxiety and alternatives fit with the mobile melodramatic mode, but also text and context enact this fluidity rather than one containing or subverting the other.

For the historians who, like Griggs and Dixon, characterize the period between Reconstruction and World War I both in relation to the explosiveness of the protean heritage of the American Revolution and through complex interconnections among the era's racial, political, and economic agendas, "race" is not the "motor of history," nor does it provide a singular, coherent explanatory account of history.[30] The historical actors of Griggs and Dixon are not simply black or white, Republican or Democrat, yeoman farmer or Bourbon aristocrat; rather, they are all of the above. Racial loyalties and divisions interact in often contradictory ways with other social and economic ties. Griggs details the wide range of debates and positions taken within the African American community—mistakenly, but strategically, characterized as singular—on black leadership and education, miscegenation and race purity, racial separatism and racial cooperation, the Spanish-American War and U.S. expansionism, and, finally, African emigration and Pan-Africanism. Dixon, too, returns obsessively in his Klan trilogy to the differences—mainly of section, class, and politics—within what comes to seem the mobile, even promiscuous, framework of white supremacy. *The Leopard's Spots* traces a long history of conflict in the South, the burden of repeated threats of "Negro domination" as well as lower-class white and New South industrialist challenges to the rule of Bourbon elites. *The Clansman* retraces some of the same terrain, narrowing its chronological focus to North-South divisions within the nation during the period of the Klan's emergence, 1865–68, and *The Traitor* (1907) concentrates on the dissension within the Klan itself that precipitated its demise in the 1870s.

Among Dixon's procrustean bedfellows are the so-called New South allies of *The Leopard's Spots,* the classic paternalist General Worth and his sometime antagonist Gaston, the representative of the younger, patrician generation. While Gaston, the faithful boyhood companion of Dick, a New Negro and "unsolved riddle" (*LS,* 240), later lynched for the alleged rape of Tom Camp's daughter, rejects the political blandishments of the Republican scalawag Allan McLeod, who is in cahoots with another New Negro, the unsuccessful labor organizer George Harris (the son of the fiery mulatta slave Eliza of *Uncle Tom's Cabin* fame), General Worth celebrates the past (especially slavery's racial paternalism) but embraces Yankee-style capitalism, a docile, poor-white labor force, and a laissez-faire future. Griggs's *Unfettered* calls on black voters to break free of the "political chains" that historically shackle them to the Republican Party, a long alliance of now-procrustean bedfellows, and inaugurate "a new emancipation" from "party slavery" in the South (*U,* 95, 98, 97). The novel features a white Republican congressman conspiring to murder a highly educated black former supporter and speechwriter whose defection threatens to expose the party's manipulation of the black vote; such manipulation will, in turn, be exploited by the Democratic campaign against Negro domination even while the party of white supremacy secretly encourages black voters in Republican ranks. Griggs's many strange political bedfellows are outdone only by such historical phenomena as the specter of blacks in the red shirts of white-supremacy night riders, noted in more than one Democratic newspaper, and Democrats who are not only Whigs, like Dixon's General Worth, but Reconstruction Radicals in disguise.[31]

Given so many contradictions, it is no wonder that, in going beyond the race-theme reading to account for the conflicting arenas and modes in which race was mobilized, both writers become embroiled in what I call *the conspiratorial imagination.* The subject of Dixon's Klan trilogy is, of course, the conspiratorial organization par excellence; and, of Griggs's five novels, three imagine a variety of conspiracies, ranging from the Imperium, an armed black organization secretly planning, in *Imperium in Imperio*, to establish a black nation in the state of Texas, to the political assassination of *Unfettered*, to a Pan-Slavic world takeover in *The Hindered Hand*. As fantastic as some of these ideas sound, the reality of political conspiracies—the prevalence of electoral fraud and demagogic manipulation of both the black and the poor-white vote by both Republicans and Democrats, not to mention the reality of the Invisible Empire—should suggest that *conspiracy* was simultaneously a state of mind and the modus operandi in postbellum racial politics. This is a historically specific flowering of the countersubversive tradition in American politics, also known as *the paranoid style*, which locates at the center, not the extremes or fringes, of American politics the habit of demonizing political foes, of attributing secret, all-pervasive power to a conspiratorial center of evil.[32]

The long and dishonorable history of conspiracy theory in American national politics has a special meaning for the turn of the century, providing a powerful explanatory account of the particular ambiguities and contradictions of post-Reconstruction history, ranging from procrustean politics' accusations of unholy political alliances, open and covert, between Republicans, Democrats, Populists, and black voters; to the paradoxes of racial terror, operating in the open forms of accusations of rape and the practice of lynching but also in the more veiled forms of the logic of disfranchisement, including electoral intimidation, violence, and ballot-box fraud; to the ubiquitous phenomenon of the many semisecret, militaristic societies and fraternal organizations that sprang up, representing virtually every political viewpoint on the spectrum. What has been called *the age of incorporation* is also an age of secret organizations. From the Masons, to the Knights of Pythias, to the Rosicrucians, the nostalgic appeal of mystic rites and secret rituals undergirded the performance of brotherhood in the era of nativism and Jim Crow. Providing mainstream reinforcement to the many popular, militarized groups, what might be called a *military-imperial* complex emerged at the turn of the century with international expansion and the allied need to control political and economic dissenters, both native and foreign, at home.[33] The common denominator among these varieties of conspiratorial experience is the simultaneous threat and promise of the different collectivities that they reveal as well as a perceived instability fostered in the boundaries between loyalty and betrayal, insider and outsider, patriot and traitor, within and between racially, nationally, and politically defined groups. All these domestic developments, lending themselves to conspiratorial explanations, played out against the international context of the Spanish-American War, seized on by popular culture on the home front as a symbol of national re-unification and rescue from the conflicts of both past and present. Yet the war also represented the culmination of the conspiratorial 1890s, highlighting and exacerbating political, economic, and social divisions within supposedly homogeneous racial groups, from the "solid South" to the black Republican Party, even as it served national rescue fantasies.

For the two novelists, American conspiracy theory affords a historical alternative to the dominant popular narrative of Manichaean racial and na-tional forces. What is most striking about the various rhetorics of a recon-stituted U.S. nationalism at this time is how they also paradoxically tapped the very divisions and conflicts, some old, some new, threatening that na-tional unity—and, thus, made themselves available to a countersubversive reading. The central events (the Spanish-American War, the American Revolution), terms (*Anglo-Saxon* unity, *the white man's burden*), and slogans ("our little brown brothers," "mystic brotherhood") that come to define the new imperial American nation point to or are themselves fields of con-tention, just as the corresponding rhetorics of racial purity (vs. miscegena-tion), imperialism, militarism, and fraternalism are unstable or promiscu-ous, aligning themselves or cohabiting with diametrically opposed groups, ideologies, and political programs.[34] The sexualized terms for the mobility of these ideologies convey the underlying, troubling fusion of race and sex in which the post-Reconstruction conspiratorial imagination specializes. The net result is a destabilizing of the rigid racial and political affiliations as-sociated with these rhetorics, which, in the volatile context of racial nation-alism, did not always divide along or correspond to the usual party lines and, thus, lent themselves to a conspiratorial reading. Adapted to the vol-atile context of racial nationalism and conspiracy theory, both texts and genre prove mobile and protean.

THE STRANGE CAREER OF THE
CONSPIRATORIAL IMAGINATION

Griggs and Dixon were not alone in turning to conspiracy theory as an al-ternative to the competing national narrative of clear-cut racial polarities. The cultural power of conspiracy theory derives from its simultaneous sta-tus as reality and fantasy, state of mind and modus operandi. No better evi-dence of the reality of the Ku Klux Klan conspiracy, as it was commonly called, can be found than the thirteen volumes issued by the Joint Select Committee to Inquire into the Condition of Affairs in the Late Insurrectionary States, an investigation into Klan activities from 1866 to 1872 conducted by the Forty-second Congress in 1872. "No one can read the mass of testimony in the various congressional reports," comments Du Bois in *Black Reconstruction in America*, "without being convinced of the organized disorder and conspiracy that accompanied this revolution" (*BRA*, 688–89).

The Klan provides only one kind of specific evidence for this conspiratorial moment. More broadly, it has been argued that Southern Democrats, Populists, and Independents alike subscribed to a late-nineteenth-century "conspiracy theory of national politics," in which the national economic policies of the Republican Party involving taxation, banking, and financial regulation were interpreted as the product of entrenched corruption, ongoing since Reconstruction, laying a special burden on the South, but also threatening the very basis of representative government and "the people."[35] In the 1880s, what quickly became a well-known conspiracy view of the Fourteenth Amendment, extending civil rights to the ex-slaves, was first purveyed. On the basis of the 1882 Supreme Court argument of Roscoe Conkling, one of the drafters of the Fourteenth Amendment, that the joint congressional committee had intentionally used the word *person* in order to include corporations, historians theorized that the drafting process had assumed the character of a conspiracy, with the due-process and equal-protection clauses "smuggled in" as double entendres.[36] Du Bois says flatly of the death knell of the specific "Negro-race" use of the Fourteenth Amendment, in favor of an expanded legislative power over the whole national economy: "Both the Fourteenth and Fifteenth Amendments were thus made innocuous as far as the Negro was concerned, and the Fourteenth Amendment in particular became the chief refuge and bulwark of corporations. It was thus that finance and the power of wealth accomplished through the Supreme Court what it had not been able to do successfully through Congress" (*BRA*, 691).

In the realm of electoral politics, the notion of a white-supremacist conspiracy of Democrats against all rival parties informed discussions of the numerous strange bedfellows making secret political deals that most everyone knew about. According to Republicans and Populists, the "white-supremacy campaign" of 1898 in North Carolina, which culminated in the so-called Wilmington race riot, a flash point in race relations and the almost-instantaneous focus of contending interpretations by Griggs, Dixon, Chesnutt, and others, represented the Democratic machine's cynical manipulation of the vote by conjuring what Democratic leaders knew to be the imaginary threat of what they called, cynically or not, "Negro domination."[37] "Indeed," comments the historian Morgan Kousser on the widespread disfranchisement campaigns of the early 1890s, "the cross-fertilization and coordination between the movements to restrict the suffrage in the Southern states amounted to a public conspiracy."[38] Finally, the Spanish-American War generated intermittent rumors of an armed uprising by blacks in support of Spain against their American oppressors, precisely the threat that, as we will see, Griggs fictionalizes in *Imperium in Imperio*.[39] More broadly, the presence of black troops in the South—a visible sign of African American manhood and patriotism that raised the accompanying specter of secret organizing and black insurrection—was often juxtaposed with accounts of race riots as a factor contributing to the cycle of violence.

The widespread obsession with, and sometime reality of, conspiratorial violence points to a central paradox of late-nineteenth-century American countersubversion: why depict as invisible and secret the open and ritualized violence of racial antagonism? Whereas earlier conspiracy theories had inveighed against Catholics, Masons, the "monster-hydra" U.S. bank, abolitionists, the slave power, and the black rapist, Griggs and Dixon focus almost exclusively on a ubiquitous and paradoxical racial violence, at once overt and masked, legal and illicit, actual and imagined. Their examples range from the figure of the openly armed and uniformed black soldier, to the state-sanctioned, extralegal militarism of white terrorist groups, to secret societies (some well-known, others covert, and still others completely fictitious) dedicated simultaneously to racial brotherhood and racial terror. From Griggs's Imperium, to Dixon's Invisible Empire, to Du Bois's "A Negro Nation within the Nation," the notion of an alien collectivity *within* the national body was a common formula for the open secret of different racial groups living parallel lives in the United States. Dixon repeatedly insisted—sometimes as a rhetorical question, sometimes as an answer—that "in a Democracy you cannot build a nation inside of a nation of two antagonistic races, and therefore the future American must be either an Anglo-Saxon or a Mulatto" (*LS*, 201, 242, 383, 433). Griggs's fictional Imperium originates as a "patriotic secret society" of blacks in Texas but ultimately becomes "nothing more nor less than a compact government [modeled on that of the United States] exercising all the functions of a nation" (*II*, 194)—a nation within the nation. Du Bois's 1935 essay "A Negro Nation within the Nation" calls for the development of separate organizations—Negro churches, Negro schools, Negro businesses—to achieve, through "voluntary and increased segregation," economic independence and solidarity among American Negroes.[40] Racial conspiracy theory extends to such volatile explanatory accounts, and philosophies, as these of the phenomenon of racial separatism. The conspiratorial analysis of the meaning and consequences of racial violence for intra- and interracial relations ultimately turns back on itself, proliferating, and confusing, enemies and allies, and rendering unstable the boundaries between inside and outside.

Conspiracy theory not only embraces but also tends to associate contradictory agents, resulting in a psychic doubling: the countersubversive's need for monsters through which to articulate his fears and his desires, that is, something that will allow him, "in the name of battling the subversive, to imitate his enemy."[41] In Dixon's *Leopard's Spots*, this antagonistic, symbiotic bond takes the striking form of an almost direct projection from the white mind to the black image, as Dixon attributes to all black collectivities, including such political organizations as the Republican Party's Union League and the Negro militias, the very details of secrecy and violence that he later proudly associates with the Klan. A chapter entitled "The Negro Uprising" summons up a conspiratorial vision of the "summer of 1867," with "a group of oath-bound secret societies, The Union League, The Heroes of America, and The Red Strings dominating society, and marauding bands of negroes armed to the teeth terrorising the country, stealing, burning and murdering" (*LS*, 100). Near the novel's conclusion, in a chapter entitled "The Red Shirts," the disfranchisement campaign that culminated in the 1898 Wilmington race riot successfully mobilized "five thousand white men dressed in scarlet shirts" to defeat "six thousand negroes watching in fear" as well as the memory of the (black) Red Strings (*LS*, 446). What we have here are not only two terrorist groups that are hard to tell apart, the Red Strings and the Red Shirts, but also two conspiracies: the Klan ("the 'Ku Klux Klan Conspiracy,' which overturned the Reconstruction régime" [*C*, 1]) and its mortal enemy, Reconstruction (vilified as "a conspiracy against human progress" [*LS*, 194]). The resemblance between the two is no accident: the logic of conspiracy demonstrates in effect that it takes a conspiracy to catch a conspiracy.

A double unmasking is necessary to identify the hidden agenda of the Invisible Empire, which was, after all, openly devoted to the cause of white supremacy. The Klan exemplifies the paradox of hyperinvisibility, with its highly visible, ritualized spectacles of terror. It was impossible to miss. During its early heyday, 1866–72, Klan night riders faced down local police in open daytime parades. Further, in the reciprocal movement of the conspiratorial imagination, black political organizations, from the Republican Union League to the Garveyites, were sometimes twinned with the Klan itself. An Alabama newspaper editorial in 1868 denounced the Union League, a Republican Party political organization often mistaken for a terrorist group, as "nothing more than a nigger Ku Klux Klan."[42] The mystic syllables *Ku Klux* thus traveled widely and openly, although, as the historian David M. Chalmers notes, many Klan members insisted they were just another fraternal organization like the Young Men's Democratic Clubs.[43] The disavowal of violence was, like the hood and the mask, a veiled threat, meant to be dimly seen through, enhancing terror through ostentatious mystification.

In one of the later chapters of *Black Reconstruction in America*, Du Bois anatomizes the paradoxical hyperinvisibility of white supremacy, a "systematized effort to subordinate the Negro," which works "by secret, hidden and underground ways, the method of the Ku Klux Klan": "the methods of night and the mask, the psychology of vague and unknown ill, the innuendo that cannot be answered for it is not openly published." There is a history to such methods. "Secret dictatorship," Du Bois concludes, "has long been a method of fastening dictatorship on the South," the "dictatorship of property over labor," with a racial mask: "It was seen in Louisiana early in the nineteenth century. . . . Senator Douglass called the whole secession movement 'the result of an enormous conspiracy.' Charles Sumner said: Not in all history . . . is there any record of conspiracy so vast, so wicked, ranging over such spaces, both in time and history" (*BRA*, 678–79). For Du Bois, conspiracy and lawlessness formed the ongoing, protean legacy of the Civil War, transmuted into a "labor war," both more secret and better organized than the earlier race war of the Klan, pitting ex-slaves against poor whites fighting for the same jobs, and, finally, joining white laborers, landowners, and capitalists together "through secret organizations and the rise of a new doctrine of race hatred" (*BRA*, 670). Organized aggression against black people, in a movement "Back toward Slavery," as Du Bois entitles his chapter, was masked by the techniques of midnight murder that substituted race war for a long-standing labor war. Moreover, Du Bois rejects the common view that white violence simply mirrored black terrorism. "There is no historic foundation for this," he says. "The Union League movement . . . employed among Negroes some ceremonies and secrecy, but it never contemplated murder and force. By no stretch of the imagination could it be called an organization similar to or provocative of the Ku Klux Klan" (*BRA*, 680). Overthrowing Reconstruction and reducing black labor to conditions of permanent exploitation, a program in open defiance of the letter of the law, required "organized disorder and conspiracy": "A lawlessness which, in 1865–68, was still spasmodic and episodic, now became organized and its real underlying industrial causes obscured by political excuses and race hatred. . . . Armed guerilla warfare killed thousands of Negroes; political riots were staged" (*BRA*, 688, 674). The staging is the key to Du Bois's demystification, just as the various phases of conspiracy are the key to his historicizing.

For Du Bois, Griggs, and others, the paradoxical visibility of the Invisible Empire unmasks white terror, demystifying it as a ritual of political and social control. Both lynching and race riots are exposed as open conspiracies, organized spectacles rather than the spontaneous products of random mob violence. In his representation of a double lynching of an innocent wife and husband in *The Hindered Hand*, Griggs provides a grim, detailed script of such rituals, in which white violence against black men and women is highly organized yet multiplied to near-phantasmic proportions. Not only are all the usual procedures of lynching followed openly. (Special trains bring spectators, including the women and children routinely in attendance at such events: "There's the train now, mother. Do let me go," pleads one little boy. "I ain't never seen a darky burned" [*HH*, 130]. And the most visible, socially symbolic spot in town is chosen: the "commander today" orders the "administration of justice to take place near the Negro church" [*HH*, 133].) But Griggs also displays in gory, almost surreal detail the gruesome, three-hour ritual torture of both male and female victims that Dixon's Klan ostentatiously masks in the mystic language of violated white womanhood and virile Anglo-Saxon manhood. Afterward, the members of the mob rush for the usual souvenirs to take home, with the little boy finding a piece of "charred flesh in the ashes" (*HH*, 134). The rest depart with fingers and eyeballs, reminding us of Du Bois's memory of his horror at the sight of Sam Hose's knuckles on exhibition in an Atlanta grocery-store window.[44] A galvanizing barbarism for Du Bois, who notes that the objectivity of the social scientist was no longer possible in such a climate, the ritualistic relics of the mutilated body point for Griggs to the everyday life of lynching, both its utter horror and its utter conventionality.[45] The display of such routine, grisly evidence exposes the barely hidden calculation and preplanning essential to producing the terrors of lynching.

The anatomy of hyperinvisible racial terror revealed different kinds of violence, both imagined and actual, orderly and random: the military discipline of the soldier and the clandestine organization in contrast to the chaos of the mob or race riot and the criminality of the rapist. It was an analysis that itself served different needs of different constituencies at different moments. On the one hand, Dixon's history of the Klan stresses, as we will see, "the danger of playing with fire" when secret societies get out of control, even as the distinction between disorderly and controlled violence justifies his hero's inability to control the lynch mob and vilifies those who would hold him responsible for leadership in the Wilmington riot (*LS*, 169). On the other hand, demystifying the fiction of lynching as a spontaneous outbreak of uncontrollable violence served Griggs and other antilynching activists, not only as an indictment of white barbarism, but also as a means of testing varieties of black resistance to the rising tide of white supremacy.

Working initially within the binary construction of black political responses divided between the poles of Washington and Du Bois—a structure of polarities in which melodrama specializes—Griggs invariably sets up pairs of opposed leaders whose clear ideological divisions break down, revealing an array of philosophical positions and political programs as varied as they are fractured.[46] The "two most conspicuous representatives" of the race vying for the leadership of the Imperium, the fiery mulatto Bernard Belgrave and the conservative black Belton Piedmont, start out as friendly school rivals ("oratorical gladiators"), the former going on to study "politics, art, religion, sociology, and the whole realm of human knowledge" at Harvard, the latter attending Nashville's "Stowe University," "scarcely more than a normal school" (*II*, 188, 32, 85, 48). Later, they take opposed views on the issue of what form the clandestine Imperium should take in the future, Belton favoring emigration to the state of Texas and there "working out our destiny as a separate and distinct race in the U.S.A.," Bernard insisting on secret infiltration of the U.S. navy and alliances with "foreign enemies" of the United States in order to establish a black empire in the state of Texas (*II*, 245, 251–52). But, as we will see, despite their differences, both end up in the same place, undone on the romance front by their obsession with racial purity in sexual matters, and betrayed by the book's frame narrator, a self-described traitor to the Imperium.

Even more starkly, in *The Hindered Hand*, the preacher Ensal and the militant Earl, "representing two types in the Negro race," espouse "opposite methods," Ensal advocating race pride and political agitation for the vote and citizenship rights, Earl calling for collective, violent resistance (*HH*, 49–50). (In a secret suicide pact, Earl's handpicked band of five hundred pledge to assault government buildings, take over the state capitol, and present a set of demands "as a race" to the American people [*HH*, 144].)

Between their "two pathways," which Griggs labels *conservative* and *radical*, lies yet a third alternative in this novel, that of Gus Martin, a Negro with "Indian hot blood" who mounts a one-man terrorist attack against a town "in a frenzy" to lynch him (*HH*, 37, 185–86). This trio is striking, not for posing a third term between two clear opposites, but, as with the Imperium's competing leaders, for interweaving among them, in nonaligned, disruptive ways, positions traditionally associated either with Washington or with Du Bois. Ensal, the so-called conservative, who touts black adaptation to slavery as evidence of evolutionary progress, argues for "political uplift" and "equality of citizenship" in the United States but emigrates to Africa, where American blacks may provide "an easily acclimated civilizing force" to work on behalf of the "world-wide awakening of the race" (*HH*, 150, 159, 197, 276). Equally ideologically murky are the views of Earl, the putative radical, ranging from his predictable insistence that blood must be shed in race war ("there had to be a John Brown and a Harper's Ferry" undergirding Mrs. Stowe), to his review of "the whole gamut of panaceas that had been proposed for a solution to the long standing race problem of America," to his final stand in favor of interracial political alliances and the cause of national unity (*HH*, 161, 259). On the issue of racial violence, then, as on virtually every other volatile question, Griggs's novels repeatedly rehearse the extremes of the debates without endorsing any of them. The Griggs narrator doubles himself, first projecting his voice into opposed protagonists, then fracturing them into multiple mouthpieces, enacting the inability either of their author or his culture to find a middle ground or even to formulate the "problem" in a less contradictory way.

For Dixon, however, the multiple politics of racial violence offers a rationale, albeit a volatile one, for the Klan when, in *The Leopard's Spots*, he stresses the distinction between chaotic mobs of poor whites, mobilized by unscrupulous scalawags against both blacks and the Bourbon elite, and the orderly, hierarchical violence of the Klan: "This Invisible Empire of White Robed Anglo-Saxon Knights was simply the old answer of organised manhood . . . , [whose] purpose was to bring order out of chaos," both black and white created (*LS*, 150). Dixon's vision of controlled, ritualized Klan violence counters the competing history that he narrates of later, renegade white-supremacy groups operating without the Klan's mystique. The novel exhibits unmistakable nostalgia for the "white terror" of the early Klan, which "sprang up like magic in a night" and, mysteriously, seemingly effortlessly, restored order (*LS*, 150–51). In contrast, the "fool later day Ku Klux Klan marauders," "wild youngsters and revengeful men," get so out of control that they provide the "scapegoat" for the U.S. army regulars to impose military order; even Reverend Durham, the novel's most unregenerate racist spokesman, "saw the glint of their bayonets with a sense of relief" (*LS*, 169–71). Still later, the "Red Shirt movement," best known of the so-called White Government Leagues to spring up during the white-supremacy campaign of 1898, produced "a race fire . . . broken into resistless fury, . . . a spontaneous combustion of inflammable racial power. . . . But there was no head to it. It had no organisation except a local one, and it spread by a spark flying from one county to another" (*LS*, 415). The point here is that even the Democratic political leaders of the notorious disfranchisement campaign of 1898, represented by Dixon's hero Charlie Gaston (Governor Charles Aycock), cannot be held accountable for the race war that they unleash but do not control.

Dixon covers this critical election, which commentators then and now have seen as the culmination of the post-Reconstruction struggle against the black franchise, near the end of *The Leopard's Spots*, in a chapter titled "Another Declaration of Independence," set in a thinly veiled version of Wilmington, North Carolina, the location of the notorious 1898 race riot. Dixon's version has its violence all ways, including, not only the "resistless" white race fire, but also a rampaging mob of black soldiers from the Third North Carolina Regiment, waiting to be mustered out after the Spanish-American War, who are contrasted to an informal guard of white elites working "under strict military discipline" that succeeds in driving away the "rioting" blacks and putting the town "under informal martial law" (*LS*, 412–13). The result of the "Revolution at Independence" is the restoration of the revolutionary legacy of both the "little city" and its leader, Gaston, "whose ancestors had been leaders in the great Revolution" (*LS*, 409). The reversals of the actual power dynamics here conclude with "a conspiracy" of local Republican scalawags and the "Negro-Farmer" alliance against Gaston, who is arrested and imprisoned for violating state election laws (his historical counterpart, however, is actually voted into office) (*LS*, 410–11). Thus do white power brokers, like Dixon, borrow black victimization to make whites into victorious victims and enhance their own standing in the cultural struggle for the moral high ground waged in the context of lynching.[47]

Dixon's account of the Wilmington race riot brings the Spanish-American war together with the themes of revolutionary violence and conspiracy. These reference points appear scattered in many interpretations of this recognized flash point in race relations of the decade, the first in a series of extralegal racial outbreaks that consolidated white power even as segre-

gation prevailed as the law of the land. Historians usually tell the tale exclusively from the standpoint of the perpetrators, but the race melodramatists,
including Dixon, complicate this narrative by introducing the conspiracy
angle, analyzing the riot and its rhetoric as modes of conspiracy and white
supremacy as a cover (Griggs, Chesnutt, Du Bois) or a unifying slogan
(Dixon) for many other, sometimes competing interests and aims. The
Spanish-American War provided, as we will see, a focal point at which these
contending forces both collided and were reconciled.

The sequence of events in Wilmington is well-known, yet the meanings
and motivations of those events are often contested. After the town's whites
(a minority), led by a group of leading local Democrats calling themselves
the "Secret Nine," succeeded in orchestrating the election of their candidates
over those favored by the black majority, the disfranchisement campaign of
the armed Red Shirts, which Dixon describes as "a spontaneous combustion
of inflammable racial power," was completed, a riot being staged in which
mobs of armed whites attacked and killed blacks and destroyed black businesses and property (*LS*, 415). The supposed original target of white rage
was the newspaper publisher Alexander Manly, who was one of the first
blacks run out of town and whose press was one of the many establishments
burned. Manly's offense? In response to a virulent speech in support of
lynching delivered the previous year by the feminist reformer Rebecca Lattimore Felton (later the first female U.S. senator), he had printed a controversial editorial in his *Wilmington Daily Record*—the only African American daily in the state—in which, in the course of attacking lynching, he
referred openly to the underground tradition of long-standing, consensual
interracial relations that many whites preferred to forget.[48]

Only three years later, in *The Marrow of Tradition*, Charles Chesnutt
was already pointedly challenging the chronology, the language, and the
very status of the Wilmington riot. Set in the fictional town of Wellington,
the novel interweaves an interracial family romance plot with a politics plot
that includes numerous thinly veiled versions of actual people and places.[49]
Chesnutt's interpretation, like Dixon's, accepts as the cause of the riot
Manly's editorial. Chesnutt also connects deepening American involvement in imperialism with the race riots that erupted between 1898 and the
summer of 1900; he based *The Marrow of Tradition*, he says in a newspaper
article of 1901, on "two recent outbreaks," one in New Orleans in 1900, the
other the 1898 Wilmington riot.[50] Critical to Chesnutt's conspiracy-theory
reading is his rearrangement of the timing of the riot from after to *before*
the white Democratic campaign in North Carolina. The effect, as Eric

Sundquist explains, is to expose the "logic of disfranchisement" as a conspiratorial secret that blurred violence and legal process in U.S. racial justice.[51] Since the election resulted in a victory for the white-supremacy campaign, Chesnutt's rearranged riot pointedly exposes what Rayford Logan calls the "illogic" of the argument of Negro domination, thus intimating that both the extralegal riot and the putatively legal tactics of the racial campaign belong to a much wider, more pervasive, and less obvious power structure.[52]

Extending the analysis to the terms by which the Wilmington disturbance was known, Chesnutt's novel rejects *riot*, asserting that this was a *"coup d'état,"* a "revolution," and a "rebellion," engineered by a group of "conspirators" calling themselves, "jocularly," the "Big Three" (*MT*, 243, 249, 80, 91). Led by Major Carteret, the classic Southern gentleman and the publisher of the town's main newspaper, and faced with a flagging disfranchisement campaign and the delayed "success of the impending 'revolution,' for which [they] had labored so long," "the little coterie of Wellington conspirators" finally decides to republish "the obnoxious article" in the "negro newspaper," which they had long before recognized as "good campaign matter" but "reserved until it [would] be most effective": "A peg was needed upon which to hang a *coup d'état,* and this editorial offered the requisite opportunity" (*MT*, 228, 241, 88, 243). Arguing with his coconspirators about the possibility of "unnecessary bloodshed"—he fears a riot, not a revolution—General Belmont, the pragmatic aristocrat among the Big Three, appeals to his experience in Nicaragua, "down in the American tropics," where he witnessed "Paterno's revolution" easily drive out "Igorroto's government." "In Central and South America," the general concludes, even with "the fiery mixture that flourishes in the tropics," "none are hurt except those who get in the way," implicitly linking racial revolution at home with the frontiers of empire abroad, or at least suggesting that the latter serve as a model for the former (*MT*, 250).[53] The group's revolutionary goal, Chesnutt shows, proliferating into unintended zones Dixonian metaphors of fire and revolution, was nothing less than "to fire the inflammable Southern heart and rouse it against any further self-assertion of the negroes in politics or elsewhere": "It only remained for them to so direct this aroused public feeling that it might completely accomplish the desired end,—to change the political complexion of the . . . government. . . . A revolution, and not a riot was contemplated" (*MT*, 243, 249).

The conspirators' heightened racial rhetoric avoids the "brutal characterization of their motives" favored by Captain McBane, the cigar-

smoking, poor-white member of the Big Three, which "robbed the enterprise of its poetry, and put a solemn act of revolution upon the plane of a
mere vulgar theft of power." To maintain revolutionary order, "a well-
defined plan" is devised, as the "conspirators . . . fixed the hour of the proposed revolution, the course to be pursued, the results to be obtained"
(*MT*, 253). And, finally, the results: "The proceedings of the day—planned
originally as a 'demonstration,' dignified subsequently as a 'revolution,' under any name the culmination of the conspiracy formed by Carteret and his
colleagues—had by seven o'clock in the afternoon developed into a mur-
derous riot" (*MT*, 299). By this point, the term *revolution* has been thoroughly eviscerated, not only emptied of the foundational authority that
Dixon wants to claim with the mantle of the founding fathers, but also extended to uncharted territory, redeployed in the more volatile, global context of empire.

The mobilization of American revolutionary rhetorics happens at crisis points in the novels, just as U.S. imperialism, most often in the form of
the Spanish-American War, comes up only at the textual margins, in ex-
tremis as it were. The war presented a kind of primal scene, both symptom
and solution, tapping hopes and fears of both national unity and division,
joining and decoupling the domestic and the foreign. In this postbellum era
of the Blue and the Gray united on battlefields relocated from the United
States to island colonies, where the site of fratricidal conflict was refigured
as one of "Anglo-Saxon rapprochement" (Griggs), a "sudden union of the
English speaking people . . . [that] . . . confirmed the Anglo-Saxon in his
title to the primacy of racial sway" (Dixon [*LS*, 408]), the black boys in
blue, or "smoked Yankees," as the Spaniards called them, posed a distinct
threat to that unity—even as dispatches from Cuba stressed the interracial,
intersectional makeup of the U.S. forces. There was no neat correspon-
dence between the racial attitudes either of the majority that supported or
the minority that opposed what John Hays called a "splendid little war."[54]
Anti-imperialists counted among themselves strange bedfellows, including
the Anti-Imperialist League, originating in Boston with roots in abolition-
ism,[55] and a vocal Southern Democratic minority, represented by such
"Racial Radicals" (Joel Williamson's term) as Senator Benjamin R. Tillman
of South Carolina, the author of the patriotic jingle quoted earlier about
Americans freeing Cuba who nevertheless opposed the annexation of the
Philippines on the racist grounds that the United States did not need "another race problem" and should oppose "incorporating any more colored
men into the body politic."[56] Noting the presence of such virulent racism in

anti-imperialist thinking, some historians have argued that the relation between Negrophobia at home and colonialism abroad was not all that close. Racism may actually have been a deterrent to imperialism.[57]

Similarly, the complex response of black Americans to the war with Spain and the Philippine crisis ranged over a great many positions: Some identified with Cuba as a black republic and racial utopia. Others proposed a variety of emigration schemes (all ultimately unsuccessful) involving both Cuba and the Philippines. Still others argued that black military participation would display not only patriotism and manhood but also the capacity for responsible citizenship and might, therefore, ameliorate the deteriorating racial situation at home. Some were disappointed over the allotted role and treatment of those blacks already in the military, whether serving at home or abroad. And some took the antiexpansionist positions that colonial acquisitions would divert attention from and perhaps worsen the racial crisis at home and, further, that the color affinities between black Americans and Filipinos (both identified as "niggers" in the popular press) dictated against support of or belief in the U.S. policy of benevolent assimilation and in favor of identification with the worldwide struggle of the darker races against colonialism. Few black Americans consistently embraced the extremes on either side. Instead, according to the historian Willard Gatewood, most took "a torturous course characterized by ambiguities, contradictions, and dramatic reversals ... stemming from [the black man's] anomalous position in American society."[58] The same could be said of the anomalous position of the Spanish-American War as a whole. Both symptom and cause of dissent on multiple fronts, the war was interpreted—"torturously" and with immense cultural effort, both then and now—as a powerful engine of sectional reunion and national reconciliation.

The conspiratorial imagination helps bring the war's contradictory, often obscured roles to the surface. Both Griggs and Dixon, whose nationalisms claim to reinvigorate American Independence, demonstrate how the era of national reunification and imperial expansion witnessed a struggle, waged at home and abroad, for control over the symbology of the Revolution.[59] The Philippine and Cuban ventures, for example, were both represented through the same complex of racialist and revolutionary rhetorics, which apparently worked equally well whether applied positively (Aguinaldo as a Filipino George Washington in the preannexation period) or negatively (Aguinaldo and his insurrectionist guerrillas as Filipino "niggers"). And this despite the distinction between the Philippine annexation, which aroused widespread public dissent, and the rescue of *Cuba libre*, pop-

ularly embraced as an exporting of the American Revolution. As we have
seen in the context of the echo Reconstruction, revolutionary rhetoric traveled readily either to condemn or to endorse violence and either to return to
or to revise the national ideals of the founding fathers. Revolutionary rhetoric encompasses, not only the star-crossed lovers of *The Leopard's Spots*,
"both children of the Revolution," and the events in Wilmington (the ul-
timatum issued by white leaders to the city's blacks was "a second Declaration of Independence") (*LS*, 219, 411), but also Griggs's Imperium,
founded to secure for the Negroes "all the rights and privileges of men according to the teachings of Thomas Jefferson," and structured as a parallel
nation within the nation, whose army, congress, constitution, and judiciary
reinvigorate rather than slavishly imitate their U.S. models (*II*, 191, 195).
Such volatile and potentially contradictory meanings, not overtly racialized, mark the revolutionary mantle as yet another of the protean and excessive terminologies so characteristic of American race melodramas.

At the same time, the conspiratorial imagination detects a series of disturbing links between revolutionary violence at home and revolutionary
violence abroad, as imperialism brought both race riots and the black military to the fore. Although it was common to perceive general parallels between racial injustice in the United States and imperial exploitation in the
Philippines, the potent race-sex complex that dominated public accounts of
the upsurge in racial violence following the end of the war in Cuba half obscured other, more proximate causes. In what might be considered the Negro Question of the Spanish-American War, the figure of the black soldier
became a flash point for both blacks and whites. In his *Autobiography*, Du
Bois comments on "the deep resentment mixed with the pale ghost of fear
which Negro soldiers call up in the breast of the white South": "It is not so
much that they fear the Negro will strike if he gets a chance, but rather that
they assume with curious unanimity that he has reason to strike" (*A*, 268).
The uniformed black man is the white conspiratorial imaginary's trigger,
signaling the threat of secret organizing among blacks; the visible marks of
manhood and patriotism translate to invisible insurrection. Dixon, remember, opens his chapter on Wilmington, "Another Declaration of Independence," with a long description of the "riot and disorder" of the Negro regiment camped at Independence and waiting to be mustered out: "Its
presence had inflamed the passions of both races to the danger point of riot
again and again" (*LS*, 409). Attributing to the black soldier all the potentially uncontrollable violence that we know he ambivalently associates with
the white mob, Dixon exposes one of white supremacy's guises and reminds

us of the varied uses of secrecy in periods of racial crisis. Analyzing white fear of black conspiracy, Griggs has Ensal, the "conservative" of *The Hindered Hand*, rebuke the "radical" Earl for his secret plan to lead an armed band and take over the state capitol, which will "provoke the passions of that [white] race" and "arouse the dormant but ever-present fear of secret plottings for a general uprising" (*HH*, 146). Chesnutt's insight, on the other hand, is to expose Wilmington's white supremacists themselves as the conspiratorial plotters and, thus, return the fear of secrecy to its sources in the white imagination.

Associated with the mere image of the armed black in uniform, the fear of black violence and insurrection led, first, to the assignment of black regulars, many of them Civil War veterans, to isolated forts west of the Mississippi (where the cavalrymen in particular, the famous "Buffalo soldiers," distinguished themselves in the Indian wars) and, later, to hostility and disturbances in the South when these troops were sent to the military posts designated as embarkation points for Cuba. Incidents such as the highly publicized Tampa riot in June 1898—in which black soldiers, angered by an accumulation of racist outrages, discharged their weapons in a violent demonstration and were brutally restrained by a white Georgia regiment— fed rumors during the war of an armed uprising of black citizens on behalf of Spain. Angered at President McKinley's silence in the wake of what blacks called the Wilmington massacre and his subsequent failure to take a strong stand against lynching, blacks often framed their responses in the language of war, empire, and armed uprising. Vocal black opponents to "McKinley imperialism" spoke of creating a colored auxiliary to the New England Anti-Imperialist League as the beginning of "an uprising of the colored race" to bring about "the downfall of McKinley, imperialism, and the Republican Party."[60] Although this generally meant simply a revolt at the ballot box, the historian Willard Gatewood notes that at least one noted black anti-imperialist claimed that, during the Spanish-American War, some black citizens had wanted to fight U.S. racism by aiding the Spaniards. "Regardless of its factual validity," Gatewood concludes, the notion of a black insurrection during the Spanish-American War inspired Griggs's *Imperium in Imperio*.[61] And no wonder. In the infamous speech that prompted Manly's fateful reply, Rebecca Lattimore Felton argued that the posting of black troops in the South (like the appointment of blacks to federal offices) by "the promoters of Negro equality" was responsible for the impending "revolutionary uprising" that would resolve the Negro Problem once and for all.[62] Revolution becomes an effect of the hall of mirrors of conspiracy theory, both imagined and acted out, rhetorically claimed by opposing sides, alternatively embracing nation and empire, as both problem and solution, symptom and cure.

No one is better suited to anatomizing that world than Sutton Griggs, who unfolds an elaborate conspiratorial analysis of imperialism and its avatars, using debates over the Spanish-American War as an index to other divisions and positions within and between black and white communities. The Imperium is strikingly divided on the question of a black revolution—as it is on the question of the Spanish-American War itself—between those wanting to support the United States in freeing Cuba and those wanting to ally with the foreign enemies of the United States, secede from the union, and found a "Negro empire" in Texas (*II*, 252). The patriotic course is advocated by the "conservative" Belton within a resolution—combining Washington's go-slow doctrines with Du Bois's early belief that the Negro Problem needed only education to be solved—that the Anglo-Saxon must be taught that he has a "New Negro" on his hands (*II*, 245). (If after four years this fails, then black Americans will peacefully emigrate to Texas and work out "our destiny as a separate and distinct race" in the United States [*II*, 245].) The subversive course is associated with the "ultra-radical" Bernard, so militant that he orders the execution of his boyhood friend Belton and, thereby, unleashes "internecine war" on the Imperium (*II*, 262).

Moreover, the novel creates multiple mirror images, twinning the internal, secret black Imperium, itself modeled on the U.S. Constitution, with the external American empire emerging with the colonization of Cuba and the Philippines. Griggs describes how the destruction of the USS *Maine* in Havana Harbor galvanized both the nation and the Imperium, in tandem, but not together. The congress of the Imperium meets in special session in the capitol at Waco on the same day on which the U.S. Congress declares war with Spain, but the requisite American flags are hung alongside black mourning cloth, to commemorate the lynching of a black postmaster appointed by KcKinley: "This incident naturally aroused as much indignation among the members of the Imperium as did the destruction of the warship in the bosoms of the Anglo-Saxons of the United States" (*II*, 203). So the Spanish-American War both precipitates interracial crisis and accentuates divisions within black communities.

The war provides a key to the varieties of black leadership in *The Hindered Hand*. The novel's leading threesome are introduced as having served together in the Spanish-American War, the moderate Ensal, who was a minister, as chaplain and Gus and Earl, who espouse different forms of resistance, as soldiers: "These three were present at the battle of San Juan Hill, and Gus, who was himself notoriously brave, scarcely knew which to admire the more, Ensal's searching words that inspired the men for that world-famous dash or Ensal's enthusiastic, infectious daring on the actual scene of conflict" (*HH*, 36–37). Accounting for Ensal's determination that America's race problem be solved by "the output of brains, rather than of veins," against Earl's insistence on bloodshed, the novel alludes to Earl's failure to secure a commission after the war (because "of the disinclination of the South to have Negro officers in the army") (*HH*, 161, 37). The war galvanizes as well as frustrates the militant Earl, who takes his inspiration for a terrorist attack on the government from the Cubans: "Look at Cuba. A handful of men stayed in the field and kept up a show of resistance until our great nation intervened" (*HH*, 145). Near the novel's end, disillusioned with "his own martial scheme" ("of his earlier, unmarried days"), the "irrepressible Earl" tries to convince a radical Southern governor to take a broad, new stand on the race question and make the Negro Question, heretofore a Southern question, "a national one" (*HH*, 259, 266). Because "you Southerners sprang to arms so gallantly in that skirmish with Spain, . . . a more opportune time for you Southern people to take a stand would be hard to conceive" (*HH*, 267). Yet, at this moment, Earl's other, Ensal, advocate of protest and patriotism, chooses to depart for Liberia to work for "the uplift of Africa, the redemption of the race" (*HH*, 279). It is as a locus of such contradiction and tension, a mosaic of conflicting inter- and intraracial positions, that the Spanish-American War can be a formative experience for Griggs's black leaders.

The larger questions of international expansion and domestic party politics structure the overall narrative—including the love plot—of *Unfettered*, Griggs's most political novel. Here, the central characters are, not opposed male leaders, but divided lovers, Morlene and Dorlan, a couple "fettered" by conflicting positions on the race question in America. Hers: "Ardent Expansionist" and "unyielding Republican," Morlene argues that "our expansion makes for universal peace," that, given our "ideal form of government," "bloody revolutions become unnecessary wherever our flag floats" (*U*, 121, 126, 87). His: Political speechwriter and the heir, it turns out, to an ancient African throne, Dorlan insists, "In view of the silence of the Republican party upon the question of the ultimate status of the Filipinos, it has been decided to organize a new party that . . . will insist that 'Old Glory' shall continue to float over human beings that can . . . shout 'We are all equals'" (*U*, 96). While, in a long letter published in the black Democratic press, Griggs himself appealed for support for William Jennings Bryan in the 1900 election, like Dorlan indicting Republican imperialism and the "chain of gratitude"⁶³ that tied black votes to the Republican Party, he also speaks through Morlene's metaphors of "chains fettering the mind" of the Negro (*U*, 174). This is the language of the epigraph to *Unfettered* taken from *Race Adjustment* (1908) by Kelley Miller, the pioneering sociologist and a dean at Howard University. One of Griggs's heroines–as–"race orators,"⁶⁴ Morlene represents both obstacle to the course of true love with Dorlan and hope of political change. The novel's romantic resolution brings together both roles: although "it is known that the Negro women of the South are, perhaps, the most ardent and unyielding Republicans in the land," Morlene nevertheless abandons her expansionism in favor of Dorlan's hand and his "plan" for solving the race problem (*U*, 126, 228). "Dorlan's Plan" (*U*, 228)—advocating, not African emigration, but race organization and "Social Cooperation" at home in the United States, theories drawn from the social Darwinists Herbert Spencer and Benjamin Kidd (*U*, 235)—is included in the form of a fifty-page addendum to the novel. The fetters preventing romance for the perfect couple may have been broken, but "Dorlan's Plan" reminds us that the chains still binding so many arenas of black life in America have not been. The couple's marriage thus highlights rather than resolves the nexus of racial issues, domestic and foreign, political and economic, raised by and represented through the narrative's romantic involvement in the Spanish-American War.

For Dixon, too, the war is both symptom of and solution to disabling divisions. Fissures in the face of white unity—the many differences, of politics, class, region, and generation, that Dixon deplores—are temporarily papered over by war fever, just as interracial rape and lynching provide another, even more volatile basis for white solidarity. The sprawling plot of *The Leopard's Spots* could be condensed into three climactic moments, each expressed through the same, excessive language of white hyperunity. What unites the race is one question, seemingly rhetorical, sometimes italicized (when attributed, as a quotation, to the racist Reverend Durham), obsessively repeated (sometimes as an assertion) at each moment of crisis in the novel: "*Shall the future American be an Anglo-Saxon or a Mulatto?*" (*LS*, 159, 198, 201, 242, 332–33, 382–83, 438–39).⁶⁵

The first crisis comes in the final days of Reconstruction, when the Klan defies the local military government and gathers before a local election in Independence. At this rally of five thousand "excited" people, "every discordant element of the old South's furious political passions was now melted into harmonious unity. Whig and Democrat . . . sat side by side. . . . Secessionist and Unionist now clasped hands. It was a White Man's Party, and against it stood in solid array the Black Man's Party. . . . The state burst into a flame of excitement that fused in its white heat the whole Anglo-Saxon race" (*LS*, 159). But the very same discordant elements, plus some new ones, resurface in the next historical phase of the New South, the "eighteen years of peace that followed the terrors" of Reconstruction, during which a "new terror" emerges in the form of the "roving, criminal negro," along with new political, social, and economic antagonisms and alliances among poor-white farmers, Bourbon planters, Populists, Republicans, and Democrats (*LS*, 200). The New Negro, the black beast of the post-Reconstruction nadir, taps the race-sex complex around which otherwise divided whites can rally. When the daughter of the old, one-legged ex-Confederate soldier Tom Camp is raped and killed, "in a moment the white race had fused into a homogenous mass. . . . The rich and the poor, the learned and the ignorant, the banker and the blacksmith, the great and the small, they were all one now" (*LS*, 368). All other differences overcome in the face of the danger of the New Negro, the one point on which they can all agree, these usually law-abiding citizens "melt" and "fuse" into a lynch mob, the "thousand-legged, thousand-eyed beast" that Gaston is powerless to stop from burning to death the alleged rapist, Dick, the slave companion of his youth (*LS*, 381). Since, however, white unity thus relies on volatile "racial fury," it is unstable and fragile, in need of continual shoring up. Thus the refrain "*Shall the future American be an Anglo-Saxon or a Mulatto?*" must be repeated over and over again throughout the novel.

Finally, near the end, the Spanish-American War provides the climactic display of both the most spectacular division and the most spectacular unity on both national and global grounds. Before the "crisis" of the war, "we were afraid that our nation still lacked unity. . . . We feared that religion might threaten the future with its bitter feud between the Roman Catholic and Protestant. . . . We feared the gulf between the rich and the poor had become impassable. . . . Sectionalism and disunity had been the most terrible realities in our national history" (*LS*, 405–6). But, during the mere hundred days of the war, "America united at last and invincible, waked to the consciousness of her resistless power. And, most marvelous of all, this hundred days of war had re-united the Anglo-Saxon race. This sudden union of the English speaking people in friendly alliance . . . confirmed the Anglo-Saxon in his title to the primacy of racial sway" (*LS*, 408). The costs of the continual effort to reimagine "the Anglo-Saxon race . . . united into one homogeneous mass" are exposed by the repetitions, both anxious and excessive, of the refrain, "*Shall the future American be an Anglo-Saxon or a Mulatto?*" (e.g., *LS,* 409). Even after the war had supposedly guaranteed "the newborn unity of national life," in the triumphant final speech of his political career, Gaston is still asking the same question, even closer to home: "Shall the future North Carolinian be an Anglo-Saxon or a Mulatto?" (*LS,* 438). While conjuring so much overwhelming evidence to the contrary, Dixon continually reenacts a white unity that proclaims itself *as* unseen, whether in the form of the Invisible Empire of the Klan, America's empire overseas, or a united body politic at home.

White fantasies of the invisible empire of whiteness tap the conspiratorial paradox of open-secret organizations (the Klan, Wilmington's Secret Nine) that trade on an imagined, unified community to counter the overt presence of division and hostility. That unity depends, not only on a common enemy, the Negro Problem, at home, but also on an ally abroad, what the historian Glenda Gilmore calls both "the racialization of manhood"—"so international, so scientific, so modern," and "the language of empire," borrowed from Kipling and others, which authorized white supremacy in the South.[66] Dixon links North Carolina's unresolved Negro Problem with that of the nation after the Spanish-American War, when empire presented democracy with the presence of apparently unassimilable new populations. The Invisible Empire covers all evidence of difference and counters the realities of social, economic, and political divisions, exacerbated by the overseas empire and the accompanying threat of new immigrant and black power, political and economic. As a solution, however, white supremacy creates new problems: the Klan spawns traitors within; the lynch mob pursuing the black beast is itself a "thousand-legged, thousand-eyed beast"; the war brings black soldiers home, a "source of riot and disorder" (*LS,* 381, 409). Just so, imperialism—one of what Gilmore calls white power's many "subtle and not so subtle disguises"—poses new, global variants of the Negro Problem and its domestic solutions.[67]

In the narrative sphere of the race melodrama, sexuality, intra- and interracial, offers a parallel resolution to the nation's race problem, a resolution that, like empire, turns out to be part of a global race problem. Fear of miscegenation brings together the romance and the political plots in both Dixon's and Griggs's representations of the Spanish-American War. Dixon's repeated reenactments of the "nation inside a nation" formula equate blacks with the tyrannical Spanish Empire that whites must overthrow; rescue from Negro domination is simultaneously to avoid becoming mulatto. The either/or logic of *"Anglo-Saxon or Mulatto"* is often explicitly sexualized through adding the term *intermarriage* to the formula: "With the Anglo-Saxon race guarding the door of marriage with fire and sword, the effort was being made to build a nation inside a nation of two antagonistic races" (*LS*, 201). Griggs's Imperium is internally rent in both the political and the romantic realms. The division between those wanting to support the United States in freeing Cuba and those wanting to secede from the Union and support foreign enemies destroys the Imperium, just as the marriage plot is undermined by the threat of miscegenation. The radical secessionist—the mulatto son of a white senator—is further radicalized and ultimately destroyed by his fiancée's suicide; she would rather die than pollute the race by marrying a mulatto. The quasi-accommodationist lives out the ambiguities of his political position by temporarily leaving his wife when she seems to have given birth to a white baby. The impossible search for racial purity in the antimiscegenation love plot is, thus, twinned with the impossibility of political homogeneity in the conspiracy plot. But, by the same token, the Spanish-American War could galvanize black patriotism and secure a black domestic sphere, as in *Unfettered*, where the "Ardent Expansionist" finally joins forces, romantically and politically, with the Pan-Africanist.

Finally, the race-purity question itself brings internationalism into both Griggs's romance and his politics plots. What seems a local conflict over race mixture disturbing the domestic tranquillity of the nation also alludes to the issue of racial purity in the project of nation building in Africa addressed by such Pan-Africanists as Edward Wilmot Blyden. Born in the Danish West Indies, and later based in Liberia, Blyden joined the leading African American activist and intellectual Alexander Crummell in a long struggle against so-called mulatto domination in nineteenth-century Liberian politics. Blyden, who argued that the fatally weak, hybrid mulatto did not possess the "race instincts" of the Negro necessary for the rigors of colonization, made several tours of the United States during the period of Griggs's career and spoke to black audiences throughout the Deep South.[68] Griggs's tragic love stories of race mixture, actual and imagined, locate his nationalist politics in a larger setting of global and diasporic conflict.

Sexuality in Griggs and Dixon also raises issues of confused boundaries, bodily and familial, inside and outside, because sexual violations are represented as coming both from within and from without, from the racial family. Just as *conspiracy* applies to all sides, black and white enemies and loyalists, confusing rather than keeping them apart, so it infects the body itself. The conventional nineteenth-century "black-blood scenario" of exposing the hidden one drop has been crossed with a conspiracy narrative of the social body as the source of both threat and revenge. White fantasies of black bodies take the form of imagining secret black collectivities poised for aggressive action. The specter of an invisible empire has supplanted that of invisible blood.[69] The black conspiratorial imagination constructs a corporealized nation within the nation, fantasizing the race's own bodily contamination from within, its secret poisoning by unknown enemies. In a series of hallucinatory scenes, Griggs represents the hanging and near dissection, in the interests of racial science, of his *Imperium in Imperio* advocate for civil and political rights (he uses the same device to introduce into the plot of *The Hindered Hand* a plan for germ warfare outlined by the Pan-Slavist conspiracy, the unleashing of a yellow-fever epidemic among white Southerners). Griggs's racist Dr. Zackland kidnaps Belton under the cover of darkness in order to obtain his body, a "fine specimen," which he'd always eyed "cadaverously," all very much in the African American folkloric tradition of rumors of "night doctors" and Klan "night riders" (*II*, 145).[70] For Griggs, of course, the suspicion of betrayal or contamination from within may just as well be turned outward onto white society, as in the Imperium, which translates fears of black betrayal into its organization as a secret society concealed from so-called Anglo-Saxons, or in the conspiratorial passing plot of *The Hindered Hand*, in which a mixed-race mother orchestrates her family's intermarriage into and, thus, infiltration of Southern society.

All these examples work to destabilize the borders between inside and outside, as racial unity appears to be both threatened and shored up by forces from within and without. What and whose inside and outside become Griggs's main questions: hence his formulation of what he never actually calls a nation within a nation provides the problematic slogan of a militant black separatism in *Imperium in Imperio*. While, for Dixon, the nation within the nation is always the alien, mulatto nation, sometimes it represents enforced separation, a viable segregation, but most often it marks the limits of race relations at the threshold of sexuality and marriage. Griggs's germ-warfare fantasy reverses the Dixonian view of blacks as contaminated "strangers within our gates," "a festering Black Death," a corrupting presence in "our body politic" (*LS*, 436–37). Finally, Griggs internalizes and individualizes the threat to black people posed by collective white violence. If, as he and many others noted, any black person would do as victim, innocence or guilt notwithstanding, then to focus as he does on the pain of individual black bodies is to counter the collectivizing of the race in the perception of lynching as a symbolic act against the whole black community.

So, in tandem with the externalized threat of a violent racial other, both writers also place center stage the problem of betrayal from within, an image central to the countersubversive imagination. It takes what the anthropologist Michael Taussig terms the *mirror dance* of conspiracy to represent the competing and contradictory fears of both internal and external foes.[71] Griggs's *Imperium in Imperio* is narrated by the self-styled traitor who exposes the Imperium in the interests of averting race war; *Unfettered* depicts the "nefarious plottings" of "Negro Republic zealots" against political independents they decry as "Negro traitors plotting to undo all that the North has done for us" (*U,* 132, 143, 145). The third novel of Dixon's trilogy, *The Traitor* (1907), addresses the period of conflict within the ranks, when the Klan, growing out of control, was disbanded by those allying themselves with its original spirit. The title *The Traitor* has at least a double meaning, referring both to the old leader, who disbands the Klan but refuses to betray its secrets to federal investigators, and to the new Klan leader, a willing government informant. Conspiracy in the novels thus paradoxically works both sides, as it were, with the threat from the racial monster outside tainting as well the putative allies inside.

The theory of racial conspiracy tends to be volatile, circling back on itself, multiplying its objects, and, finally, traveling imitatively both from victim to victimizer and from accuser to accused. Rather than simple twinning, the Griggs-Dixon conspiratorial imagination engenders Taussig's mirror dance. If Griggs's patriotic Imperium mirrors the actions of the founding fathers by reconstructing a new, black American revolution, the Klan in turn claims to reflect both the terror tactics of black insurrection and the chivalric rituals of white fraternalism. Incorporating a passage from the Klan "Konstitution" in *The Leopard's Spots,* Dixon describes the "Invisible Empire of White Robed Anglo-Saxon Knights," we remember, as "simply the old answer of organised manhood to organised crime. Its purpose was to bring order out of chaos." The distorted conception of the Klan as "simply" reactive, created in the image of its opposite ("organised manhood" in response to "organised crime"), is matched by the distorted logic that distanced the opposite as enemy ("organised crime" as chaos). First identification, then disavowal: that is the mirror dance of racial conspiracy theory.

How to deal with the "criss-crossing racial and class tensions that threatened the implantation of the solid South" and shook the Southern political, economic, and social order to its foundations?[72] As we have seen, the answer to this question—mobilize white supremacy—only intensified the problem. Racial attitudes are, as Fields puts it, "promiscuous critters" that "do not mind cohabiting with their opposites," and white solidarity is not a belief but a "slogan" to be repeatedly invoked as the need arises.[73] Fields's "promiscuous critters"—and Woodward's "procrustean bedfellows"— join with Gilmore's "sex and violence in Procrustes' bed" to point to the contradictions in the racial-sexual complex of white supremacy in the 1890s.[74] For Chesnutt, the contradictions are most literally visible in the dual meanings of *fusion*, which refers, not only specifically to the interracial-coalition party of the Fusionists, but also colloquially to miscegenation.[75] For Woodward, in a Dixonian vein, the fabled national reconciliation was fragile, consisting, especially in the South, of unstable coalitions among politically, geographically, and economically divided groups. Only the "old cry of white supremacy" could even hope to solidify the white factions— from Black Belt gentry to poor-white commoners, from hard-money, Negro-rights Republicans to conservative, white-supremacist Democrats and agrarian, antimonopolist Populists—yet "boasts of white solidarity that impressed outsiders were often loudest in the presence of division."[76] For Fields, as for Chesnutt, white supremacy was "a set of political programs, differing according to the social position of their proponents" but "so far from providing a unifying element" that "they were as likely as not to accentuate the latent possibilities for discord."[77] For Gilmore, in a Griggsian mode, summing up the significance of all these interpretations, and speaking from outside the view of the white supremacists, "white power was contingent, the master of a thousand subtle and not so subtle disguises."[78] No literary mode was better suited than the paternal race melodrama to charting the mobility of white supremacy, interacting with sexuality and nationalism as asymmetrical substitutions that alternately masked, neutralized, and displaced one another.

Likewise, all the central tropes and figures of American racial-national discourse—from white supremacy to the Spanish-American War's Negro Question, fraternalism's mystic brotherhood, and imperialism's white man's burden—reveal the many fissures, shifting alignments, and cross- and countercurrents that form the polarized racial realities of the turn of the century. In response, the melodramatized tropes of race, nation, and empire attempt to bring, in Dixon's terms, order out of such chaos. But, at the same time, particularly when mobilized in the forms of popular fiction, these figures demonstrate, not simply either the potential to travel in surprising company or the political flexibility and mobility of generic form, but also—

by rupturing the ordering structures and conventions of the melodramatic mode—the very disorderliness fundamental to the American racial scene.

OCCULT TRACES

As a social theory and narrative mode, conspiracy enables both Griggs and Dixon to explore, more or less successfully, the occult—both invisible and secret—relations among race, sex, and politics: both writers expose the manifold uses of the race issue to fight what are properly political and economic battles, although they part ways when it comes to an analogous demystifying of the sex-race-politics equation. But, to return to the question with which this chapter begins, Is it any good? How are we finally to judge the aesthetic and political work of the paternal race melodrama? Working through an incomplete structure of double plots, in which history and politics are intertwined with romance and love as integral, even equal, partners in the narrative, both writers construct, not separate spheres, in which political problems may be managed or resolved through love, but rather coalescing plots that merge in the key problems of interracial rape and sexuality, protean figures for racial and national purity articulating radically opposed visions of the American future. Unlike the classic allegorical resolution of erotics and politics in Doris Sommer's foundational Latin American fictions,[79] with Griggs and Dixon the two worlds refuse either to parallel neatly or to diverge in the final resolution of political conflict through the romance of marriage. The Griggs-Dixon love plots cannot provide the conventional resolution of social and political conflicts because both interracial sexuality and intraracial sexuality have always been at the historical center of the race problem. Fusion politics, "procrustean bedfellows," and "promiscuous critters" all remind us of that.

Hence, the melodramatic polarities are ruptured, and romantic resolutions are either too little, too late, or nonexistent. We have arrived here at the "incomplete happy ending" of the paternal race melodrama, symptomatically both irresolute and excessive. Griggs's proliferating couples do not all end up together, nor do they provide neat foils for one another; the narratives of their largely tragic, unresolved romances are supplemented by the novelist's many tracts and "dissertations on the race problem" (as "Dorlan's Plan" is subtitled [U, 217]). Dixon's arranged marriages fail to answer or to still the narrator's anxiously repeated refrain, "Shall the future American be an Anglo-Saxon or a Mulatto?" But, whereas Griggs's multiple doublings consistently twin the sexual and the political, Dixon wavers between intertwining racial-sexual politics and forcibly asserting that love will out, and outweigh, political conflict. *The Leopard's Spots* concludes with the marriage of Gaston and Sallie Worth but draws attention to the remaining loose end, the "one unresolved problem" of "the Negro," which was, for Dixon, inextricably linked to that other great question, the "conflict between Labor and Capital" (*LS*, 331). (The last few pages reopen the novel's long-standing argument about whether, like the Negro, the leopard can change his spots, this time making black education and labor the issue.) Dixon condemns his trilogy, in a kind of excess, to return to the same, vexed post-Emancipation history while failing to make the story come out right. The broad chronological sweep of *The Leopard's Spots*, from the Civil War to the Spanish-American War, narrows down to a focus on Klan history, its beginnings in *The Clansman* and its demise in *The Traitor*, both moments already covered in *The Leopard's Spots*. If Dixon's melodramas thus become ever narrower, Griggs's vision grows correspondingly more expansive, accommodating everything from Darwinian social science to Ethiopianism and racial mysticism in his various efforts to synthesize the extremes of contemporary thinking into a science of collective efficiency. Both writers' excess—whether that of singularity or that of multiplicity—ironically underscores the racial impasse at which they both finally arrive.

But, at the same time, Griggs and Dixon point toward a possible, alternative approach to the race problem through traces of the occult scattered throughout their writings. The most familiar of these occult discourses would have to be the "ersatz mysticism" that characterizes the Ku Klux Klan, from the "three red mystic letters, K. K. K.," to the mystical titles and rites of cross burning and night riding, to the Klan's origins as, in Dixon's words, the "reincarnated souls of the Clansmen of Old Scotland" (*C*, 2).[80] In addition, there are medical and scientific discourses of the occult, most prominently drawing on theories of the unconscious from the practice of hypnosis. Dr. Cameron, the unreconstructed Southerner of *The Clansman*, uses the "powers of hypnosis" to establish the guilt of his ex-slave Gus as the novel's criminal black rapist: "like an ancient alchemist ready to conduct some daring scientific experiment," Cameron first sees with the "mystic light" of his eyes the image of Gus—"the bestial figure of a negro"— etched on the retina of the murder victim, later hypnotizing Gus ("a negro peculiarly sensitive to hypnotic influence") into reliving the crime "with fearful realism." Accounting for this kind of occult science, Cameron alludes to "the world of spiritual phenomena . . . , sleep and dreams, or second-sight, or the day-dreams which we call visions" (*C*, 313, 213, 321–22).

Griggs, too, links race, hypnotism, and even hysteria to formulate a variety of sociological theories tinged with the mystical: the Southern practice of "racial hypnotism" (to "engender in the darky a sense of his inferiority and . . . paralyze his aggressiveness") has created "a sort of sociological hysteria," with "more and more pathological manifestations as a result of the strain upon the people" (*HH*, 255). Such traces of the racial occult in both Dixon and Griggs suggest a different account of race relations, one that focuses on unconscious structures of feeling as well as on the socioeconomic, political realities that dominate the paternal melodramas.

More broadly, the racial occult flowers in the form of a cultural fascination with secret organizations, armed and terrorist, extending into the legitimate realm with the military rituals and branches of the many fraternal organizations and secret orders, both black and white, that flourished during the late-nineteenth-century American "Golden Age of Fraternity." As both Griggs's and Dixon's detailed representations of secret organizations suggest, fraternalism provided yet another cultural locus in which the crosscurrents of racial, sexual, and nationalist politics could play themselves out. From defending the Klan as simply another fraternal organization, to attacking black political organizations as versions of the Klan, the conspiratorial rhetoric of fraternalism generates the racially and politically conflicted crosscurrents of the twin complex of imperialism and militarism.[81] Promoting ties of mystic and revolutionary brotherhood through fraternal drill teams and parade units as well as through elaborate, secret initiation rituals, often drawing on "primitive" rites of the past, whether medieval/ chivalric (as in Dixon) or Native American or American revolutionary (as in Griggs), such organizations as the Masons (including the black Prince Hall Masons), the Oddfellows, the Red Men (a fraternal group that incorporated reworked Indian legends in its ritual), and the Knights of Pythias participated in the broader militarism, as well as the conspiratorial bent, of the new postbellum American empire. Fraternal brotherhood, both mystical and militarist, thus connected what were seen as the occult practices of the past with the presentist theme of the nation at arms.

Locating and explicating the various cultures of the racial occult is one of my tasks throughout this book. A few provisional comments may help make the transition from Griggs and Dixon to my final two, thoroughgoing racial occultists, Twain and Du Bois. In the paternal melodramas, race operates in both occulting and occulted modes: the frustrating visibility of "blackness," in which racial science seeks to detect race on the body (in fingerprints, facial characteristics, or, at the very least, the one drop of black blood), must be paired with a compensatory invisibility of "whiteness," which says that true unity among American whites is invisible, deeper than surface differences of politics, region, and class. This formulation, however, slights the global culture of the racial occult, the international dimensions of the study of hypnotism, hysteria, and the unconscious as racialized phenomena that are only partially evident in Griggs and Dixon. They acknowledge the interplay of the domestic and the foreign, we know, but that traffic is confined largely to the sphere of race and empire. The following chapters will trace the interplay of racial meanings, both local and global, national and transnational, attributed to and derived from the culture of the occult.

CHAPTER FOUR

MARK TWAIN AND FELLOW
OCCULT TRAVELERS

BOTH MARK TWAIN and W. E. B. Du Bois were, oddly enough, mistaken for Jews—Du Bois while traveling as a student in Germany, Twain during a little-known smear campaign conducted in Germany after his death. These cases of mistaken identity—both only slightly ironic— point to a complicated set of relations emerging in the late nineteenth century between the U.S. "Negro Question" and the international "Jewish Question." Black-Jewish parallels, based on the biblical account of pharaonic bondage and the Exodus, were a long-standing source of symbolic, interethnic affinities, but the international connections at the turn of the century between worldwide anti-Semitism and racism fostered more complex misidentifications as well. For Twain and Du Bois, the Jew as a wandering scapegoat, located both within and beyond the borders of the contiguous United States, provided a third term between black and white that tested, and sometimes exploded, the social boundaries and discursive limits of domestic racial conflict. Not simply a one-way traffic that produces what Sander Gilman calls, in the context of his work on comparative scientific racisms, "too black Jews and too white Blacks," the Jewish medium that they envision speaks to the diaspora concept as Paul Gilroy has defined it: a "global perspective on the politics of racism" that "enables one to think about the issue of racial commonality outside of constricting binary frameworks."[1] In this case, for two American writers at the turn of the century, the context of Continental anti-Semitism, visible especially in the Dreyfus case in France and in conflicts over German nationalism in the Austrian Empire, served to mediate and reorient their experience of race relations at home.

For Du Bois, the Jewish Question pointed to a complex matrix of associations between what he calls in the autobiographical *Dusk of Dawn* (1940) "the colored world within," a social and psychic community based on group solidarity—"like the Jews," he remarks—and "the race developments throughout the world" (*DD*, 173, 207, 29). We might trace this identification back to Du Bois's years as a student in Germany (1892–94), when, he writes in his last autobiography, "I was several times mistaken for a Jew; arriving one night in a town of north Slovenia, the driver of a rickety cab whispered in my ear, 'Unter die Juden?' [among Jews?]. I stared and then said yes. I stayed in a little Jewish inn. I was a little frightened as in the gathering twilight I traversed the foothills of the dark Tatras alone and on foot" (*A*, 175). Countering what he characterizes a few pages later as the gulf between the supposedly racially unmarked idyll in Germany—remembered as a place and time when, he says, he could build "great castles in Spain"—and his return to "'nigger'-hating America," this episode suggests how the encounter abroad would ultimately break Du Bois's national focus (*A*, 183). At the time of his graduation from Fisk in 1888, he was, as he said of himself, "blithely European and imperialist in outlook," "democratic as democracy was conceived in America" (*DD*, 32). Yet, despite his admiration for Bismarck ("he had made a nation out of a mass of bickering peoples" [*DD*, 32]), his self-identification as the "dark-faced" Jewish traveler in Europe presages the global sympathies that begin to emerge in the very midst of his "Days of Disillusion" back in the United States (*A*, 183).

Once again, the medium of Du Bois's emergent internationalism is a black-Jewish connection, this time via European anti-Semitism and the Dreyfus case:

> It was a disturbed world in which I landed; 1892 saw the high tide of lynching in the United States. . . . The Dreyfus case had opened in France with his conviction and imprisonment, and he was destined for twelve years to suffer martyrdom. The war between China and Japan broke out the year of my return. I recognized the blow democracy received when Congress repealed the so-called Force Bills in 1894, refusing any longer even to try to protect the legal citizenship rights of Negroes. But on the other hand, I did not at all understand . . . how the gold and diamonds of South Africa . . . and especially the black labor force were determining and conditioning the political action of Europe. (*DD*, 48–49; *A*, 184)

Despite his protestations, even before he enshrines what would, he says in *Dusk of Dawn*, later become his own more systematic understanding of how American Negroes were part of "the race developments throughout the world," the Dreyfus case clearly initiated both a chain of associations and a medium of awareness of the gaps in his own "knowledge of the race problem" (*DD*, 29–30). From lynching in America and pogroms in Russia to the Dreyfus case and "the struggle between East and West in the Sino-Japanese War": this is the litany of events that Du Bois repeatedly invokes as having raised his political and racial consciousness (*DD*, 30). It was in no small measure the Dreyfus case, and, by extension, the Jewish Question, that both revealed Du Bois's own nationalist blind spots and reoriented his perspective toward global political and economic exploitation.

If, for Du Bois, the international Jewish Question became a medium of refiguring the Negro Question at home, with enslavement and diaspora as only the most evident commonalties, for Twain the Jew proved to be a medium of a different, more occult kind. Mark Twain was always intensely engaged by two important nineteenth-century cultural conversations, one addressing issues of race, the other theories of the unconscious. His later writings in particular are known both for their explicit anti-imperialism—and the charged racial awareness that it produced—and their flirtation with spiritualism, dream theory, and a variety of occult phenomena. Each of these cultural arenas, the racial and the psychological, has been individually recognized as a major force shaping Twain's imagination, but how they might have interacted to produce his large body of late, mostly unfinished (and some unpublished) writings has yet to be determined. The later works—the group of fantastic, quasi-philosophical pieces now published in volumes with such titles as *Which Was the Dream? and Other Symbolic Writings of the Later Years* and *Mark Twain's Fables of Man*, all written roughly around the time of Twain's 1895–96 world lecture tour and after—are themselves part of the challenge in that they have always raised for readers and scholars a range of fundamental problems: at issue are their textual status and generic location, their aesthetic incoherence, and their apparent retreat from both the humor and the social and political engagement that make Mark Twain one of our best-loved national authors.

Twain himself made, in a series of diary entries for March 1906, a loose association among these various elements—race, spiritualism, imperialism—the kind of free association that he called "the methodless method of the human mind."[2] Moving from Monday the twelfth to Wednesday the twenty-first, he touches first on newspaper reports of the "slaughter" of six hundred Moros, men, women, and children, by U.S. troops in the Philippines: "'Slaughter' is a good word. . . . They were mere naked savages, and yet there is a sort of pathos about it when that word 'children' falls under your eye, . . . and by help of its deathless eloquence color, creed, and nationality vanish away." He then moves on to boyhood memories of the Levin boys, "the first Jews" he had ever seen: "It took me a good while to get over the awe of it." And he finishes by touching on what he calls "mental telegraphy": "I imagine that we get most of our thoughts out of somebody else's head, by mental telegraphy—and . . . in the majority of cases, out of the heads of strangers; strangers far removed—Chinamen, Hindus, and all manner of remote foreigners whose language we should not be able to understand, but whose thoughts we can read without difficulty."[3]

Despite this intriguing evidence of the free-associative sort as well as the similarly suggestive evidence of the whole of Twain's later writings, it has not been easy to see how, or even that, the arenas of the racial and the psychological intersect for Twain. But, following the lead of Pauline Hopkins and W. E. B. Du Bois, both of whom, we know, applied the vocabulary of double or divided consciousness to the race question, we may ask, If the New Psychology, as it was known, proved in their adaptations a racialized science, then why not in Twain's, too? Following their lead, we may even take as given the occulted presence of "race"—Toni Morrison's "ghost in the machine"[4]—in much of Twain's late writing, ranging from the travel narrative *Following the Equator*, the record of his 1895–96 world lecture tour and of his views on race and colonial relations in the "hot belt of the equator";[5] to the body of all the "dream tales," the fables of nightmarish voyages to alternate worlds and states of mind, only one of which ("Which Was It?") charts the kind of openly racial nightmare characteristic of his explicit narratives of passing and hidden racial identity; to the very last and greatest dream tale, *The Mysterious Stranger*, a collection of texts in which an angelic stranger, alternatively the nephew or the son of Satan and variously named (Young) Satan, No. 44, and Philip Traum (*traum* being the German word for "dream"), draws on an array of psychic powers to offer a series of dream-like meditations on the fallen human race.

It is rare to group these works together, except in the form of their footnotes, which are like a series of cross-references to their shared cultural context: the repeated, but often unincorporated and unelaborated, allusions throughout Twain's late writing to the various imperial ventures of the 1890s (including Great Britain in India, the United States in Cuba and the Philippines, and most of the world's powers in China). What connects these works, however, goes beyond even the context of empire and its underlying racial practices. Far from being simply the literary manifestations of Twain's retreat into personal despair that they are so often made out to be, the dream tales, like their companion travel narrative *Following the*

Equator, written during the same period, invoke and adapt the notions of spirit communication and disembodied space-time travel, made newly respectable at this time by the investigations of psychical researchers, as a means of revisiting the old terrain of U.S. slavery and linking it to the newer global imperialism, the worldwide nationalisms, nativisms, and racisms of the late 1890s.

These "travel" writings transform a variety of locales, from the American South both before and after the war, to the equatorial colonies of Africa, to Austria of both 1490 and 1702, to the veins of a "tramp" named Blitzowski, into the worlds elsewhere through which Twain reimagines the Negro Question: now located both at home and abroad, in the empires of the world, as a jarring continuation of the U.S. past into the global present. Starting with "Which Was It?" and several other little-known, unfinished stories of racial passing, and ending with *The Mysterious Stranger,* the late, unfinished series of manuscripts on the travels of the youthful Satan (named in honor of his older relative) among the human race, Twain variously reimagines "race": as a tragic family romance of denied kinship, role reversal, and revenge; as a hidden source of taint and disease; as a set of customs deforming both slave and master, native and colonizer; and, ultimately, as a particular subset of what throughout his writings he called the "damned human race," universally enslaved to necessity and its own nature.[6]

In arguing that Twain's late writings return, via the occult, to the familiar subject of race, I am myself going back over the literary terrain of the dream tales that I have already described both as broadly historicized and as escapist: immersed in the contexts of the New Psychology and global empire, the tales are divided between the twin impulses to acknowledge racial issues and to turn away from them.[7] But Twain goes much farther here in his engagement with contemporary politics than I first recognized. His transformation of the occult into a specifically racial register in these late works underscores the different uses—ranging from the personal to the cultural—to which he put the available psychological discourses. Theories of spiritualism and occult phenomena gave Twain access to a particularly rich source to mine, not only, as I argued earlier, for questions of authorship and selfhood, but also, and more important in this context, for cultural images of otherness.

That is, when in *Following the Equator* he uses as the epigraph to a chapter on South African politics the maxim from "Pudd'nhead Wilson's New Calendar," "Everyone is a moon, and has a dark side which he never shows to anybody," he is not thinking simply of double personality or the hidden side of the mind, as it is usually read (*FE,* 654). Rather, he is referring explicitly to what he speaks of in the chapter as his own inability, as a "stranger," to understand the Boer "side of the quarrel" with the British over control of the Transvaal—the ruling Boers themselves in conflict with their native-born subjects, known as *Uitlanders* (which Twain translates as "strangers, foreigners") in their own land (*FE,* 657). The point here is that there are actually many more than two sides, the light and the dark, to "The Political Pot" of imperial politics in South Africa, as an accompanying Dan Beard illustration of that title suggests with the following labels on the wooden logs stoking the boiling pot of "Africa": "Syndicate," "Trusts," "Spanish," "French," "Dutch," "English," "Negro," "Half Breed," "Gold Bugs" (*FE,* 655). Complicating this already-overflowing, not to say overdetermined, usage of *dark side* is our discovery a few chapters later that it may also apply to Cecil Rhodes, the premier of the British Cape Colony and the architect of British expansionist policy in South Africa, who is described as "deputy-God on the one side, deputy-Satan on the other," "an Archangel with wings to half the world, Satan with a tail to the other half" (*FE,* 708, 710). The rich, even perplexing constellation of meanings that Twain associates with the notion of the dark side demonstrates at the very least how culturally, and politically, mobile a metaphor it was. Extending *dark side* to include the occult, as it was being investigated, theorized, and popularized by a variety of researchers at the time, from Charcot and Bernheim to Freud to William James, we can begin to see the complex system of cultural references that Twain is constructing in what we might call his *travels in the racial occult.*

The question of genre is also key to reading this group of Twain's late writings, for, as so many readers, following his lead, have recognized, the series of unfinished manuscripts that he left largely unpublished at his death reflect repeated efforts to find a form adequate to his later vision—to what he called his "pen warmed up in hell."[8] In this respect, too, my own earlier reading of these texts failed fully to appreciate the high stakes for Twain in the writing of history, in the content of the historical form, as it were. Although an interest in history, primarily that of his own boyhood, the era of Southern slavery, is generally taken for granted as a fixture of the Mark Twain persona and canon, all his work features a more expansive and anomalous historical consciousness that goes beyond the realm of representing acceptable historical subjects—even such unconventional representations as *Huckleberry Finn* and *Pudd'nhead Wilson.* From my perspective now, the most intriguing examples of Twain's history writing are neither his classics set in the antebellum South nor the more conventional historical novels (*The Prince and the Pauper, Joan of Arc*) but, rather, the fragmentary, fantastic, and parodic fictional histories of his later years. These are mock epics in which the history of the damned human race is sardonically reviewed by some kind of controlling narrative authority—the "Creator" in "Letters from the Earth," the "Father of History" in "Papers of the Adam Family," Twain himself as the supposed editor of "The Secret History of Eddypus, the World-Empire," a narrative of the rise, decline, and fall of the great American civilization. Together, these works convey the conflicting conceptions of historical time—divided between a Whiggish conception of progress and a darker view of history as mechanical repetition—that characterize Mark Twain's fractured philosophy of history.[9]

The figure of Civilization, imaged variously and repeatedly throughout Twain's writings, appears, most often, insistently vilified, as though Twain could neither get over nor get beyond a deep sense of promise betrayed, even rage at the betrayal of history encoded in the term *progress*. The "Mad Philosopher" or "Mad Prophet," who contributes several "extracts" to the archive of the "Adam Family," asserts that, by the "Law of Periodical Repetition," nothing can happen one time only but must happen again and yet again—"monotonously."[10] Yet, as "the distinguished Professor of the Science of Historical Forecast," he speaks to a yearning for the lost art of prophecy in a world where the future is less certain and the possibility of progress not foreclosed ("PAF," 89). The Mad Prophet "got his nickname long ago, and did not deserve it; for he merely builds prognostications, not prophecies. . . . Builds them out of history and statistics, using the facts of the past to forecast the probabilities of the future. It is merely applied science" ("PAF," 84). As the "Father of History," ultimately responsible for collecting the "Papers of the Adam Family," Twain, too, appears condemned to repeat the conflict between historical progress and historical repetition, in what amounts to a series of deeply chaotic fragments, even more symptomatically incomplete than the rest of the unfinished late writings.

But, if the Professor of the Science of Historical Forecast can do little more than produce what are entitled "Fragments from a Suppressed Book called 'Glances at History' or 'Outlines of History'" ("PAF," 96), he is countered by the microbic narrator inhabiting the body of the tramp Blitzowski and other narrators of the dream tales and science fiction. Their fantastic voyages manage to sidestep the impasse of the fragmented, fictional histories by conceiving history, not as temporal movement, forward or back, up or down, but through what we might call a Twainian variant of occult time in which time and space are imagined as simultaneous dimensions. The very basis of temporal thinking about history—the question of whether historical time moves forward, teleologically, or repeats itself in a cycle of civilizational rise and fall—shifts when time is defined, as it is in the dream tales, both spatially and temporally. Past, present, and future are disrupted, located—or, more accurately, dislocated—on both spatial and temporal axes in the dream tales, which imagine a series of alternate worlds on parallel temporal planes within a single, densely occupied universe. The tramp's body harbors, hidden within, swarming microbic worlds, representing widely varying times and places, coexisting or colliding in a single instant.

Purportedly a "History translated from the Original Microbic by Mark Twain," as the title page reads, "Three Thousand Years among the Microbes" cultivates the comparative perspective of translation to demonstrate the relativity and the density of both time and space. "I could observe the germs from their own point of view," the microbe narrator begins. "At the same time, I was able to observe them from a human being's point of view. . . . Another thing: my human measurements of time and my human span of life remained to me, right alongside of my full appreciation of the germ-measurements of time and the germ span of life."[11] Not only does he provide a table of "Time-Equivalents" (one human year is "roughly" equal to 52,416 microbe years), but he also describes the densely occupied physical space of the tramp's body (in which whole worlds, "alive and in energetic motion," are visible, down to individual molecules and atoms that to the human eye exist "only in *theory*") through comparative reference to human geography ("TTYM," 447). "Our tramp is mountainous, there are vast oceans in him, and lakes that are sea-like for size, there are many rivers (veins and arteries) which are fifteen miles across, and of a length so stupendous as to make the Mississippi and the Amazon trifling little Rhode Island brooks by comparison" ("TTYM," 437). This series of asymmetrical, nested scales, defined by spatial and temporal distortion, adds up, finally, to an inverted chain of being, an infinite regress of victims and victimizers: the spectacle of billions of cholera germs unsuspectingly feeding on the body of the tramp whom they perceive as their planet and deity, himself a social parasite, "hints at the possibility that the procession of known and listed devourers and persecutors is not complete. . . . [B]elow that infester there is yet another infester that infests *him*—and so on down and down and down till you strike the bottommost bottom of created life—if there is one, which is extremely doubtful" ("TTYM," 454, 526–27). "It doesn't make any difference who or

what we are," the microbe narrator concludes toward the end of his narrative. "There's always somebody to look down on!" ("TTYM," 479).

Even if few, then or now, have found such views on God and the
damned human race as shocking as Twain thought they were, still the formal question that he raises is a telling one. If, as I will argue, the classic plot
of racial passing proved a dead end for Twain, then it was a cross between
the travel narrative, the form with which he made his literary reputation,
and the occult-oriented dream tale that produced the richest of his late writing on the race question.

RACE MELODRAMAS MANQUÉ

Twain's most successful narrative approach to the problem of U.S. race slavery was always through voice: the counterpoised comic and poignant ver-
naculars of Huck and Jim; the vernacular outrage of Roxana in *Pudd'nhead
Wilson* (1894), next to *Huckleberry Finn* (1885) Twain's best-known novel
on race. Almost equally central to his representation of the Negro Question
was the context of institutional, medicojuridical discourses on race, those
that enabled him to grapple in *Pudd'nhead Wilson* with the "fiction[s] of law
and custom" constituting racial identity.[12] Yet, alongside these strategies,
another, competing racial narrative operated as well, one that foregrounds
the figure of what I call the *avenging mulatto,* Twain's adaptation that inverts
the conventional tragic mulatto as figured in works by white "romantic
racialists" (e.g., Harriet Beecher Stowe, George Washington Cable, and
Kate Chopin) as well as by some black writers (e.g., William Wells Brown,
Charles Chesnutt, and Nella Larsen). Between the 1880s and the early
1900s, Twain wrote three little-known, unfinished sketches of racial tragedies in which the son of a white master father and slave mother takes revenge on the father, the stories culminating in patricide. While essentially
operating within the conventional narrative boundaries of the tragic-
mulatto tale, these sketches reverse the terms of that plot. It is not the tragic mulatto himself (and gender is part of the reversal) who comes to a
tragic end—typically death or forced separation from a love object, either
because the relationship is revealed to be incestuous or because one of the
lovers is deported, usually to Europe—but the white father, whose murder
is the mulatto's aggressive response to his biracial heritage. At this point in
the plot, the story breaks off, unconcluded.

What stands out here is the problem of Twain's apparently constitu-
tional inability to complete this particular racial story. It has always been

something of a related critical puzzle that *Pudd'nhead Wilson,* a novel that raises textual questions of aesthetic coherence or completeness, contained in manuscript form much racial material that never appeared in the published editions.[13] Indeed, of Twain's three avenging-mulatto sketches, the best known—if such a notion applies to what amounts only to a shadow plot of what Hershel Parker would call a "flawed text"[14]—is a series of passages contained in the manuscript version of *Pudd'nhead Wilson* but deleted by Twain from the published version, passages that outline a vestigial patricide plot hatched by the vengeful "white" Tom Driscoll, following his slave mother Roxana's revelation that he is a black slave, the son of an aristocratic white man. These canceled passages confirm what several readers and critics of the novel itself have always asserted, that, although the novel culminates with Tom's murder of Judge Driscoll, his white benefactor and supposed uncle, from what Henry Nash Smith calls "the standpoint of imaginative coherence" Judge Driscoll is Tom's father just as clearly as Roxana is his mother.[15] And the suppressed patricide plot thus remains in the novel, barely disguised despite Twain's double stratagem, recognized by Smith and others, of making Roxana the slave of a shadowy brother of Judge Driscoll at the time of Tom's birth and then creating an even more shadowy figure, Colonel Cecil Burleigh Essex, to be Tom's biological father. In fact, in the working notes for the novel, to return once again to the repressed, Twain made Judge Driscoll himself the father of Tom.

What are we to make of this almost impossibly thin disguise? It will help here to consult a range of contemporary writings on the race question, writings that will tell us what people in the late nineteenth century could say about race relations and how they could say it. Put another way, Twain's personal difficulties with saying what he wanted to say reveal as much about the limits and possibilities of American racial rhetorics as they do about those of Twain himself. Most critics have read Twain's well-recorded self-censorship biographically and psychologically rather than culturally, seeing in it either his squeamishness about the fact of miscegenation or his ambivalence toward his own father, John Marshall Clemens, whom he clearly identified with the gentlemanly Driscolls, Essexes, and other "F. F. V.'s" (first families of Virginia) humorously and lovingly satirized in *Pudd'nhead Wilson.* If we place Twain's suppressed patricide plot in the context of other possible plots offered by contemporary race narratives, it emerges strikingly as a telling variant of the tragic-mulatto story.

Blackness is conceived in this story as hidden taint, with the conventions of the search for origins and the revelation of kinship that are central to much race literature resulting here in fearful exposure, identity destroying rather than affirming. *Pudd'nhead Wilson* only touches on this process, briefly representing the volcanic "irruption" in Tom Driscoll's psyche on being made aware (by his mulatto mother) of "the 'nigger' in him" (*PW*, 44). But the manuscript plays with an extended moment of realization in passages such as these:

> I must begin a new life to-day—but not outside; no, only inside. I must be the same slangy, useless youth as before, outside, but inside I shall be a nigger with a grievance. . . . I wish I knew my father. . . . I will wheedle it out of her some day; and if he is alive, then let him not go out at night. (MMS, 234–35)

> He loathed the "nigger" in him, but got pleasure out of bringing this secret "filth," as he called it, into familiar and constant contact with the sacred whites. . . . [And there was one thought that sang always in his heart. He called that his father's death-song.] (MMS, 246–47)

Even in the manuscript the bracketed last sentences are crossed out, emphasizing that the repeated references to the son killing the father are both the object and the threat. Similarly problematic is the revelation of Tom's blackness, which brings, not the conventional resolution of ambiguous identity, but rather a continuation, and intensification, of the former disjunction between white outside and black inside. In Twain's fantasy, which culminates in the specter of violence against the white father, the knowledge of hidden blackness becomes, if anything, more of a threat to, than a consolidation of, white dominance—and, indeed, to the boundaries of whiteness itself—which so readily harbors the "secret 'filth'" of blackness.

Race is envisioned here almost entirely as a structure of domination and subordination, as relations of power between familial power brokers, father and son. The slave mother is subordinated in the role of victim to the master father, the source and object of the primary emotion. So, too, are racial-sexual relations almost entirely suppressed, not simply, however, because of Twain's prudery, but also because of the narrative focus on the filial relation, figured as taboo. This is the vision that Twain pursued in his two other race narratives, one a four-page outline, dated to the 1880s, for a story about a mulatto ("1/16 negro"), "his father his master & mean," who, after the war, "at last, seeing even the best educated negro is at a disadvantage, . . . clips his wiry hair close, wears gloves always (to conceal his telltale nails) & passes for a white man." The mulatto falls in love with his cousin—"he used to 'miss' her on the plantation." And then the notes break off at the climactic moment of revelation: "At the time of the climax he is telling the stirring story of the heroic devotion of a poor negro mother to her son—of course not mentioning that he was the son & that *his* is the mother who bears the scar which he has described. Then she steps forward and shows the scar she got in saving him from his own father's brutality. So this gassy man is *his* father, & it is his niece whom XX loves, & who with (perhaps) his daughter, supports him."[16] Although the genealogical ramifications of the plot are confusing—again, the revelation of kinship is far from clarifying—they seem to suggest that others in the story also live under the illusion that they are white—a shared illusion, the sketch suggests, that is part and parcel of the protagonist's knowing, aggressive passing.

The latest and longest of the three race narratives comes, significantly, at the end of the unfinished novel "Which Was It?" published only many years after Twain's death in a collection of his late dream writings.[17] The basic plot resembles that of Twain's major dream tales: a respected and successful family man has a momentary dream of disaster, seeming to last for many years, in which he experiences financial reversal and social disgrace and is even accused of murder. All Twain's dream tales break off before the dreamer finally awakens, but only "Which Was It?" concludes with a specifically racial nightmare: the specter of black supremacy, the total reversal of racial power relations.

The protagonist of "Which Was It?" is George Louisiana Purchase Harrison. ("It is a curious name, but in a way patriotic. He was born on the date of the signing of the Purchase-treaty" ["WWI," 179].) Harrison, a respectable community leader, reveals what his middle name suggests is the criminal side of American Manifest Destiny when he commits forgery and murder, evidence of which are obtained by the free mulatto Jasper, who then blackmails Harrison for the rest of the story. The payment exacted is steep: Jasper, whose slave mother is sold down the river and who is himself swindled out of his freedom by his white master father, George Harrison's uncle, takes revenge on the nephew by "enslaving" him. Publicly master and servant, in private they exchange roles. "You b'longs to me, now. You's my proppity, same as a nigger. . . . Get up and fetch yo' marster a dram!" exults Jasper, exposing Harrison's self-image as upright citizen in control of his family's destiny for the illusion that Harrison himself already knows it to be: "I was proud of my invincible uprightness . . . and all the time was rotten to the soul. . . . I am an exposed sham; I have found myself out" ("WWI," 413, 219). Jasper is a projection of unresolved guilt, not simply Harrison's own for the murder that he has committed, but more broadly a collective guilt for the national hypocrisy of slavery and, more pointedly, of

the post-Emancipation reinstitution of slavery in the form of legalized segregation. Jasper's predicament as a slave who, having bought himself from
"the meanest white man dat ever walked," ends up in his "second slavery"
owing to the treachery of that master ("he took 'vantage of me en stole [my
freedom] back") mimics precisely the national betrayal of the ex-slaves—
even to the complicity of the law (which "sells and banishes free niggers")
and the courts ("a white man's court") in eroding the rights of the ex-slaves
("WWI," 415, 320, 308).

To this racial nightmare the story envisions only one response: another
nightmare, the master's fantasy of his victim's revenge, the exchange of
roles between black and white. "'You is my meat,'" says the black ex-slave
become master of the white ex-master. "Jasper contemplated his serf's misery . . . , his mind traveling back over bitter years and comparing it with the
thousand instances wherein he himself had been the unoffending victim and
had looked like that, suffered like that" ("WWI," 410, 416). Jasper inflicts
on George Harrison the masquerade of freedom that he himself had experi-
enced: "When dey's anybody aroun', I's yo' servants, en pow'ful polite . . . ;
en when dey ain't nobody aroun' but me en you, you's *my* servant, en if I
don't sweat you!" ("WWI," 417). Harrison's response—"Slave of an ex-
slave! it is the final degradation"—underlines the extent to which the central insight here into race relations involves the desire for, and certainly the
threat of, the absolute exchange of power from white to black. As early as
the 1880s, Twain had predicted "Negro supremacy—the whites underfoot
in a hundred years."[18] Jasper embodies narratively the fulfillment of that
prediction: "The meek slouch of the slave was gone from him. . . . He
looked the master; but that which had gone from him was not lost, for his . . .
humble mien had passed to his white serf, and already they seemed not out
of place there, but fit, and . . . at home" ("WWI," 415).

At this point of completed racial role reversal, of "Negro supremacy,"
the narrative breaks off. To pursue the narrative logic beyond this moment
would inevitably expose the moral dilemma that the slave must now become
like the master and the past repeat itself. Of course, this is a dilemma only
from the standpoint that assigns one-dimensionality to blackness, dividing
docility from aggression—the white response to black vengefulness. It is as
if there was simply no more that could be said on race conceived through
this binary, as if Twain had reached a dead end, the limits both of his own
moral dilemma and of this particular narrative form. He had also reached
the limits of what he characterized elsewhere as the "Law of Periodical Repetition," that is, the limits of the curve of rise and fall as a model for histori-

cal time. Despite the numerous gestures made in these three pieces toward rewriting the story of the tragic mulatto—the cruel master father, the heroic slave mother, the vengeful mulatto son—Twain's racial vision, itself bifurcated, ultimately could not be accommodated by that popular form. It would take the global vision of international travel as well as the increasing pressures of world imperialism for Twain to return, with a new, more expansive vision, to the American racial scene.

Traveling the Equatorial Black Belt

Following the Equator (1897), the travel book based on Twain's 1895–96 around-the-world lecture tour, which took him from the Pacific Northwest to Australia, New Zealand, Ceylon, India, and South Africa, announces its connection to the U.S. racial context of *Pudd'nhead Wilson* with the maxims from "Pudd'nhead Wilson's New Calendar" that head each chapter. But, engaging as it does a variety of racial and national groups, the travel narrative moves beyond the claustrophobic world of the prewar South in more than simply a geographic sense. Here, the black-white binary that defines the U.S. racial system and the master narrative of U.S. race relations gives way to the multiplicities of race and nation in the colonial context: like Du Bois's equation of race and nation in "The Conservation of Races," Twain is struck by the variety of "nationalities and complexions" in Mauritius ("island under French control"), including "French, English, Chinese, Arabs, Africans with wool, blacks with straight hair, East Indians, half-whites, quadroons—and great varieties in costumes and colors" (*FE*, 617). And, here, the race-sex nexus that, in the avenging-mulatto sketches, Twain largely shies away from emerges more fully, in the images of blackness and sexuality that are repeatedly associated in his focus on the sensuality of black skin, bodies, and clothing. Most important, however, this around-the-world travelogue establishes a mode of occult travel, of travel across time and space, that links the U.S. and global racial contexts through a disjunctive temporality reminiscent of Twain's dream tales. The result is a penetrating, and often exuberant, satiric meditation on the racial practices that undergird the institutions of empire and U.S. slavery alike.

When Twain crosses the equator and arrives in Ceylon, he enters a dream-like state of "Oriental charm and mystery" that forms, in one respect, the heart of *Following the Equator* (*FE*, 336). Much as one in a mediumistic trance, Twain cultivates a susceptibility to the spirit(s) of the place, a sensitivity that signals ironically, not simply otherworldly escape, but also engagement with the cultures confronting him—extending back to the world elsewhere of his own American past. Twain's mode of occult travel oscillates between dreamy nostalgia for the past and an exoticizing Orientalism in the present, on the one hand, and confrontation with the criminality and corruption of both, on the other. And race is central to both modes as well, to the attraction and to the threat of past and present.

Ceylon is "utterly Oriental" in comparison to the "tempered Orient" of Cairo, "an Orient with an indefinite something wanting," much as Florida or New Orleans is, we are told in the kind of cross-cultural comparison that will become increasingly frequent, "a modified South, a tempered South" (FE, 339). One hallmark of Twain's Orientalism is the exotic aura of black and brown skin: in Ceylon "that wilderness of rich color, that incomparable dissolving-view of harmonious tints, and lithe half-covered forms, and beautiful brown faces"; in Bombay the "sprinkling of white people" among the million inhabitants that is "not enough to have the slightest modifying effect on the massed dark complexion of the public" (FE, 340–43, 345). Another hallmark is the explicit dreaminess—the sense of a distant and decaying world—of the Oriental, or "tropical," experience: in Ceylon, "this dream of fairyland and paradise," "there was that swoon in the air . . . , and in the remoteness of the mountains were the ruined cities and mouldering temples, the mysterious relics of a forgotten time and a vanished race"; in India, "a bewitching place, a bewildering place, an enchanting place," we enter "the land of dreams and romance, of fabulous wealth and fabulous poverty, of splendor and rags, of palaces and hovels" (FE, 339–40, 343, 345, 347). Here, on the "hot belt of the equator," we have clearly arrived at the very center of the voyage, Twain's own paradoxical heart of darkness, where this remote Orientalized land of dream and romance merges, both pleasurably and disturbingly, with memories of Twain's boyhood in the antebellum South.

The drowsy, dreamy atmosphere itself that heralds the "real" Orient for Twain should be familiar to his readers as the incarnation of Hannibal, summoned up the same incantatory way he summons up all the images of his boyhood village in his fiction, from the St. Petersburg of *Huckleberry Finn,* to the Dawson's Landing of *Pudd'nhead Wilson,* to the Eseldorf of *The Mysterious Stranger.*[19] Even more explicitly, however, Twain links "your long-ago dreams of India rising in a sort of vague and luscious moonlight above the horizon-rim of your opaque consciousness" to "a thousand forgotten details which were parts of a vision that had once been vivid to you when you were a boy, and steeped your spirit in tales of the East"

(*FE*, 357). The elements of this Oriental vision—"the princely titles," "the romances" of the exchange of princes and paupers in their cradles—are all also familiar parts of the world of *Pudd'nhead Wilson,* where aristocratic Southerners with pretentious, English-sounding names and pseudomilitary titles are confronted with robberies and murder originating in the exchange of "black" and "white" babies in their cradles (*FE*, 357–58). Indeed, at one point, in a series of chapters on native crime in India, Twain humorously insists that criminality, in the form of "Indian Thuggee," forms a fundamental space-time continuum between his American past and the equatorial present. Remembering how, fifty years ago, as a boy in "the then remote and sparsely peopled Mississippi valley," he had heard "vague tales and rumors of a mysterious body of professional murderers come wandering in from a country which was constructively as far from us as the constellations blinking in space—India," he then recounts how he has just now on his trip come across a copy of the very "Government Report" that originated the "Thuggee" tales: "It is full of fascinations; and it turns those dim, dark fairy tales of my boyhood days into realities" (*FE*, 426–27).

Among those dim, dark tales of professional murderers was the story of Murell's Gang, American thugs "once celebrated," Twain says in his 1883 travel book *Life on the Mississippi,* as "a colossal combination of robbers, horse-thieves, . . . and counterfeiters" but most notorious for trading in slaves, stealing and then reselling them along the Mississippi River. Twain immortalizes Murell as a "wholesale" rascal to Jesse James's "retail rascal" in *Life on the Mississippi,* specifically because of Murell's exploitation of both the profits and the fears engendered by slavery. Engaged in the slave trade, Murell and his associates also planned to foment "negro insurrections and the capture of New Orleans." A long passage quoted from the account of "this big operator" (as Twain calls him) in Marryat's *Diary in America* documents how the gang would sell the same slave three or four times over (inciting him to run away from each master with promises of money and freedom) and then murder him (to get rid of the only possible witness against them), while their "ultimate intentions" were "on a very extended scale, having no less an object in view than raising the blacks against the whites, taking possession of, and plundering New Orleans, and making themselves possessors of the territory."[20] This specifically racial criminality, predicated on slave rebelliousness, is reiterated in *Tom Sawyer,* where the vengeful half-breed Injun Joe's buried treasure is said to have been the booty of Murel's Gang. The dim, dark fairy tales of Twain's boyhood are revealed, in the context of the Indian "Thuggee," to be just that, dreams as dim and dark as the nightmare of black revenge in "Which Was It?"

If we continue to pursue the notion that criminality marks an occult, racialized connection between Twain's Oriental present and his American past, then the paradigmatic episode establishing the occult mode in *Following the Equator* is his recounting of the beating of a native servant that he witnesses at his hotel on his first night in Bombay. The hotel is full of "dark native servants," all looking as though "dressed for a part in the Arabian Nights," "turbaned, and fez'd and embroidered, cap'd, and barefooted, and cotton-clad" (*FE*, 348). A white man, "a burly German," dissatisfied in some way with one of the natives, gives him a "brisk cuff on the jaw," which, Twain notes, the native took with "meekness," showing no apparent resentment (*FE*, 351). The sight triggers the return of a long series of repressed memories, again of his boyhood in the antebellum South: "I had not seen the like of this for fifty years. It carried me back to my boyhood, and flashed upon me the forgotten fact that this was the *usual* way of explaining one's desires to a slave. I was able to remember that the method seemed right and natural to me in those days, I being born to it and unaware that elsewhere there were other methods; but I was also able to remember that those unresented cuffings made me sorry for the victim and ashamed for the punisher" (*FE*, 351).

The punisher is none other than Clemens's father. Here, rather than demonize the father, as Twain does in the mulatto sketches in order, fundamentally, to reject his own past, he cultivates the more forgiving cultural relativism induced by the "elsewhere" of travel. Continuing his environmental line of argument regarding his own warped, childhood sense of what seemed "right and natural," he explains that his father was "a refined and kindly gentleman, very grave . . . and upright," who rarely laid a hand on his family; however, he "had passed his life among the slaves from the cradle up, and his cuffings proceeded from the custom of the time, not from his nature" (*FE*, 352). The father and son share the same flawed birthright, "the custom of the time," which the son unequivocally rejects as an adult, and yet which enables his identification with his father and his past.

Why are the sins of the Southern father viewed so sympathetically in this travelogue? More than simply the comparative cultural perspective or the relativism of actual travel, it is the occult mode of travel that makes the difference here. Twain concludes his long meditation on the punishment of natives and slaves by saluting the thrill of mental travel, of space-time travel: "It is curious—the space-annihilating power of thought. For just one second, all that goes to make the *me* in me was in a Missourian village, on the other side of the globe, vividly seeing again these forgotten pictures of fifty years ago, and wholly unconscious of all things but just those; and in the next second I was back in Bombay, and that kneeling native's smitten cheek was not done tingling yet! Back to boyhood—fifty years; back to age again, another fifty; and in a flight equal to the circumference of the globe— all in two seconds by the watch!" (*FE*, 352). The sheer exuberance of this representation of the experience of occult travel nearly outweighs the pain, and the implied condemnation, of the specific triggering event, the beating of the native. There is also a hint of the kind of Benjaminian cessation of happening that we have already seen in Pauline Hopkins's use of occult time, although the messianic or redemptive strains are quite muted here. Indeed, we might say that such time traveling enables both a recovery of the past, steeped in conflict and guilt as well as dreamy nostalgia, and a retreat from it. It is precisely the oscillation from the dream vision of the Missouri village, itself a source of both pleasure and anxiety, to the reality of Bombay, itself divided between both the exoticism and the otherness of the racialized Orient, that enacts the central rhythm of *Following the Equator*: the movement, alternately reassuring and unsettling, between U.S. race slavery and global imperialism, both social structures that Twain condemns absolutely even as they bring into focus ambivalent desires (simultaneous attraction and repulsion for the Other and for the father).

Of the racial practices that connect these institutions, Twain focuses, as we have seen, on the role of custom in deforming the master as well as the slave and, by implication, the colonizer as well as the colonized. Even some of the book's best-known, most-overt anti-imperialism appeals, ironically, to the "law of custom" as the justification for the "laying on" of European civilization around the world: "Dear me, robbery by European nations of each other's territories has never been a sin. . . . All the territorial possessions of all the political establishments in the earth—including America, of course— consist of pilferings from other people's wash. . . . In Europe and Asia and Africa every acre of ground has been stolen several millions of times. A crime persevered in a thousand centuries ceases to be a crime, and becomes a virtue. This is the law of custom, and custom supersedes all other forms of law" (*FE*, 623–24). We are now in a global version of the world of *Pudd'nhead Wilson*, where the "custom" of territorial robbery becomes analogous to the practice of racial classification, defined in the novel as a "fiction of law and custom." The question of racial grouping by skin color forges a final, important relation between Twain's antebellum past and the imperial present.

The Orientalizing of blackness throughout *Following the Equator* does not go much beyond a conventional exoticizing of difference—until Twain constructs a comparative vision of white and black complexions. In India, struck once again by the sight of native costume and color, Twain muses on the comparative disadvantage of "Christian" clothing and white skin: "Where dark complexions are massed, they make the whites look bleached-out, unwholesome, and sometimes frankly ghastly. I could notice this as a boy, down South in the slavery days before the war" (*FE*, 381). Then, in a classic moment of occult travel, Twain looks outside his window in London, where he is writing the book, and compares the white passersby with the picture in his mind of "the splendid black satin skin of the South African Zu-lus of Durban" ("I can see those Zulus yet") (*FE*, 381). The result is a list of the gradations of whiteness, complete with cartoon-like illustrations of various deformed-looking white faces, entitled "The Passers-By," that comes close to parodying the racial classifications of degrees of blackness that were standard throughout most of the colonial world, from Latin America to South Africa—almost everywhere, in fact, except in the United States. Ranging from "complexion, new parchment" and "old parchment," to "grayish skin, with purple areas" and "whitey-gray," to "ghastly white," and, finally, to "unwholesome fish-belly skin" (shades of Pap Finn's fish-belly white?), the list of the "tint which we miscall white" brings to mind nothing so much as the terms for fractional degrees of racial mixture, which Twain satirizes in his description of the French colony of Mauritius, the very place, we remember, whose variety of "nationalities and complexions" he also so admired (*FE*, 382–83, 617). "The majority [of the population] is East Indian; then mongrels; then negroes . . . ; then French; then English. There was an American, but he is dead or mislaid. The mongrels are the result of all kinds of mixtures; black and white, mulatto and white, octoroon and white. And so there is every shade of complexion" (*FE*, 620). The passage concludes with another list of skin colors, this one the mirror image of the white passersby, ranging from "ebony" and "horse-chestnut," to "molasses-candy," and ending, finally, with "fish-belly white—this latter the leprous complexion frequent with the Anglo-Saxon long resident in tropical cli-mates" (*FE*, 620). The repetition of "fish-belly white," Twain's immortal term of disgust for the abusive, poor-white Pap Finn, forges the final oc-cult link between the antebellum South and the imperial Orient. The logic of U.S. racial division, based on the one-drop rule and, therefore, assum-ing degrees of blackness only (white is a "pure" category), is exploded within the context of colonial race relations, where nation competes and blurs with race and whiteness is made to appear alien, defamiliarized by the "massed dark complexion of the public."

TRAVELING THE EMPIRE — WITHIN

If, in *Following the Equator,* Twain moved away from the notion of blackness as hidden taint, so central to the tragic-mulatto plot, he returned to that vision, with a different, spiritualist-inflected angle, in the long, unfinished "Three Thousand Years among the Microbes," written in 1905, just before the end of yet another imperial conflict, the Japanese defeat of Czarist Russia. Narrated by the human subject of a failed experiment who has been transformed into a microbe, specifically a cholera germ, "infesting" the blood of a "tramp" named Blitzowski—a Hungarian immigrant!—this bizarre travel narrative catalogs the microbe's journey among the "swarming nations of germ-vermin" within the "planet" of the tramp's body ("TTYM," 435). Although it may seem strange to place this fantastic tale in the context of *Following the Equator,* it was on the trip narrated therein—in Sydney, to be precise—that Twain says he dreamed his "large" microbe dream: "That the vast worlds that we see twinkling millions of miles apart in the fields of space are the blood corpuscles in [God's] veins; and that we and the other creatures are the microbes that charge with multitudinous life the corpuscles" (*FE,* 132). This particular dream, which Twain had first recorded in his notebook in August 1884, when he was preparing *Huckleberry Finn* for publication, establishes a series of links between the microbe story and Twain's various narratives of travel and race relations. First, elaborating on the notion of the diseased, hidden self that constitutes one version of the racial unconscious for Twain, he stresses how unaware the microbes are that their planet ("their world, their globe, lord of their universe") is the "mouldering" body of an undesirable Hungarian tramp ("he was shipped to America by Hungary because Hungary was tired of him") and how they are themselves infecting his blood and tissue ("TTYM," 436, 504). Then, extending this notion of infinite regress into a further response to the increasing pressures of global imperialism, particularly the U.S. annexation of the Philippines in 1899 and the subsequent military occupation of the islands, he transforms all the microbic nations into thinly disguised versions of the world's empires and colonies, one "feeding on" another ("TTYM," 437), just as, as young Satan explains in *The Mysterious Stranger,* England has "swallowed" India and Europe is "swallowing" China.[21]

This homology represents a strategy of historical identification across time that we saw earlier in the fragments of the "Adam Family Papers," which were to have constructed from the biblical past a prophetic typology of contemporary world events (the Flood and the annexation of the Philippines, etc.). But, there, the possibilities for a fully diachronic view are foreclosed by the stalemate between theorizing historical time as progress or as repetition. It would take a different form to realize the potential of occult travel. Most pointedly and exuberantly, "Three Thousand Years among the Microbes" refashions the mode of occult travel in the dream work of *Following the Equator* by inverting the spiritualist notion of out-of-body travel: instead of multiple personalities or levels of consciousness inhabiting one mind, we get alternate worlds coexisting within the tramp's body. Moreover, this is a spiritualist's paradise, where alternate forms of life continue on after death. To the microbe narrator, who can see molecular activity invisible to the human eye, the "charnel house" of the tramp's body is full, not of death, but of life and motion: "With my microbe-eye I could see *every individual* of the whirling billions of *atoms* that *compose* the speck. . . . Many have wandered away and joined themselves to new plasmic forms, and are continuing their careers in the bodies of . . . other creatures. . . . And so our people here have no word to signify that either a person or his spirit is dead, in our sense of that term" ("TTYM," 447, 457). In part a reference to one of Twain's favorite objects of satire, Mary Baker Eddy's Christian Science ("Kitchen Science"), this spiritualist's fantasy alludes explicitly, the narrative acknowledges, to the work of "a man like Sir Oliver Lodge," the well-known British physicist and the original sponsor of the British Society for Psychical Research (SPR), of whom the microbe narrator asks rather sardonically, "What secret of Nature can be hidden from him?" ("TTYM," 447). As a member of the SPR's Committee on Physical Phenomena, Lodge conducted a series of experiments with the notorious medium Mrs. Piper, experiments designed in part to verify the phenomena of "psychic excursions" or "traveling clairvoyance," in which, the theory goes, a spirit from outside can enter the organism or the spirit from inside can go out—both of which Twain transforms into his own mode of occult travel in the microbe story.[22]

"Three Thousand Years among the Microbes" not only adapts the spiritualist psychic excursion but also inverts Twain's own dream plot by beginning with the narrator's having awakened into another existence, this one incorporating a mirror image of America, his former country, in the "Republic of Getrichquick": "Under its flag is the whole of Blitzowski's

stomach, which is the richest country, . . . the most prodigally and variously endowed with material resources in all the microbic world"
("TTYM," 442). Here, the dream frame clearly serves as a window on the
world rather than on the mind, as an avenue not so much to the individual
unconscious—as it is, for example, in the theory of the waking and dream
selves adumbrated in the "Print Shop" manuscript of *The Mysterious
Stranger*—as to the cultural unconscious of the late-nineteenth-century
world of empire.[23]

Parodying a variety of anti-immigrant sentiments, the microbe narrator, an "instantly naturalized" citizen, calls himself "Huck" ("an abbrevia-
tion of my American middle name, Huxley") but compensates for this for-
eignness through his microbic "patriotism," which "out-natived the natives
themselves": "I was become intensely, passionately, cholera-germanic; . . . I
was the germiest of the germy" ("TTYM," 435, 471). This assimilation does
not stop him from trading on his exoticism, entertaining his microbe family
with a program of "sentimental music" from the minstrel shows of his past
("I don't 'low no Coon to Fool roun' Me") ("TTYM," 462). In a further par-
ody of the nativist view of the immigrant as permanently alien, he straddles
the borders of his two worlds, constantly translating, linguistically, chronologically, and otherwise, between them, and amusing the microbic "boys"
(among them his friend the yellow-fever germ with an unpronounceable
name, which he "had to modify to Benjamin Franklin") with Old World stories of the "Cuban skirmish" and the "Jap-Russian War" ("TTYM," 448,
538–39). In Twain's larger satire, of course, the international aggressions of
the early twentieth century correspond to their mirror images in the "planet
Blitzowski": a particular focus is the Republic of Getrichquick, which ends
an era of "selfish isolation" with the "high and holy policy" of "Benevolent
Assimilation," in which a "collection of mud islets inhabited by harmless
bacilli" "was first ingeniously wrested from its owners, by help of the unsus-
picious owners themselves," then "purchased from its routed and dispos-
sessed foreign oppressors at a great price" ("TTYM," 443). Thus did Twain
articulate, in ostentatious disguise, "hooded if not masked," as Du Bois says
of the Klan, in this fantastic narrative of 1905, his by then well-known criticism of the ongoing U.S. intervention in the Philippines.

The spotlight on American imperialism in "Three Thousand Years
among the Microbes" raises a number of questions. One, to which I will return in my conclusion, is the problem of history in Twain's dream tales, always sufficiently submerged that they are generally misread as escapist, retreating from the world of reality. Another is the question raised by William

Gibson, the textual editor of *The Mysterious Stranger*, about the complete absence of the Spanish-American War from those stories, many of which are permeated by equally submerged allusions to world empires, past and present.[24] "Three Thousand Years among the Microbes" was written in May–June 1905, just as Twain was returning to further work on the last *Mysterious Stranger* manuscript, "No. 44, the Mysterious Stranger," or the "Print Shop" version, where he would add chapters burlesquing a minstrel show and satirizing both Mary Baker Eddy and imperial Russia—all of which material he had just included in some form in "Microbes," along with the long section on Getrichquick's Benevolent Assimilation of the archipelago of the Philippines. It is as though the two works, "Three Thousand Years among the Microbes" and *Mysterious Stranger*, are, like so many of Twain's later writings, intertwined, each partaking of the imaginative and cultural engagements of the other. Reading them together, along with several other contemporary, allied texts, as a kind of continuous work enables us to see the three, unfinished manuscripts of *The Mysterious Stranger* as an ensemble, if not a "coherent whole," joining what Henry Nash Smith calls the "Matter of Hannibal" to world empire at the turn of the century,[25] and moving toward a broad-ranging meditation on ethnic, religious, and nationalist violence throughout world history.

Written between 1897 and 1908, *The Mysterious Stranger* exists in at least four versions that survive in three manuscripts, all set either in antebellum Hannibal or in Austria during what Twain considers the Middle Ages (whether 1702 or 1490). The settings tend to blend together, in part all variants on the "Matter of Hannibal," as Henry Nash Smith long ago noted: the Austrian settings of the two longest manuscripts, "Chronicle of Young Satan" and "No. 44," are both initially invoked through identical dream openings, evocations of the same willed state of drowsy, partial consciousness that was always essential to Twain's literary representations of boyhood, whether in *Tom Sawyer, Huckleberry Finn,* or *Pudd'nhead Wilson:* "Austria was far from the world, and asleep, and our village . . . drowsed in peace in the deep privacy of a hilly and woodsy solitude where news of the world hardly ever came to disturb its dreams" (*MS*, 35, 221).[26] This is also, of course, virtually the same dreamy sensibility that Twain cultivates in *Following the Equator*, not, however, as a mode of remote distancing, but as a mode of occult connection, a summoning up of the worlds of both his U.S. past and the global present. Similarly, the *Mysterious Stranger* settings add up to more than simply a series of images of Hannibal, for they signal a new link between U.S. race slavery of the past and global imperialism of the present: crudely put, Hannibal brings up the Negro Question, Austria brings up the Jewish Question, and Twain draws once again on the occult matter of spiritualism, embodying it in the array of psychic powers attributed to Satan, the "spirit control" (in the parlance of psychical research) of all *The Mysterious Stranger* stories, in order to bring together the two questions, and their separate times and places, in a vision of universal human enslavement. Indeed, as we will see, the *Mysterious Stranger* manuscripts, together with the several allied texts, forge a matrix of associations: between the "mild domestic slavery" of Hannibal and the more brutal racisms of turn-of-the-century empire; between the ancient bondage of the Jews and the contemporary enslavement of blacks, particularly African Americans; between race and the occult.[27] Finally, like so much of the history permeating Twain's late dream writing, all the contexts listed above are articulated, not directly or explicitly, but in a fragmented, associative mode characteristic of the cultural life of stereotypes, racial and otherwise.

Twain began *The Mysterious Stranger* in Vienna in the winter of 1897, when anti-Semitism was reaching new extremes on the Continent, with both the notorious Dreyfus case in France (which made world headlines for more than ten years after Dreyfus was convicted of treason in 1894 and which Twain discussed frequently) and periodic attacks on Austrian Jews, scapegoats for the many political and nationalist conflicts between Austria and Hungary. The Austrian context, identified with the "Jewish Problem," clearly found its way into the first, and, some believe, most influential, of the *Mysterious Stranger* manuscripts, "Chronicle of Young Satan," a reworking of an earlier fragment set in the St. Petersburg of the 1840s, now transmuted into the Austrian village of Eseldorf, the site of the adventures of three young boys, their good and evil priests, and the stranger known both as Philip Traum and as Satan, after his uncle. Several textual scholars have noted that Twain derived his portrait of the evil priest, Father Adolf, from several of the Austrian political figures whom he lambasted, in part for their anti-Semitism, in "Stirring Times in Austria," an essay published in the March 1898 issue of *Harper's* magazine.[28]

But a far more substantive link between the Hannibal and the Austrian contexts, and, by extension, between the Negro and the Jewish Questions, emerges in a better-known companion article, "Concerning the Jews," written in the summer of 1898 in response to letters from Jewish readers alarmed by Twain's report of the persecution of Austrian Jews, and published in the September 1899 issue of *Harper's*.[29] What Twain called "the Jew article," and what I see as one of the allied texts of *The Mysterious Stranger*, invokes Satan as a figure of the persecuted Jew.[30] The connection would, of course, have been ready-made in the nineteenth century, given the long tradition of condemning the Jews as the murderers of Christ. Twain, however, rings his own change on that connection, reclaiming both Satan and the Jews as victims of religious hatred. Beginning with the question of his own "race, color, caste, and creed prejudices," Twain asserts that he is not prejudiced against Satan and perhaps even "leans a little his way on account of his not having a fair show" ("CJ," 236). As a persecuted innocent, Satan explicitly raises the context of the Dreyfus case. Condemned by "all religions" without having presented his "side" or his "case," he provides the "precedent" for the condemnation of Dreyfus ("CJ," 236)—whom Twain elsewhere consistently defended as an "innocent man," "a persecuted and unoffending man."[31] If Satan is here virtually identified as a Jew, at the end of the essay the Jew—meaning, Twain specifies, "both a religion and a race"—becomes an analogue for Satan ("CJ," 237). Characterizing the eternal race prejudice against the Jew as rooted in his being a "foreigner in the German sense—stranger," Twain notes that "even the angels dislike a foreigner": "You will always be by ways and habits and predilections substantially strangers—foreigners—wherever you are, and that will probably keep the race prejudice against you alive. But you were the favorites of Heaven originally" ("CJ," 248).

As if this were not enough to re-create the Jew in the image of Twain's own fallen angel and stranger, Satan, Twain concludes the essay with an extravagant, world-historical vision of Jewish immortality that sounds for all the world like the cosmic displays of Satan's own immortal mind in several versions of *The Mysterious Stranger* (e.g., the theatrical "History of the Progress of the Human Race" from the Egyptian, Greek, and Roman wars to the present, from Cain and Abel to Queen Victoria, in the "Chronicle of Young Satan" and the "Assembly of the Dead," a procession of skeletons going backward in time, each labeled with name, date, and major accomplishments, in "No. 44" [*MS*, 134, 400]): "The Egyptian, the Babylonian, and the Persian rose, filled the planet with sound and splendor, then faded to dream-stuff and passed away; the Greek and the Roman followed, and made a vast noise, and they are gone. . . . The Jew saw them all, beat them all, and is now what he always was, exhibiting no . . . infirmities of age, . . . no dulling of his alert and aggressive mind. All things are mortal but the Jew; all other forces pass, but he remains. What is the secret of his immortality?" ("CJ," 249). If on one level this tribute to the Jews inadvertently trades on the anti-Semite's stereotypical image of the successful Jew, still

Twain's "Jew article" was a powerful enough defense to elicit attempts in Germany, from his death in 1910 through the Nazi era, to prove that he was a Jew, "Salamon Clemens."[32]

Twain's procession of the living dead of history, his theatrical spectacle consisting of blood, battles, and the Missing Link, may seem a fantastic invention, perhaps even sui generis, but it must surely belong as well to the tradition of historical pageantry and the popular-history movements that characterize the culture of the racial occult in the early twentieth century. Like Pauline Hopkins's mystical pageant of royal Ethiopian and Old Testament figures, and even more like her clairvoyant images of the past under American slavery that flash up in "modern" Ethiopia, Twain's occult performances return us with characteristic satiric force to the world of the twentieth century. During the years of writing *The Mysterious Stranger* under the pressure of world events—the "despotisms and aristocracies and chattel slaveries, and military slaveries, and religious slaveries, . . . all about the globe"—the Jewish Question came, ironically, even closer to home, to Hannibal itself.[33] In Twain's autobiographical dictations for March 1906, we recall, he moved from discussions of the U.S. military occupation of the Philippines to childhood memories of the Levin boys, "the first Jews" he had ever seen. The rest of the entry suggests how Hannibal's Jews were linked in Twain's imagination, first, and most directly, to U.S. race slavery and, second, although far less explicitly, to his meditation on universal human enslavement in the *Mysterious Stranger* stories. Of those "first Jews," he says: "To my fancy they were clothed invisibly in the damp and cobwebby mold of antiquity. They carried me back to Egypt, and in imagination I moved among the Pharaohs. . . . The name of the boys was Levin. We had a collective name for them. . . . We called them Twenty-two—and even when the joke was old and had been worn threadbare we always followed it with the explanation, to make sure that it would be understood, 'Twice Levin—twenty-two.'"[34] To locate these Jews, with their special aura of biblical enslavement, in the midst of Hannibal, "a slave-holding community," as Twain calls it elsewhere in the autobiography, that is, in the heart of the antebellum South, is to gesture toward the identification between the pharaonic bondage of the Israelites and U.S. chattel slavery that is characteristic of the nineteenth-century American racial imagination, both black and white.[35] A number of narratives, mythical and historical, were used, especially in the elaboration of slave identity, to bring into focus the black-Jewish parallel: biblical tales of cooperation between blacks and Jews and the stories of Solomon, the Queen of Sheba, and the Exodus, in particular the heroic figure of Moses.[36] But, if the analogue in most abolitionist and postbellum African American writing was to the deliverance of the Jews from Egypt, for Twain the identification between Jewishness and blackness focused specifically on the fact of enslavement itself.

This is the analogical or allegorical association made in two nearly identical stories, written during the late 1890s but set in the 1840s, in which a young Jew rescues a slave girl who has been won in a poker game by a notorious gambler and is to be sold away, not from her family, but from her white mistress. In both "Newhouse's Jew Story" and "Randall's Jew Story," the slave girl is beautiful and nearly white, maid and mistress are as close as sisters, and the Jew's defeat of the gambler in a duel marks him as "a man." The Jew's story is, thus, expressed through a series of racial stereotypes by a frame narrator whose stated intention is to tell a tale of one Jew that explains why the narrator, himself once a Jew "hater," can no longer tolerate such prejudice.[37] Like the Levin boys entry, these stories mobilize a number of ethnic and racial stereotypes of both Jewishness and blackness in the service of rejecting the body of those stereotypes.

All Twain's Jew stories, then, including the Levin boys entry, forge a partially articulated connection between anti-Semitism and race slavery. This is also how the Jewish Question enters *The Mysterious Stranger:* through indirection and analogy, as Henry Nash Smith acknowledged in his tentative suggestion that Satan's name of "Quarant-quatre or Forty-four" (in both "Schoolhouse Hill," actually set in Hannibal, and "No. 44, the Mysterious Stranger") may derive from extending the Levin joke to twice twenty-two.[38] But the Satan-as-Jew analogue need not rely only on Smith's ingenious numerical argument or only on the Satan-Dreyfus figure of "Concerning the Jews." The *Mysterious Stranger* manuscripts themselves, as well as the working notes, provide a series of equally suggestive, equally tentative allusions to a black-Jewish association, one that ultimately crosses or intersects with the occult as that specific ethnic pairing is generalized into the work's universal vision of human enslavement to what throughout his late writings Twain sardonically calls the "Moral Sense," God, and history.

Although, or perhaps because, Satan is endowed with virtually every psychic power ever investigated by spiritualists, from clairvoyance and telepathy, to the mediumistic ability to summon the spirits of the dead, he is the stranger, misunderstood and feared by most human authorities, the priests in particular. As the stranger, he is both exoticized (by the boys he befriends) and outcast (by the rest)—the classic division of attraction toward and repulsion from the Other. Twain's working notes make Satan

almost more of an explicit figure of otherness than the *Mysterious Stranger*
stories themselves do, persistently associating him with "disease-
germs"—"he is to find the diseases & tortures & microbes"—in a fantasy
that found expression in "Three Thousand Years among the Microbes"
(*MS*, 416, 421). At the same time, these notes touch on numerous references to Jews. Planning "Chronicle of Young Satan" while he lived in Vienna, Twain listed the following in close proximity: a set of apparently parallel settings ("Village," "Castle on heights," "Ghetto, Jew J. Goldschmidt,
I. Nussbaum," "New Jerusalem"); Satan's decline ("disease invades him,
. . . he is persecuted, but remains a heretic; so they torture him, convict
him, damn him & burn him"); and, finally, "Stoning the Jews. (passing remark)" (*MS*, 418, 421). Without making too much of too little evidence, I
would suggest that the various faces of Twain's Satan, a long-standing icon
of his imagination, reflect what Sander Gilman calls "the protean nature of
stereotypes," the tendency of such major categories of difference as *race*,
sexuality, and *pathology* to become associated, to stand in for one another,
even when "their association demands a suspension of common sense."[39]
Thus, Satan, the fallen angel, is the Jew, at once the persecuted, the diseased, and the chosen, just as, we will see, as No. 44 he transforms himself
into the specter of a black slave playing both Bones and Banjo in a minstrel
show.[40] In the context of this genealogy, one of the most striking of Twain's
various lists of ideas for *The Mysterious Stranger* starts with "Old Ship of
Zion" and moves to "Mesmerism, Nigger Minstrels, Spirit rappings, Mate-
rializing . . ." (*MS*, 436).

Thus, Satan becomes Twain's medium, his conduit to the racial spirits
haunting both his present and his past. It is telling that "Schoolhouse Hill,"
the only manuscript set in Hannibal, and the only one to address directly the
question of U.S. slavery, is also explicitly steeped in the occult. A village
among whose citizens are a "'nigger' trader" and a newly converted spiritualist, this fictionalized Hannibal provides the setting for the manuscript
described by the textual editor William M. Gibson as "apparently . . . both
an essay in the correction of ideas and a comedy set in the world of Tom
Sawyer and Huck Finn, whose boy-hero would like to reform and save it."
Gibson also speculates that there is even a possible Jewish connection in this
story of the village that needs reforming. In his notebook for June and July
1897, Gibson says, Twain wrote "some notes for a 'New Huck Finn' in
which the 'Lev'n' boys were to be suspiciously regarded by the town."[41]
Then Twain has, "Instead of 11, call them 9 (Nein) and 18" (*MS*, 473). This
protean black-Jewish association, locating the Jewish Question in the world

of Hannibal, where the Negro Question was paramount, was never fully re-
alized, but, in the story as Twain wrote it, not only is "Marse" Oliver Hotch-
kiss, the slaveowning head of the household in which young "Forty-four"
appears (and a figure of the Clemens brother Orion), a sometime spiritualist ("the latest thing in religions was the Fox-girl Rochester rappings; so
he was a Spiritualist for the present"), but also during a snowstorm he
stages a séance to materialize the spirit of the lost Forty-four during which
"slave-State etiquette" is breached: as a newly converted abolitionist, he
insists that all around the table—including the two slaves who are present—hold hands (*MS*, 191, 205). This promising foray into the racial occult breaks off just as the slaves Aunt Rachel and Uncle Jeff are arguing
with Marse Oliver about what he calls their "ignorant prejudice" against
devils like Forty-four (*MS*, 219).

In the last *Mysterious Stranger* manuscript, however, the cross between
matters racial and spiritual becomes for Twain a means of extended identification with the enslavement and suffering of African Americans. Near the
end of "No. 44," in yet one more exhibition of 44's supernatural powers, he
materializes as a "black man," "Cunnel Bludso's nigger fum Souf C'yarlina,"
and performs "'th'ee hund'd en fifty year ahead o' time'" the traditional song
and dance of the minstrel show (*MS*, 355). Simultaneously a figure of humor
and pathos, he plays the banjo and sings "Buffalo Gals" ("in a sort of bastard
English"), addresses the young boy narrator as "honey," and, finally, sings
"Swanee River" (in "a sweet voice, such a divine voice") (*MS*, 354–55): "And
so on, verse after verse, sketching his humble lost home, . . . and the black
faces that had been dear to him, and which he would look upon no more—
and by the magic of it that uncouth figure lost its uncouthness and became
lovely like the song, . . . whereas a silken dress and a white face and white
graces would have profaned it, and cheapened its noble pathos" (*MS*, 356).

The narrator concludes by stressing the spiritualist side of this minstrel
vision. Closing his eyes to try to picture that lost home, he opens them,
suddenly to find himself right there, in front of a log cabin in "a mellow summer twilight," only to feel the vision "fading, fading, . . . like a dream," as
his room and furniture dimly reappear, "spectrally, with the perishing home
showing vaguely, through it, as through a veil" (*MS*, 356). We do not really
need the reminder of Du Boisean double consciousness, with its similarly
racialized invocation of the veil, to affirm the meaning of Twain's location in
the racial occult here. For, in the very next chapter, he himself makes explicit
the significance of the minstrel-show vision with the plea of the narrator's
duplicate, his "dream-creature," named appropriately Emil Schwarz,

linking blackness and Jewishness in the German, to "free me from . . . these bonds of flesh" (*MS*, 369). Asserting that, like other dream spirits, "we do not know time, we do not know space"—"we live, and love, and labor, and enjoy, fifty years in an hour, while you are sleeping, snoring, repairing your crazy tissues"—he pleads with the narrator to "be my friend and brother" and "take away this rotting flesh and set my spirit free!" (*MS*, 370): "Oh, here I am a servant!—I who never served before; here I am a slave—slave among little mean kings and emperors made of clothes, the kings and emperors slaves themselves, to mud-built carrion that are *their* slaves!" (*MS*, 369). This is the work's final vision of universal human enslavement, containing and collapsing within it all the historically specific nationalist, religious, and ethnic persecutions encompassed by *The Mysterious Stranger*, from the medieval witch-hunt, to the French Revolution, to European missionary and colonial violence in China and India.

PROVISIONAL OUTCOMES

What is at stake in paying so much critical attention to a body of writing that Mark Twain never completed? And why focus particularly on the presence in this collection of fragments of a history of race and colonial relations that is so easy to miss? Despite the aspersions cast on Twain's personal inability to confront or acknowledge issues of slavery, miscegenation, and race, what he and his late writings have to teach us is not idiosyncratic to him. Rather, in both their generic and their formal "messiness"—the critical and aesthetic challenges that they pose—these texts are, strange to say, characteristic of much race literature of the period. From Du Bois's *Souls of Black Folk*, to black women's sentimental fiction, to the historical romances of Thomas Dixon and others, these works present Twainian problems of hybrid, or mixed, generic boundaries: Are they art or propaganda? Turn the question around into Du Bois's famous, if contested, answer: "All Art is propaganda."[42] We have seen how these texts engage document and vision, sometimes discrepantly, alternating, as Twain's do, between fictional and factual registers, the fictive elements often competing with the network of allusions to and representations of contemporary events and debates. As in Twain's, the history in many of the texts tends, thus, to be problematic, either awkwardly incorporated into the fictional plot, or partially submerged, hyperinvisible, in the form of thinly disguised references to actual people and events, or else, at the other extreme, too dominant, leading the work to be considered propaganda, not art. Perhaps we might even say that the generic and historical problems in the literature are actually symptoms of the race problem itself: the struggle to produce alternative racial discourses testifies to the pervasiveness of nineteenth-century racist ideology and its very capacious rhetorics. Finally, the very aesthetic difficulties that have led so many readers to dismiss both Twain's late writings (as products of personal despair) and much late-nineteenth-century race literature (as propaganda) place him at or near the very center of the literary effort to represent the race question at this time—exactly where we always knew Mark Twain belongs.

CHAPTER FIVE

W. E. B. Du Bois
and Occult History

"It is a dream come true," Du Bois writes in the preface to Herbert Aptheker's *A Documentary History of the Negro People in the United States* (1951), "to have the history of the Negro in America pursued in scientific documentary form."[1] To hear Du Bois speak in one breath of dream, science, and history may sound contradictory. Yet no one contributed more to that paradoxical intellectual project than he, working, however unexpectedly, as a race melodramatist in what I call *occult history*. The term is meant to convey the paradoxes of Du Bois's lifelong struggle to reconfigure the social-scientific study of the "Negro Problem" into what he called in 1915 "a complete history of the Negro peoples" (*N*, vi). In so doing, Du Bois had to be both historian and history maker (to paraphrase Herbert Aptheker), for, as he put it in 1939, "few today are interested in Negro history because they feel the matter already settled: the Negro has no history."[2] Such a project in such a context is inherently a work of activist scholarship.

The ubiquitous term *Negro Problem*, cited repeatedly in the derogatory language of social science, becomes, as we saw in chapter 1, a call to arms, seized on by Du Bois for numerous reformulations, only the best known of which is his rejoinder at the opening of *The Souls of Black Folk*: "How does it feel to be a problem?" The very question gestures toward the grounds of its solutions, by bridging the divide between those who study feelings and their expressions (humanists and artists) and those for whom social problems define the area of study (social scientists). Bringing together apparently antagonistic interests in race consciousness, racial mysticism, and racial science, occult history bridges the variety of disciplines, knowledge fields, and structures of feeling necessary at that moment to "unveil" the hidden histories of "the problem of the color-line." To rediscover the occluded past of "a race concept" was a project of prophetic unveiling meant simultaneously to redress the present and to reimagine the future.

It may surprise some to hear Du Bois speak so affirmatively of scientific history so late in his life when he is supposed, after the turning point of the 1910 Atlanta riots, to have abandoned academics and research for politics and the editorship of *The Crisis*. But Du Bois represents the culmination of my study of turn-of-the-century race melodramas precisely because he embodies so many of its contexts and contradictions. In his multiple autobiographies, Du Bois fashions himself both as historian and as history maker, collapsing the history of the race and the self, for example, in *Dusk of Dawn*, characteristically subtitled *An Essay toward an Autobiography of a Race Concept*. Alternatively, he sometimes presents himself, not as a race representative, but as sui generis, from the brilliant *isolato* of Great Barrington to the scholarly lone ranger, conducting all his own survey work in *The Philadelphia Negro*.[3]

Undoubtedly the best-known Du Bois self-fashioning, however, is that of the divide that he constructs between the social scientist and the poet-activist, located at the juncture when "my work in Atlanta and my dream of the settlement of the Negro problem by science faded" (*DD*, 94; *A*, 253). The turning point reappears, framed in virtually the same before-and-after terms, in both *Dusk of Dawn* (1940) and the *Autobiography* (1968). "In 1905," Du Bois says, "I was still a teacher at Atlanta University and was in my imagination a scientist, and neither a leader nor an agitator," but soon, he notes with some ambivalence, "my career as a scientist was to be swallowed up in my role as master of propaganda" (*DD*, 94; *A*, 236). This split repeatedly appears in his work, as he produces and reproduces the divide, locating it at different temporal junctures, in his various autobiographies. Both the pattern of self-citation, in which Du Bois quotes his own earlier accounts of this signature event, and the heightened language of polarities and incommensurable alternatives with which he frames those accounts reflect the Du Boisean will to melodramatic style that I will explore later in this chapter.

In another episode that is also repeated, almost verbatim, in the two autobiographical works, Du Bois pinpoints precisely the moment and place of rupture. This is the famous account of the Sam Hose lynching outside Atlanta in April 1899, which opens with the striking metaphor of a "red ray": "At the very time when my studies were most successful, there cut across this plan which I had as a scientist, a red ray which could not be ignored." The rest is a brief, understated account of the Georgia Negro Sam Hose's arrest; of Du Bois's effort to protest, by writing "a careful and reasoned statement concerning the evident facts"; and, finally, of the lynching of Sam Hose and the exhibition of his knuckles in a grocery store on Mitchell Street in Atlanta. The narrative ultimately comes to two conclusions: "First, one could not be a calm, cool, and detached scientist while Negroes were lynched, murdered and starved; and secondly, there was no such definite demand for scientific work of the sort that I was doing as I had confidently assumed would be easily forthcoming" (*DD*, 67–68; *A*, 221–22). Following Du Bois's own lead, the historian Wilson J. Moses asks, "Can Du Bois the social scientist be reconciled with Du Bois the poet and prophet of race?"[4] Many critics and readers have said no, echoing Du Bois's tale of reluctant derailing, or fashioning it into a narrative of enlightenment.[5]

A few, however, do not take Du Bois at his word. Thomas Holt observes simply that, despite Du Bois's celebrated account of turning aside from his scholarly work, he did not, in fact, turn away from his confrontation with race.[6] In his review of Du Bois's magisterial history *Black Reconstruction in America* (published in 1935, long after Du Bois had left the academy), Charles H. Wesley, a scholar of black history and fraternalism, twins the professional historian with the poet of race, considering the book to be the poetic work of a "lyric historian."[7] Even in Du Bois's own accounts, the divide in his career becomes a moving target. Taking its inspiration from Holt and Wesley (among others), and not least from the force of Du Bois's own repeated disavowals, this chapter was inspired by a desire to rethink the traditional periodization of Du Bois studies, divided between the early years of education and research in the social sciences and the mature devotion to art and activism.[8] Rather than think in terms of before and after, I argue that Du Bois's work displays a lifelong engagement with the limits and possibilities of historicizing race consciousness itself, an engagement based on a shifting set of turning points rather than a single divide.

As a historian, Du Bois fits in readily with other nineteenth-century figures, who present themselves as mediators between science and art but who, according to Hayden White, assume too much for the divide that they claim to bridge. When Du Bois bemoans the break that he himself repeatedly reproduces, that between art and propaganda, science and politics, we might think of him as one of White's modernist historians, challenging the epistemological status of the science-art divide.[9] These questions suggest the pressures, social and historical, surrounding the concept of the racial occult: a heuristic and a mixed form as well as a set of historical and social practices that characterize both Du Bois's experimental writings and his repeated reconstructions of the symbolic divide that is eroded by the very sweep of his life's work.

To think of Du Bois as an occult historiographer may be the way to begin redressing this split. *Occult history* captures the contradictions inherent in Du Bois's history of the race concept: each of the two component terms encompasses both a traditional or emerging knowledge field and an aesthetic, or what Raymond Williams calls *a structure of feeling*. Both terms, *occult* and *history*, represent both sides of the equation: at the turn of the century, both those who studied history and those who investigated the occult laid claim—on different and, apparently, paradoxical grounds—both to scientific standing and to mystical authority. Du Boisean occult history holds in tension the oppositions between a rational empiricism and a mystical faith in unseen correspondences between the darker peoples of the world, defined sometimes socioculturally, and sometimes geographically, but most often historically. "What is Africa to me?" asks Du Bois (quoting Countee Cullen), in one of the most often-quoted lines of *Dusk of Dawn.* "One thing is sure": his ancestors and their descendants have had "a common history; have suffered a common disaster and have one long memory" (*DD,* 116–17). In tapping that memory, Du Boisean occult history synthesizes most of the major figures and discourses of the contemporary race melodramas discussed in this book, including Hopkins's maternal melodramas of mystical, race psychologizing and racial sciences, Griggs's and Dixon's secret societies, Twain's spiritualist traveling on the Black Belt, and, most important, all these authors' collective uses of melodrama as a historiographic mode. A quasi-mystical, quasi-scientific knowledge field, Du Boisean occult history developed through the struggle to move between and among the modes of science, activism, art, and mysticism. It derives simultaneously from the refutation of racial science, the practice of scientific history, and the production of an emerging mystical history of a race consciousness that is pan-racial, transnational, and metahistorical. In historicizing race consciousness, Du Bois sought to reveal the ideological and geopolitical contours of racial thinking.

Du Bois's histories of race consciousness skirt the preserve of romantic Afrocentrism, especially, as we will see, in his research on the race and civilization of ancient Egypt. But Du Bois's is not the mystical "pseudo-history"—"occult, irrational, and fantastic"—that the historian Stephen Howe lambasts in his critique of Afrocentrism.[10] Nor is the Du Boisean mysticism that most interests me the transcendent, ahistorical phenomenon commonly derived from the recurrent references in *The Souls of Black Folk* to second sight, the veil, and, most infamously, double consciousness. Rather, through the medium of occult history, Du Bois demonstrates the uses of mysticism in historical research and writing. Most prominently, only the mystical language of "souls" and "spiritual strivings" can conjure fully the long, historical development of the Negro in America and beyond. Of the four fields for future study of the Negro (including historical, statistical, and anthropological methods) that Du Bois outlined in "The Study of the Negro Problems" (his 1897 address to the American Academy of Political and Social Sciences, which may be seen as one possible ur-text of his lifelong research program—if, indeed, there could be said to be *one*), the last one, "sociological interpretation," studies "those finer manifestations of social life which history can but mention and which statistics can not count." In short, to make legible the expressions of "a distinct social mind" requires something more than science alone—something akin to the hybrid of magic and science in the occult ("SNP," 81–83).

The results of such an occult history appear throughout Du Bois's writings, embracing all genres, as we will see, from *The Philadelphia Negro* (1899), the multivalent study of a black group defined at once as a community, built of familial, social, and economic institutions, and as a folk, "palpitating" and "striving," to *Darkwater* (1920) and its clairvoyant historian and seer, whose analysis of world imperialism makes legible both "The Souls of White Folk" (chapter 2) and "The Hands of Ethiopia" (chapter 3). Thus, as it did for Pauline Hopkins and Mark Twain, occultism represented for Du Bois less a singular, mystical belief system than a set of knowledge fields, institutions, and social movements that could posit hidden—occulted—correspondences uniting, or dividing, the peoples on the global color line. What specific kinds of occultism provide the cultural context for Du Bois? Rather than the syncretic Africanist or Afro-Caribbean blend that some might expect, it is the protean Western occult tradition, traveling (as we saw in chapter 1) the international circuits of pseudosecret brotherhoods and revolutionary societies that are based on a variety of supposed ancient Egyptian, Indian, and Eastern wisdoms. Of the periodic waves of occult revivals, the most immediately relevant to Du Bois are the turn-of-the-century popular occultisms distinguished by their common racial valence.

Du Bois's place among such disreputable company may not be obvious, but a few preliminary connections should be suggestive. First, the context of German nationalism, of which Du Bois was so aware during his graduate study at Berlin, combined *Volk*-ish ideology and race history with less-recognized occult notions, borrowed from Theosophy, to produce both an antimodern revival of the lost wisdom and racial purity of the ancient Germans and the corresponding imagined community of a new pan-German empire. Second, the Theosophists were involved in desultory ways with the anti-imperial project that was so central to Du Bois's work: after Madame Blavatsky moved the headquarters of the Theosophical Society to India in 1879, she was frequently accused of, or praised for, participating in the fledgling Indian National Congress, and the Theosophist (and radical socialist) Annie Besant joined Du Bois at the 1911 Universal Races Congress. Equally problematically, the Theosophical movement also offered an extensive history of world civilizations, traced through the evolution of a series of "root races," marking the racist subtext that so many historians have noted in the popular occultisms of the imperial age.[11]

Third, and perhaps most unlikely, the Masonic connection is best established through Du Bois's presence in the black-popular-history project of the early twentieth century, led by the prominent Prince Hall Masons Arthur A. Schomburg and John E. Bruce, among others.[12] (Of these, Carter Woodson stands out as a major figure who was *not* a Mason.) The Freemasons have been known since their origins in seventeenth-century Scotland for their mystical ritual and symbology as well as for their international membership and, paradoxically, an association with revolutionary, Enlightenment ideals, but less so for their avid interest in recording Masonic history. British Masonry has a central historiographic body, a lodge dedicated to the preservation of materials related to the history of Masonry, local and national.[13] Many Lodges include among the Masonic degrees that of grand historian, and, as touched on briefly in chapter 1, it is as the grand historian of his New York lodge that Schomburg demonstrates the overlap between the black-popular-history project and Prince Hall Masonry of the 1910s and 1920s. During this period, the Masonic historical imperative was reinterpreted by African Americans to produce a global history of black peoples worldwide—precisely the kind of diasporic history of the peoples on the color line that Schomburg, Du Bois, et al. sought to produce. The legitimacy of black institutions, both black Masonry and the study of global black history, was, thus, keyed to both these coextensive imperatives.

If the modern occult revivals thus combined racial mysticism and race history with the internationalism and political activism for which Du Bois is so well-known, the study of the occult had, from its inception, always bridged, as Du Bois also sought to do, the separate spheres of magic and science. In the Renaissance, the occult arts and sciences (the terms themselves are indicative) sought to break down distinctions between "legitimate sciences" and "pseudosciences" (between, e.g., chemistry and mathematics, on the one hand, and alchemy and astrology, on the other) just as they crossed the magic-science divide. The historian Frances Yates quotes the seventeenth-century alchemist Robert Fludd explaining that, if good magic is condemned or driven underground, then "we take away all natural philosophy," that is, Yates says, all science.[14] Rosicrucianism—the occult movement that originated in seventeenth-century Germany and Bohemia with a series of tracts, widely circulated, on a secret brotherhood, putatively founded by a German mystic in the fourteenth century, dedicated to magical powers, scientific knowledge, and general social reform—influenced such important Renaissance mathematicians as John Dee and also provided key elements of Theosophic and Masonic symbology.

The fin de siècle popular occultisms under consideration here were all specifically marked both by racial mysticism and by racial science. Drawing on the sciences of race and of consciousness, the racial occult of modernity is characterized by the displacement of notions of race onto the structures of paranormal belief systems. Madame Blavatsky founded the Theosophical Society in 1875 as what she called a "spiritual Science" or "Science of magic," subsuming Darwinian evolution, she claimed, into a mysticism purportedly sympathetic rather than hostile to prevailing scientific theories.[15] The subtitle of her masterwork *The Secret Doctrine* (1888) proclaims the work to be a *Synthesis of Science, Religion, and Philosophy*. From the close identification of magic and science that had always characterized occultism emerged a parallel interest in secret brotherhoods and root knowledges, especially among such fraternal organizations as the Freemasons and the Rosicrucians, whose symbolism focused on the esoteric knowledge of "Egyptian mysteries."[16] American occultisms, mediated through the internationalist forms of mesmerism, Swedenborgianism, Theosophy, Freemasonry, and Rosicrucianism, were part of what some historians characterize as a renewed interest at the turn of the century in reconciling science and religion.[17]

The renaissance of scholarly interest in Hellenistic mystery cults intersected with the contributions of Egyptology, both popular and scholarly, to provide, as we know from Pauline Hopkins's work, a common basis for the opposing sides in debates over the racial origins of Western civilization.[18] The many Egypts of Du Bois's work also bridge separate spheres, adding up to a total greater than the sum of its parts: the archaeological Egypt of skull measurements and racial science; the historical Egypt of classical and later scholars (Herodotus, Volney); the black Egypt of African Americans, the ancient origin of Western civilization; the prophetic Egypt of biblical Ethiopianism; and, finally, the revolutionary (black) Masonic Egypt with its gendered identity derived from the Osiris-Isis myth (about which more later). Du Bois's many Egypts distinguish him from what Arthur A. Schomburg scathingly criticizes in his essay "The Negro Digs Up His Past" as the "Ethiopian counterpart" of the "blatant Caucasian racialist"—"the rash and rabid amateur who has glibly tried to prove half of the world's geniuses to have been Negroes and to trace the pedigree of nineteenth-century Americans from the Queen of Sheba."[19] In contrast to such one-dimensional, amateur history, Du Bois explores the multivalent uses of Egypt in "the history and sociology of the Negro race," as he subtitled his 1939 *Black Folk Then and Now*—and does so despite his confession in the preface: "I am no Egyptologist. That goes without saying" (*BF*, vii). Rather than simply digging up a black Egypt, Du Bois takes a metahistorical position, implicit in the subtitle of *Black Folk Then and Now*, a work philosophically guided by the "effort to ascertain and publish the verifiable history and social condition of the Negro race, according to the best scholarship of the world, regardless of race, nation or color" (*BF*, viii).

To articulate Du Bois's philosophy of history from the perspective of the racial occult will be the burden of this chapter. First, the major texts and contexts of Du Boisean occult history must be established. Constructing the context—the main figures, events, and locations essential to placing Du Bois as a historian in what I call *the culture of the occult* during the war decade, 1910–20—will itself form one locus of my argument. While so much is already known of Du Bois and World War I, my object is to trace the interplay among his major historiographic projects of the period and a variety of political and cultural phenomena, movements, and activisms, political, intellectual, and social, that are not generally associated yet form the basis of the culture of the occult at that moment. Of the set of Du Bois texts from the 1910s and 1920s that tell "the history of the development of the race concept" (*DD*, 97), the best-known, *Darkwater* (1920), is joined by two, perhaps less-familiar works: *The Negro* (1915), a world history of black people, tracking the diasporic and transnational histories of the Negro from ancient Africa (Egypt and Ethiopia) to contemporary New World black cultures (the Caribbean, Latin America, and the United States); and "The Star of Ethiopia" (1913), a "pageant of Negro history."[20] Grouping these texts as an

ensemble, rather than reading them generically (the usual approach), puts
Du Boisean historicism in a popular-cultural context quite different from
the elite intellectual confines in which it is generally placed, the culture of
the occult that flowered during the period of World War I, the long war
years of the early twentieth century.

In the United States, the war decade presented many contradictions—
epitomized by that between the violence of those who espoused nativism
and lynching and the pacifism of those, including some of the former,
who opposed involvement in the European war. (Griffith's *Birth of a Nation* embodies all such contradictions.) Equally striking is the increasing internationalism of public culture on the home front, embracing such disparate political and social movements and cultural formations as black
internationalism (including Du Bois's and Garvey's brands of Pan-
Africanism), the uses of political theater and pageantry on behalf of world
causes, and the popularization of black history. At the same time, in this era
of occult revivals and intensified fraternalism (the resurgence of the Klan in
the 1920s, the emergence of women's auxiliaries), a reinvigorated black
Freemasonry—known for mystical symbology, theatrical ritual, and community voluntarism but less for its historicism and international activism—
comes out of the lodges and into the streets and onto the pages of the press,
enlisting its ranks in the cause of race history. What all these movements
share is, as I hope to show, a racial consciousness at once mystical, historical, and political. Placing these disparate cultural formations and developments under the broad umbrella of the occult, and, ultimately, addressing
the political significance of the culture of the occult, constitutes the central
objective of the chapter.

Following this extended cultural and chronological mapping, I will
look closely at the pattern of strategic self-citation in Du Bois's work, focusing on a body of his sociological texts that are cited, reworked, and rein-
corporated in the autobiographies. These core passages repeatedly return
to and reformulate the inaugural intellectual project that he is supposed to
have abandoned: "put[ting] science into sociology" (*A*, 206) through the
study of his own racial group. As these citations are incorporated into different textual and disciplinary modes, they form, I will argue, a body of historiographic manifestos. Finally, the chapter will conclude with a look at
Darkwater as the Du Boisean race melodrama par excellence, the race melodrama of the culture of the occult in the war decade, especially revealing of
the possibilities and pressures—social, historical, and, above all, political—surrounding the concept of the occult for Du Bois.

THE DU BOISEAN OCCULT: TEXTS AND CONTEXTS

As far as the key texts are concerned, Du Bois's work in occult history emerges throughout his career in what should be thought of as an ensemble of paired works crossing autobiographical narratives with histories of the race. Extending chronologically from *The Negro* (1915) and *Darkwater* (1920), to *Black Folk Then and Now* (1939) and *Dusk of Dawn* (1940), and, finally, to *The Autobiography of W. E. B. Du Bois* (1968) and *The World and Africa* (1965), these texts constitute an experimental historiography in a variety of registers and modes (social science, history, fiction, autobiography, and prose essay). In contrast to the well-known genre-busting, autobiographical narratives (*Dusk of Dawn, Darkwater,* and the *Autobiography,* to which must be added, of course, *The Souls of Black Folk*), the others (*The Negro* and its expanded version, *Black Folk Then and Now,* as well as *The World and Africa*) are less familiar, surveys of diasporic history ranging from the (obligatory) Nile Valley and the (less common) Congo and Cape, to the "black United States," the West Indies, and "black Europe," to modern Africa and the future of "world democracy." Although these global historiographies of the Negro peoples of the world are unconventional, pioneering texts, they are not generally associated, as are the multigenre narratives, with Du Bois the "lyric historian." Yet, commenting on how "scholarly detachment and a hortatory posture" often coexist in Du Bois's writing, Adolph Reed lists as examples of texts that display both such poses *The Negro, Black Folk Then and Now,* and *The World and Africa.*[21] And, further, because Du Bois's historiographic work and his sociological work share a common base with his more lyrical social and cultural commentary, they ought to be read in tandem, pairing specifically the lyric anticolonialism of *Darkwater* with his "history of the Negro peoples," *The Negro,* as works of the war decade, the watershed that represents the culmination of the period under study.[22]

To complete the textual ensemble of the war decade, we must add to the lyric historicism of these works the theatrical race history of Du Bois's historical pageant "The Star of Ethiopia." Written and performed in the middle of the war decade, "The Star of Ethiopia" portrays, according to the pageant program, "the history of the Negro race and its work and sufferings and triumphs in the world" by combining "historic accuracy and symbolic truth." It was, Du Bois says in his last autobiography, one of two projects of the 1920s (the other, significantly, was the *Brownie's Book,* "a little magazine for Negro children") that he recalls with "infinite satisfaction," "most especially my single-handed production of the pageant 'The Star of Ethiopia' . . . , an attempt to put into dramatic form for the benefit of large masses of people, a history of the Negro race" (*A*, 270). "The Star of Ethiopia" clearly fits with and extends Du Bois's approach in *The Negro* and *Darkwater* to historicizing race consciousness.

What emerges from this cluster of texts, produced during the war decade and crossing the genres of history, drama, and autobiography, is a suggestive conflation of racial mysticism, global historiography, and Masonic Egyptology and symbology. To read the texts as an essential ensemble helps us see how Du Bois's different generic experiments should be read, not in isolation, producing Du Bois the historian or Du Bois the activist-dramatist, but rather as parts of overlapping projects. *The Negro* extends in global directions Du Bois's ongoing historical study of the Negro in America (*The Philadelphia Negro*, *The Negro American Family*, and his monographs published in the Atlanta University "Studies of the Negro Problems" series), drawing on the work of archaeologists, anthropologists, historians, and novelists to construct an unconventional transnational, pan-racial history of the peoples on the worldwide color line. "The Star of Ethiopia" stages this world history of the color line as a spectacle divided into six "episodes," each featuring a parade of historical figures dramatizing a different "gift of the Negro to the world." *Darkwater* incorporates global history with an explicit mysticism, traditionally read as primarily an aesthetic of the lyrical and the poetic, thus reinforcing and deepening the activism that Du Bois attributed (sometimes with and sometimes without question) to the practice of scientific history. Finally, *The Negro* shares with *Darkwater* a set of critical citations that outline Du Bois's lyric anticolonialism, ranging from a short poem praising Egypt, "the motherland of human culture," as "that starr'd Ethiop queen" to the Latin line (italicized in *Darkwater*, where it is attributed as a quotation from the Roman proconsul, but not in *The Negro*) that also frames his famous essay "The African Roots of War" (1915), "*Semper novi quid ex Africa!*" (*N*, 46, 242; *D*, 511, 520).

To read all three as companion texts, in the tradition of pairing the 1899 essay "The Conservation of Races" and *The Souls of Black Folk*, accentuates the pageantry of *The Negro*, the popular and scholarly ambitions of "The Star of Ethiopia," and the historicism of *Darkwater*. Reflecting these multiple identities, a full-page advertisement for *The Negro* that ran for several numbers of *The Crisis* in 1915 calls it "the authentic romance of the black man, . . . a history of him at once scholarly and eloquent."[23] At the very same time, Du Bois was touting the advantages of the dramatic arts for historical representation. "The Pageant is the thing," Du Bois commented in 1915, just as he was taking "The Star of Ethiopia" on the road.[24] In the "fabulous dramaturgy" of Du Bois's pageant, David Levering Lewis sees "the basics of an Afrocentric aesthetics and historiography—the sweeping interpretive claims [Du Bois] was just then inserting into the scholarship on which the forthcoming books *The Negro* and *The Gift of Black Folk* were based."[25] *Dark Princess*, Du Bois's 1928 historical romance, further develops the "historic accuracy and symbolic truth" of his pageantry with a messianic finale in the form of a pageant celebrating the birth of the "Messenger and Messiah to all the Darker Worlds."[26] And, of course, Du Bois would later (in the year of his seventieth birthday) write yet another version of his own life in the form of a historical pageant, *A Pageant in Seven Decades, 1878–1938*. Later still, he would again yoke his dramatic muse to the narrating of his life and subtitle his final autobiography *A Soliloquy on Viewing My Life from the Last Decade of Its First Century*.

The pageantry of pan-African history works its way into the autobiographical *Darkwater* in what we will see is another, more indirect type of self-citation, including but not limited to Du Bois's own "Star of Ethiopia." His "pageant of Negro history," featuring (according to the ads in *The Crisis*) "1000 actors, 53 musical numbers, scenery and costumes," dramatizes the history of blacks in Africa and the Americas (from the "Gift of Iron" from Africa, to the "Gift of the Nile" from Egypt, to the "Gift of Struggle" from the Maroons of the West Indies and the slaves of the United States). A three-hour extravaganza in six episodes, "The Star of Ethiopia" staged black history on the steps of a papier-mâché Egyptian temple in a series of performances, starting in New York in 1913 as part of the city's commemoration of the fiftieth anniversary of the Emancipation Proclamation, and then traveling to Washington, D.C. (1916), and Philadelphia and Los Angeles (1924). The "Master of the Pageant," Du Bois both supervised the performances and theorized their cultural significance. He was also attentive to their statistics. Du Bois wrote enthusiastically of this extravagant effort, first, in the December 1915 Christmas *Crisis* (specially titled *Pageant Number*), where he noted that the pageant attracted "audiences aggregating 14,000" ("SE[2]," 90), and, later, in the August 1916 *Crisis*, where he reported, "The Pageant is the thing . . . to teach on the one hand the colored people themselves the meaning of their history and their rich emotional life . . . and on the other, to reveal the Negro to the white world as a human, feeling thing."[27] Still later, Du Bois quoted himself in *Dusk of Dawn* and waxed lyrical as well as analytic and quantitative about his "historic pageant of the history of the Negro race": "Suddenly a great new spirit seemed born. It sweeps on and you hang trembling to its skirts. Nothing can stop it. It is. It will. . . . You have simply called it, and it comes. I shall never forget that last night. Six thousand human faces, shifting blaze of lights, shimmering streams of color. . . . It was no mere picture: it was reality" (*DD*, 273). The arts of pageantry, autobiography, and self-citation merge suggestively here, as Du Bois incorporates his review essay into the 1940 *Dusk of Dawn,* reminding us how his historicist uses of dramatic form extend to his histories of the self, including *A Pageant in Seven Decades.*[28]

The mystical "it" of the black-history pageant, "in which the message of education and reasonable race pride can deck itself," puts the Du Bois of the *Darkwater* years—the "long" war decade—in different intellectual company than the usual arena of academic, high culture ("SE[2]," 91). It reveals how he ought also to be read in the much less well-known context that he himself illuminates, that of black popular history, political activism, and popular occultisms, which coalesced at this time. For John E. Bruce (a militant journalist and Garveyite, well-known for his writing under the pseudonym "Bruce Grit") and Arthur A. Schomburg, the cofounders in 1911 of the Negro Society for Historical Research (later a stronghold of black-nationalist lay historians), the importance of black history lay in its uses for the widespread education and politicization of black people. If "Race is the key to History," as Bruce would say, quoting Disraeli (a line that formed the centerpiece of the society's logo, framed by the Egyptian pyramids and palm trees), then the key to the organized study and popular dissemination of black history is "to popularize the movement now taking form, of a chair of Negro history" (Bruce), and "to have a history, well-documented, widely known at least within race circles, and administered as a stimulating and inspiring tradition for coming generations" (Schomburg). The aim of the black-popular-history project was to wake black people "to the importance of thinking black." Garvey's parades and street-corner performances garnered audiences far larger than those of what Bruce called the "Socialist Orators" on other corners, in part because, according to Woodson and Wesley, his mission was to dramatize Africa in history.[29] What is Du Bois's role in this context? As we already know in connection with Garvey and will further see in relation to the others, Du Bois's was a vexed presence in these intellectual and activist circles, his relation to them often competitive, yet Du Bois shared with Schomburg, Bruce, Woodson, Garvey, et al., not only the same mission, but also many of the same methods.

The textual ensemble of *Darkwater* and "The Star of Ethiopia" helps

outline these connections. Not only does Du Bois excavate the ancient civilizations of Egypt and Ethiopia that constituted the preferred past for
Pauline Hopkins and so many of his contemporaries, but also, as *The Negro*
establishes, he seeks to write a modern history of a diasporic, global Africa.
His plan to produce a multivolume *Encyclopedia Africana*—a project conceived in 1909 and boasting an international advisory board that included
the West Indian Edward Blyden in Sierra Leone ("the doyen of black nationalism," in David Levering Lewis's words) and the Gold Coast journalist and lawyer Casely Hayford—represents another manifestation of Du
Bois's commitment to a study "covering the chief points in the history and
condition of the Negro race."[30] The fact that his vision was ultimately to be
frustrated—briefly revived twenty-five years later (as the *Encyclopedia of
the Negro*) and then again in Nkruma's Ghana, never successfully in Du
Bois's lifetime—demonstrates both the limits and the possibilities of such a
lyric "African" history.[31]

If the formal medium of Du Bois's historiography is the multigenred
text, the context is defined by what were for him coextensive projects and
fields of inquiry: the scientific study of the Negro, racial mysticism, and
transnational activism. Du Bois's training and practice in history bridged
separate spheres, as he drew on well-known, sometimes competing historiographic traditions and methodologies. Of these, the most familiar is
what is alternatively called "the 'race uplift' or 'vindicationist' tradition,"
associated in the early nineteenth-century with William Wells Brown, a
bit later with George Washington Williams, and, much later, with Carter
Woodson. This long-standing, mainstream African American philosophy
of history, Cedric Robinson says, "began in the shadow of the national
myths and as their dialectical negation."[32] In addition, Du Bois was formally trained in academic, professional history and several allied disciplines: the positivist empiricism of Albert Bushnell Hart at Harvard and
Gustav von Schmoller at Berlin, which was based on documentary research and the inductive method; the Dunning school of Southern history;
the practices of the empirical, sociological survey (as exemplified in *The
Philadelphia Negro*, the Atlanta University "Studies of the Negro Problems" series, etc.); the cultural relativism of Boasian anthropology (Boas's
1906 Atlanta University commencement address, on African history, representing another watershed for Du Bois). The varieties of black historicism in vogue also included the mystical (e.g., Hegelian *Volk*-ish history,
which attempted to capture the spirit of a people/nation), the messianic
(where long-standing political-religious traditions of Ethiopianism and

black messianism provided the religious undergirding for black nationalist movements as well as for the development of black political consciousness), and the amateur and the popular (e.g., Schomburg's and Woodson's research societies and journalism).

Linking all these historiographic traditions is an activism distilled by black historians' global excavation of neglected racial histories and what David Blight characterizes as Du Bois's local "struggle for American historical memory."[33] The heterogeneous range of sources for Du Bois's philosophy of history reminds us of how the disciplines were differently, more fluidly, arrayed at the turn of the century. Du Boisean occult historiography is ultimately a concatenation of "histories," a shifting synthesis of religious mysticism and racial messianism with various historical theories and practices, both popular and professional, that emerged or dominated the scene during his lifetime.[34] All these histories were reworked and reinterpreted during the 1910s in *The Negro* and *Darkwater* (and later revisited in *Black Folk Then and Now* and *The World and Africa*).

Emerging from such a crucible, Du Boisean historiography never abandoned scientific methodology but rather continually reframed it as the grounds on which to adjudicate the competing demands of objectivity and advocacy in a lifelong "study of the Negro Problems." Du Bois's long career could be tracked through a series of ongoing appeals to a protean, plural entity called *science*. Looking back, first in *Dusk of Dawn* and later in the *Autobiography*, on his motivation for conducting the many interviews and the massive research required for *The Philadelphia Negro* (1899), Du Bois comments, "The Negro problem was in my mind a matter of systematic investigation and intelligent understanding. The world was thinking wrong about race, because it did not know. . . . The cure for it was knowledge based on scientific investigation" (*DD*, 58; *A*, 197). This passage, and others like it, is typically quoted to establish Du Bois's early position, the scientific faith of his professional youth, from which he was irrevocably to break.[35] But witness *Black Reconstruction in America* (1935), where the equally often-cited final chapter, "The Propaganda of History" ("which in logic should be a survey of books and sources" but which becomes "an arraignment of American historians and an indictment of their ideals"), argues passionately for the value of "scientific history" as a means of rescuing the field from distortions and lies (*BRA*, 725). For Du Bois, such "scientific historians" as Benjamin Brawley, Carter Woodson, and George W. Mitchell are counted among the contributors to Negro art and literature.[36] Even his earliest sociological studies, such as *The Philadelphia*

Negro and *The Negro American Family,* incorporate nontraditional, non-documentary forms of evidence (e.g., evidence having its source in black cultural and literary life), initiating the mixed mode that would later characterize some of his best-known lyrical and autobiographical works. Du Bois's foundational essay of 1898, "The Study of the Negro Problems," in which he sets forth the principles and parameters of the field that he will occupy, defines the primary sources for the kind of "historical study" that should be undertaken: "the material at hand for historical research is rich and abundant," he says, including, not only colonial statutes and records and congressional reports and documents, but also "the personal narratives and opinions of various observers and the periodical press covering nearly three centuries" ("SNP," 81–82).

Du Boisean scientific history is not itself neutral. It is inherently an interested disciplinary practice, just as science is inevitably an enterprise of advocacy and social reform, not only for Du Bois, but also for others, such as the proponents of racial science, with very different political goals. Just so, Du Bois's earliest sociological studies were fashioned to "put science into sociology" (*DD,* 96). Du Bois's "Sociology Hesitant" includes a similarly revealing take on the unacknowledged contradictions in his own earlier, half-spoken determination to put history as well as science into sociology.[37] What kind of history? Du Boisean sociology is historicized and reframed into a history of human action. Whereas, according to Du Bois, the sociological enterprise subordinates the goals of reform and uplift to the primary aim of scientific truth, the practice of history is more explicitly politicized (as in the Dunning school and other approaches) and, hence, lends itself to the paradoxical combination of objectivity and activism, detachment and engagement, that comes to define Du Bois's philosophy of history. Du Bois's best formulations stress rather than smooth over the paradoxes of his position and hold in suspension the tensions between science and politics.

If, Du Bois argues in "The Propaganda of History," "we are going to use history for . . . inflating our national ego, and giving us a false but pleasurable sense of accomplishment, then we must give up the idea of history either as a science or as an art using the results of science. . . . Today, in the name of new slavery established elsewhere in the world under other names and guises, we ought to emphasize this lesson of the past. . . . Our histories tend to discuss American slavery so impartially, that in the end nobody seems to have done wrong and everybody was right" (*BRA,* 714). Citing as evidence of such a mechanistic interpretation the Beards' *Rise of American*

Civilization, Du Bois offers a sweeping list of the conflicting forces, "magnificent and selfish," that make up "the real plot of the story" and asks rhetorically, "Can all this be omitted or half suppressed in a treatise that calls itself scientific?" (*BRA*, 715). He concludes: "We have spoiled and misconceived the position of the historian," who as "the chronicler of human action" must adjudicate between two functions, that of the scientist to provide the facts and that of "the philosopher and prophet" to interpret them (*BRA*, 722).[38] Science here is redefined, subordinated as the handmaiden of history and the agent of both the "authentic romance" and the "scholarly eloquence" necessary to the writing of history (to recall the formula used to advertise *The Negro*).

Just such a paradoxical appeal to science, both as methodology and as symbology, opens *Black Folk Then and Now*. Putatively apologizing for the fact that "this is not a work of exact scholarship" ("far too few studies in history and sociology are"), the 1939 preface concludes even more bitingly that, predisposed as he is by his "Negro descent" to a favorable interpretation of Negro history, Du Bois will hardly be an especially misleading historian: "The Negro has long been the clown of history; the football of anthropology; and the slave of industry. . . . I realize that the truth of history lies not in the mouths of partisans but rather in the calm Science that sits between" (*BF*, ix). "Science," gendered female in the following sentence ("Her cause I seek to serve" [*BF*, ix]), ultimately embraces but does not reconcile the contradictions between claims of objectivity and disclaimers of partisanship. Du Bois's Science sits, then, personified as woman, between unnamed opponents and unspecified oppositions, a liminal location that, for Du Bois, sanctions the use of structures of feeling, not only as evidence, but also as the scientific investigator's modus operandi.

The preface also raises the question of Du Bois's extensive reliance on secondary sources, for which he is so often criticized, particularly in relation to his Africanist work. That reliance makes methodological sense as much because he is devoted to constructing and analyzing the historiography of these neglected and misrepresented fields as because he is devoted to excavating them himself. In articulating such paradoxes, Du Bois has had to come some distance even from the position that he took in the 1915 preface to *The Negro* (the earlier version of *Black Folk Then and Now*). Explaining there why "the time has not yet come for a complete history of the Negro peoples," Du Bois argues that racial prejudice still prevents "judicial appraisement," concluding that "much intensive monographic work in history and science is needed to clear mooted points and quiet the controversialist who mistakes present personal desire for scientific proof" (*N*, vi). It took, at least, the two prefaces—that of 1915 to *The Negro* and that of 1939 to *Black Folk Then and Now*—plus the time in between for Du Bois to adumbrate his philosophy of scientific history as both an impartial methodology and a partisan imperative.

The key moment in that development was the war decade, when we find an even more contradictory, and compelling, reformulation of the history-science relation in Du Bois's famous anticolonial interpretation of World War I, "The African Roots of War." First published in the May 1915 issue of the *Atlantic Monthly*, and then revised and incorporated in *Darkwater* under the new title "The Hands of Ethiopia," this essay takes, as we will see, new shape in the new context of the maternal genealogy and feminist historiography of *Darkwater*. Modernity's systematic campaign of exploitation of the world's colored peoples "has unconsciously trained millions of honest, modern men into the belief that black folk are sub-human. This belief is not based on science, . . . the belief is not based on history, . . . nor is the belief based on any careful survey of the social development of men of Negro blood to-day in Africa and America. . . . Modern contempt of Negroes rests upon no scientific foundation" (*D*, 519–20). The negative evidence of the "not-science" and "not-history" is essential to proving the existence of unconscious forces, which are in turn essential to accounting for the historical persistence of racism.

Du Bois's conception of science, always wedded to reform, becomes more explicitly and deeply historicized, shifting, on the one hand, from the empiricism of the sociological enterprise and, on the other, from the local knowledges and historical particulars of Schmoller and Hart to, first, the "mysticism, authoritarianism, civilizationism and collectivism"[39] of classical black-nationalist historiography and, then, his own version of scientific history, reinfused with a lyrical activism, in which what counts as evidence extends to things occulted: the neglected histories, unconscious phenomena, and structures of feeling that determine race relations as well as political and economic conflict. Even as late as the 1960s, however, Du Bois stresses that this is an unfinished revolution. Du Bois's 1951 preface to Aptheker's *Documentary History* (with which this chapter starts) praises the work for its "rescue from oblivion and loss" of the kind of research that historical scholarship does all too infrequently: "We have the record of kings and gentlemen ad nauseam . . . ; but of the common run of human beings, and particularly of the half or wholly submerged working group, the world has saved all too little." The missing "record of revolt or struggle" is what the unscientific or "car-window" social scientist, lambasted by Du Bois in *The Souls of Black Folk*, could never see and what the Du Boisean occult history determines to unveil (*SBF*, 180).[40]

Occultism bridges, as we have seen, a variety of separate spheres. The political valence of turn-of-the-century occultisms ranges, it is fair to say, even more wildly, from the most thoroughgoing racism to a variety of anti-racist views. Masonic, Theosophical, and Rosicrucian sources have been linked, via their focus on ancient Egypt, to Afrocentric views of history, the latter themselves ranging ideologically from the "vindicationist" tradition of early African American historians to the later "stolen-legacy" school of George G. M. James and others. Imanuel Geiss even argues that Prince Hall's founding of the first black Masonic lodge in 1787, with its ideology of equality and fraternity as well as its emphasis on education (the Prince Hall school was founded in 1798), was an indirect source of Pan-Africanism.[41] The traveling politics of Masonry in the eighteenth and nineteenth centuries are also frequently noted. E. J. Hobsbawm's primitive rebels track the relations between Freemasonry and the international, revolutionary movements of 1789–1830, including the Italian Carbonari and the Russian Decembrists.[42] Other historians comment on the affiliation of the revolutionary leaders Simon Bolivar, Giuseppe Mazzini, and Giuseppe Garibaldi with "Egyptian Masonry" and Rosicrucianism as well as the involvement in American socialist and labor movements of Charles Sotheran, one of the original founders and the first librarian of the Theosophical Society.[43] Similarly, the reformist and feminist claims of nineteenth-century American spiritualism, broadly construed, have long been apparent, as has the dominant presence of women in spiritualist circles, from the Fox sisters during the 1840s to Mark Baker Eddy and Helena Blavatsky herself.[44] Ever since Henry James lampooned in *The Bostonians* the zany mix of spiritualism and feminist politics, the fearful asymmetry of these causes and passions has been recognized as constitutive, although their ultimate political efficacy has always been in doubt.[45]

Perhaps most strikingly, many turn-of-the-century occult movements embraced a variety of international political causes on the Right and the Left. Madame Blavatsky's autocratic leadership relied on a mysticism that was both raced and gendered, one that produced, in the political sphere, Theosophy's unofficial influence in the Indian home-rule movement, the Indian nationalism of some of her followers, as well as the participation of the Theosophist Annie Besant, with Du Bois, at the 1911 Universal Races Congress. Yet Blavatsky's politics were far from antiracist: the white-supremacist cast of her "root races" concept in *The Secret Doctrine* (1888), most prominently the "Aryan race," has not been lost on some historians, who underline the racist side of occultism. Most important, she is seen as a symptom of the ties between occultism and nineteenth-century European *Volk*-ish nationalism, two movements linked by their common interests in the notion of a mystical *Volk* connection with ancient Aryan peoples (especially the Teutons), in neopagan rituals, and in the study of the Aryan roots of occult symbolism (such as the swastika, popularized in the writings of Blavatsky, used as a decorative border in *The Crisis*, and becoming only later a Nazi symbol). Many *Volk*-ish groups, especially Pan-German groups, elevated notions of racial purity to a quasi-scientific, quasi-mystical ideal that many historians see as a central foundation for Nazism.[46] The occult revivals at the turn of the century thus synthesized the deeply contradictory racial politics of the protean traditions of mysticism, science, and international activism—the very same cultural formation that brings together Du Bois's major projects of the war decade. To say that this is a confusing and ambiguous historical context is to say the very least. The racial valence of the occult defines both its threat and its promise.

By the same token, to read Du Bois as an occult historian reveals the underground context of the key decade of World War I, after he left Atlanta and the academic world for New York and *The Crisis*. The key works of this turning point—"The Star of Ethiopia," *The Negro*, and *Darkwater*—help summon and body forth the larger occult nexus to which they belong but in which they are rarely placed. It is a process of reciprocal influence and illumination: if Du Bois's work in the war decade is indebted to the occult synthesis of different sciences, mysticisms, and activisms, then, even more provocatively, the Du Boisean perspective brings into view, under the umbrella of what might be called *activist occultism*, a variety of temporally contiguous but otherwise apparently disparate cultural and political formations. Most prominent among these popular-cultural vectors is the vogue, among political groups such as the Lyrical Left and others, including Du Bois and Garvey, for public performance as a mode of political intervention and popular historiography. "Street historians" and "stepladder radicals" invented another kind of public theater in the street-corner oratory that reflected syncretic African American and Caribbean traditions.[47] The black-popular-history movement, including such major milestones as the founding of the Negro Society for Historical Research (by Bruce and Schomburg) in 1911, the Association for the Study of Negro Life and History (by Woodson) in 1915, and the *Journal of Negro History* (again by

Woodson) in 1916 and the inauguration of Negro History Week in 1926, capped a remarkable popularization of African American history in which mass culture and consumption played a central role.

The solidification of the field of black history took place largely under the auspices of public intellectuals without regular academic affiliations, including Du Bois, Carter G. Woodson, Arthur A. Schomburg, and John E. Bruce. The latter two were, perhaps not coincidentally, active Masons, both vocal during this period on the issue of Prince Hall legitimacy as well as the importance of black history. Further linking Masonic to historicist imperatives, the centrality of ancient Egypt to the advance of knowledge was a source common both to the traditions of Masonic history and to black popular history.[48] The parade as a display of fraternal and political solidarity took its place alongside the public oratory and pageantry of the spectacles staged at Madison Square Garden and other major urban venues. Garvey, too, built his movement as an amalgam of political theater, public pageantry, and race history, with ancient Egypt providing the symbolic, ceremonial icons for the Garveyite regalia.

All these disparate formations, studied as freestanding subjects, generally isolated within different scholarly fields (Afro-American studies, colonialism and postcolonialism, the history of fraternalism), have not yet appeared as a cultural ensemble joined by more than their common location (the greater New York area) or their common moment (the war decade). Perhaps in part for this reason, the occult nexus of popular and professional concerns is not ordinarily one in which Du Bois's historiography would be located. Du Bois is, as we know, usually placed, following as always his own lead, within the elite academic and intellectual confines of Harvard and Berlin (his influences being Hart at Harvard, Schmoller at Berlin, and Hegelian idealism generally). Instead, thinking of Du Bois as an occult historian and race melodramatist helps reveal his indebtedness to the more mundane, popular, middle-class culture—which he himself regularly plays down as incompatible with his vision—of popular history, mysticism, fraternalism, and political theater. If none of the players combines all the defining elements of this cultural moment, it is Du Bois, no soapbox orator or stepladder radical, who reveals the occult context as another defining context, which he both recorded and reshaped.

Most notably, Du Bois's own "penchant for the dramatic form," his operatic sense and "fabulous dramaturgy," converged with the many uses of political pageantry at the time.[49] The educational possibilities for black history attracted Du Bois, and others, to the art of pageantry. Among these possibilities, Claude McKay's 1940 study *Harlem: Negro Metropolis* singles out the "gorgeous show" of the first Universal Negro Convention "staged" in 1920 by Marcus Garvey: "This was the dramatic occasion that made the City of New York fully aware of the movement in Harlem. The convention went over with theatrical éclat. . . . Harlem adores colorful, colossal demonstrations. Garvey borrowed generously from cult manifestations and fraternal rituals in painting his political mission in gay colors."[50] McKay explicitly acknowledges the debt to fraternal and occult symbologies of the Garvey movement, as historians would later confirm.[51]

Even more presciently, McKay's portrait of the 1920 theatrical spectacle in Madison Square Garden, a few short years after the staging of Du Bois's own pageant there, suggests that the strained Garvey–Du Bois relationship was based as much on their similarities as on their differences. It is a comparison that others, among them Du Bois himself, have since made.[52] This recognition must be balanced against the more commonly accepted view of Du Bois's antagonism toward Garvey, which follows Du Bois's own account. Most commonly cited is the disclaimer in *Dusk of Dawn:* "My first effort was to explain away the Garvey movement and ignore it; but it was a mass movement that could not be ignored." It was "a grandiose and bombastic scheme," yet "Garvey proved not only an astonishingly popular leader, but a master of propaganda" (*DD*, 277–78). What Du Bois takes such pains to put at a distance, however, we should neither accept at face value nor automatically dismiss.

Du Bois's editorship of *The Crisis* during the war decade helps map the cultural landscape and place him in the unremarked spatial and temporal contiguity of its popular occultisms, fraternalism, political activism, and historicism. Regular monthly issues of the magazine appearing from 1913 to 1916 feature, cheek by jowl, repeated references to Du Bois's pageant "The Star of Ethiopia" and to his historical work *The Negro* as well as to books on Masonry and to companies selling fraternal regalia. Starting near the end of 1914, and running for about a year and a half, full-page advertisements for Du Bois's *The Negro* and George Crawford's *Prince Hall and His Followers* (1914) alternate on the end pages of "The Crisis Advertiser" (the Crawford ads occasionally replaced by two half-page notices, one each for the *Journal of Negro History* and Woodson's *The Education of the Negro Prior to 1861* [1915]) (see plates 1–4). *The Crisis* seal of approval ("Mention *The Crisis*" appears at the bottom of notices for a vast array of texts) was explicitly extended to the Prince Hall book in an end-page announcement in the October 1914 issue: "The CRISIS has the honor to announce the publication of the most important book on Negro Masonry . . . the only book written by an authority from our own point of view." The ad copy for *The Negro* always remains the same: "This is the authentic romance of the black man. It is a history of him at once scholarly, earnest and eloquent." Crawford's *Prince Hall*, however, is alternatively advertised to the Masonic fraternity ("Attention, Masons! A New Book of Interest to You") and to a wider readership ("The character and work of this great man have been admirably set forth in a new book of vital interest to Masons and laymen"). Still, both ads characterize Prince Hall as "One of the Great Figures in Negro History," demonstrating that Crawford, a thirty-third-degree grand master from Connecticut, belongs to the ranks of the historians and grand historians of Masonic lodges who assumed the task, not only of recording the history of black American Masons, but also of writing a global history that would champion the "race" as a whole, thereby going far beyond the injunction to preserve Masonic history that characterized their white counterparts. Elsewhere, in the smaller, cheaper, and less-visible spaces of "The Crisis Advertiser," where beauty products, shorthand courses, pianos, teaching posts, and a vast array of books, including the scholarly monographs of the Atlanta University "Studies of the Negro Problems" series, are all advertised, the Central Regalia Company ("The Negro Regalia House") regularly hawks its wares: "A Race Enterprise Manufacturing Badges, Banners and Supplies for All Fraternal and Church Societies"; "Cheapest Badge House in the Country"; "If It Is for Your Lodge We Have It!" (see plates 5–6).

During the same extended period, Du Bois covered "The Star of Ethiopia" in a variety of *Crisis* columns and notices: from a full prose version, "People of Peoples and Their Gift to Men," in the November 1913 issue; to "The Star of Ethiopia" in the December 1915 issue, featuring pageant photographs and a report on the trials and triumphs of the first performance at the Emancipation Exposition in New York; to "The Drama among the Black Folk" in the August 1916 issue, a position paper (frequently anthologized) on the social efficacy of "Negro drama." Studded throughout with passages from "The Star of Ethiopia" (a classic case of Du Boisean self-citation), the latter argues for the development of Negro drama "to teach on the one hand the colored people themselves the meaning of their history . . . , and on the other, to reveal the Negro to the white world as a human, feeling thing" ("DBF," 171). Such an explicit commitment to race history in the very broadest sense is clearly the common denominator linking *The Crisis* coverage of "The Star of Ethiopia," *The Negro,* and the Masons.

Yet, if the connection seems obvious once the evidence is put together, what does it all add up to? Still unanswered is the fundamental question of the racial politics of occultism and fraternalism: What, and how, do these related structures of knowledge and feeling ultimately contribute to the fin de siècle politics of race? The specific political valence of Masonry is as volatile and questionable as that of the broader occultism of which it is a subset. On the one hand, the revolutionary and Enlightenment ideals of the Masons, often traced to the American and French Revolutions as well as to Italian radicalism, are thought to buttress the progressive internationalism of the war decade; similarly, the reformist Masonic tradition has been seen in the active role played by Prince Hall Masons in the struggle for civil rights.[53] On the other hand, whether there is, in fact, any such "major tradition" of activism within black Freemasonry is a subject of some debate. Black fraternalism, from colleges to the business community, is seen both as an imitative counterpart to the predominantly middle-class, white fraternal movement, producing parallel orders such as the Prince Hall Masons or the Colored Knights of Pythias, and as a separatist, quasi-nationalist movement that spawned various self-help programs for racial pride and advancement. In other variants of this divide, some see Masonic and other fraternal male orders as traditional bulwarks of black middle-class life; others characterize black Freemasonry as politically quiescent, refusing to participate institutionally in community affairs; and a few claim outright that a major tradition within black Freemasonry has been one of activism.[54]

Du Bois himself weighs in on all sides of the debate. A full section of *The Philadelphia Negro* is devoted to "Secret and Beneficial Societies and Co-Operative Business," counting nineteen Odd Fellow lodges, nineteen Masonic lodges, three Scottish Rite temples, and one drill corps in the city. Commenting (without elaboration) that secret orders "naturally had great attraction for Negroes," Du Bois concludes that the importance of such societies lies in the "art of social organized life" that they foster, but, as far as the "experiment of organization" goes, he finally condemns secret societies, among them the Masons ("not so well organized and well conducted as the Odd Fellows"), for diverting members "from their better ends" by "the temptation of tinsel and braggadocio."[55]

Echoing Du Bois's divided position, some scholars stress the "conservative," middle-class values of the Prince Hall Masons, construed primarily as a voluntary association, while others either celebrate or critique the more radical impulses of fraternal organizations in general. Historians trace the remarkable success of early-twentieth-century fraternal organizations, black and white, to their broad engagement with cultural contradiction, arguing that, like the discourses of white supremacy and militarism, fraternalism provided a tenuous, symbolic resolution of conflicts—among religious sectarians, between old and young, workers and entrepreneurs, and, most important, men and women.[56] Arguing that fraternalism's appeal drew on the "gendered identity" of the artisan, the historian Mary Ann Clawson also connects the militarism of the turn-of-the-century fraternal movement to the particular moment in U.S. history of renewed nativism, unprecedented labor unrest, and conspicuous lack of involvement in international hostilities, when the primary threat appeared to be internal. Similarly, the theatricality that always characterized fraternalism, to which black Freemasonry was no exception, transmutes at the turn of the century, in a form of "product diversification" in the "business of brotherhood," into military branches with drill teams and parade units, as the chivalric image of the crusader knight and the theme of the nation at arms replaced the artisanal symbolism of the craft workshop.[57] As a uniquely black male subculture, Maurice Wallace argues, Prince Hall Freemasonry, with its alternating artisanal and historical consciousness, illustrates in microcosm the "dialectics of African-American male identity construction."[58]

As we have seen in chapter 1, Paul Gilroy offers by far the most compelling critique of the masculinist military-fraternal complex, citing examples that range from the 1850s, with Frederick Douglass's attack on black Masonry as a diversion from antislavery politics, to Marcus Garvey's Universal Negro Improvement Association (UNIA) and its kinship with the fascist political movements of the 1920s, to, most recently, the Nation of Islam's transformation of Masonic teachings for its own authoritarian purposes. Gilroy argues that the model of solidarity provided by these groups is an older, premodern concept of belonging grounded in the masculinist and militarist culture shared with fraternalism. Linking fascist groups and brotherhood movements, Gilroy notes how their common emphasis on racial purity and solidarity relies on the opposite, a conspiratorial consciousness of the political possibilities of secrecy and betrayal.[59]

Gilroy's focus on fraternalism's exclusionary masculinity is further substantiated by the history of Masonic women's auxiliaries. Despite the rhetoric of Masonic equality, women were not permitted as members of Masonic lodges—a practice based on the revolutionary notion of *fraternité*—and even the establishment of the ladies' auxiliaries in the late nineteenth century, the best known of which is the Daughters of the Eastern Star, meant in practice little more than a set of "various female orders attached to" the chief secret societies, as Du Bois says of them (*PN*, 224). There is significant counterevidence, however. Tracing the overlap among Masonic, Theosophical, and Rosicrucian works, Stephen Howe comments that the Theosophists founded Masonic lodges that admitted women—the first and only lodges to do so.[60] Charles Wesley notes that, as a "man of vision," Prince Hall would have black women strive to attain goals similar to those of male Masons: "And they heard his message in the Eastern Star, the Daughters of Isis, . . . and the women at home, school, and abroad, all of whom have constituted a unity of purpose under the leadership of the life and spirit of Prince Hall."[61] Members of the Eastern Star produced their own historiographic accounts—for example, Mrs. S. Joe Brown's *The History of the Order of the Eastern Star among Colored People* (1925)—that mirror the Prince Hall Masons' histories. Feminist historians read these histories of black female Masonry—which call for the separation of women's history from that of (in the words of Mrs. Brown) "Colored Men" and of "white Americans"—as essential to the historical record of black women's activism.[62] Similarly, the historian Mark Carnes insists on the broad, gendered appeal of fraternalism, arguing that, for young men, fraternal ritual, particularly its secrecy, proclaimed the emotional self-sufficiency of men and, thus, facilitated the transition to a "problematic conception of manhood," while women's auxiliaries, which seemed to represent an acceptance of male dominance, were the products of women's struggles and the targets of masculine resistance.[63] This is a deeply ambiguous context, and legacy, in which to locate, or with which to burden, Du Bois. And what he, in turn, makes of it will become apparent only in *Darkwater,* an examination of which represents the culmination of this study of race melodramas.

Central as a Masonic connection is to the culture of the occult, the Masonic connection to Du Bois is, however, neither readily apparent nor easily established. Du Bois himself is, as far as I know, utterly (and uncharacteristically) silent on the question. His best biographer, David Levering Lewis, makes no mention of it. Only a handful of scholars, most interested specifically in Freemasonry, address the question of whether Du Bois was a Mason, and all arrive at slightly different answers, sometimes no more than a mention in a footnote.[64] Most informatively, Charles H. Wesley tells us precisely where he believes Du Bois was inducted (Widow's Son Lodge, No. 1, New Haven, Connecticut) but finds the significance less in the fact of Masonic membership per se than in Du Bois's uses of the "Masonic style," specifically in "Credo," the prose poem that Du Bois wrote in 1904 on his fiftieth birthday (first published in *Independent* magazine in October 1904 and later incorporated into *Darkwater*). "Credo" became an artifact of everyday black life, memorized by black children and frequently framed and displayed in black homes. Wesley quotes the 1904 version in full, laying it side by side with the Prince Hall Credo drawn up by George W. Crawford (the author of the classic Masonic text so frequently advertised in *The Crisis*) to demonstrate their stylistic parallels. Wesley's genealogy gestures toward a Masonic imprint on Du Bois's writing, characteristic of a wider Masonic presence among the African American middle classes, an imprint that I will further explore in *Darkwater,* the most important of Du Bois's works from the war decade.[65]

The point is neither to uncover a secret Du Bois nor to claim him as a Mason (although identifying important black members has long been a major strategy in the controversy over the legitimacy of black Masonry). Du Bois's own Masonic affiliation is, in my reconstruction of this understudied (but not unknown) context, appropriately no more than a simple note to a fraternal history that stands on its own without his presence, just as the fact that he was a Mason is neither necessary nor sufficient to authorize the Masonic imprint on his writing. Du Bois did not need induction into the Masons to produce his lyrical history, just as the history of Prince Hall Masonry, and, more broadly, of occult history, in the war decade does not need Du Bois.

This historiographic point has historical resonance in the relations among the main players, who tended to downplay or disavow each other's parallel work. The increasing professionalization of the discipline of history produced a split between scholars and (so-called) amateur historians that rendered less visible the contributions of Prince Hall Freemasonry—those of, for example, such leading Masons and advocates of black popular history as John E. Bruce and Arthur Schomburg—to the synergy of historical practices (the collection, preservation, and dissemination of black history in primary and secondary source materials) and public spectacle that constituted the black-history movement in the early twentieth century.[66] It is known, for example, that Du Bois borrowed from Arthur Schomburg's collection of books and manuscripts, often without acknowledging the favor. On the other hand, Du Bois singled out "Carter Woodson's 'Negro History Week'" as perhaps the "greatest single accomplishment" of "the artistic movement among American Negroes" (*DD*, 203). McKay's *Harlem: Negro Metropolis* credits the "incomparable" Schomburg collection at the Negro Division of the 135th Street Library as "the most distinctive contribution of Puerto Rico to the literary culture of Harlem" (refer-

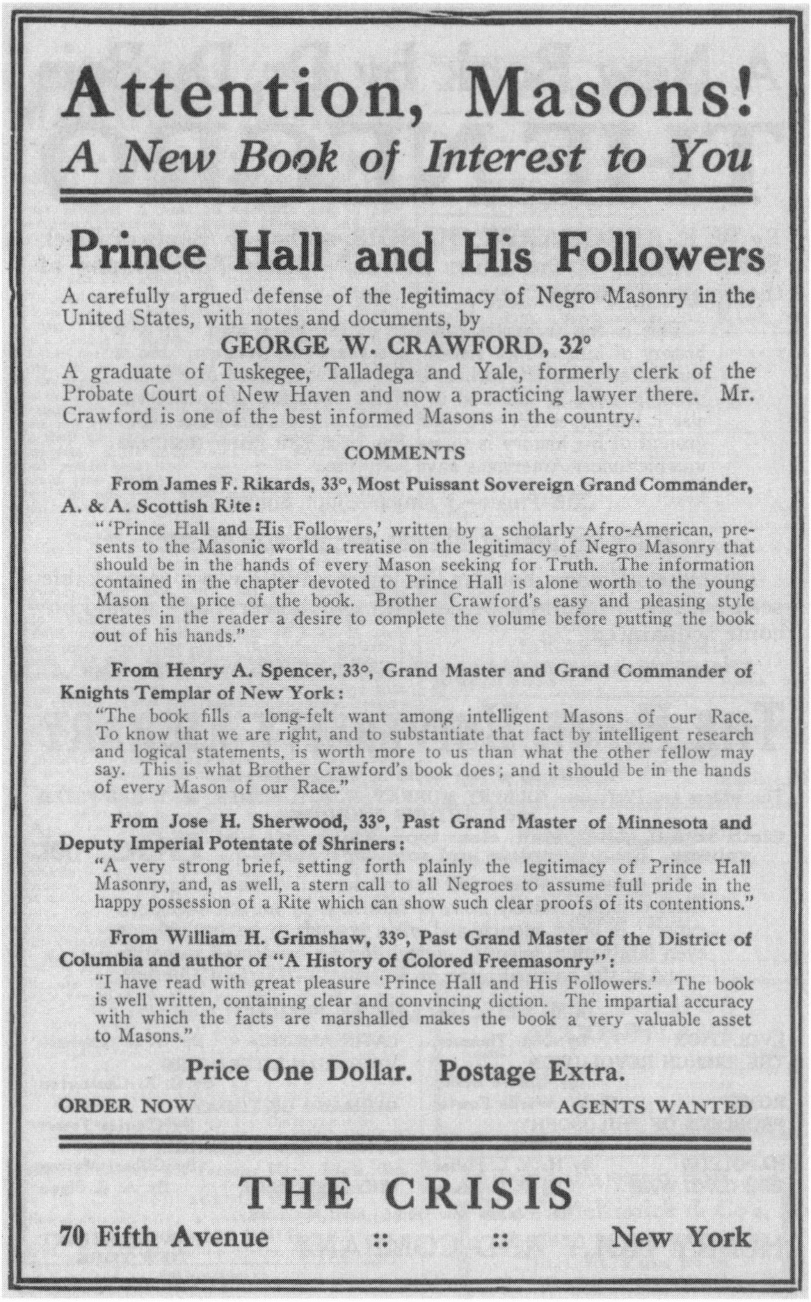

Attention, Masons!

A New Book of Interest to You

Prince Hall and His Followers

A carefully argued defense of the legitimacy of Negro Masonry in the United States, with notes and documents, by

GEORGE W. CRAWFORD, 32°

A graduate of Tuskegee, Talladega and Yale, formerly clerk of the Probate Court of New Haven and now a practicing lawyer there. Mr. Crawford is one of the best informed Masons in the country.

COMMENTS

From James F. Rikards, 33°, Most Puissant Sovereign Grand Commander, A. & A. Scottish Rite:

"'Prince Hall and His Followers,' written by a scholarly Afro-American, presents to the Masonic world a treatise on the legitimacy of Negro Masonry that should be in the hands of every Mason seeking for Truth. The information contained in the chapter devoted to Prince Hall is alone worth to the young Mason the price of the book. Brother Crawford's easy and pleasing style creates in the reader a desire to complete the volume before putting the book out of his hands."

From Henry A. Spencer, 33°, Grand Master and Grand Commander of Knights Templar of New York:

"The book fills a long-felt want among intelligent Masons of our Race. To know that we are right, and to substantiate that fact by intelligent research and logical statements, is worth more to us than what the other fellow may say. This is what Brother Crawford's book does; and it should be in the hands of every Mason of our Race."

From Jose H. Sherwood, 33°, Past Grand Master of Minnesota and Deputy Imperial Potentate of Shriners:

"A very strong brief, setting forth plainly the legitimacy of Prince Hall Masonry, and, as well, a stern call to all Negroes to assume full pride in the happy possession of a Rite which can show such clear proofs of its contentions."

From William H. Grimshaw, 33°, Past Grand Master of the District of Columbia and author of "A History of Colored Freemasonry":

"I have read with great pleasure 'Prince Hall and His Followers.' The book is well written, containing clear and convincing diction. The impartial accuracy with which the facts are marshalled makes the book a very valuable asset to Masons."

Price One Dollar. Postage Extra.

ORDER NOW **AGENTS WANTED**

THE CRISIS

70 Fifth Avenue :: :: New York

PLATE 1

"Attention, Masons! *A New Book of Interest to You*," *The Crisis*, November 1915, n.p.

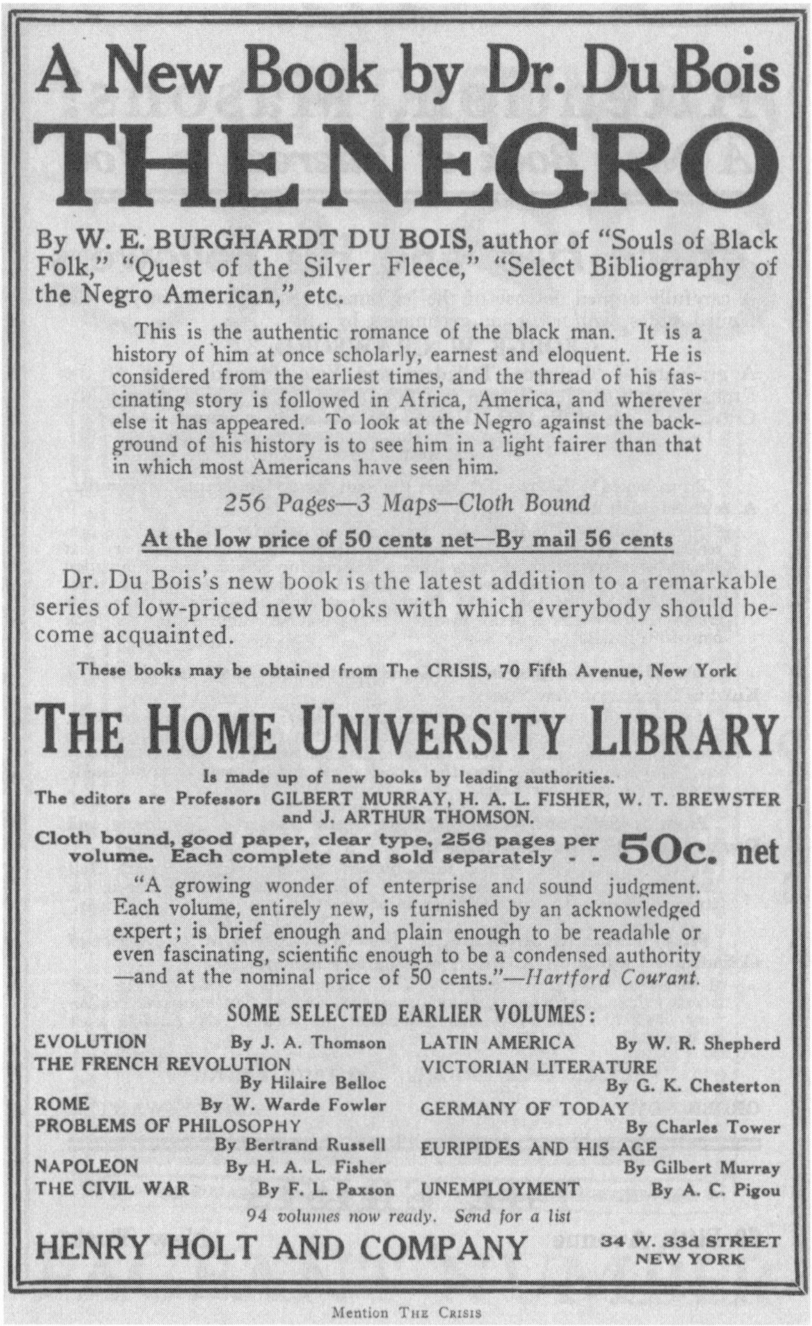
A New Book by Dr. Du Bois
THE NEGRO

By **W. E. BURGHARDT DU BOIS**, author of "Souls of Black Folk," "Quest of the Silver Fleece," "Select Bibliography of the Negro American," etc.

This is the authentic romance of the black man. It is a history of him at once scholarly, earnest and eloquent. He is considered from the earliest times, and the thread of his fascinating story is followed in Africa, America, and wherever else it has appeared. To look at the Negro against the background of his history is to see him in a light fairer than that in which most Americans have seen him.

256 Pages—3 Maps—Cloth Bound

At the low price of 50 cents net—By mail 56 cents

Dr. Du Bois's new book is the latest addition to a remarkable series of low-priced new books with which everybody should become acquainted.

These books may be obtained from The CRISIS, 70 Fifth Avenue, New York

THE HOME UNIVERSITY LIBRARY

Is made up of new books by leading authorities.
The editors are Professors GILBERT MURRAY, H. A. L. FISHER, W. T. BREWSTER and J. ARTHUR THOMSON.

Cloth bound, good paper, clear type, 256 pages per volume. Each complete and sold separately - - 50c. net

"A growing wonder of enterprise and sound judgment. Each volume, entirely new, is furnished by an acknowledged expert; is brief enough and plain enough to be readable or even fascinating, scientific enough to be a condensed authority —and at the nominal price of 50 cents."—*Hartford Courant.*

SOME SELECTED EARLIER VOLUMES:

EVOLUTION By J. A. Thomson
THE FRENCH REVOLUTION By Hilaire Belloc
ROME By W. Warde Fowler
PROBLEMS OF PHILOSOPHY By Bertrand Russell
NAPOLEON By H. A. L. Fisher
THE CIVIL WAR By F. L. Paxson
LATIN AMERICA By W. R. Shepherd
VICTORIAN LITERATURE By G. K. Chesterton
GERMANY OF TODAY By Charles Tower
EURIPIDES AND HIS AGE By Gilbert Murray
UNEMPLOYMENT By A. C. Pigou

94 volumes now ready. Send for a list

HENRY HOLT AND COMPANY 34 W. 33d STREET NEW YORK

Mention The Crisis

PLATE 2
"A New Book by Dr. Du Bois. THE NEGRO," *The Crisis*, November 1915, n.p.

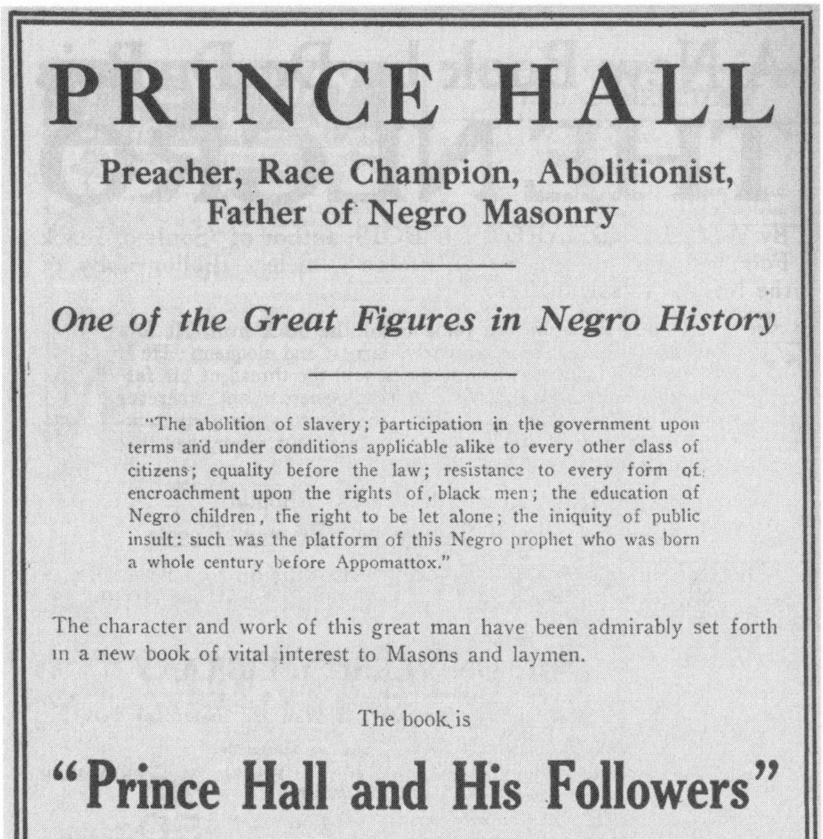

PRINCE HALL

**Preacher, Race Champion, Abolitionist,
Father of Negro Masonry**

One of the Great Figures in Negro History

"The abolition of slavery; participation in the government upon terms and under conditions applicable alike to every other class of citizens; equality before the law; resistance to every form of encroachment upon the rights of black men; the education of Negro children, the right to be let alone; the iniquity of public insult: such was the platform of this Negro prophet who was born a whole century before Appomattox."

The character and work of this great man have been admirably set forth in a new book of vital interest to Masons and laymen.

The book is

"Prince Hall and His Followers"

The author is

George W. Crawford, 33°
Grand Master of Connecticut

Price One Dollar. Postage Extra.

ORDER NOW AGENTS WANTED

THE CRISIS

70 Fifth Avenue :: :: New York

Mention THE CRISIS

PLATE 3
"PRINCE HALL. Preacher, Race Champion, Abolitionist, Father of Negro Masonry. . . . [A] new book of vital interest to Masons and laymen," *The Crisis*, March 1916, n.p.

The Horizon Guild

in conjunction with a committee of citizens announces the presentation of

A Pageant

illustrating the history of religious faith in the Negro race, and commemorating the 100th anniversary of the meeting of the General Conference of the African Methodist Episcopal Church, entitled

The Star of Ethiopia

In the City of Philadelphia

May 15, 17 and 19, 1916

One Thousand Actors——Fifty-three Musical Numbers——Scenery and Costumes

W. E. BURGHARDT DU BOIS, Master of the Pageant, 70 Fifth Avenue, New York City.

This pageant, which has already been given in New York City and Washington, D. C., will be repeated in Boston, Baltimore, and other cities South and West.

PLATE 4
"The Star of Ethiopia," *The Crisis*, April 1915, n.p.

PLATE 5
"REGALIA. A Race Enterprise," "The Crisis Advertiser," *The Crisis*, November 1915, 48.

PLATE 6

"If It Is For Your Lodge WE HAVE IT!" "The Crisis Advertiser," *The Crisis*, November 1916, 46.

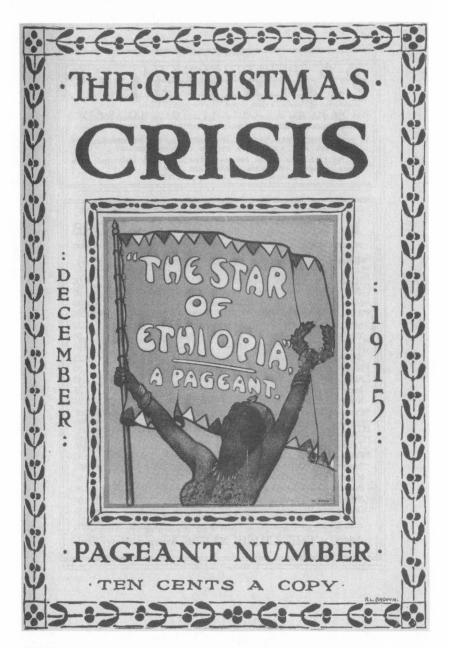

"The Christmas Crisis. Pageant Number," *The Crisis*, December 1915, front cover.

THE QUEEN OF SHEBA
(Miss Adella Parks)

ETHIOPIA
(Miss Eleanor Curtis)

CANDACE OF MEROE
(Miss Gregoria Fraser)

PLATE 8

"From the Pageant: 'The Star of Ethiopia,'" *The Crisis*, December 1915, 90.

PLATE 9

"THE PAGEANT, 'STAR OF ETHIOPIA,' IN PHILADELPHIA. Leading characters, and Temple built and decorated by Richard Brown and Lenwood Morris," *The Crisis*, August 1916, 172.

ring to Schomburg's Puerto Rican roots) but concludes: "Yet Schomburg was not typically literary. . . . He could not discourse like a scholar, but he could delve deep and bring up nuggets for a scholar which had baffled discovery."[67] The gulf between scholar and bibliophile, professional academic and amateur archivist, that dogged the black-history scene during this period may also account for why, as secretary of the Negro Society for Historical Research, Schomburg tartly characterized Carter Woodson's *Journal of Negro History* as "a very creditable" effort that was "stealing our thunder."[68] We thus get a sense of the rivalries—the mutual suspicion and the multiple cleavages—that make it difficult to reconstruct the context of the black-history movement in the 1920s, especially the links among apparently antagonistic actors and projects (e.g., Du Bois, Garvey, and Bruce).[69]

Neither a simple footnote to the Du Bois biography nor an idiosyncratic subculture, the Masonic connection is, instead, a landmark of the commitment to historiography that characterizes mainstream Freemasonry and the Prince Hall Masons alike. The continuing preoccupation of Freemasons with their own history, measured by the extensive corpus of Masonic historical literature generated continuously since the organization's founding in 1717, is simultaneously accompanied by its opposite, what the historian of religion Alexander Piatigorsky sees as Freemasonry's conservatism, a resistance to historical change. Masonic historicism presents history—the Masons' own and that of the world at large—as a symbolic manifestation of divine power, which is itself transhistorical. For Freemasons, the combination of historicism and theatricality has always had a special significance; Piatigorsky argues that the Ritual of Master Mason is itself a "theatrical performance" establishing the connection between the Freemason and his biblical past.[70] But, whereas Freemasonic historical consciousness amounts to a paradoxical antihistorical history, Prince Hall Masons reinterpret the Masonic historical imperative by rejecting its ahistoricity, broadening it to include the history of the "race," meaning primarily Africans in America but also Africans throughout the diasporic world—the Masons "scattered through the territory of 40 states, Germany, Alaska, Canada, the West Indies, Liberia in West Africa and the Bahama Islands, with the linkage between them constituting a black brotherhood," as Charles Wesley puts it in his history of Prince Hall.[71]

Tracking much the same geographic spread, Du Bois's "The Star of Ethiopia," *The Negro*, and *Darkwater*—his major works of the war decade—also contribute to the historical imperative of the black-popular-history movement, with its leading Masonic figures and stepladder radicals, staged spectacles and street theater. All the main players and texts of this occult context come together, as I have already suggested, in the pages of *The Crisis*, most strikingly in the December 1915 issue. Titled *The Christmas Crisis: Pageant Number*, this issue features a woodcut of a female figure holding aloft a banner emblazoned with "The Star of Ethiopia" on the cover, photographs of and an article on the pageant, as well as the usual advertisements for Masonic and Du Boisean works of history (see plate 7). It is here that Du Bois exulted, "The Pageant is the thing," concluding, "This is the gown and paraphernalia in which the message of education and reasonable race pride can deck itself" ("SE[2]," 91). The December 1915 issue of *The Crisis* marks the middle of the decade in which, as we will see, Du Bois repeatedly returned to his pageant and other *Crisis* texts, citing, incorporating, and, ultimately, refashioning them into the historical consciousness, gendered female, of *Darkwater*.

STRATEGIC SELF-CITATION: PUTTING SCIENCE INTO AUTOBIOGRAPHY

One important key to reading Du Bois is, as I have argued, keeping attuned to his strategic uses of repetition, particularly specific forms of self-citation that constitute his adaptation of the melodramatic style, itself given to repetition in plot, character, and language. It was common practice for Du Bois to incorporate into his autobiographies passages from his own speeches or from essays and other writing that he had done for various magazines and journals and even to re-cite, in the later autobiographies, his own earlier autobiographical recollections. This textual recycling ranges from the multiple uses of signature lines in a variety of contexts (his multiple invocations of the famous color-line aphorism, "The problem of the twentieth century is the problem of the color-line");[72] to the recounting in his various autobiographical and multigenred texts of formative life events (the visiting-card episode in *The Souls of Black Folk*, when he says he realizes his own blackness and asks, "How does it feel to be a problem?" [*SBF*, 101]); to the wholesale recasting of essays and articles, originally published as freestanding pieces, and later incorporated into the omnivorous autobiographical writings. *The Souls of Black Folk*, for example, brought together what Du Bois calls "a number of my fugitive pieces" (*DD*, 80): nine of the fourteen essays had, Levering Lewis points out, already appeared in major and specialized publications of the day.[73] It is also well-known that Du Bois's famous essay on world war and world imperialism, "The African Roots of War," is transformed in *Darkwater* into the longer, and lyrically retitled, "The Hands of Ethiopia."[74] These signature citations stand out because they ring changes on the foundational term and concept *the Negro Problem*.

To this set of reusable materials, I would add a group of sociological citations from Du Bois's seminal early academic work that are also repeatedly folded into his last two autobiographical texts, *Dusk of Dawn* (1940) and *The Autobiography of W. E. B. Du Bois* (1968). Representing his most important reformulations of the Negro Problem, in which the Negro *has* problems rather than *being* the problem, these passages originate in Du Bois's sociological classics "The Study of the Negro Problems" (his November 1897 address to the American Academy of Political and Social Sciences) and *The Philadelphia Negro* (1899). Both texts formulate what he describes in the autobiographies as his basic project: "to put science into sociology through a study of the condition[s] and problems of [his] own group" (*DD*, 51 [with singular "condition"]; *A*, 206 [with plural "conditions"]). That this most often-quoted statement of purpose, invoked as a pithy summary of Du Boisean social science, originates with, and appears only in, the autobiographical rather than the sociological texts is revealing. It took the autobiographical retrospective to provide the comparative readings—juxtaposing the *then* and the *now*—that would make fully visible the meanings of Du Bois's work in social science.

This was the work of the thirteen years from 1897 to 1910, the period of the Atlanta University "Studies in the Negro Problems" series that Du Bois remembers as being devoted to "the development at an American institution of learning, of a program of study on the problems affecting the American Negroes" (*A*, 213). A ten-year series of studies on a variety of aspects of black life in the United States, the program was ambitiously designed, he recalls, quoting the statement of aims included annually in the reports, as a century-long set of "recurring decennial inquiries into the same general set of human problems" (*DD*, 63–64). The autobiographies raise this point only to lament that the studies were not to be carried out as envisioned; nonetheless, Du Bois notes, the project did produce what he considered to be "a current encyclopaedia on the American Negro problems" (*DD*, 65; *A*, 217).[75] In short, this is the same body of academic research from which Du Bois distances himself in his "red-ray" narrative, the account of the turning point in his career that constitutes the culmination of these social-scientific sections of the autobiographies (*DD*, 67–68; *A*, 221–22). Yet the sheer length and quantity of the sociological citations, not to mention the force of their repetition, do not so much outweigh as remain in an uneasy state of unresolved tension with the subsequent repudiations.

What are the effects of the change of venue from the academic to the autobiographical context? Most obvious are, first, the issue of audience and, second, the effect of quotation out of context. The autobiographical location makes visible a signal change in audience. Although both sociological texts were explicitly addressed to scholars and specialists, the implicit intent of Du Bois's intellectual work as a whole—"to find a way of applying science to the race problem"—was always to persuade the public at large to support "the utilitarian object of reform and uplift" (*DD*, 54–55; *A*, 206).[76] Du Bois, we know, ultimately abandoned the academy and its scholarly audience, but not his intellectual project, the study of the Negro Problems, itself. In the autobiographies, when he re-cites substantial passages from his sociological classics, not only are these passages now addressed to the broad-based readership that had been built over the years through *The Crisis* and other magazines, but they are also, by definition, quoted out of context. In so doing, Du Bois himself inaugurates the practice of signature quotation out of context—citing himself without much regard for provenance—that has since become a hallmark of Du Bois criticism.[77] In both *Dusk of Dawn* (in a chapter entitled "Science and Empire," a thematic representation of the sixteen years from 1894 to 1910) and the *Autobiography* (in the geographically located set of chapters "University of Pennsylvania" and "Atlanta University"), the long sociological quotations, taken out of context, stand out in bold relief to emerge as a set of manifestos that make explicit what was latent in the original texts: first, that the Negro Problems must be defined as "a contradictory group of forces, facts and tendencies," ranging from the "conscious and rational," to "physical, biological and psychological forces," and, finally, and most significantly, to "unconscious and irrational urges" of race prejudice (*DD*, 133, 96, 304); and, second, that to study such a contradictory group of forces—especially to make visible the "hidden and partially concealed causes of race hate" (*DD*, 284)—requires an analogous set of investigative methodologies that bridge the separate spheres of science and politics, objectivity and partisanship, the lyrical and the scientific. In short, it is occult history—attuned equally to all the contradictory forces, the rational and irrational, the visible and the veiled—that allows Du Bois access to what he calls in *Dusk of Dawn* the "twilight zone" of race prejudice (*DD*, 282).

When Du Bois brought the then of his scientific work in Atlanta into the now of the autobiographies, what came to the surface were the submerged, radical implications of making plural the singular Negro Problem. Implicitly, he also explained how such a radical subtext would have been missed in the original, scholarly venue by an audience not attuned to those implications: how it was, for example, that the pioneering *Philadelphia Negro* so quickly established a reputation as a classic, rather than a maverick, of American sociology. We know that the 1899 study, as well as the Atlanta University "Studies of the Negro Problems" series, was well received in part because Du Bois himself tells us so: "It may be said without undue boasting that between 1896 and 1920 there was no study made of the race problem in America which did not depend in some degree upon the investigations made at Atlanta University" (*A*, 217–18). The *Autobiography* amplifies the brief description in *Dusk of Dawn* of this intellectual and professional success by quoting numerous accolades from well-known figures (William James, Jane Addams, even Booker T. Washington) and positive reviews in international journals.[78] David Levering Lewis argues that the positive reception of *The Philadelphia Negro* comes from Du Bois's canny nesting or embedding approach in the book, which "tended to understate its major premises, inserting them unobtrusively between data and analysis." Du Bois's "great, schizoid monograph" had to be "almost two books in one: one that would not be immediately denounced for its transparent heterodoxy," and a second one, read between the lines of Victorian moralizing, that would, over time, penetrate the social sciences and improve race relations through its "not-immediately apparent interpretive radicalism."[79]

What could be read only between the lines of *The Philadelphia Negro* and of its companion piece, "The Study of the Negro Problems," is the implied thesis of the latter's title: the plural nature of the Negro Problem.[80] Although that basic claim is advanced many times throughout "The Study of the Negro Problems," it is done so in a series of scattered lines, dispersed throughout the essay, that could be, and, indeed, were, readily (dis)missed. The titles of three of the essay's five sections, for example, repeat the "Problems" formulation, incorporating and subordinating it within the conventional structures of social-scientific research: "1. Development of The Negro Problems"; "2. The Present Negro Problems"; "3. The Necessity of Carefully Studying These Problems" ("SNP," 71–74). Or else the "Problems" thesis appears midparagraph, buried within a mass of evidence and statistics, points and counterpoints. So, for example, discussing how "the Negro problems" are apt to be differently defined by a Negro and a Southern white man, Du Bois notes, in passing, as it were, "And yet each calls the problem he discusses *the* Negro problem, leaving in the dark background the really crucial question as to the relative importance of the many problems involved" ("SNP," 75). Only the italics provide the stress, quietly make the point.

If Du Bois thus succeeded in veiling the radical subtext of his sociological essays, he lifted the veil in his autobiographies. And recognizing that, in the autobiographies, he quotes the social-scientific thesis statements out of context, stripped of their textual camouflage—documentation, statistical analysis, the superstructure of headings and subsections—provides the key to these statements' newly emergent meanings. When Du Bois re-cites in both *Dusk of Dawn* and the *Autobiography* several long passages from the opening and closing sections of *The Philadelphia Negro* and "The Study of the Negro Problems," he makes visible the "Problems" thesis embedded there. The aim of his study, he emphasizes in the autobiographical now, was to follow "the development of the Negro problem not as one problem, but"—quoting, and highlighting, what he had said in the social-scientific then—"'rather a plexus of social problems, some new, some old, some simple, some complex'" (*DD*, 60; *A*, 200). The autobiographical re-citations shift the focus of this key passage to emphasize the change from the singular to the plural. So, too, the shift in textual location foregrounds the plural ("Problems") thesis, gathering together the dispersed references in the earlier work to "the Negro problems," and concentrating their argumentative force in an unfolding series of interlocked citations, repeated verbatim in both the 1940 and the 1968 autobiographies.

Finally, the autobiographical context, which foregrounds rather than underplays the development, over time, of the "I," allows Du Bois to continue in *Dusk of Dawn* to repeat, to revise, and, finally, to place on center stage his formulation of the fundamental "Problems" thesis. At the end of the key chapter "The Concept of Race," Du Bois seizes the climactic moment to present as the centerpiece of his life story what had been relegated to, and veiled within, the closing sentences of the first of five subsections in the earlier social-scientific paper.[81] Here, Du Bois the autobiographer reflects self-consciously and self-critically on the "race concept" that dominated his life, "the history of which I have attempted to make the leading theme of this book," concluding, "Perhaps it is wrong to speak of it at all as 'a concept' rather than as a group of contradictory forces, facts and tendencies" (*DD*, 133). With this explicit, autobiographical statement of the thesis of "The Study of the Negro Problems," Du Bois underscores the plural already grammatically present in the title of that essay and unveils its "interpretive radicalism." It is no longer possible to see through, or to miss, the "transparent heterodoxy" of Du Bois's study.

The effects of the autobiographical foregrounding of the Negro Problem*s*, plural, are profound. Both the object of study and the investigator come into view in fundamentally different ways than they did in the social-scientific texts. What had seemed in the sociological then to be conceived narrowly, as a singular problem, emerges in the autobiographical now as a set of plural possibilities. And, re-cited in the autobiographies, what had once seemed, in Du Bois's "calculated"[82] writing style in *The Philadelphia Negro,* an unqualified rejection of subjectivity—"some personal bias, some moral conviction or some unconscious trend of thought" that "distorted" the investigator's view (*DD,* 59; *A,* 199)—is revealed as the essential core of the research project itself. The inevitability, if not the principle, of the investigator's subjectivity is accepted—and, not just lamented, but embraced—as the essential boundary condition of the study of the Negro Problems. Only the autobiographical context makes fully visible this argument, camouflaged in the social-scientific originals, as well as the implications that could not be articulated for the academic audience. Readers of autobiographies expect what Herbert Aptheker (one of Du Bois's best critics) calls "the intense subjectivity that inevitably permeates autobiography," in contrast to the scholarly audience that never fully accepted the implications of Du Bois's work—perhaps one explanation for why he continually insists on the opposition between scientist and activist/artist.[83]

When Du Bois looks back in both autobiographies at his sociological classics, he exposes the internal contradictions in his own, earlier critique of the scientific investigator's objectivity that his contemporaries had been led to miss.[84] He quotes two relevant passages, one from an introductory subsection of *The Philadelphia Negro* headed "The Credibility of the Results," the other from the conclusion to "The Study of the Negro Problems," both of which address, in highly equivocal and troubled terms, the objectivity question. In the 1899 monograph, developing the argument that we have already seen on how the careful student "must tremble lest some personal bias . . . distort the picture," Du Bois seems almost to argue with himself. On the one hand, he begins, "Convictions on all great matters of human interest one must have to a greater or less degree," and, on the other hand, he continues the thought, "and they will enter to some extent even into the most cold-blooded scientific research as a disturbing factor. . . . Nevertheless, . . . the utmost that the world can demand is, not lack of human conviction, but rather the heart-quality of fairness and an earnest desire for the truth despite its possible unpleasantness" (*DD*, 59; *A*, 199–200). Not only is the pejorative *personal bias* replaced here by the positive *human conviction*, but also *fairness* and *truth* shift in meaning from the realm of scientific objectivity to the subjective virtues of *heart-quality* and *earnest desire*. The effect is troubling but readily overlooked, a slippage in, rather than a fundamental redefinition of, terms.

Similarly equivocal is the concluding exhortation (taken from "The Study of the Negro Problems") on the necessity of "keeping clearly before students the object of all science, amid the turmoil and intense feeling that clouds the discussion of a burning social question" (*DD*, 62; *A*, 201–2). Once again, Du Bois's conflicted position on the assumptions of objectivity ruffles the surface of his logic. Alluding somewhat cryptically to current "flippant" criticism of scientific work and to "sneers at the heroism of the laboratory," he laments that "the truth-seeker is too often pictured as devoid of human sympathy and careless of human ideals" and urges that "at such times true lovers of humanity can only hold higher the pure ideals of science" (*DD*, 62–63; *A*, 202). If Gustav Schmoller and others accepted the compatibility of the inductive method and the collection of empirical data with the formulation of social policy, still they would not have been receptive to the far more radical position of Du Bois's implied thesis: love of humanity, not simply social uplift, constitutes, not simply an accessory to, but the very foundation of pure science.

The equivocation of these passages—the strained logic, the slippery terms, the reluctant tone—is both underscored and explained by the commentary of the autobiographical "I." What Du Bois had been ambivalent and troubled about then, he embraces unequivocally now: the necessary "personal bias," the inevitable "moral conviction" of the scientist. First, Du Bois frames both autobiographical accounts of his work as assistant professor at the University of Pennsylvania by assuming from the outset the non-neutrality—the interestedness—of the city of Philadelphia in commissioning the study. As he says in *Dusk of Dawn* (in a passage that he saw fit to omit in the parallel material in the *Autobiography*): "The fact was that the city of Philadelphia at that time had a theory"—that the city was "going to the dogs" because of "its Negro citizens." "Philadelphia wanted to prove this by figures and I was the man to do it" (*DD*, 58). Both autobiographies conclude: "Of the theory back of the plan, I neither knew nor cared. I saw only here a chance to study an historical group of black folk and to show exactly what their place was in the community. I did it despite extraordinary difficulties both within and without the group. Whites said, Why study the obvious? Blacks said, Are we animals to be dissected and by an unknown Negro at that?" (*DD*, 58; *A*, 197). Strikingly conjoined here are the two reconceived roles, Du Bois's as investigator and that of the black people of Philadelphia as his object of study. Du Bois unveils himself as a deeply engaged, far from disinterested investigator and dignifies his object of study as "an historical group of black folk." Just as Du Bois is liberated from the bonds of scientific methodology to speak openly of his own position in the study, so do the "black folk" whom he studies talk back.

Second, as if to ensure that his later readers would not, as had the earlier, scholarly audience, miss the radical implications of this reconception, in the *Autobiography* Du Bois amplifies the account given in *Dusk of Dawn* of the work that he did in Philadelphia's Seventh Ward. This passage, spotlighting his own contradictory role as participant-observer in the research, originates much earlier, first written for *Darkwater,* and then re-cited in the *Autobiography:*

> Few persons ever read that fat volume on *The Philadelphia Negro,* but they treat it with respect, and that consoles me. The colored people of Philadelphia received me with no open arms. They had a natural dislike to being studied like a strange species. I met again and in different guise those curious cross-currents and inner social whirlings. They set me to groping. I concluded that I did not know so much as I might about my own people. . . . I became painfully aware that merely being born in a group, does not necessarily make one possessed of complete knowledge concerning it. I had learned more from Philadelphia Negroes than I had taught them concerning the Negro Problem. (*D,* 493; *A,* 198)

Alternately inflating and mocking himself, Du Bois acknowledges both the limits and the possibilities of his conflicted connection to the group that he studies. Declaring his dependence on them, he declares their independence from him. The "curious cross-currents and inner social whirlings," which the autobiographical Du Bois remembers set him "to groping," reiterate, and deepen, another earlier formulation in "The Study of the Negro Problems" to which Du Bois alludes in the autobiographical accounts, but always without directly incorporating. This is "sociological interpretation," one of the four divisions of study, devoted to "those finer manifestations of social life . . . which statistics cannot count": the "expressions of Negro life . . . that manifest the existence of a distinct social mind" ("SNP," 83). That the "social mind" also always includes unconscious forces, or "inner social whirlings," the *Autobiography* makes clear. While the scientific investigator emerges in the autobiographies with his own sympathies fully invested and fully visible, just as important his object of study also comes into view, now defined both as a problem and as a people. The investigator is foregrounded for his subjectivity, the objects of study for their historicity.

In the process, it is the objects of study—the "Philadelphia Negroes"—who take the place of the Negro Problem and emerge as historical subjects in their own right. The autobiographies reveal, not an "inert changeless mass" ("SNP," 78), a fixed object of study, or a problem, but the latent subject of Du Bois's sociological study, "a changing racial group" in "a changing, developing society" (*DD*, 51: *A*, 206). That black people have a history and that they should be studied as "a long historic development" (e.g., *DD*, 59; *A*, 199) are two axioms of Du Bois's sociology, but only in the autobiographical re-citation of these axioms is the radical import of his historicism fully unveiled. Much as with the "Problems" thesis, the autobiographies gather together as a concentrated force the repeated references, scattered throughout "The Study of the Negro Problems," to what the autobiographies term the "historic development" of the Negro "Problems." Among the far-reaching consequences of such historicism, the key is Du Bois's methodological insight that to historicize the problem is also to make it plural. As he argues in a passage buried within a subsection of "The Study of the Negro Problems" (headed, significantly—and, in the light of the later autobiographical citation, misleadingly—"Development of the Negro Problems"): "Though we ordinarily speak of the Negro problem as though it were one unchanged question, students must recognize the obvious facts that this problem . . . has had a long historical development, has changed with the growth and evolution of the nation; moreover, that it is not one problem, but rather a plexus of social problems" ("SNP," 71–72). Here, we have arrived at the formulation of the plural "Problems" thesis that Du Bois cites and foregrounds in both autobiographies.

The final autobiographical word on *The Philadelphia Negro* identifies as its greatest accomplishment this fundamental reconception of its own object of study: "It was as complete a scientific study and answer as could have then been given, with defective facts and statistics, one lone worker and little money. It revealed the Negro group as a symptom, not a cause; as a striving, palpitating group, and not an inert, sick body of crime; as a long historic development and not a transient occurrence" (*DD*, 59; *A*, 198–99). In language reminiscent of his 1903 classic *The Souls of Black Folk*, Du Bois has refashioned his 1899 sociological study into a lyric history of race consciousness, one in which "spiritual strivings," located in the community of Philadelphia, become "a striving, palpitating group," "an historical group of black folk." At the same time, Du Bois reaffirms his own commitment as a social scientist to the importance of "historical study" (the first of the four divisions in "The Study of the Negro Problems"). Because "sociology was history abstracted," notes David Levering Lewis,[85] Du Bois framed his study of the Seventh Ward in a two-hundred-year time span, a necessary move given that "one cannot study the Negro in freedom and come to general conclusions about his destiny without knowing his history in slavery" ("SNP," 76). The ultimate end point of such historicizing is finally located only in *Dusk of Dawn,* where Du Bois explains the "clash of ideologies" (among which are those of Booker T. Washington, and others) as the expression of social forces, reasoned, habitual, and unconscious: "The total result was the history of our day. That history may be epitomized in one word—Empire" (*DD,* 96). In a word, Du Bois links his "laboratory experiment" on the streets of Philadelphia to the global political and economic forces of world imperialism ("the domination of white Europe over black Africa and yellow Asia")—or, better yet, in the two words of the chapter title, "Science and Empire" (*DD,* 96).

The autobiographies thus make legible the "soul" of *The Philadelphia Negro:* its revelation, from within the veil, of the "spiritual strivings"— "those curious cross-currents and inner social whirlings"—of "black folk." We know that this is really nothing new for Du Bois the sociologist, who had always been studying the "social mind" of the Negro, long relying on such nonconventional, nondocumentary forms of evidence as fiction and poetry (Frances E. W. Harper's *Forest Leaves* and *Iola Leroy* are included, along with more traditional social-scientific sources, in the bibliography of *The Philadelphia Negro*) to reveal what "statistics cannot count." Similarly, Du Bois devotes extended attention in his Philadelphia monograph to the elusive presence of secret societies ("it is almost impossible to get accurate statistics of all these orders" [*PN,* 224]) and their role in fostering broad-reaching political and community organization. "Mastery of the art of social organized life" is the art "hardest for the freedman to learn," but it is also evidence of "a long, slow process of growth" as well as of hope for the future (*PN,* 221, 233). Most important, to reveal "the long historical development" of the Negro is to displace the Negro Problem with "the souls of black folk" and to unveil the lyric historicism that constitutes the subversive methodology of all Du Bois's work in social science.[86]

Du Bois's great schizoid monograph points more broadly to the hybridity of the larger black sociological enterprise. Writing on the late-nineteenth-century "prehistory" of black sociology, the historian Paul Jefferson argues that academic sociology emerged in the midst of an omnibus reform movement, demonstrating the yoking of scientific objectives with moral and polemical imperatives. Given what Jefferson calls the "practical idealism" of mainstream academic sociology, the minority counterpart must be thought of as even more thoroughly "Janus-faced," producing "rival conceptions of the cultural function of science." The Hampton-Tuskegee approach was to favor rhetoric—the effective communication of ideas to the foundations and donors of the day—over research, the latter associated with the Atlanta conferences and the ultimate failure of Du Bois's project to "put science into sociology."[87] The hybridity of Du Bois's project emerges most fully when he locates his social-scientific texts within the autobiographical context, reading them both with and against the grain. The subjectivity of autobiography as genre merely provides the grounds for the passionate defense of scientific advocacy that had always permeated and troubled the surface of Du Bois's sociology. The "Apology" to *Dusk of Dawn* acknowledges without resolving the autobiographical paradox: "I have written then what is meant to be not so much my autobiography as the autobiography of a concept of race, elucidated, magnified and doubtless distorted in the thoughts and deeds which were mine" (*DD*, viii).[88]

Citing Egypt/Egyptian Sites

Reading *Darkwater* in the textual context of self-citation and the cultural context of the racial occult will provide the conclusion, and final challenge, of this chapter. The second of Du Bois's multigenred histories of a race concept—what he calls in *Dusk of Dawn* "three sets of thoughts centering around the hurts and hesitancies that hem the black man in America"—*Darkwater* is assessed, in comparison to the others, as "an exposition and militant challenge, defiant with dogged hope" (*DD*, vii). Also operating within a similar mode of autobiographical self-citation, *Darkwater* begins, as does *The Souls of Black Folk*, with the standard acknowledgment of prior publications: "Many of my words appear here transformed from other publications and I thank the *Atlantic* [magazine etc.] . . . for letting me use them again" (*D*, 483–44). Half the nine chapters of *Darkwater* devoted to social criticism and fiction had appeared in shorter versions in a variety of publications; following each chapter are shorter interludes of poetry and allegorical vignettes, several of which had previously been published; and the autobiographical sketch at the opening ("I was born by a golden river and in the shadow of two great hills . . . " [*D*, 485]) was derived from the account in *The Souls of Black Folk*. The unorthodox formal structure of both works—collage (a combination of essays and poems or lyric interludes)—defines the interpretive challenge of reading Du Bois's multi-genred texts, but, as Eric Sundquist remarks, the pieces of *Darkwater* function pivotally—even more than do those of *The Souls of Dark Folk*—to connect surrounding texts through a kind of impressionistic logic, one in which rigorous "economic analysis can suddenly give way to an intense lyric moment."[89]

Yet, in addition to the familiar Du Boisean collage of previously published work, *Darkwater* features another, much more elusive form of self-citation, one that clusters around two textual sites: the consciousness of Egypt and the consciousness of pageantry that pervade the text. Harder to pin down, more of an echo or an aura than anything else, these sites of consciousness would be less visible, as citations, without some familiarity with the larger pattern of self-citation in Du Bois. But there is no doubt that *Darkwater* is striking for what Sundquist calls a "pageantlike theatricality," in which a series of theatricalized scenes lift the veil, "like a stage curtain," to reveal the African past and diaspora history.[90] Both a dramatic form and a historical content, the pageants "cited" in the text, most notably including but not limited to Du Bois's "Star of Ethiopia," extend outward to the context of the culture of pageantry in the war decade with which we are already familiar. The two cites/sites are interlocked in both text and context, for ancient Egypt, as variously imagined by black popular and academic historians as well as by many racial occultists and fraternalists, provides a jumping-off point, in time, if not in space, for the racial pageantry of *Darkwater*. Because the invention of Egypt was so instrumental both to Du Bois's text and to his context, tracing the presence of the concept in its various forms in *Darkwater*, and beyond, is an essential beginning.

One of Du Bois's signature sites, Egypt serves as a refrain throughout his writings. All the Egypts that proliferate in an interpretive line throughout Du Bois's works from 1903 to the post–World War II period also illustrate his changing uses of a single body of evidence. Egypt is invoked in a variety of ways: mystically and spiritually, as in *The Souls of Black Folk;* historically, as in *The Negro*, where it is treated as a body of evidence and interpretation produced by secondary sources; archaeologically and ethnographically, as in the *Encyclopedia Africana*, where Du Bois would have collaborated with the English ethnographer William Matthew Flinders-Petrie and the American anthropologist Franz Boas.[91] Best known, perhaps, are the sphinxes that frame *The Souls of Black Folk:* "the tale of Ethiopia the Shadowy and of Egypt the Sphinx" at the opening and the "veiled, unanswered sphinxes on the shores of science" at the closing (*SBF*, 102, 238). In between, "the Egypt of the Confederacy" (his term [*SBF*, 163, 165]) raises the "Egypt Problem" (my term), noted by many.

What is the Egypt Problem? If the notion of Egypt lends itself to universal metaphors (e.g., the riddle of the sphinx), Egypt is also a specific place in time and space, representing the prehistory of Du Bois's Pan-Africa, what Sundquist describes as a nation consisting of "a transhistorical consciousness" rather than a particular geography or racial body.[92] Foregrounding the multivalence of "Egypt," Du Bois uses the sphinx in *The Suppression of the African Slave Trade* (1896) as a warning, an allusion to the "pressing questions" still unanswered in the "lesson for Americans" of the struggle against the slave trade: "The riddle of the Sphinx may be postponed, it may be evasively answered now; sometime it must be fully answered."[93] But, as a figure of submerged history, Egypt poses yet another problem. Many critics note the fundamental contradiction in the metaphoric relation of Egypt to Africa-America: how it can be both the place of bondage, the prison house before liberation, and the source of civilization, the site of pharaonic grandeur, monumental history, and imperial political forms?[94] As the touchstone for Masonic history, Egypt is equally ambiguous: although most historians regularly assume a Masonic connection with ancient Egypt—asserting that references to Egypt, and to the thesis of the origins of Masonic symbology and myth in the Egyptian mysteries, were central to Freemasonry at the outset—Wilson Moses questions whether there is such a thing as Masonic Egypt at all or whether Masonic Egypt has been manufactured by Afrocentric historiography.[95] Echoing this view, but with a more favorable spin, Stephen Howe notes that a Masonic influence has continued, "more or less underground," into twentieth-century Egyptology, including its Afrocentric versions. It is the enigma of Egypt, the multiple and polyvalent riddles of the sphinx, I would argue, that makes it so fertile a location for Du Boisean historiography.[96]

Most striking, from my perspective, is the "Egypt" effect of *Darkwater*. There, amid a confluence of Egypts—ancient and modern, archaeological and Masonic, historical and mystical—Du Bois produces what is, by virtually any measure, the single, most sustained intervention in gender of his career. But the Egypt citations of *Darkwater* are as difficult to locate as they are critical to the female-gendered pageant of world history on the color line that is unique to this text. Nowhere else in his writing is Du Bois so tangibly committed to constructing a feminist, diasporic history, yet even here it is located between the lines, so to speak, in the interstices between two pieces derived from earlier texts (the poem "The Riddle of the Sphinx" and the essay "Hands of Ethiopia") and an entirely new essay, written expressly for this text, "The Damnation of Women." Frequently excerpted and anthologized, "The Damnation of Women" has a kind of exceptional standing in Du Bois studies, often treated as though it literally stands alone as a feminist manifesto. Yet the essay also, perplexingly, fits with the contradictions characteristic of Du Bois's thinking on gender and sexuality.[97] Eric Sundquist, however, argues that, in a "far-reaching and powerful trope" of the body of Pan-Africa ("a simultaneously geographical and physiological body," violated by the slave trade and colonial rule), Du Bois made more pronounced than any previous writer the "feminist dimensions of anticolonial ideology."[98]

So it does a disservice to such "a pivotal chapter"[99] as "The Damnation of Women" to read it out of its original context in *Darkwater*, a crucible text in which Du Bois's views of black womanhood emerge in all their contradictions. Not only should "The Damnation of Women" be read back into the text of *Darkwater*, where, as chapter 7, it follows from and moves beyond the moments of womanist history in the previously published pieces, but, as I have already argued, it should also be placed in the context of the war decade, the era of political pageantry, internationalist race history, and assorted racial mysticisms. Doing so will demonstrate how constitutive Du Bois's practice of textual bricolage is, both to the transformative uses and meanings of his essays and to the specific historical circumstances that coalesced to produce *Darkwater*.

Constructed, like *The Souls of Black Folk*, of "fugitive pieces," *Darkwater* is a textual collage, or, better yet, a cannibal, a text that feeds on many published works, not all of them Du Bois's own, and not all equally acknowledged. Du Bois's well-known citation, without attribution, of the passage "when and where I enter," from Anna Julia Cooper's *A Voice from the South* (1892), inserted right in the middle of "The Damnation of Women," marks one unmistakable limit of the text's advocacy of black women. Du Bois, Joy James notes, advocated women's rights but "veiled" the achievements of individual women such as Cooper.[100] Yet, at the same time, the articulation of the feminist politics of *Darkwater* could not have been achieved without Du Bois's many uses of citation, both of himself and of others. The best example of this is the chain of re-citation set off by the poem "The Riddle of the Sphinx," originally published in the November 1907 *Horizon* as "The Burden of Black Women," and reprinted under the same title in the November 1914 *Crisis*, where it followed an editorial, "World War and the Color Line." That editorial, which identifies "the wild quest for Imperial expansion" as the larger cause of the war in Europe,[101] is a rehearsal for the influential analysis that Du Bois would offer a year later in his May 1915 *Atlantic Monthly* essay about the global competition of colonialism, "The African Roots of War." Finally, when Du Bois incorporated the 1915 essay into *Darkwater*, he used much of it for a new piece, "The Hands of Ethiopia" (chapter 3), as well as for "The Souls of White Folk" (chapter 2), actually an amalgam of three essays, one of the same name first published in 1910, a second, "Of the Culture of White Folk," published in 1917, and a third, "On Being Black," published in 1920.[102] These chapters, in their final form, frame the renamed "The Riddle of the Sphinx," which has reappeared (seemingly out of nowhere) on the radar screen. Such is the life history of one of Du Bois's complex chains of re-citation.

These revised chapters, linked by the crying voices of the dark daughter and black mother in the poem, now titled "The Riddle of the Sphinx" and functioning as an interlude between chapters, present the maelstrom of a world war of the races as an expository call-and-response generated in relation to the poem's riddle. The multiple textual locations of this cluster of writings—as well as the multiple contexts, shifting from war and anti-colonialism, to feminism, to race consciousness and mysticism—are paradigmatic of how instrumental the practice of self-citation is to the extended meditation in *Darkwater* on the role of woman in race history and world civilization.

Equally central to the dense texture of the feminist historicism of *Darkwater* is the political and cultural context in which it was written. Reading *Darkwater* as part of the cultural ensemble of the war decade shows how the text's representation of a female-centered black history relied on and adapted particular discourses of popular occultisms. We have already seen evidence of a Masonic imprint on *Darkwater* in Du Bois's opening citation of his "Credo," written (according to Charles Wesley) in the characteristic style of a Masonic pledge.[103] Claudia Tate sees a further connection between the "Credo" and "The Star of Ethiopia," twin expressions of "African American political confidence" that, she argues, are consolidated in Du Bois's 1928 *Dark Princess*, with its finale of messianic pageantry.[104] *Darkwater* also draws specifically on Egyptological occult discourses, derived from the myth of Osiris and Isis, to produce both an Egypt and an Africa that are notably gendered female. Equally influential, the variety of feminisms competing during the decade—associated both with popular fraternalism and with political reformism, and often compromised by racial and class divisions—provide an explanatory context for the possibilities and the compromises in Du Bois's own feminist politics. Indeed, we could go so far as to say that the feminist vision of *Darkwater* was made possible by the conjunction of these particular forces at this particular moment. Only in this sense is it an exceptional work. Whatever the limitations of the cultural context, it produced in *Darkwater* an extended engagement with a lyrical feminist historicism the likes of which Du Bois was never to achieve again.

Although "The Damnation of Women" is the centerpiece of the feminist vision of *Darkwater,* the first of the text's prominently gendered locations coalesces, rather unexpectedly, around the revised version of Du Bois's famous essay on war and colonialism, "The African Roots of War." Grouped with two other previously published works, the essay forms the center of a cluster of citations, arranged to introduce the black-feminist historical sensibility that comes to full flower in "The Damnation of Women." Retitled, substantially revised, and transformed into "The Hands of Ethiopia," in its new form the essay is flanked by two vignettes—a poem, "The Riddle of the Sphinx," and the allegorical "The Princess of the Hither Isles" (taken from the October 1913 *Crisis*)—both of which foreground female voices and figures. For Sundquist, the overall narrative strategy of juxtaposition, alternating lyric and analytic sections, makes for a "nearly complete fluidity between the aesthetic and political spaces" of *Darkwater.*[105] The specific effect of the rearranged texts and contexts is, I would argue, to foreground the question of gender: the revised "Hands of Ethiopia," framed by the feminist symbology of the lyric interludes that surround it, not only emerges as far more "militant" and "defiant" (to use Du Bois's own terms, formulated later in the preface to *Dusk of Dawn,* for *Darkwater* as a whole) than the original "African Roots of War," but also accentuates the moment, at the very end of the essay, where, we will see, woman takes precedence over war.

The new militancy of "The Hands of Ethiopia," to which the exemplary "demand" "Africa for Africans" has been added, should not be all that surprising, given the deep disillusionment suffered by African Americans in the aftermath of World War I.[106] The temporal distance alone of five years between the publication dates of "The African Roots of War" and *Darkwater* is sufficient to account for the more defiant, prophetic mode of "The

Hands of Ethiopia." Heralded by its new, biblical title, the essay prophesies global revolutionary action as the only possible response to worldwide racial oppression and economic exploitation. For "the trained man of darker blood," who represents "the vast majority of mankind," "there is but one thing . . . to do and that is definitely and openly as possible to organize his world for war against Europe" (D, 513). Openly espoused in 1920 are those things that had been posed in 1915 as rhetorical questions or veiled abstractions for future consideration: "But is this inevitable? Must we sit helpless before this awful prospect?" "We are calling for European concord to-day; . . . but . . . the colored peoples will not always submit passively to foreign domination."[107] In an entirely new, highly figurative paragraph, added to the *Darkwater* version of the essay, Du Bois underscores the political threat of the biblical prophecy: "The hands which Ethiopia shall soon stretch out unto God are not mere hands of helplessness and supplication, but rather are they hands of pain and promise; hard, gnarled, and muscled for the world's real work; they are hands of fellowship for the half submerged masses of a distempered world; they are hands of helpfulness for an agonized God!" (D, 520). The riff on *hands,* from "helplessness" to "helpfulness," from empty to full, provides one measure of the metaphoric distance from the 1915 essay to the 1920 *Darkwater.*

Another equally striking measure is the deepened historicism of "The Hands of Ethiopia." Although both essays begin with the same words, the cry of the Roman proconsul, "*Semper novi quid ex Africa!*" (the very line that concludes *The Negro*), and at the same intellectual starting point, the place of Africa in world history, the 1915 version truncates its analysis of "human empire" with the dismissive "so much for the past."[108] The *Darkwater* version, however, fills in the "four-hundred year" "indictment of Africa against Europe," asserting that "the present problem of problems is nothing more than democracy beating itself helplessly against the color bar" (D, 511–12). Most important, thanks to this extended historicism, the final paragraph of the chapter, identical to that of the 1915 essay, takes on new life in the larger context of *Darkwater.* What is an "incidental element" in "The African Roots of War" becomes, Sundquist notes, "by the juxtaposition of the essay with 'The Riddle of the Sphinx' the commanding figure for the colonial devastation of the 'body' of the African continent."[109]

Following the passage on the hands of Ethiopia that Du Bois added to "The African Roots of War," the concluding paragraph traces an inverted world history, a tragedy of the destruction of civilizations, from ancient Egypt to present-day Africa, figured as a "weeping and waiting" black woman, and closing with the prophetic question, "What shall the end be?" (*D*, 520). It is a kind of incipient pageant, in microcosm, of a black, female-centered past and a prophetic future, a dramatic enactment of the Ethiopianist promise of the chapter title. The pageant begins in Africa, twenty years before Christ, with the "blotting out" of the culture of Egypt; shifts to five hundred years later, when Egypt was "redeemed" by "a black woman, Queen Nefertari, 'the most venerated figure in Egyptian history'"; and ends, finally, twenty centuries after Christ, with black Africa "prostrated, raped, and shamed" by the conquering Philistines of Europe and "beyond the awful sea a black woman . . . weeping and waiting, with her sons on her breast." "What shall the end be?" The answer: a repetition of the opening line, "*Semper novi quid ex Africa!*" (*D*, 520). That this is also the concluding line of Du Bois's *The Negro* confirms how integral the practice of citation is to the feminist and diasporic historicism of *Darkwater*.

Here is our first glimpse of the constitutive black woman of *Darkwater*, summoned forth in a dramatic moment of historical invocation. It is a frozen moment, both a foreshadowing of and a gateway to the elaborate pageant of world history presented in "The Damnation of Women." There, Du Bois stages a veritable parade of female figures—"from the primal black All-Mother of Men down through the ghostly throng of mighty womanhood, who walked in the mysterious dawn of Asia and Africa, . . . from black Neith down to 'That starr'd Ethiop queen . . . ,' through dusky Cleopatras, dark Candaces, and darker, fiercer Zinghas, to our own day and our own land,—in gentle Phillis; . . . the sybil, Sojourner Truth; and the martyr, Louise De Mortie" (*D*, 565–66). Not only is the Queen Nefertari of "The Hands of Ethiopia" a harbinger of the "starr'd Ethiop queen" of both *The Negro* and "The Damnation of Women," but the earlier chapter, focused on world war, also prefigures the pattern of time in the pageant proper in "The Damnation of Women," where Du Bois unfolds the chronology of world history as a movement "down-from-through-to."

Hints of pageant time emerge in the poetic interlude, "The Riddle of the Sphinx," that precedes "The Hands of Ethiopia." The poem, originally entitled "The Burden of Black Women," first recasts the location of the burden of the "Dark daughter of the lotus leaves" (*D*, 509) from the original, shadowy "out of the past of the Past's grey past"[110] to the *Darkwater* version, "out of the South,—the sad, black South" (*D*, 509). Relocated from a time to a place, the South of the poem, Sundquist says, is both African and American, just as slavery and colonial rule are "coterminous" in Du Bois's imagination.[111] Then, in a series of apocalyptic lines, each beginning with the word *down,* the speaker prophesies the dark daughter's redemption from "the white man's burden": "And they that raised the boasters / Shall drag them down again,— / Down with the theft of their thieving / . . . / Down with their barter of women / . . . / down/down/deep down" (*D,* 510). The movement downward toward retribution gives way in the next several lines to the prophetic fullness of time, with the temporal *till* ("Till the devil's strength be shorn, / Till some dim, darker David . . . / Bid the black Christ be born!") and the biblical *shall* ("Then shall our burden be manhood") (*D,* 510). Having transformed "the white man's burden" into "our burden," "The Riddle of the Sphinx" concludes with images of both the black Messiah and the "black mother of the iron hills that ward the / blazing sea" (*D,* 510).

As an avatar of the black woman invoked at the end of "The Hands of Ethiopia," weeping and waiting, beyond the awful sea, the black mother of "The Riddle of the Sphinx" is also a harbinger of the historical pageant of black women in "The Damnation of Women." The earlier group of pieces that cluster around "The Hands of Ethiopia," all versions of previously published material, provides a preview of Du Bois's full-blown pageantry in "The Damnation of Women": both of its temporal form, a procession down, from, and through history, and of its historical content, the figures of black women, "darker sisters," "daughters of sorrow," who dramatize their own history (*D,* 565).

The incorporation of pageantry as a dramatic form and as historical content in "The Damnation of Women" represents a mode of self-citation radically different from the practices that we have seen thus far. No passages from Du Bois's own writings are quoted wholesale, nor is his pageant "The Star of Ethiopia" referred to. Nonetheless, his "penchant for pageantry" suffuses the entire chapter. As a mode of spatial and temporal organization, the pageant structures both the opening account of the four women of Du Bois's boyhood ("they represented the problem of the widow, the wife, the maiden, and the outcast") and, especially, the ensuing staging of "the great black race in passing up the steps of human culture," through a procession of black female figures, mythical, historical, and little known (*D,* 564, 566). The parade of dramatis personae clearly draws, in spirit, form, and content, on Du Bois's own "Star of Ethiopia," first performed in 1913 and reviewed, by Du Bois, in 1915, the same year as "The African Roots of War." We already know how formative the citing of the war essay was to the shape of *Darkwater.* Yet, as is common with Du Bois's self-citation, when "The Star of Ethiopia" is filtered through the historical consciousness of *Darkwater*, in this case explicitly gendered female, the effect looks different, as though the pageant had been rewritten to unveil its own latent, female-centered history.

The historical pageant of black women in "The Damnation of Women" repeats the geotemporal structure of "The Star of Ethiopia," its six episodes of race history each associated with a different gift. But these "gifts of black men to this world" ("SE[1]," 306) do not make visible the womanist history of "The Damnation of Women," so Du Bois adapts, as he repeats at the opening of the chapter, the civilizational image of "passing up the steps of human culture" (*D*, 566). It is "as if," he remarks, in "The Damnation of Women," "the great black race . . . gave the world not only the Iron Age . . . but also, in peculiar emphasis, the mother-idea" (*D*, 566). To stage world history through and as a maternal genealogy fundamentally revises the monumental history of "The Star of Ethiopia." Most of the predominantly male figures of black history dramatized in the six episodes of the pageant, from Ra and Mohammed, to Crispus Attucks and Frederick Douglass, to Toussaint and Turner, fade away in "The Damnation of Women"; instead, the female figures, some already present in the cast of characters of "The Star of Ethiopia," come to the fore, taking center stage more there than they do anywhere else in *Darkwater*. The "Queen of Sheba" and "Candace of Ethiopia," who in "The Star of Ethiopia" merely "join the procession at intervals" while Ra is crowned "Priest and King" ("SE[1]," 307), define the great middle period of women's history in "The Damnation of Women" (the *through* of the "down-from-through-to") and are renamed there "dusky Cleopatras, dark Candaces, and darker, fiercer Zinghas" ("SE[1]," 307; *D*, 566). Sojourner Truth plays a part in both works, even speaking the same line in the same setting, an abolitionist meeting where Frederick Douglass is onstage and Sojourner Truth a member of the audience. In both texts, she asks, in implicit rebuke to his message of violent rebellion, "Frederick, is God dead?" ("SE[1]," 309–10; *D*, 572). But, while in "The Star of Ethiopia" he thunders back an answer, reiterated by the heralds of the pageant, in "The Damnation of Women" she has the last word. Her question, left unanswered, concludes the scene. Finally, the "Veiled Woman"—dimly present in most of the six episodes of "The Star of Ethiopia," but not "unveiled in her chariot" until the end, when she is revealed as "the All-Mother, formerly the Veiled Woman" ("SE[1]," 310)—functions in "The Damnation of Women" as "the primal black All-Mother," heading the procession from the very beginning of time (*D*, 565).

The "All-Mother" of "The Damnation of Women" presides over her "daughters of sorrow"—the "darker sisters" of the world that "worships womankind" but "studiously forgets" them—who "typify that veiled Melancholy" (*D*, 565). To unveil their forgotten history, not simply a history of famous black women, but an explicitly gendered and sexualized race history of womanhood, is the fundamental project driving "The Damnation of Women." It is a "history of insult and degradation," but, Du Bois emphasizes, with results "both fearful and glorious" (*D*, 569). Dramatized in stages that parallel but revise the chronology and geography of "The Star of Ethiopia," the history of "the black motherhood of this race" is traced from the "African mother-idea," down through the "crushing weight" of the westward slave trade and American slavery, to five million granddaughters "of Negro descent" in 1910, "an efficient womanhood, whose strength lies in its freedom" (*D*, 568–69). It is also a hidden history: "the outward numerical fact of social dislocation"—measured by such statistics as the ratio of males to females in the American black population—tells little of "the hell beneath the system," where "within lay polygamy, polyandry, concubinage, and moral degradation" (*D*, 567). To unveil, and to dramatize on the textual stage, such a specific social and economic history of reproduction, "The Damnation of Women" combines pageantry with sociology, statistics with passion, and scholarly sources with the voices of ordinary women.

The cast of characters shifts dramatically from the roll call of the mythical and the famous of "The Star of Ethiopia," with the Cleopatras and Candaces playing bit parts, subordinated to the real stars of the pageantry of "The Damnation of Women," the largely unknown and unsung black women of everyday life in the modern race history of the Americas. Among these, announced by the unattributed Anna Julia Cooper quotation, are "a cousin of my grandmother, whom western Massachusetts remembers as 'Mum Bett,'" a runaway in Great Barrington, "scarred for life by a blow received in defense of a sister" and one of the first slaves to be freed under the Bill of Rights of 1780; Kate Ferguson, born in New York long before the Declaration of Independence, who established the first modern Sunday School in Manhattan; Mary Shadd, "out of Delaware," teacher, editor, lecturer, and recruiting agent for black soldiers in the West; and Louise De Mortie, "a free-born Virginia girl" and "a woman of feeling and intellect," who worked with "the orphaned colored children New Orleans,—out of freedom into insult and oppression and into the teeth of the yellow fever" (*D*, 569–73). Unlike the mostly mute, largely symbolic figures of "The Star of Ethiopia," these ordinary black women live in the concrete detail of local histories and speak, where possible, in their own voices. On the "strong women that laid the foundations of the great Negro church of today," Du Bois quotes a long passage from "one of the early mothers of the church, Mary Still," writing in the 1840s (D, 570). Even when he brings onstage such well-known, representative women as Harriet Tubman and Sojourner Truth ("two striking figures of wartime"), he gives or invents for them extended speeches of their own, creating the effect of an imagined oral history (D, 571). Of Phillis Wheatley, whose "muse was slight" by today's measure, he insists: "We call to her still in her own words: 'Through thickest glooms look back, immortal shade'" (D, 572). Layered onto the women's voices is statistical evidence from sociological studies of the kind that Du Bois had conducted—measuring literacy, employment, and "death, divorce, [and] desertion" within the black community—invoked to ground the passionate affirmations of "The Damnation of Women" ("These women are passing through, not only a moral, but an economic revolution") and the equally impassioned laments ("Down in such mire has the black motherhood of this race struggled") (D, 573, 569). Whether citing a line from a Wheatley poem, or incorporating fugitive-slave bills, or quoting the son of the judge who freed Mum Bett (as well as "a sister of a president of the United States" and George Washington himself), or referring to the scholarly authorities on African tribal life (Mungo Park, Schweinfurth, Ratzel), Du Bois draws on all the available sources to give life as well as authority to his pageant of the "mother-idea" as race history (D, 572, 570, 567).

That the figures of black women, and the particular, hidden history that they dramatize, had always been constitutive of Du Bois's historical pageantry becomes apparent when we read backward to "The Star of Ethiopia" from the *Darkwater* perspective. In the advertising imagery and *Crisis* coverage of "The Star of Ethiopia," visual images of women—what Levering Lewis calls the pageant's display of "the flower of Talented Tenth pulchritude"—dominate those of the men by at least two to one.[112] The December 1915 *Crisis* features photographs of Miss Adella Parks, Miss Eleanor Curtis, and Miss Gregoria Fraser in costume as, respectively, the Queen of Sheba, Ethiopia, and Candace of Meroë as well as a photograph of Mrs. Dora Cole Norman, the pageant's director of dancing (see plate 8). (Du Bois appears only in the photograph taken of the local pageant committee.)[113] And, accompanying Du Bois's long essay in the August 1916 *Crisis*, "The Drama among Black Folk," in which he incorporates passages from "The Star of Ethiopia," are group photographs that place front and center the white-robed female participants in the pageant (see plate 9). In the essay,

Du Bois also adds the figure of the mother, not present in the 1913 version, when he cites the opening and closing cry of "the dark and crimson-turbaned Herald" at the pageant. "Hear ye, hear ye!" the herald begins, "learn the ancient Glory of Ethiopia, All-Mother of men, whose wonders men forgot," concluding with the injunction: "And remember forever and one day the Star of Ethiopia, All-Mother of Men, who gave the world the Iron Gift and Gift of Faith" ("DBF," 169, 173). At the very headwaters of black history and the source of race gifts, the maternal presence stands, both forgotten and remembered. The female-only pageantry of "The Damnation of Women" confirms, and compensates for, what this imagery from "The Star of Ethiopia" suggests, that the absence or silence of black motherhood from and in most accounts of race history haunts it nevertheless.

As a syncretic figure standing for this history in "The Damnation of Women," Du Bois's Isis, "the mother," "still titular goddess, in thought if not in name, of the dark continent," brings together the fertility goddess of Madame Blavatsky's *Isis Unveiled* with Africanist myth and ritual as well as the uses of Egyptological symbology in Masonic and black popular history (*D*, 566). In "The Drama among Black Folk," Du Bois comments that "all through Africa pageantry and dramatic recital is close mingled with religious rites and in America the 'Shout' of the church revival is in its essential pure drama" ("DBF," 169). Du Bois's unveiling of Isis as a symbol for "the land of the mother" and "the spell of the African mother" also adapts the Masonic grafting of ancient Egypt onto the Bible (*D*, 566). (Both Solomon's Temple and the Pyramids are standard Masonic emblems.) In the traditional account of biblical history narrated by the Order of the Eastern Star, the five-point star on which the Eastern Star degree is based consists of five biblical figures, "eminent female characters," according to Grimshaw's *History of Freemasonry*, symbolizing the five roles of woman's life—daughter, widow, wife, sister, and mother—as well as the virtues that they embody (Ruth represents devotion, Esther fidelity, and so on). As such, the Eastern Star points, first, to Du Bois's own boyhood history, with the four women who represented the "problem" of the widow, the wife, the maiden, and the outcast, and, second, to the collective history of global black sisterhood dramatized in *Darkwater*. Just as the Eastern Star joins with the Star of Ethiopia to produce "The Damnation of Women" in *Darkwater*, so, too, does "The African Roots of War" become "The Hands of Ethiopia."[114] The discourses of occult mysticism, from Ethiopianism to Freemasonry, underlying the text as a whole form a central organizing principle in the feminist historiography and pageantry of "The Damnation of Women."

Finally, in "The Damnation of Women," Du Bois takes a long, global view of the maternal line of descent, going back to *The Souls of Black Folk*, that he repeats in tracing his personal history in each subsequent autobiography. Here, the sorrowful song of "the little, far-off mother of my grandmothers," cited in the "Bantu" lyrics of "Do bana coba" in the first chapter of *Darkwater*—just as it had been in the final chapter of *The Souls of Black Folk*—does not represent simply his own individual family heritage (*SBF*, 233; *D*, 486); rather, it taps his incantatory memories of world mothers: "As I remember through memories of others, backward among my own family, it is the mother I ever recall. . . . All the way back in these dim distances it is mothers and mothers of mothers who seem to count, while fathers are shadowy memories" (*D*, 567). Dramatizing race-conscious history means making visible the occult history of the African "mother-idea," but not, Du Bois says in "The Damnation of Women," solely as "a survival of the historic matriarchate through which all nations pass,—it appears to be more than this" (*D*, 566). The "more than this" is the world-historical gift of the "mother-idea."

We have, finally, come full circle, back to the maternal melodramas with which we began this book, with Du Bois's global pageant of black history dramatized *as* a maternal melodrama. Du Bois thus concludes my book as a great synthesizer, explicitly historicizing and internationalizing the race melodramas of Cable and Chesnutt, Griggs and Dixon, Twain and Hopkins, as well as contextualizing them in the culture of the occult.[115] The melodramatic synthesis that Du Bois produced is great, however, not for its seamlessness, but rather because it emerges out of the uncertainty, paradox, and irresolution characteristic of the world racial scene at the turn of the century. Nowhere are the tensions more visible than in Du Bois's many formulations of the race concept as a product both of nature and of culture. And, although it is dangerous to rely for long on any single moment of Du Bois's thinking, the synthesis of *Darkwater* provides a passage with which we might conclude. Writing about race antagonism, Du Bois begins with a question that he answers in familiar terms, negating the racist meaning of the only words that he has. First, his answer: "There are no races. . . . There are great groups, . . . and the world today consists, not of races, but of the imperial commercial group of master capitalists . . . ; the national middle classes . . . ; the international laboring class of all colors; the backward, oppressed groups of nature-folk." What was his question? "How should we think such a problem through, not simply as Negroes, but as men and women of a new century, helping to build a new world?" (*D*, 532).

The Politics of Occult Time;
or, But Is It Any Good?

THIS BOOK could not conclude without returning to the link between bad art and bad politics with which I began my discussion in chapter 3. In a sense, this is simply a subset of a larger question on the aesthetics and politics of the race melodrama that has been my central concern from the outset. The political reading of black writers on the race question, for example, is as vexed, we know, as the internal contradictions of Hopkins's blood talk or Du Bois's multiple variants of the Negro Problem. And the political symmetries of Griggs and Dixon—their equally conspiratorial imaginations, their two versions of a nation within a nation—are, if anything, far outweighed by the byzantine plots, stereotypical characterizations, and sheer bad writing of which both are guilty. The question of the politics of race literature is not unrelated to the question of literary evaluation. If Twain's late dream writings have seemed so solipsistic as to negate the very presence of an urgent political engagement, then perhaps the politics have something to do with the aesthetic failure of the texts. An answer may be suggested by what Peter Osborne calls "the politics of historical time" or by what Paul Gilroy, even more pointedly, calls "the racial politics of temporality."[1] The complex temporal arrangements that we have encountered in the texts, all of which are grouped under the sign of the (racial) occult, may provide a key to the politics of time in the race melodramas.

Here is where we have ended up: issues of genre and historical consciousness are linked in the disorder, formal and historical, of the race melodramas. A central manifestation of the historical disorder of the American race experience at the turn of the century is the mix of genres that characterizes the race melodrama. The fictional competes, as we have seen, with the complex network of references to contemporary debates and historical events, with the result that the historical enters the text awkwardly, either cryptically or excessively. At the same time, the race melodramas clearly articulate a vision, or versions, of *race history* inspired by and dependent on popular occultisms of the moment. We might say broadly of the genre's invention of occult history what Du Bois says specifically in "The Conservation of Races": "The American Negro has always felt an intense personal interest in discussions as to the origins and destinies of races."[2] Racial origins *and* destinies: intertwining past and future, racial thinking at the turn of the century produced specific conceptions of time and time consciousness. Among the complex temporal arrangements that we have seen emerge from the various occult perspectives of the race melodramas are the following: Griggs and Dixon cultivate the conspiratorial exposure of what they both fear and desire, both the betrayal and the reincarnation of a revolutionary past that prophesies a possible apocalyptic future of race war; Twainian time travel creates a spatiotemporal simultaneity of past and present; the revolutionary eruption of the past of slavery into the post-Reconstruction present of Hopkins's America and Africa enacts what Du Bois calls an image of "second slavery" as, in Benjamin's terms, it "flashes up" at "a moment of danger."[3] Symptomatic of the disjunctive multidimensionality of all the time frames is the temporality of Ethiopianism, a virtual simultaneity of past and future, prefiguring and fulfillment.

What kind of politics do these conceptions of time add up to? Occult time, a kind of futurology based on the esoteric wisdom of the past, constructs mystical interrelations among past, present, and future; in the race melodramas, the multidimensionality of occult time accounts for hidden intrusions of the past into the present as well as for ongoing and unredeemed claims of the past on the present. The time consciousness of the transtemporal, interspatial, often transoceanic imagined communities of the race melodramas is necessarily disjunctive, reflecting their extraterritorial makeup: Hopkins's matriarchal, interracial families bridging the United States and Africa; Twain's masters and slaves twinned, improbably, in the time and space of antebellum Missouri and colonial India; Dixon's Invisible Empire of reincarnated ancient Scots; Griggs's *imperium in imperio* of modern black American revolutionaries; Du Bois's matrilineal genealogies, narrated in the autobiographies and dramatized in the pageants. Both within and beyond the boundaries of nation and race as well as of the archaic and the modern, these imagined communities resonate with the ambivalent and disjunctive temporalities characteristic of a later moment of national consciousness in an emerging postcolonial world, what Frantz Fanon calls the "zone of occult instability where the people dwell." Fanon writes against the teleology of historical progress, which produces only a sterile conception of time as homogeneous and empty, in favor of a view of history that acknowledges the fundamental instability of tradition during the "period of struggle."[4] Does the language of "occult instability" have a relevance outside the situation of anticolonial struggle? Homi Bhabha asks.[5] Fanon's "occult zone" locates the differential temporalities of the racial occult in an unstable relation of the present to the past, neither the past out of which "the people have already emerged," nor the archaic past of a static traditionalism, but rather "that fluctuating movement which they are just giving a shape to."[6] This is the disjunctive present time of the race melodramas, the battleground, as we have seen, between Benjaminian images of the past, with a claim to present recognition, and "chips of Messianic time" shot throughout the present.

The occult time of the race melodramas is, thus, like Benjamin's angel of history in the Klee painting *Angelus Novus,* who looks backward as he is propelled into the future but sees it all as "one single catastrophe."[7] The angel of occult history is both more and less: Janus-faced, looking simultaneously backward and forward at the wreckage of the racial past and its reenactments, repetitions, and reincarnations in the present, the occult vision does not guarantee either foreknowledge or the outcome of the future itself. Occult history concentrates, not on prophecy or futurology, but rather on a hermeneutic of the past's relation to the present. Rather than beginning at the beginning and postulating an origin, occult time works relationally from the present backward. From their location in the present, the race melodramas face toward the past rather than the future to construct constitutive relations between present and past, with the future a signal pressure, if not presence, charged both with messianic and with apocalyptic possibilities. In the context of the many reinterpretations of U.S. history that characterize the so-called era of national reconciliation, the occult histories—even Dixon's Klan trilogy—refuse the redemption of prophecy in favor of redeeming the past in relation to the present and leaving provisional the outcome of history itself.

This is neither a conservative invocation of tradition that would advocate return to the homeland (à la Garvey) nor the recovery of an earlier moment of purity in the ancient roots that would guarantee a utopian future (whether in Africa, the United States, or anywhere else). Instead, like the "non-traditional tradition" of Paul Gilroy's black Atlantic, which is "irreducibly modern," the messianism of Hopkins's and Du Bois's occults, as well as the apocalyptic strain in the Griggs-Dixon imaginary of race war, is rooted in an ongoing past tense.[8] The prophetic mode of the occult runs counter to the far greater weight accorded the genealogical in their race histories, in which the future remains resolutely open and uncertain while limning the possible—weird and unexpected—saturations of the past in the present. Both Hopkins's maternal spirit writing and Du Bois's performances of a broken matrilinearity work to foreground tensions over where to draw the ever-shifting line between past and present. Likewise, Twain's dream tales within tales of journeys inside archaic and moldering bodies, medieval strangers, and microbes turn out to harbor the most modern, up-to-the-minute evidence of imperial and racial oppressions. These seemingly magical pasts of occult time, which refuse the binaries of tradition and modernity, may even approach what Bhabha calls the "strange temporality of the future perfect," a historical time in which "the deeply repressed past" returns, again and again, in a "strategy of repetition" that disrupts the solidity of modernity.[9]

These multidimensional configurations of past, present, and future articulate an anomalous historical consciousness, neither a linear and periodized chronology that sequesters the past from the present, nor a progressive teleology that subsumes the past into a relentless march forward toward progress. Rather than enshrining what Benjamin decries as the "homogeneous empty time" that characterizes both the "dead" historicism of the conservative and the futurist perspective of the socialist-democrat (as well as the conventional alternatives in mainstream historiography of the modern era), the occult history practiced by the race melodramatists works within a simultaneity of time in which temporal relations both correspond to and exceed the dimensions of past, present, and future.[10] The concept of simultaneity itself has taken on a life of its own, defining for Benjamin, and Benedict Anderson after him, both medieval and modern views of time. The Benjaminian concept of messianic time, a simultaneity of past and future in an instantaneous present, is both revised and superseded by Anderson's idea of simultaneity, or the "transverse, cross-time" of modernity, "marked not by prefiguring and fulfillment [the archaic form of imagining, associated with the religious communities and dynastic realms that precede the modern, imagined community of the nation], but by temporal coincidence, and measured by clock and calendar."[11] Occult time is marked by a disjunctive fusion of both types of simultaneity. The messianism of occult time, however, driven less by a futurist imperative than by the challenge of making visible the partially occluded interrelations of past and present,

leaves open the question of redemption in a mode correspondingly more urgent and less quietist than traditional religious messianism.

This is, paradoxically, what Benjamin would consider a redemptive
philosophy of history in which images of the past are not permitted to dis-
appear, "lost for history," but rather recognized *by* the present as concerns
of the present.[12] To "articulate the past historically," in the Benjaminian
sense, is to recognize the past as an image that "flashes up" in the present—
the maternal spirits and birthmarked bodies haunting the modern Ethiopia
of *Of One Blood* (in which ancient Meroë lies embedded, preserved as a living anachronism), the antebellum South in India of Twain's *Following the
Equator,* the grandmother's song, sung in incomprehensible African words,
that continually resurfaces in Du Bois's autobiographies—and to grasp the
"constellation" formed by our own era with "a definite earlier one," taking
"a revolutionary chance in the fight for the oppressed past." The net result:
to establish a conception of the present as the "'time of the now' which is
shot through with chips of Messianic time."[13] The race melodramatists con-
strue history as just such a revolutionary mode, combining and bridging the
genealogical and prophetic with the messianic and apocalyptic. Their occult temporality does not simply recover an occluded past—although the
drive to excavate alternative histories and counter mainstream narratives
(Africa as the land without history) is certainly a major motivation of the
revisionists in the literature of national reconciliation as it is of the practitioners of African American historiography. For all our writers, bringing
into view the presence of the past in the present (a move that often requires
plumbing the paradoxes of a hidden, hypervisibility that eludes full detec-
tion) is the means by which to stake a claim on the future, the outcome of
which remains resolutely uncertain, a call to action superimposed on the qui-
etism of conventional messianic expectations. Such a cross-generational
continuity in the "now" (*Jetzeit,* which, according to Benjamin's translator,
means, not simply "the present," but "the mystical *nunc stans*") enacts the
"temporal index" that marks the redemption of the past: "There is a secret
agreement between past generations and the present one."[14]

Narrative is the key to the hermeneutics of occult history: the tracing of
genealogical lines along with the prefiguring of the future constructs a history without teleological logic but *with* meaning. History for the race melodramatists *is* narrative. The proliferation that we have seen in their texts of
frame narratives and interpolated tales (especially the maternal genealogies
inset and set off in Hopkins, Chesnutt, Cable, and Du Bois) is the primary
means by which history is both constituted and represented in the race

melodrama. The opening frame of *Contending Forces* is paradigmatic: "A Retrospect of the Past," we recall, set in the time and place of slavery, offers an initially disjunctive temporality that ultimately and explosively takes on meaning in relation to the novel's present through a tale told in post-Reconstruction Boston. There are also the conspiratorial tales of night riding and black riots in Griggs and Dixon, the inset narratives layered within the onion skins, or the bodies, of Twain's science fiction, and the multiple re-narrations of Du Bois's maternal genealogy. The narratives trace an explicitly nonsequential set of temporal relations based on rupture (Mabelle Beaubean becomes Sappho, permanently) and disruption (the archaic body of the tramp contains the corruption of the imperial present) without conclusion or even future resolution. Rather than the full-blown messianism of a Garvey, for example, which approaches both pure ideology and power grab, the race melodramatists opt instead to provide a frame of interpretation that foregrounds the contradictions, the irresolution, of the history that they narrate. Even Dixon's threatening question "*Shall the future America be Anglo-Saxon or Mulatto?*" remains, as we have seen, conspicuously unanswered. It is a presentist call to arms rather than an apocalyptic vision of the future.

Here, at the end of the book, we must return to what finally may now emerge, "posthumously as it were," in Benjamin's terms, as a definitive "constellation" of signature phrases, repeated throughout most, although not all, of the race melodramas. Rather than telling the sequence of these phrases "like the beads of a rosary," we are now in a position to read them *as* a constellation in which the variability of the verb tenses enacts the multiplicity and plasticity that define the politics of occult time.[15] First, the *shall* of Psalm 68:31 ("Princes shall come out of Egypt, and Ethiopia shall stretch out her hands unto God")—and of the refrain of *The Leopard's Spots* ("*Shall the future American be an Anglo-Saxon or a Mulatto?*")—speaks with the force simultaneously of prophecy and of injunction (predictive and imperative), while, even more paradoxically, the portion of the passage that is rarely quoted emphasizes the *was*, the suppressed past of Egypt and Ethiopia ("After God shall have scattered the fierce nations who delight in war, and who have carried the destructive science to a height never before conceived of, then Princes . . . "). Even Ethiopianism, that most resolutely future directed of traditions, thus works through the need continually to redeem the images of the past, lest they be lost to history. Egypt and Ethiopia are invoked through the multiple layers of their past and present, the Egypt of the house of bondage in the Exodus narrative and the Ethiopia of modern-day Africa.[16] Dixon's *shall* speaks in the interrogative, posing a question whose repetitions increase the urgency of the repeatedly absent answer. Last, but far from least, the Du Boisean *is* (of "the problem of the twentieth century is the problem of the color-line") takes us back to the problem with which we started; only in the most literal sense the "Negro Problem," Du Bois's signature line activates, posthumously as it were, in the verb *is* the past, present, and future of race history as we in the twenty-first century know it. Written in 1903, at the dawn of the twentieth century, in the second chapter of *The Souls of Black Folk*, entitled "Of the Dawn of Freedom," Du Bois's *is* requires the past ("it was a phase of this problem that caused the Civil War," reads the next sentence [*SBF*, 107]) for its predictive force. And Du Bois uses *is*, not *will* or *shall be:* the future remains provisional, as all historical outcomes must be. As it turned out, from a vantage point only three years into the turn of the new century, Du Bois was both right for the moment and prescient: the Problem of the Twentieth Century (to use Du Bois's other set of capitals) *was to be* and *has been* the problem of the color line. What other simple present tense than his *is* could have both recognized the past and foretold, but not foreclosed, the future?

NOTES

1. W. E. B. Du Bois, "The Study of the Negro Problems" (address to the American Academy of Political and Social Sciences, November 1897; published as "The Study of the Negro Problems," *Annals of the American Academy of Political and Social Science* 11 [January 1898]: 1–23; reprinted in *W. E. B. Du Bois on Sociology and the Black Community*, ed. Dan S. Green and Edwin D. Driver [Chicago: University of Chicago Press, 1978], 70–84; hereafter "SNP," with page numbers [keyed to the Green and Driver collection] given in the text), *The Souls of Black Folk* (1903), in *The Oxford W. E. B. Du Bois Reader*, ed. Eric J. Sundquist (New York: Oxford University Press, 1996), 99–240, 101 (hereafter *SBF*, with page numbers given in the text), and "To the Nations of the World" (address to the Pan-African Congress, July 1900; reprinted in Sundquist, ed., *Du Bois Reader*, 625–27, 625).

2. Du Bois also varies the capitalization, alternating between uppercase ("Twentieth Century" [*SBF*, 121, 160]) and lowercase ("twentieth century" [*SBF*, 107]).

3. W. E. B. Du Bois, *Dusk of Dawn: An Essay toward an Autobiography of a Race Concept* (1940; reprint, New York: Schocken, 1968), 60, 133 (hereafter *DD*, with page numbers given in the text). The formulation of "a plexus of social problems" was first coined in 1897 in "The Study of the Negro Problems," as Du Bois acknowledges here in *Dusk of Dawn*.

4. *DD*, 51; W. E. B. Du Bois, *The Autobiography of W. E. B. Du Bois: A Soliloquy on Viewing My Life from the Last Decade of Its First Century*, ed. Herbert Aptheker (New York: International, 1968), 206 (hereafter *A*, with page numbers given in the text).

5. See Larzer Ziff, *The American 1890s* (New York: Viking, 1966).

6. Barbara Jeanne Fields, "Ideology and Race in American History," in *Region, Race, and Reconstruction: Essays in Honor of C. Vann Woodward*, ed. J. Morgan Kousser and James M. McPherson (New York: Oxford University Press, 1982), 143–77, 143–44, 152–55, 168. See also Fields's later, related essay, "Slavery, Race, and Ideology in the United States of America," *New Left Review* 181 (May/June 1990): 95–118. Fields's classic, still controversial essays provide a touchstone throughout this introductory chapter for my arguments on race and historiography.

7. Stephen Holden, "Reverend's Wrongs Unrighted," *New York Times*, 23 September 2002, arts and ideas section, A26. The critique of melodrama symptomatically extends from an aesthetic to a political objection, often focusing on the tragic mulatto/a, a stock character in nineteenth-century race melodramas. Judith Berzon argues, e.g., that George Washington Cable

was "unusual" in "presenting the tragic mulatto not only as a figure of romance and melodrama but also as a social and political being," while James Kinney asserts that, because Cable "escapes from stereotypes of the mulatto," he produces race fiction of "literary merit." See Judith R. Berzon, *Neither White nor Black: The Mulatto Character in American Fiction* (New York: New York University Press, 1978), 109; James Kinney, *Amalgamation! Race, Sex, and Rhetoric in the Nineteenth-Century American Novel* (Westport, Conn.: Greenwood, 1985), 133.

8. Rayford W. Logan, *The Betrayal of the Negro: From Rutherford B. Hayes to Woodrow Wilson* (New York: Collier, 1972), 79.

9. W. E. B. Du Bois, *Darkwater: Voices from within the Veil* (1920; reprint, with an introduction by Herbert Aptheker, Millwood, N.Y.: Kraus-Thomson, 1975) (hereafter *D*, with page numbers given in the text).

10. James C. Scott, *Domination and the Arts of Resistance: The Hidden Transcript* (New Haven, Conn.: Yale University Press, 1990). Scott works on peasant resistance in Southeast Asia.

11. The most readily available version of the full text of the pageant "The Star of Ethiopia" is W. E. B. Du Bois, "The Star of Ethiopia," in Sundquist, ed., *Du Bois Reader*, 305–10 (hereafter "SE[1]," with page numbers given in the text). This version is derived from and, with the exception of the title (which Du Bois changed), identical to the prose version (the only contemporary published version of the full text), which appeared under the title "The People of Peoples and Their Gifts to Men" in "The National Emancipation Exposition in New York City, October 22–31, 1913," *The Crisis*, November 1913, 339–41. A review of the pageant by Du Bois later appeared under the same title: W. E. B. Du Bois, "The Star of Ethiopia," *The Christmas Crisis: Pageant Number*, December 1915, 89–94 (hereafter "SE[2]," with page numbers given in the text). (The interested reader should note that, in the contents of the December 1915 *Crisis*, the title of the review is given as "From the Pageant, 'The Star of Ethiopia,'" not as "The Star of Ethiopia," which is the version used on the first page of the review.)

The phrase *Lyrical Left* is from John P. Diggins, *The American Left in the Twentieth Century* (New York: Harcourt Brace Jovanovich, 1973), 73–105. George Hutchinson has argued that studies such as Diggins's have paid little attention to the interracial dynamics that produced the cultural nationalist Lyrical Left of the early twentieth century—hence the prevailing assumption that race is not an issue in their work. See George Hutchinson, *The Harlem Renaissance in Black and White* (Cambridge, Mass.: Harvard University Press, 1995), 14, 94–124.

12. Thomas Dixon Jr., *The Clansman: An Historical Romance of the Ku Klux Klan* (Lexington: University Press of Kentucky, 1970), 321, 212–13 (hereafter *C*, with page numbers given in the text).

13. See Sutton Griggs, *Unfettered* (Nashville: Orion, 1902), 31 (hereafter *U*, with page numbers given in the text); Pauline Hopkins, *Of One Blood; or, The Hidden Self* (1902–3), reprinted in *The Magazine Novels of Pauline Hopkins*, with an introduction by Hazel Carby (New York: Oxford University Press, 1988), 439–621, 442 (hereafter *OOB*, with page numbers given in the text).

14. On the trope of the veil as derived from occult thinking, see Eric J. Sundquist, *To Wake the Nations: Race in the Making of American Literature* (Cambridge, Mass.: Harvard University Press, 1993), 576–77.

15. E. J. Hobsbawm, *Primitive Rebels: Studies in Archaic Forms of Social Movement in the Nineteenth and Twentieth Centuries* (New York: Norton, 1965), 163–65.

16. For histories of early-modern occultism, see Frances A. Yates, *The Rosicrucian Enlightenment* (London: Routledge & Kegan Paul, 1972); David Stevenson, *The Origins of Freemasonry: Scotland's Century, 1590–1710* (Cambridge: Cambridge University Press, 1988); Keith

Thomas, *Religion and the Decline of Magic* (New York: Scribner's, 1971); Mircea Eliade, *Occultism, Witchcraft, and Cultural Fashions: Essays in Comparative Religions* (Chicago: University of Chicago Press, 1976).

17. For histories of the occult synthesis, in the nineteenth- and twentieth-century context, from a variety of perspectives, see Philip Jenkins, *Mystics and Messiahs: Cults and New Religions in American History* (New York: Oxford University Press, 2000), 78–79; Robert S. Ellwood Jr., "The American Theosophical Synthesis," in *The Occult in America: New Historical Perspectives,* ed. Howard Kerr and Charles L. Crow (Urbana: University of Illinois Press, 1983), 111–34; Richard Noll, *The Jung Cult: Origins of a Charismatic Movement* (Princeton, N.J.: Princeton University Press, 1994); Peter Washington, *Madame Blavatsky's Baboon: Theosophy and the Emergence of the Western Guru* (London: Secker & Warburg, 1993); Nicholas Goodrick-Clarke, *The Occult Roots of Nazism* (New York: New York University Press, 1992); K. Paul Johnson, *The Masters Revealed: Madame Blavatsky and the Myth of the Great White Lodge* (Albany: State University of New York Press, 1994), 4–5, 81–83; Bruce F. Campbell, *Ancient Wisdom Revived: A History of the Theosophical Movement* (Berkeley and Los Angeles: University of California Press, 1980).

18. See Howard Kerr, *Mediums, Spirit-Rappers, and Roaring Radicals: Spiritualism in American Literature, 1850–1900* (Urbana: University of Illinois Press, 1972).

19. Fields, "Slavery, Race, and Ideology in the United States of America," 102.

20. The best-known example is probably the multiple connotations of *nation* in Du Bois's work, most of which are already present in his powerful 1897 essay "The Conservation of Races." There, he argues, first, that "the history of the world is the history, not of individuals, but of groups, not of nations, but of races"; second, that a race is "a vast family of human beings, generally of common blood and language, always of common history"; and, third, that "Negroes, members of a vast historic race . . . in the dark forests of its African fatherland[,] . . . are the first fruits of this new nation, the harbinger of that black tomorrow which is yet destined to soften the whiteness of the Teutonic today" (W. E. B. Du Bois, "The Conservation of Races," Occasional Paper no. 2 [Washington, D.C.: American Negro Academy, 1897], reprinted in Sundquist, ed., *Du Bois Reader,* 38–47, 40, 44). Du Bois's intertwining of biological, sociohistorical, and national concepts of race has been brilliantly, and controversially, analyzed in Kwame Anthony Appiah, "The Uncompleted Argument: Du Bois and the Illusion of Race," in *"Race," Writing, and Difference,* ed. Henry Louis Gates Jr., a special issue of *Critical Inquiry* 12 (autumn 1985): 21–37, reprinted in *"Race," Writing, and Difference,* ed. Henry Louis Gates Jr. (Chicago: University of Chicago Press, 1986), 21–37 (for an expanded version of this essay, see Kwame Anthony Appiah, "Illusions of Race," in *In My Father's House: Africa in the Philosophy of Culture* [New York: Oxford University Press, 1992], 28–46).

21. Eric Foner, *Reconstruction: America's Unfinished Revolution, 1863–1877* (New York: Harper & Row, 1988).

22. On "procrustean bedfellows," see C. Vann Woodward, *Origins of the New South, 1877–1913* (1951; 2d ed., Baton Rouge: Louisiana State University Press, 1971), 75–106.

23. Thomas Dixon Jr., *The Leopard's Spots: A Romance of the White Man's Burden, 1865–1900* (New York: Doubleday, Page, 1903), 41 (hereafter *LS,* with page numbers given in the text).

24. On "the propaganda of history," see W. E. B. Du Bois, *Black Reconstruction in America* (1935; reprint, with an introduction by David Levering Lewis, New York: Touchstone, 1995), 731 (hereafter *BRA,* with page numbers given in the text).

25. There is a long tradition of feminist theory and film criticism dealing with the family

melodrama or women's film, including Thomas Elaesser, "Tales of Sound and Fury: Observations on the Family Melodrama," *Monogram* 4 (1975): 1–15, reprinted in Christine Gledhill, ed., *Home Is Where the Heart Is* (London: British Film Institute, 1987), 43–69, and in Marcia Landy, ed., *Imitations of Life: A Reader on Film and Television* (Detroit: Wayne State University Press, 1991), 68–91; Mary Ann Doane, *The Desire to Desire: The Women's Film of the 1940s* (Bloomington: Indiana University Press, 1987); Ann E. Kaplan, *Motherhood and Representation: The Mother in Popular Culture and Melodrama* (London: Routledge, 1992); Tania Modleski, *Loving with a Vengeance: Mass-Produced Fantasies for Women* (New York: Methuen, 1982); Barbara Klinger, *Melodrama and Meaning: History, Culture, and the Films of Douglas Sirk* (Bloomington: Indiana University Press, 1994); Linda Williams, "'Something Else Besides a Mother': Stella Dallas and the Maternal Melodrama," *Cinema Journal* 24, no. 1 (fall 1984): 2–27, reprinted in Gledhill, ed., *Home Is Where the Heart Is*, 299–325. For two excellent overviews of the history of approaches in film and theater studies to melodrama, see Gledhill, ed., *Home Is Where the Heart Is;* and Jacky Bratton, Jim Cook, and Christine Gledhill, eds., *Melodrama: Stage, Picture, Screen* (London: British Film Institute, 1994).

26. Jane M. Gaines, *Fire and Desire: Mixed-Race Movies in the Silent Era* (Chicago: University of Chicago Press, 2001); Linda Williams, *Playing the Race Card: Melodramas of Black and White from Uncle Tom to O. J. Simpson* (Princeton, N.J.: Princeton University Press, 2001).

27. Henry James quoted in Williams, *Playing the Race Card*, 6.

28. Toni Morrison, "Unspeakable Things Unspoken: The Afro-American Presence in American Literature," *Michigan Quarterly Review* 28 (winter 1989): 1–34, 3, 11.

29. Williams, *Playing the Race Card*, 6.

30. Peter Brooks, *The Melodramatic Imagination: Balzac, Henry James, Melodrama, and the Mode of Excess* (New York: Columbia University Press, 1985).

31. Ibid., 202–3, 5, 41, 42, 202.

32. Ibid., 9. Addressing an episode in Balzac, James argues that the whole representation is "either a magnificent lurid document or the baseless fabric of a vision" but, ultimately, Brooks contends, we cannot tell which (see ibid.).

33. Ibid., 62. I am indebted here to Tom Gunning's argument that Brooks's concept of "communicating excess" allows a rehabilitation of the mode yet simultaneously "'tames' this spectacular excess by defining it as 'expressive.'" See Tom Gunning, "The Horror of Opacity: The Melodrama of Sensation in the Plays of André de Lorde," in Bratton, Cook, and Gledhill, eds., *Melodrama*, 50–61, 50–51.

34. W. E. B. Du Bois, "The Shape of Fear" (1926), in Sundquist, ed., *Du Bois Reader*, 385–94, 385, 388.

35. Morrison, "Unspeakable Things Unspoken," 11, 3. See also Gates, ed., *"Race," Writing, and Difference.*

36. I take my language here from Fields, "Ideology and Race in American History," 168–69; and Foner, *Reconstruction.*

37. Sometimes known as the "Dunning school," the *"Birth of a Nation* school"—associated with such academic historians as William A. Dunning, Claude G. Bowers, and Ulrich B. Phillips—formulated the interpretation of Reconstruction as a failure, a "tragic era" (as Bowers termed it in his influential *The Tragic Era: The Revolution after Lincoln* [Cambridge, Mass.: Houghton Mifflin, 1929]) of black misrule, that dominated American historiography until the mid-twentieth century. On Du Bois's relation to the prevailing Reconstruction historiography, see chapter 5.

38. Fields, "Slavery, Race, and Ideology in the United States of America," 113, 117.

39. Morrison, "Unspeakable Things Unspoken," 3.

40. Fields, "Ideology and Race in American History," 152, 154.

41. Brooks, *The Melodramatic Imagination*, 17.

42. Christian Viviani, "Who Is without Sin? The Maternal Melodrama in American Film, 1930–39," *Les Cahiers de la cinématheque*, vol. 28 (July 1979), reprinted in Gledhill, ed., *Home Is Where the Heart Is*, 83–99, 86.

43. Laura Mulvey, "Notes on Sirk and Melodrama," *Movie* 25 (winter 1977–78): 53–56, reprinted in Gledhill, ed., *Home Is Where the Heart Is*, 75–79, 76. On the impossibility of reconciliation in melodrama, see also Jane Gaines, "The Melos in Marxist Theory," in *The Hidden Dimension: Film and the Question of Class*, ed. David James and Rick Berg (Minneapolis: University of Minnesota Press, 1995), 56–71.

44. Doris Sommer, *Foundational Fictions: The National Romances of Latin America* (Berkeley and Los Angeles: University of California Press, 1991). My discussion of allegory is especially indebted to Sommer's excellent theoretical introduction (ibid., 30–51).

45. The latter cite (that on p. 438) represents a variant question: "Shall the future North Carolinian be an Anglo-Saxon or a Mulatto?"

46. Brooks, *The Melodramatic Imagination*, 15.

47. Judith Butler, *Bodies That Matter: On the Discursive Limits of "Sex"* (New York: Routledge, 1993), 10, 12–15, 232.

48. Homi Bhabha, "Of Mimicry and Man: The Ambivalence of Colonial Discourse," in *The Location of Culture* (London: Routledge, 1994), 85–92, 88.

49. See C. Vann Woodward, *The Strange Career of Jim Crow* (1955; 3d rev. ed., New York: Oxford University Press, 1974), and *Tom Watson: Agrarian Rebel* (New York: Macmillan, 1938). On the *Birth of a Nation* (or Dunning) school, see the discussion in n. 37 above.

50. For two of the best-regarded accounts of the history of this revisionist interpretation, see Foner, *Reconstruction*, xix–xxvii; and J. Morgan Kousser and James M. McPherson, introduction to Kousser and McPherson, eds., *Region, Race, and Reconstruction*, xiii–xxxvii.

51. Du Bois annotates the bibliography with such section headings as "Standard—Anti-Negro" and "Historians (Fair to Indifferent on the Negro)" (see *BRA*, 731–37).

52. W. E. B. Du Bois, "A Portrait of Carter G. Woodson" (1950), in Sundquist, ed., *Du Bois Reader*, 277–82, 280.

53. The journal's aim appears as stated in an advertisement in the back pages of the July 1916 issue of *The Crisis*.

54. I take the phrase *nation-time* from the discussion of time and history in Paul Gilroy, *The Black Atlantic: Modernity and Double Consciousness* (Cambridge, Mass.: Harvard University Press, 1993), 196–201. On temporality and the nation, see also Homi K. Bhabha, "Dissemi-Nation: Time, Narrative, and the Margins of the Modern Nation," in *Nation and Narration*, ed. Homi K. Bhabha (London: Routledge, 1990), 291–322.

55. Most commentators do not directly address the question of how and why the Masons paid such sustained attention to constructing their own history, with the notable exception of historians of Afrocentrism. On the Masonic connection, see Stephen Howe, *Afrocentrism: Mythical Pasts and Imagined Homes* (London: Verso, 1998), 66–72; Wilson J. Moses, *Afrotopia: The Roots of African American Popular History* (Cambridge: Cambridge University Press, 1998), 7–17. For one of the few discussions of Masonic historicism in general, see Alexander Piatigorsky, *Who's Afraid of Freemasons? The Phenomenon of Freemasonry* (London: Harvill, 1997), 198–229.

56. W. E. B. Du Bois, *The Negro* (1915; reprint, Millwood, N.Y.: Kraus-Thomson, 1975) (hereafter *N*, with page numbers given in the text).

57. George W. Crawford, *Prince Hall and His Followers; Being a Monograph on the Legitimacy of Negro Masonry* (New York: The Crisis, 1914).

58. Arthur A. Schomburg, "The Negro Digs Up His Past," in *The New Negro: An Interpretation,* ed. Alain Locke (1925; reprint, New York: Johnson Reprint, 1968), 231–37, 236.

59. See Du Bois, "The Shape of Fear."

60. Robert A. Hill, "Making Noise: Marcus Garvey," *Dada,* August 1922, reprinted in *Picturing Us: African American Identity in Photography,* ed. Deborah Willis (New York: New Press, 1994), 181–205, 194.

61. W. E. B. Du Bois, "Marcus Garvey" (1923), in Sundquist, ed., *Du Bois Reader,* 265–76, 265 (hereafter "MG," with page numbers given in the text). Commenting on a Garvey ceremony in which he knights his followers, Du Bois says: "What did it all mean? A casual observer might have mistaken it for the dress-rehearsal of a new comic opera, and looked instinctively for Bert Williams and Miller and Lyle" (265).

62. On fraternalism and theatricality, see Mary Ann Clawson, *Constructing Brotherhood: Class, Gender, and Fraternalism* (Princeton, N.J.: Princeton University Press, 1989), 42–45, 228–31. On the "pseudomilitarism" of black fraternal associations, see Wilson J. Moses, *The Golden Age of Black Nationalism, 1850–1925* (New York: Oxford University Press 1978), 197–98, 217–19. On Greenwich Village and the Lyrical Left, see Edward Abrahams, *The Lyrical Left: Randolph Bourne, Alfred Stieglitz, and the Origins of Cultural Radicalism in America* (Charlottesville: University Press of Virginia, 1986), 1–11. For the terms *stepladder radical* and *street historian,* I am indebted to Ralph Crowder. On Du Bois's role in the popular black-history movement, see Manning Marable, *W. E. B. Du Bois: Black Radical Democrat* (Boston: G. K. Hall, 1986), 83–91. A much more lengthy discussion of this context can also be found in chapter 5 below.

63. Paul Gilroy, *Against Race: Imagining Political Culture beyond the Color Line* (Cambridge, Mass.: Harvard University Press, 2000), 38, 146–47, 211.

64. Delany quoted in ibid., 222.

65. Ibid., 222–23. On the rise of the women's auxiliary in nineteenth-century fraternalism, see Clawson, *Constructing Brotherhood,* 178–210. On spiritualism as a feminist movement with a coherent worldview, see Ann Braude, *Radical Spirits: Spiritualism and Women's Rights in Nineteenth-Century America* (1989; 2d ed., Bloomington: Indiana University Press, 2001). Arguing that the "gloriously racialized and gendered narrative of Masonic history" has not yet been told, Maurice Wallace laments "how little the historical and cultural impact of black Freemasonry has caught the scholar's attention. . . . Academic neglect of its historical and cultural impact has been the rule" ("'Are We Men?': Prince Hall, Martin Delany, and the Masculine Ideal in Black Freemasonry, 1775–1865," *American Literary History* 9 [fall 1997]: 396–424). Wilson J. Moses has also argued that "an interest in mysteries, legends, and speculative Freemasonry is important to the cultural history of black Americans" (*Afrotopia,* 92).

66. On "the racial politics of temporality," see Gilroy, *Against Race,* 334, part of an extended discussion of temporal disjunction (ibid., 329–44). On modernity and tradition in black political discourse, see Gilroy, *The Black Atlantic,* 187–201.

67. Ralph Ellison, *Invisible Man* (1947; reprint, New York: Vintage, 1972), 8.

68. Ishmael Reed, *Mumbo Jumbo* (Garden City, N.Y.: Doubleday, 1972), 186, 194.

69. See, e.g., Peter Brooks, "Melodrama, Body, Revolution," in Bratton, Cook, and Gledhill, eds., *Melodrama,* 11–24; and Fredric Jameson, "Reification and Utopia in Mass Culture," *Social Text,* no. 1 (1979): 130–48.

70. See Stuart Hall, "The Problem of Ideology: Marxism without Guarantees" (1983), in

Stuart Hall: Critical Dialogues in Cultural Studies, ed. David Morley and Kuan-Hsing Chen (London: Routledge, 1996), 25–46.

71. T. J. Jackson Lears, *No Place of Grace: Antimodernism and the Transformation of American Culture, 1880–1920* (New York: Pantheon, 1981), 301.

72. For a range of views on the role of Theosophy in social and political movements, see Hobsbawn, *Primitive Rebels;* Goodrick-Clarke, *The Occult Roots of Nazism;* Janet Oppenheim, *The Other World: Spiritualism and Psychical Research in England, 1850–1914* (Cambridge: Cambridge University Press, 1985); Jenkins, *Mystics and Messiahs;* Campbell, *Ancient Wisdom Revived;* and Washington, *Madame Blavatsky's Baboon.*

73. Gilroy, *Against Race,* 38–39, 146–47, 218–25, 231–37.

CHAPTER TWO

1. *Of One Blood* originally appeared in serial form in the *Colored American Magazine,* vol. 6 (November–December 1902, January–November 1903).

2. Pauline Hopkins, *A Primer of Facts Pertaining to the Early Greatness of the African Race and the Possibility of Restoration by Its Descendants* (Cambridge, Mass.: P. E. Hopkins & Co., 1905).

3. "Editorial and Publishers' Announcements," *Colored American Magazine* 1 (May 1900): 60–64, 60. I attribute this particular editorial to Hopkins because it appeared during her tenure as the magazine's literary editor.

4. "Editorial and Publishers' Announcements," *Colored American Magazine* 6 (May–June 1903): 467. The series "Ethiopians of the Twentieth Century," by A. Kirkland Soga, appeared regularly in the *Colored American Magazine* starting with vol. 6 (May–June 1903).

5. For an excellent discussion of Hopkins's broad-ranging use of "countercultural science," see Thomas J. Otten, "Pauline Hopkins and the Hidden Self of Race," *ELH* 59 (1992): 227–56, 237–42. Not only was Otten the first to identify Hopkins's sources in William James's writings on psychology, but he also provides what still remains one of the best overall discussions of the complex of sciences that Hopkins brings together under the umbrella of *the unconscious.* For a more recent analysis of the novel's uses of eugenics and theories of heredity as a response to scientific racism, see Shawn Michelle Smith, *American Archives: Gender, Race, and Class in Visual Culture* (Princeton, N.J.: Princeton University Press, 1999), 187–205.

6. For the evidence of Candace's heritage, see Hopkins, *Primer of Facts,* 13, where she notes: "Queens frequently reigned in Ethiopia, and royal women were treated with greater respect in the united kingdom than in any other ancient monarchy."

7. "Back toward Slavery" is the title of the penultimate chapter of *Black Reconstruction.*

8. Sundquist sees Twain's novel, obsessed with racial twinning and doubling, as creating a chronological doubling in "the dual layering of antebellum and post-Reconstruction (or Old South and New South) ideologies, the recreation of the dynamics of slavery in new masquerade, . . . imposing upon antebellum dramatic action an allegory of the 1880s and 1890s" (*To Wake the Nations,* 231–33).

9. George Washington Cable, *The Grandissimes: A Story of Creole Life* (1880; reprint, New York: Penguin, 1988), 45, 114 (hereafter *G,* with page numbers given in the text).

10. Frances E. W. Harper, *Iola Leroy; or, Shadows Uplifted* (1892; reprint, with an introduction by Hazel V. Carby, Boston: Beacon, 1987), 95 (hereafter *IL,* with page numbers given in the text).

11. Charles W. Chesnutt, *The Marrow of Tradition* (1901), ed., and with an introduction by,

Eric J. Sundquist (New York: Penguin, 1993), 264–65 (hereafter *MT*, with page numbers given in the text).

12. Ellison, *Invisible Man*, 8.

13. Walter Benjamin, "Theses on the Philosophy of History," in *Illuminations: Essays and Reflections*, ed., and with an introduction by, Hannah Arendt, trans. Harry Zohn (New York: Schocken, 1968), 253–64, 254.

14. Pauline Hopkins, *Contending Forces: A Romance Illustrative of Negro Life North and South* (1900; reprint, with an afterword by Gwendolyn Brooks, Carbondale: Southern Illinois University Press, 1978), 245 (hereafter *CF*, with page numbers given in the text).

15. Benjamin, "Theses on the Philosophy of History," 255, 262–63.

16. Ibid., 262, 263.

17. See Houston W. Baker Jr., *Workings of the Spirit: The Poetics of Afro-American Women's Writing* (Chicago: University of Chicago Press, 1991), 26.

18. Much of the best work on African American women writers of the late nineteenth century has emerged from within the framework of the domestic and the sentimental as the dominant women's genres adapted by the Afro-American woman novelist. See, e.g., Hazel Carby, *Reconstructing Womanhood: The Emergence of the Afro-American Woman Novelist* (New York: Oxford University Press, 1987); Barbara Christian, *Black Women Novelists: The Development of a Tradition, 1892–1976* (Westport, Conn.: Greenwood, 1980); Anne duCille, *The Coupling Convention: Sex, Text, and Tradition in Black Women's Fiction* (New York: Oxford University Press, 1993); Claudia Tate, *Domestic Allegories of Political Desire: The Black Heroine's Text at the Turn of the Century* (New York: Oxford University Press, 1992); Mary Helen Washington, *Invented Lives: Narratives of Black Women, 1860–1960* (New York: Anchor-Doubleday, 1987). The sentimental model has not, however, been able to account for—or, perhaps, because of its popular-cultural lens has been uninterested in accounting for—the use of mainstream scientific discourses in these texts.

19. For a discussion of early "race movies," focusing on Oscar Micheaux's films and on the ways in which African American artists have historically used melodramatic devices, especially the inverted power hierarchy characteristic of melodramatic structure, see Jane Gaines, "Fire and Desire: Race, Melodrama, and Oscar Micheaux," in *Black American Cinema*, ed. Manthia Diawara (New York: Routledge, 1993), 49–70 (a revised and much-expanded version of this article can be found in Gaines, *Fire and Desire*, 161–218).

20. On the "semiotics of blood" in the novel, see Jennie A. Kassanoff, "'Fate Has Linked Us Together': Blood, Gender, and the Politics of Representation in Pauline Hopkins's *Of One Blood*," in *The Unruly Voice: Rediscovering Pauline Elizabeth Hopkins*, ed. John Cullen Gruesser (Urbana: University of Illinois Press, 1996), 158–81. On a discourse of blood based on "an essential notion of race," see Cynthia D. Schrager, "Pauline Hopkins and William James: The New Psychology and the Politics of Race," in *Female Subjects in Black and White: Race, Psychoanalysis, Feminism*, ed. Elizabeth Abel, Barbara Christian, and Helene Moglen (Berkeley and Los Angeles: University of California Press, 1997), 307–29. On *blood* as a comparative black-Jewish term, see Thomas F. Gossett, *Race: The History of an Idea in America* (Dallas: Southern Methodist University Press, 1963), 10–12, 319; Sander Gilman, *Freud, Race, and Gender* (Princeton, N.J.: Princeton University Press, 1993), 19–22.

21. Some critics read Hopkins as trapped by, rather than heightening and making legible, these contradictions. Walter Michaels, e.g., argues that *Of One Blood* advances a "no-race" position even while insisting on the passing down of racial distinction through "mysticism" and "occult powers" that transcend biology (see Walter Benn Michaels, *Our America: Nativism, Modernism, and Pluralism* [Durham, N. C.: Duke University Press, 1995], 58–60).

22. I am working here with Jane Gaines's idea of "transformation without change" in her characterization of early African American novelists as working within the existing formulas of sentimentality, which were "left intact at the same time that they were transformed." See Gaines, "Fire and Desire," 65. On the split in the novel's title, see also Schrager, "Pauline Hopkins and William James," 322; Michaels, *Our America*, 59 (where Michaels argues that "one blood is turned into two").

23. Carl E. Schorske, "Freud's Egyptian Dig," *New York Review of Books*, 27 May 1993, 35–40.

24. Director of the Bureau of Ethnology quoted in Gossett, *Race*, 83. For Gossett on the hopes of "many anthropologists," see ibid., 82–83. On the history of ethnology in general, see ibid., 54–83. On nineteenth-century racial science in the United States, see also William Stanton, *The Leopard's Spots: Scientific Attitudes toward Race in America, 1815–1859* (Chicago: University of Chicago Press, 1960), 24–72; John Higham, *Strangers in the Land: Patterns of American Nativism, 1860–1925* (New York: Atheneum, 1968), 149–57; George M. Fredrickson, *The Black Image in the White Mind: The Debate on Afro-American Character and Destiny, 1817–1914* (New York: Harper & Row, 1971), 71–96; Stephen Jay Gould, *The Mismeasure of Man* (New York: Norton, 1981), 30–72.

25. For a critique of the dismissive term *pseudoscientific*, so often applied by historians of science to the nineteenth-century racial sciences, see Nancy Leys Stepan, *"The Hour of Eugenics": Race, Gender, and Nation in Latin America* (Ithaca, N.Y.: Cornell University Press, 1991), 5, 25–26; George W. Stocking Jr., *Race, Culture, and Evolution: Essays in the History of Anthropology* (New York: Free Press, 1968), 42–43.

26. James George Frazer, E. E. Evans-Pritchard, and E. B. Tylor quoted in Michael Taussig, *Mimesis and Alterity: A Particular History of the Senses* (New York: Routledge, 1993), 48–49. On Theosophy as an occult science, see R. Laurence Moore, *In Search of White Crows: Spiritualism, Parapsychology, and American Culture* (New York: Oxford University Press, 1977), 230–32. On the "occult evolutionists," see Theodore Roszak, *Unfinished Animal: The Aquarian Frontier and the Evolution of Consciousness* (New York: Harper & Row, 1975), 115–51. On the anthropological work by E. B. Tylor, Frazer ("principles of thought"), Evans-Pritchard ("ideational logic"), and others, of Frazer, Evans-Pritchard, Tylor, and others interested in the (occult) "magic of mimesis," see Taussig, *Mimesis and Alterity*, 47–49.

27. SPR "mission statement" quoted in Renée Haynes, *The Society for Psychical Research, 1882–1982: A History* (London: Macdonald, 1982), 6.

28. On Blavatsky as an "occult evolutionist," see Roszak, *Unfinished Animal*, 118–19. In addition to Theosophy's scientific connections, there is an important political connection to the anti-imperialism movement: after Blavatsky's death in 1891, under the leadership of Annie Besant, the Theosophists, based in India as well as in Europe and America, were known for their support of Indian nationalism and the struggle for independence from Britain. (For a brief overview of the history of Theosophical science and politics, see Oppenheim, *The Other World*, 185–95.) The possible links between this mystical anti-imperialism and the uses of the occult in the struggle against racism in the United States have yet to be worked out. I am indebted to George Fredrickson for pointing out this fascinating area of research.

29. Tylor quoted in Taussig, *Mimesis and Alterity*, 48–49.

30. Henri F. Ellenberger traces a "continuous chain" from exorcism, magnetism, and hypnotism to "the great modern dynamic systems" (*The Discovery of the Unconscious: The History and Evolution of Dynamic Psychiatry* [New York: Basic, 1970], vi). On mind cures and mysticism as part of the popular context for psychoanalysis, see also Nathan G. Hale Jr., *Freud and the Amer-*

icans: The Beginnings of Psychoanalysis in the United States, 1876–1917 (New York: Oxford University Press, 1971).

31. Although I stress how these unresolved, epistemological contradictions produce the novel's imperfect, happy ending, at least one other reader has concluded that Hopkins achieves a "synthesis of universalism and racialism" in her "antirace race text" (see Ross Posnock, *Color and Culture: Black Writers and the Making of the Modern Intellectual* [Cambridge, Mass.: Harvard University Press, 1998], 67–69).

32. Sundquist, *To Wake the Nations*, 553; Gilroy, *The Black Atlantic*, 114.

33. Moses, *The Golden Age of Black Nationalism*, 19–20. See also Wilson J. Moses, *The Wings of Ethiopia: Studies in African-American Life and Letters* (Ames: Iowa State University Press, 1990), 229. For my basic understanding of what is at stake in the issues addressed by Hopkins, I am deeply indebted to Gilroy, Moses, and Sundquist.

34. George Shepperson, "Ethiopianism and African Nationalism," *Phylon* 14, no. 1 (spring 1953): 9–18.

35. Robert G. Weisbord, "Black America and the Italian-Ethiopian Crisis: An Episode in Pan-Negroism," *Historian* 34 (February 1972): 230–35; Imanuel Geiss, *The Pan-African Movement: A History of Pan-Africanism in America, Europe, and Africa*, trans. Ann Keep (1968; reprint, New York: Africana, 1974), 132–33.

36. Dickson D. Bruce Jr., "Ancient Africa and the Early Black American Historians, 1883–1915," *American Quarterly* 36 (1984): 684–99, 695. Sterling Stuckey addresses the same problem with regard to Du Bois's own insistence on the Africa origins of "the fair superstructure of modern civilization" (see Sterling Stuckey, *Slave Culture: Nationalist Theory and the Foundations of Black America* [New York: Oxford University Press, 1987], 279–80).

37. Gould comments that the doctrine of polygeny "was one of the first theories of largely American origin that won the attention and respect of European scientists—so much so that Europeans referred to polygeny as the 'American school' of anthropology" (*The Mismeasure of Man*, 42). See also Fredrickson, *The Black Image*, 74.

38. The term *transculturation* was coined by the Cuban sociologist Fernando Ortiz, working on Afro-Cuban culture in the 1940s, to describe how subordinated groups select and invent from materials transmitted to them by a dominant or metropolitan culture. See Mary Louise Pratt, *Imperial Eyes: Travel Writing and Transculturation* (London: Routledge, 1992), 6.

39. Moses, *The Golden Age of Black Nationalism*, 30.

40. Kevin Gaines, *Uplifting the Race: Black Leadership, Politics, and Culture in the Twentieth Century* (Chapel Hill: University of North Carolina Press, 1996).

41. Appiah, *In My Father's House*, 176.

42. Moses, *The Golden Age of Black Nationalism*, 23.

43. Baker, *Workings of the Spirit*, 22, 33.

44. Carby, *Reconstructing Womanhood*, 159. The continuing importance of Carby's groundbreaking book to the field of African American women's writing cannot be overestimated.

45. Pauline Hopkins, "Venus and the Apollo Modelled from Ethiopians," *Colored American Magazine* 6 (May–June 1903): 465; Stuckey, *Slave Culture*, 278.

46. Martin Bernal, *Black Athena: The Afroasiatic Roots of Classical Civilization* (New Brunswick, N.J.: Rutgers University Press, 1987), vol. 1. For perhaps the most notoriously vitriolic response to Bernal, see Mary Lefkowitz, *Not Out of Africa: How Afrocentrism Became an Excuse to Teach Myth as History* (New York: Basic, 1996).

47. See Appiah, *In My Father's House*, 176.

48. W. E. B. Du Bois, *The World and Africa* (New York: International, 1965), 99.

49. See Frank Snowden, *Blacks in Antiquity: Ethiopians in the Greco-Roman Experience* (Cambridge, Mass.: Harvard University Press, 1970), vii, 2–3, 109, 119–20. Snowden argues that the whole, long-standing debate over the "blackness" of the Ethiopians is utterly anachronistic since they did not share the modern conception of "race" (see ibid., ix).

50. Hopkins, *Primer of Facts*, 8–9.

51. On American Egyptomania as a general, cultural phenomenon, see Robert C. Young, *Colonial Desire: Hybridity in Theory, Culture, and Race* (London: Routledge, 1995), esp. chap. 5. On Egyptomania in art and architecture, see Bruce, "Ancient Africa," 688; John A. Wilson, *Signs and Wonders upon Pharaoh: A History of American Egyptology* (Chicago: University of Chicago Press, 1964), 36–37. On the history of polygeny and its Egyptological connections, see Stanton, *The Leopard's Spots*, 47; Fredrickson, *The Black Image*, 74–75; Gould, *The Mismeasure of Man*, 42.

52. Wilson, *Signs and Wonders*, 42; Gossett, *Race*, 64.

53. Nott's "niggerology" remark is quoted in Gould, *The Mismeasure of Man*, 69, his "Egyptian ethnography" remark in Fredrickson, *The Black Image*, 78.

54. On what is twice called the *eclectic* use of sources by early black historians, see Bruce, "Ancient Africa," 690–91.

55. Gliddon, e.g., is summed up in the biographical notes to one history of American Egyptology simply as "an enlightened man in an age of greed" (Wilson, *Signs and Wonders*, 220), a reference to what was seen as his proconservation position on the indigenous pillaging of Egyptian monuments (see also ibid., 41–42). On Gliddon as conservationist rather than racist, see also Brian Fagan, *The Rape of the Nile: Tomb Robbers, Tourists, and Archaeologists in Egypt* (New York: Scribner's, 1975), 267–70.

56. Gould's presence in the two camps is both symptomatic of the contradictions that I argue beset this historiography and not at all inexplicable. Gould sees a split between the polygenists, who offer a potentially strong proslavery argument, and the defenders of slavery, who were forced into a quandary (science vs. religion in support of slavery) but who ultimately, he says, did not need polygeny. See Gould, *The Mismeasure of Man*, 69–72.

57. On the persistence of polygenist thought in post-Darwinian anthropology, see Stocking, *Race, Culture, and Evolution*, 42–68.

58. Gould, *The Mismeasure of Man*, 42–43.

59. William James, "The Hidden Self" (1890), in *Essays in Psychology* (Cambridge, Mass.: Harvard University Press, 1983), 247–68, 247 (hereafter "HS," with page numbers given in the text). ("The Hidden Self" was first published in *Scribner's Magazine* [March 1890] and later revised as "What Psychical Research Has Accomplished" and incorporated into *The Will to Believe* [1897].) For three different discussions, all excellent, of Hopkins's use of James, see Otten, "Pauline Hopkins and the Hidden Self of Race"; Sundquist, *To Wake the Nations*, 570–71; Schrager, "Pauline Hopkins and William James," 307–9.

60. These remarks were added to James's essay in its revised form, "What Psychical Research Has Accomplished" (in *William James on Psychical Research*, ed. Gardner Murphy and Robert O. Ballou [New York: Viking, 1960], 25–47, 44, 41).

61. Hopkins's Ethiopian adaptation of the birthmark, a conventional device for identifying the long-lost heir to a fortune or a throne in popular fiction, is itself a sign of her syncretism. For an excellent discussion of the birthmark as combining Egyptian symbolism with the tradition of African American conjure, see Otten, "Pauline Hopkins and the Hidden Self of Race," 249–50.

62. William James, "The Last Report: The Final Impressions of a Psychical Researcher" (1909), in Murphy and Ballou, eds., *William James on Psychical Research*, 309–325, 324.

63. On the concept *diasporic consciousness,* see Sundquist, *To Wake the Nations,* 570–73.

64. Alan Gauld, *The Founders of Psychical Research* (New York: Schocken, 1968), 286, 288.

65. Moore, *In Search of White Crows,* 138.

66. Gauld, *The Founders of Psychical Research,* 286, 288.

67. Gould, *The Mismeasure of Man,* 114–19, 148–58.

68. Gossett, *Race,* 154–58, 364–68. See also Hale, *Freud and the Americans,* 99–105. Of the substantial literature on the influence of evolutionary theory on psychology, I have found that of Gould, Gossett, and Hale especially relevant to the Hopkins context. The most important work on Freud and evolutionary theory is Frank J. Sulloway, *Freud, Biologist of the Mind: Beyond the Psychoanalytic Legend* (New York: Basic, 1979).

69. On some writings of minority groups responding to and resisting the claims of scientific racism, see Nancy Leys Stepan and Sander L. Gilman, "Appropriating the Idioms of Science: The Rejection of Scientific Racism," in *The Bounds of Race: Perspectives on Hegemony and Resistance,* ed. Dominick LaCapra (Ithaca, N.Y.: Cornell University Press, 1991), 72–103.

70. James, "The Last Report," 324.

71. Michaels, *Our America,* 59–60; Posnock, *Color and Culture,* 66–67.

72. On the creation of an "alternative ideology," see Stepan and Gilman, "Appropriating the Idioms of Science," 99.

73. Butler, *Bodies That Matter,* 122. For the terms *occupied* and *occupying* as well as the fundamental idea, informing the whole of my reading here, of the strategic use of citational excess, I am indebted to Butler (see ibid., 36–38, 122–24). Of many other African American writers working terrain similar to Hopkins's, two examples come to mind here: the astonishing riff on genealogy and blue and red blood in the chapter "Woman versus the Indian" in Anna Julia Cooper, *A Voice from the South* (1892; reprint, with an introduction by Mary Helen Washington, New York: Oxford University Press, 1988); and Charles Chesnutt's Blue Vein Society, one among many seemingly transparent internalized racisms in his famous short story "The Wife of His Youth" (1899), in *The Wife of His Youth and Other Stories of the Color Line* (Ann Arbor: University of Michigan Press, 1968).

74. Gwendolyn Brooks, afterword to *Contending Forces,* 404.

75. The dedication to *Contending Forces* reads, "To the friends of humanity everywhere I offer this humble tribute written by one of a proscribed race." The same broad-based audience was envisioned for the *Colored American Magazine,* not so much at its beginning in 1900, but a few years later, when the question of global race relations influenced its coverage. Included, e.g., in the "Editorial and Publishers' Announcements" of the March–April 1903 issue are a letter from an irate white reader, a response from Hopkins, and the comment, "It gives us a great deal of pleasure to note how warm a reception is given our publication among all classes and races" (*Colored American Magazine* 6 [March–April 1903]: 398–99).

76. Du Bois's discussion of the question "How does it feel to be a problem?" opens up the famous lead essay, "Of Our Spiritual Strivings," of *The Souls of Black Folk;* he discusses his early, sociological views of "the complete Negro problem" (quoting from his 1897 academy address) in *DD,* 59–60. See my discussion of these passages in chapter 1.

77. Stuart Hall, "Notes on Deconstructing 'the Popular,'" in *People's History and Socialist Theory,* ed. R. Samuel (London: Routledge & Kegan Paul, 1981), 239, 237.

78. See Hobsbawm, *Primitive Revels.*

79. Hall discusses how "traditionalism" has been unfairly maligned in studies of popular culture (see "Notes on Deconstructing 'the Popular,'" 227).

80. Benjamin, "Theses on the Philosophy of History," 254.

81. Ibid.

82. Ibid., 263; Toni Morrison, "Home," in *The House That Race Built: Black Americans, U.S. Terrain*, ed. Wahneema Lubiano (New York: Pantheon, 1997), 3–12, 3.

83. Hall, "The Problem of Ideology," 45.

CHAPTER THREE

1. On reunion after the Civil War and Reconstruction, see Paul Buck, *The Road to Reunion* (New York: Vintage, 1937). On "the nationalization of race," see Fields, "Slavery, Race, and Ideology in the United States of America," 115.

2. On the new nation as "essentially racial," see Walter Benn Michaels, "Race into Culture: A Critical Genealogy of Cultural Identity," in *Identities*, ed. Kwame Anthony Appiah and Henry Louis Gates Jr., a special issue of *Critical Inquiry* 18 (summer 1992): 655–63.

3. Sutton Griggs, *Life's Demands; or, According to Law* (Memphis: National Public Welfare League, 1916), 15.

4. This brief overview of Griggs is taken from Sutton Griggs, *The Story of My Struggles* (Memphis: National Public Welfare League, 1914); Moses, *The Golden Age of Black Nationalism*, 171–72, 100–104, and *The Wings of Ethiopia*, 235.

5. On the Union League and the Klan, see Allen W. Trelease, *White Terror: The Ku Klux Klan Conspiracy and Southern Reconstruction* (New York: Harper & Row, 1971); David M. Chalmers, *Hooded Americanism: The First Century of the Ku Klux Klan, 1865–1965* (Garden City, N.Y.: Doubleday, 1965).

6. On "procrustean bedfellows," see C. Vann Woodward, *Origins of the New South*, 75–106.

7. On the Garvey-Klan contacts, see Gilroy, *Against Race*, 231–37.

8. The paradigmatic critical assessment: "By praising the merits and palliating the failings of the Negro, most of these early writers proved themselves as guilty of tedium and literary distortion as were Dixon and [Thomas Nelson] Page. Their works are usually poor novels, because they are more polemic than fiction, and often poor polemic because they melodramatically plead the case" (Hugh M. Gloster, *Negro Voices in American Fiction* [New York: Russell & Russell, 1965], 99–100).

9. W. E. B. Du Bois, "Negro Art and Literature," in Sundquist, ed., *Du Bois Reader*, 311–24, 318. ("Negro Art and Literature" first appeared in W. E. B. DuBois, *The Gift of Black Folks: The Negro in the Making of America* [Boston: Stratford, 1924].) For biographical details on Griggs, see Moses, *The Golden Age of Black Nationalism*, 171–72; Dickson D. Bruce Jr., *Black American Writing from the Nadir: The Evolution of a Literary Tradition, 1877–1915* (Baton Rouge: Louisiana State University Press, 1989), 156; Randolph Meade Walker, *Metamorphosis of Sutton E. Griggs: The Transition from Black Radical to Conservative, 1913–1933* (Memphis: Walker, 1990).

10. For Dixon's biography, see Raymond Allen Cook, *Fire from the Flint: The Amazing Careers of Thomas Dixon* (Winston-Salem, N. C.: John F. Blair, 1968), 67–107, and *Thomas Dixon* (New York: Twayne, 1974), 66–67. On the link between the Spanish-American War and the consolidation of Dixon's views on the racial question at home, see Michael Rogin, *Ronald Reagan, the Movie and Other Episodes in Political Demonology* (Berkeley and Los Angeles: University of California Press, 1987), 194.

11. Sutton Griggs, *The Hindered Hand; or, The Reign of the Repressionist*, 1st ed. (1905; reprint, Miami: Mnemosyne, 1969), 206 (hereafter *HH*, with page numbers given in the text).

12. The third revised edition of *The Hindered Hand* was issued in 1905, the expanded review

of Dixon following the conclusion of the novel proper. The few critical discussions of this essay focus either on the content or on how it disrupts the "unity" of the novel.

13. Because the third revised edition of *The Hindered Hand* is, as far as I have been able to ascertain, unavailable, I quote this passage from its original place within the body of the text of the first edition (*HH*, 202, 206–7).

14. Woodward, *Origins of the New South*, 249: "A cult of racism disguised or submerged cleavages of opinion or conflicts of interest in the name of white solidarity."

15. Eric J. Sundquist, introduction to Chesnutt, *The Marrow of Tradition*, xxi.

16. Woodward, *Origins of the New South*, 81–82 (see also 157, 373). Kousser's analysis of these odd phenomena is even more extended: "The Democrats' employment of white supremacy rhetoric may have been cynical. . . . Nevertheless, they undoubtedly internalized their campaign cries, so intertwining the Democratic party with the idea of white domination in their own minds that partisanship and racism became indistinguishable" (J. Morgan Kousser, *The Shaping of Southern Politics: Suffrage, Restriction, and the Establishment of the One-Party South, 1880–1910* [New Haven, Conn.: Yale University Press, 1974], 37).

17. Foner, *Reconstruction*, 430. The political experience in the states in which Dixon and Griggs set their novels differed from that in the rest of the South: only in North Carolina did Democrats lose control during the 1890s, thanks to coalitions of ex-Unionist, upland whites, lowland blacks, and, gradually, Piedmont manufacturers wanting a protective tariff; in Texas, farm parties were stronger and Black Belt Democratic politicians weaker than elsewhere. See Kousser, *The Shaping of Southern Politics*, 182–84.

18. Tillman quoted in Woodward, *Origins of the New South*, 369.

19. See Sommer, *Foundational Fictions*.

20. The limits of the national allegory emerge even in Sommer's extended application of the formula to the nineteenth-century Latin American canon, specifically in the Cuban context, where the classic antislavery fiction ends with tragedy rather than reconciliation (see Sommer, *Foundational Fictions*).

21. Sutton E. Griggs, *Imperium in Imperio* (1899; reprint, New York: AMS, 1975), 62 (hereafter *II*, with page numbers given in the text).

22. On the long-lasting legacy of white Republicanism and black political activity—as well as, ironically, a deeply entrenched Ku Klux Klan—in the Southern up-country, see Foner, *Reconstruction*, 300–304, 431.

23. Woodward, *Origins of the New South*, 259. Woodward quotes several Southern newspaper editorials from the summer of 1890 on Henry Cabot Lodge's (ultimately defeated) force bill for federal control of elections, all of which associated the "horrors of reconstruction days" with the twin threat of the force bill and third-party revolt. "The practical uses of the alarm over the force bill were not lost on the old party," Woodward concludes, quoting several more editorials that credit Lodge's bill with preventing the appeal of the new parties and welding the South more solidly together (ibid., 254–55).

24. Joel Williamson, *The Crucible of Race: Black-White Relations in the American South since Emancipation* (New York: Oxford University Press, 1984), 226–27. As Williamson asks, Why did white Southerners pass laws and commit violence to accomplish what had, in substance, already been accomplished? Williamson contends that such contradictions make it possible to argue for a second Reconstruction, followed by still another Redemption, in the upper South during the 1880s and 1890s. In such enclaves as the gerrymandered black Second Congressional District in North Carolina, a "growing, grass roots variety of black power was killed ultimately only by the white power that it, itself, unwittingly engendered in a state that was 75 percent white" (ibid., 227).

25. Woodward, *The Strange Career of Jim Crow*.

26. Probably no other period of American history has been the subject of such varied and conflicting interpretations as has Reconstruction. On Reconstruction historiography, see Foner, *Reconstruction*, xix–xxvii; Kousser and McPherson, introduction to Kousser and McPherson, eds., *Region, Race, and Reconstruction*, xiii–xx.

27. For consensus histories, see William A. Dunning, *Reconstruction, Political and Economic, 1865–1877* (New York: Harper, 1935); Ulrich B. Phillips, *Life and Labor in the Old South* (Boston: Little, Brown, 1929); Bowers, *The Tragic Era;* E. Merlton Coulter, *The South during Reconstruction, 1865–1877* (Baton Rouge: Louisiana State University Press, 1947).

28. Woodward, *The Strange Career of Jim Crow*, 32–33; and Foner, *Reconstruction*.

29. To understate or deny the significance of such multiple, often nonaligned differences, as do the traditional historical labels, is to narrate U.S. history through what Barbara Fields calls "the great, overarching theme of race": racism is America's "tragic flaw," race America's "tragically recurring central theme" ("Ideology and Race in American History," 143, 169). The inescapable fatalism of according race such transhistorical status is apparent in Walter Michaels's "race-into-culture" thesis, which "traces" the "invention" of a racialized Americanness in a virtually unbroken line, from its emergence in the American nativism and white supremacism of the Progressive period, to the cultural pluralism of the modernist ("i.e., racialized") 1920s, and, finally, to the multiculturalism of our own day (see Michaels, *Our America*, 141). To accord race what Fields calls "a transhistorical, almost metaphysical status" and to treat race "as a phenomenon outside history is to take up a position within the terrain of racialist ideology and to become its unknowing—and therefore uncontesting—victim" ("Ideology and Race in American History," 144). Quoting from the historian Charles Flynn's challenge to Woodward's work on "procrustean politics" in *Origins of the New South*, without acknowledging the meanings of the larger, historiographic debate, Michaels simply cites Flynn's point that there were no significant ideological differences between Georgia Democrats and Populists (see Michaels, *Our America*, 148 n. 36).

30. I take my language here from the influential anatomy of racial ideology in Fields, "Ideology and Race in American History," 168.

31. Woodward, *Origins of the New South*, 80; Kousser and McPherson, introduction to *Region, Race, and Reconstruction*, xviii, xxiii.

32. Richard Hofstadter, *The Paranoid Style in American Politics* (New York: Knopf, 1965); Rogin, *Ronald Reagan, the Movie*, xiii–xx.

33. On the culture of militarism, see Lears, *No Place of Grace*.

34. Fields invents the "promiscuous critter" in "Ideology and Race in American History," 155–59. I am also indebted to her argument that, like the slogans of imperialism, militarism, etc., white supremacy encapsulated "a set of political programs, differing according to the social position of their proponents . . . but so far from providing a unifying element, they were as likely as not to accentuate the latent possibilities for discord" (ibid., 156).

35. Charles L. Flynn Jr., "Procrustean Bedfellows and Populists: An Alternative Hypothesis," in *Race, Class, and Politics in Southern History: Essays in Honor of Robert F. Durden*, ed. Jeffrey J. Crow, Paul D. Escott, and Charles L. Flynn Jr. (Baton Rouge: Louisiana State University Press, 1989), 81–105.

36. Howard Jay Graham, "The 'Conspiracy Theory' of the Fourteenth Amendment," in *Reconstruction: An Anthology of Revisionist Writings*, ed. Kenneth M. Stampp and Leon F. Litwack (Baton Rouge: Louisiana State University Press, 1969), 107–31.

37. Eric Anderson, *Race and Politics in North Carolina, 1872–1901: The Black Second* (Baton Rouge: Louisiana State University Press, 1981), 252, 336.

38. Kousser, *The Shaping of Southern Politics*, 39. Kousser offers a long note giving evidence that "Democrats in various states conspired with those in others and that the leaders of disfranchisement were cognizant of developments throughout the South" (ibid., 39).

39. Willard B. Gatewood Jr., *Black Americans and the White Man's Burden, 1898–1903* (Urbana: University of Illinois Press, 1975), 211.

40. W. E. B. Du Bois, "A Negro Nation within the Nation" (1935), in Sundquist, ed., *Du Bois Reader*, 431–38, 437–38.

41. Rogin, *Ronald Reagan, the Movie*, xiii.

42. Editorial quoted in Gloster, *Negro Voices in American Fiction*, 103. Gloster also notes that, during the 1920s, the Garvey movement was decried as an effort to develop among blacks a counterpart of the Klan, or what was called "a black version of that same 100% mania that now afflicts white America, that emboldens the prophets of a 'Nordic blood renaissance'" (ibid., 103).

43. Chalmers, *Hooded Americanism*, 15.

44. For the recounting of this incident, see *DD*, 67.

45. For Du Bois on the impossibility of objectivity in the context of lynching and racial terror, see *DD*, 67.

46. For the classic historical view of these oppositions, see Moses, *The Wings of Ethiopia*, 227–29.

47. As the historian Glenda Gilmore and the film theorist Linda Williams note, melodrama's elevation of the victim works for Dixon to reverse actual power dynamics and make subjugated blacks the villains and a resurgent white majority the heroic victims (see Glenda Elizabeth Gilmore, *Gender and Jim Crow: Women and the Politics of White Supremacy in North Carolina, 1896–1920* [Chapel Hill: University of North Carolina Press, 1996], 135–36; Williams, *Playing the Race Card*).

48. The Wilmington race riot has been extensively studied; see, e.g., Gilmore, *Gender and Jim Crow*; Henry Leon Prather, *We Have Taken a City: Wilmington Racial Massacre and Coup of 1898* (Rutherford, N.J.: Associated Universities Press, 1984); Helen G. Edmonds, *The Negro and Fusion Politics in North Carolina, 1894–1901* (Chapel Hill: University of North Carolina Press, 1951).

49. On the double plots and complex chronology of the novel, see Sundquist, introduction to Chesnutt, *The Marrow of Tradition*, vii–xliv.

50. Charles Chesnutt, "Chesnutt's Own View of His New Story, *The Marrow of Tradition*," *Cleveland World*, 10 October 1901, reprinted in *Charles W. Chesnutt: Essays and Speeches*, ed. Joseph R. McElrath Jr., Robert C. Leitz III, and Jesse L. Crisler (Stanford, Calif.: Stanford University Press, 1999), 169–70.

51. Sundquist, introduction to Chesnutt, *Marrow of Tradition*, xxxii.

52. Logan, *The Betrayal of the Negro*, 98.

53. Sundquist believes that Chesnutt must have invented the names, which refer to no real persons or events that he has been able to document (see Sundquist, introduction to Chesnutt, *Marrow of Tradition*, 343). According to one of my graduate students, however, *igorot* is a derogatory term for "bushmen" that is used colloquially in the Philippines. This possible etymology preserves and, perhaps, even extends what we might call the *imperial frame of reference* of *Marrow*. For this information I am indebted to Robert Kuwada.

54. See Amy Kaplan, "Black and Blue on San Juan Hill," in *Cultures of U.S. Imperialism*, ed. Amy Kaplan and Donald E. Pease (Durham, N. C.: Duke University Press, 1993), 219–36; Christopher Lasch, "The Anti-Imperialists, the Philippines, and the Rights of Man," *Journal of Southern History* 24 (August 1958): 319–31.

55. It is worth noting that newspapers frequently charged the membership of the Anti-Imperialist League with collective treason.

56. Williamson, *The Crucible of Race*, 6. Tillman quoted in Richard E. Welch Jr., *Response to Imperialism: The United States and the Philippine American War, 1899–1902* (Chapel Hill: University of North Carolina Press, 1979), 43–62, 62.

57. See, e.g., Fredrickson, *The Black Image*, 305–11.

58. Gatewood, *Black Americans and the White Man's Burden*, 320–21. I am indebted to Gatewood's detailed coverage of the various phases of the war and corresponding changes in opinion and especially to his work on the black soldier, the army regulars, the volunteers, and the state militia (see ibid., 64–153, 261–92).

59. See Amy Kaplan, "Romancing the Empire: The Embodiment of American Masculinity in the Popular Historical Novel of the 1890s," *American Literary History* 2 (winter 1990): 659–90.

60. Quoted in Gatewood, *Black Americans and the White Man's Burden*, 209–10. Gatewood is quoting "prominent figures in Boston's black community, including Archibald H. Grimké; the Reverend W. H. Scott, minister to a suburban Baptist congregation; and Clifford H. Plummer, an attorney who was secretary of the National Colored Protective League" (209).

61. Ibid., 211. Gatewood adds that, between the Wilmington riot in 1898 and several notorious race riots in the summer of 1900, there was "considerable sentiment" among some African Americans for appealing to foreign powers to protect black Americans from lynching (ibid., 197–98).

62. Felton quoted in Williamson, *The Crucible of Race*, 129.

63. Griggs's letter to the editor of the *Indianapolis World* cited in Gatewood, *Black Americans and the White Man's Burden*, 249.

64. See Sterling Brown, *The Negro in American Fiction* (1937; Port Washington, N.Y.: Kennikat, 1968).

65. Rephrased as an assertion, the question becomes "*The future American must be an Anglo-Saxon or a Mulatto.*"

66. Gilmore, *Gender and Jim Crow*, 61, 63.

67. Ibid., 92.

68. Edward Wilmot Blyden, "Africa and the Africans" (1878), quoted in Gilroy, *The Black Atlantic*, 209. On Blyden, race mixture, and possible links with Griggs, see Moses, *The Wings of Ethiopia*, 172–73, 209–10, 230.

69. In the most recent of her series of fascinating essays on "race" movies, Jane Gaines argues that new, post-Reconstruction narratives of respectability and professionalism supersede the older, black-blood scenario; she also notes that interracial sex is imagined as a secret invasion that always takes place offstage, out of sight, "an unseen but largely hallucinated crime" ("*Within Our Gates:* From Race Melodrama to Opportunity Narrative," in *Oscar Micheaux and His Circle: African-American Filmmaking and Race Cinema of the Silent Era*, ed. Pearl Bowser, Jane Gaines, and Charles Musser [Bloomington: Indiana University Press, 2001], 67–80, 68). We never see the rape of little Flora Camp, either in Dixon's *The Leopard's Spots* or in Griffith's *Birth of a Nation;* her bruised and dead body provides synecdochic evidence.

70. Patricia Turner, *I Heard It through the Grapevine: Rumor in African-American Culture* (Berkeley and Los Angeles: University of California Press, 1993), 68–69.

71. According to Taussig, who is speaking in the context of the "culture of terror" of the rubber industry in nineteenth-century colonial Colombia, the "colonial mirroring of otherness . . . reflects back onto the colonists the barbarity of their own social relations, but as imputed to the savagery they yearn to colonize" (Michael Taussig, *Shamanism, Colonialism, and the Wild Man: A Study in Terror and Healing* [Chicago: University of Chicago Press, 1987], 134; see also Pratt,

Imperial Eyes, 249–50 n. 28). The accusation of racial terror thus relies, not just on the distorted conceptions that each side holds of its enemy, but also on the distorted conceptions that each side holds about its enemy's distorted conceptions of it.

72. Jeffrey J. Crow, "Cracking the Solid South: Populism and the Fusionist Interlude," in *The North Carolina Experience*, ed. Lindley S. Butler and Alan D. Watson (Chapel Hill: University of North Carolina Press, 1984), 334–54, 334.

73. Fields, "Ideology and Race in American History," 155–56. According to Fields—working in the tradition of Woodward's *Origins of the New South*—racial attitudes (those "promiscuous critters") are contradictory, unable to contain the differences among Southern whites, yet also fluid, meaning different things to different people at different times. And, among racial attitudes, "prejudice is as promiscuous as any other" and "can make itself at home within a variety of ideologies and programs." This is race as ideology, but with "fluidity," mobility, and the ability to adapt to changing temporalities and programs (Fields, "Ideology and Race in American History," 168, 159; see also Woodward, *Origins of the New South*, 75).

74. Gilmore, *Gender and Jim Crow*, 91.

75. Sundquist, introduction to Chesnutt, *Marrow of Tradition*, xx. On fusion politics as a persistent and destabilizing challenge to the political, social, and economic order in North Carolina and other Southern states, see Anderson, *Race and Politics in North Carolina;* Crow, "Cracking the Solid South"; Kousser, *The Shaping of Southern Politics;* Woodward, *Origins of the New South*, 75–106; Fredrickson, *The Black Image*, 262–64.

76. Woodward, *Origins of the New South*, 103, 76. Woodward provoked long-lasting scholarly debate with his thesis that between "Redemption" and disfranchisement there were "forgotten alternatives" for the South. For all the ensuing arguments over the temporal and spatial variations of Jim Crow's career, historians have repeatedly returned to Woodward's basic description of the ambiguous character of the era's race relations. Even his detractors shore him up, Flynn and Michaels, e.g., using his "procrustean" thesis to mount a new challenge based on the old unity issue, Flynn arguing (in "Procrustean Bedfellows and Populists") that Democrats and Populists were not really all that different, Michaels extending Flynn's revision of Woodward to focus on the "nonideological character of loyalty to the Democratic Party" (*Our America*, 148 n. 36). On the phenomenon of Southern Democrats and Populists alike subscribing to "a conspiracy theory of national politics," see Flynn, "Procrustean Bedfellows and Populists," 83.

77. Fields, "Ideology and Race in American History," 156–57.

78. Gilmore, *Gender and Jim Crow*, 92.

79. See Sommer, *Foundational Fictions*.

80. Mark C. Carnes, *Secret Ritual and Manhood in Victorian America* (New Haven, Conn.: Yale University Press, 1989), 11.

81. On this whole nexus, see Gilroy, *Against Race*, esp. chap. 4.

CHAPTER FOUR

1. Gilman, *Freud, Race, and Gender*, 20. Gilroy, *The Black Atlantic*, 120.

2. Albert Bigelow Paine, Twain's literary editor and biographer toward the end of his life, described Twain's process of dictating his autobiographical reminiscences in his later years: "He went drifting among episodes, incidents, and periods in his irresponsible fashion; the fashion of table conversation, as he said, the methodless method of the human mind" (Albert Bigelow Paine, *Mark Twain: A Biography*, 3 vols. [New York: Harper, 1912], 3:1268).

3. *Mark Twain's Autobiography*, ed. Albert Bigelow Paine, 2 vols. (New York: Harper, 1924), 2:193, 218, 222.

4. See Morrison, "Unspeakable Things Unspoken."

5. Mark Twain, *Following the Equator: A Journal around the World* (Hartford, Conn.: American, 1897), 339 (hereafter *FE*, with page numbers given in the text).

6. For a selection of Mark Twain's writings on the damned human race, see *Mark Twain on the Damned Human Race*, ed., and with an introduction by, Janet Smith (New York: Hill & Wang, 1962).

7. See my *Dark Twins: Imposture and Identity in Mark Twain's America* (Chicago: University of Chicago Press, 1989).

8. Mark Twain referred to his "pen warmed-up in hell" in a letter to William Dean Howells written on 22 September 1889, just after the completion of *A Connecticut Yankee in King Arthur's Court* (see Henry Nash Smith and William M. Gibson, eds., *Mark Twain–Howells Letters* [Cambridge, Mass.: Harvard University Press, Belknap Press, 1960], 287).

9. For a comprehensive view of Twain's engagement with history, see Roger B. Salomon, *Twain and the Image of History* (New Haven, Conn.: Yale University Press, 1961).

10. Mark Twain, "Papers of the Adam Family," in *Letters from the Earth*, ed. Bernard DeVoto, with a preface by Henry Nash Smith (Greenwich, Conn.: Fawcett, 1962), 56–102, 89 (hereafter "PAF," with page numbers given in the text). (The "Papers of the Adam Family" were written between 1870 and 1907 or 1908 but first published only in 1939.)

11. Mark Twain, "Three Thousand Years among the Microbes" (1905), in *Which Was the Dream? and Other Symbolic Writings of the Later Years*, ed. John S. Tuckey (Berkeley and Los Angeles: University of California Press, 1968), 433–553, 435 (hereafter "TTYM," with page numbers given in the text).

12. Mark Twain, *Pudd'nhead Wilson and Those Extraordinary Twins*, ed. Sydney E. Berger (New York: Norton, 1980), 9 (hereafter *PW*, with page numbers given in the text).

13. What I am referring to here is known today as the "Morgan Manuscript" of *Pudd'nhead Wilson* (J. Pierpont Morgan Library, New York; hereafter MMS, with page numbers given in the text). On the textual issues raised by *Pudd'nhead Wilson*, see Hershel Parker, *Flawed Texts and Verbal Icons: Literary Authority in American Fiction* (Chicago: Northwestern University Press, 1984), 115–36.

14. See Parker, *Flawed Texts and Verbal Icons*.

15. See Henry Nash Smith, *Mark Twain: The Development of a Writer* (Cambridge, Mass.: Harvard University Press, 1962), excerpted as "*Pudd'nhead Wilson* as Criticism of the Dominant Culture" in Twain, *Pudd'nhead Wilson*, ed. Berger, 248–49.

16. Mark Twain, ["The Man with the Negro Blood"] (4 MS pp.), box 37, Mark Twain Papers, Bancroft Library, University of California, Berkeley.

17. Mark Twain, "Which Was It?" in Tuckey, ed., *Which Was the Dream?* 179–429 (hereafter "WWI," with page numbers given in the text).

18. Mark Twain, notebook 18, typescript p. 19, Mark Twain Papers, Bancroft Library, University of California, Berkeley.

19. On the "Matter of Hannibal," see Henry Nash Smith, "Mark Twain's Images of Hannibal: From St. Petersburg to Eseldorf," *Texas Studies in English* 37 (1958): 3–23.

20. Mark Twain, *Life on the Mississippi* (1883; reprint, with an introduction by John Seelye, New York: Oxford University Press, 1990), 199–202.

21. Mark Twain, *The Mysterious Stranger* (1916), ed., and with introduction by, William M.

Gibson (Berkeley and Los Angeles: University of California Press, 1969), 134, 136 (hereafter cited as *MS*, with page numbers given in the text).

22. On Lodge's relation to psychical research, especially to the work of F. W. H. Myers, see Gauld, *The Founders of Psychical Research*, 142, 255–58, 289–93. On Twain's relation to Myers's theory of the "subliminal self" in particular and to psychical research in general, see my *Dark Twins*, 136–62.

23. The "Print Shop" manuscript is the last of four versions of Twain's "Mysterious Stranger" tales, the only one with that official title and the one in which contemporary theories of the unconscious are most explicitly visible.

24. See Gibson, introduction to Gibson, ed., *The Mysterious Stranger*, 1–34.

25. Henry Nash Smith, "Mark Twain's Images of Hannibal."

26. For one of the best commentaries on the conjunction of the dream mode with the topic of slavery in *The Mysterious Stranger*, see Forrest G. Robinson, *In Bad Faith: The Dynamics of Deception in Mark Twain's America* (Cambridge, Mass.: Harvard University Press, 1986), 228–37.

27. *Mark Twain's Autobiography*, ed. Paine, 1:124.

28. See Gibson, introduction to Gibson, ed., *Mysterious Stranger*, 12; John S. Tuckey, *Mark Twain and Little Satan: The Writing of "The Mysterious Stranger"* (West Lafayette, Ind.: Purdue University Press, 1963), 17–23.

29. Mark Twain, "Concerning the Jews" (1899), in *The Complete Essays of Mark Twain*, ed. Charles Neider (Garden City, N.Y.: Doubleday, 1963), 235–50 (hereafter "CJ," with page numbers given in the text).

30. Twain used the phrase "the Jew article" in a letter to Henry Huttleston Rogers, quoted in Philip S. Foner, *Mark Twain, Social Critic* (New York: International, 1958), 297.

31. Mark Twain, "A Word of Encouragement for Our Blushing Exiles" (1898), in Neider, ed., *The Complete Essays of Mark Twain*, 682–84, 683; and "My First Lie, and How I Got Out of It" (1899), in *The Writings of Mark Twain*, Definitive Edition, 37 vols. (New York: Gabriel Wells, 1922–25), 23:159–70, 161.

32. Smith, ed., *Mark Twain on the Damned Human Race*, 159.

33. Twain, "My First Lie," 148.

34. *Mark Twain's Autobiography*, ed. Paine, 2:218.

35. Ibid., 1:123.

36. On the black-Jewish connection, see Sundquist, *To Wake the Nations*, 559, 574; and esp. Gilroy, *The Black Atlantic*, 574–78.

37. Mark Twain, "Newhouse's Jew Story," in John S. Tuckey, ed., *Mark Twain's Fables of Man* (Berkeley: University of California Press, 1972), 279–82, and "Randall's Jew Story," in ibid., 283–89. Tuckey notes that "Newhouse's Jew Story" may be a discarded portion of *Following the Equator*, both written during roughly the same period, October 1896–May 1897 (see Tuckey, ed., *Mark Twain's Fables of Man*, 279).

38. See Smith, "Mark Twain's Images of Hannibal," 20.

39. Sander Gilman, *Difference and Pathology: Stereotypes of Sexuality, Race, and Madness* (Ithaca, N.Y.: Cornell University Press, 1985), 12.

40. For my thinking on stereotypes here and earlier in *Dark Twins*, I am indebted to Gilman's fascinating work in *Difference and Pathology*. Gilman has also written on Twain's relation to the cultural iconography of the Jew (see Sander Gilman, "Mark Twain and the Diseases of the Jews," *American Literature* 65 [March 1993]: 95–115).

41. Gibson, explanatory notes to Gibson, ed., *Mysterious Stranger*, 473.

42. W. E. B. Du Bois, "Criteria of Negro Art" (1926), in Sundquist, ed., *Du Bois Reader*, 324–28, 328.

CHAPTER FIVE

1. W. E. B. Du Bois, preface to *A Documentary History of the Negro People in the United States*, ed. Herbert Aptheker (New York: Citadel, 1951; rev. ed., New York: Citadel, 1969), vii.

2. W. E. B. Du Bois, *Black Folk Then and Now: An Essay in the History and Sociology of the Negro Race* (New York: Henry Holt, 1939), vii (hereafter *BF*, with page numbers given in the text). "Historian and history maker" is a paraphrase of Herbert Aptheker, "The Historian," in *W. E. B. Du Bois: A Profile*, ed. Rayford W. Logan (New York: Hill & Wang, 1975), 249–73, 249.

3. "I studied it personally and not by proxy. I sent out no canvassers. I went myself. Personally I visited and talked with 5,000 persons" (Du Bois, *Autobiography*, 198). Taking a skeptical view of this account, David Levering Lewis comments dryly that Du Bois had unacknowledged help in producing "his great work of urban sociology" (*W. E. B. Du Bois: Biography of a Race, 1868–1919* [New York: Henry Holt, 1993], 191).

4. Moses, *The Golden Age of Black Nationalism*, 169.

5. On Du Bois as "Apollonian social scientists" and "Dionysian prophet," see Levering Lewis, *W. E. B. Du Bois* (1993), 408. On Du Bois as intellectual turned propagandist, see ibid., 468. On Du Bois as at once cerebral and mystical, see ibid., 423. On Du Bois's transition from scholar to activist, see Marable, *Du Bois*, 52. On Du Bois's turn from empirical science to a pragmatic politics, see Arnold Rampersad, *The Art and Imagination of W. E. B. Du Bois* (1996; reprint, New York: Schocken, 1990), 49, 67. On strands of the scientific, historical, and lyrical giving way one to the other, see Shamoon Zamir, *Dark Voices: W. E. B. Du Bois and American Thought, 1888–1903* (Chicago: University of Chicago Press, 1995). On *Dusk of Dawn* as autobiography recomposed as polemic, and on Du Bois's early lyricism being replaced by his scientific materialism, see Sundquist, introduction to Sundquist, ed., *Du Bois Reader*, 29. On Du Bois vs. Boas and faith in science, see Julia E. Liss, "Diasporic Identities: The Science and Politics of Race in the Work of Franz Boas and W. E. B. Du Bois, 1894–1919," *Cultural Anthropology* 13, no. 2 (1998): 127–66, 128.

Ironically enough, one significant challenge to this account has been Appiah's critique of the persistence of Du Bois's biologism. Appiah points out that Du Bois's break with racial science was not as complete as he characterized it, but he disparages Du Bois's inability to break from the biologism that compromises his "uncompleted argument" on the "illusion of race." Appiah's account also narrows the considerable field of racial science to biological conceptions of race. See Appiah, "The Uncompleted Argument," and "Illusions of Race."

6. See Thomas C. Holt, "The Political Uses of Alienation: W. E. B. Du Bois on Politics, Race, and Culture, 1903–1940," *American Quarterly* 42 (June 1990): 301–23, 307, and "Marking: Race, Race-Making, and the Writing of History," *American Historical Review* 100 (February 1995): 1–20, 3–4.

7. Charles Wesley's review is quoted in Aptheker, "The Historian," 250. In addition to Holt, among those who read Du Bois's career in terms of continuities rather than rupture are Aptheker, "The Historian," 249–50; and Zamir, *Dark Voices*, 70–71.

8. Du Bois's often-quoted formula for reconciling the aesthetic and the political, "All art is propaganda," has done little to question the related dichotomies of science and politics.

9. See Hayden White, *Tropics of Discourse: Essays in Cultural Criticism* (Baltimore: Johns Hopkins University Press, 1978), esp. 27–41. Put another way, Du Bois's career exemplifies what

Adolph L. Reed Jr. calls the "unity of scholarship and activism" (*W. E. B. Du Bois and American Political Thought: Fabianism and the Color Line* [New York: Oxford University Press, 1997], 43 [see also 43–51]). To Shamoon Zamir, it is "a continuity between Du Bois's work in philosophy and his social-scientific work" (*Dark Voices*, 70). Or, in the words of Thomas Holt, Du Bois's "multiple careers" provided "multiple perspectives and multiple voices" crucial to his life project of developing "a theory of society interactively with and through social and political practice" ("The Political Uses of Alienation," 307).

10. Howe, *Afrocentrism*, 7. See also Bruce, "Ancient Africa," 695; Rampersad, *The Art and Imagination of Du Bois*, 228–34; Sundquist, *To Wake the Nations*, 544, 548–49.

11. Philip Jenkins argues that Theosophy and New Thought were at their height "exactly in the 1890s, from the vogue for eastern mysticism following the World Parliament of Religions (Chicago, 1893) to 1898" (*Mystics and Messiahs*, 49).

12. The Prince Hall Masons, founded under the auspices of the British Masons during the American Revolution, were at the time the major black Masonic group in the United States.

13. On Masonic historicism, see Piatigorsky, *Who's Afraid of Freemasons?* xiii–xiv, 198–229.

14. Yates, *The Rosicrucian Enlightenment*, quoted in Clawson, *Constructing Brotherhood*, 57–58.

15. Blavatsky quoted in Campbell, *Ancient Wisdom Revived*, 42.

16. Clawson, *Constructing Brotherhood*, 59–60.

17. Historians of Theosophy and religion echo Blavatsky's view, noting that many Victorian and early-twentieth-century occultists saw themselves in the vanguard of scientific research but that others aligned themselves with the contemporary drive to integrate religion with science. See Campbell, *Ancient Wisdom Revived*, 13–20; Jenkins, *Mystics and Messiahs*, 78–79; Ellwood, "The American Theosophical Synthesis"; Ann Taves, *Fits, Trances, and Visions: Experiencing Religion and Explaining Experience from Wesley to James* (Princeton, N.J.: Princeton University Press, 1999), 207–22.

18. Noll, *The Jung Cult*, 123; Clawson, *Constructing Brotherhood*, 57–59.

19. Schomburg, "The Negro Digs Up His Past," 236.

20. Du Bois refers to "The Star of Ethiopia" as a "pageant of Negro history" in "The National Emancipation Exposition in New York City," 339.

21. Reed, *Du Bois and American Political Thought*, 43, 201 n. 1. Zamir (*Dark Voices*, 102–3) makes much the same point about *Souls of Black Folk*.

22. As an expanded version of *The Negro, Black Folk Then and Now* has, I would argue, a similar textual and contextual relation to *Dusk of Dawn*, both works published (a year apart) on the eve of World War II.

23. See, e.g., *The Crisis*, November 1915, unpaginated section following "The Crisis Advertiser."

24. Du Bois quoted in Levering Lewis, *W. E. B. Du Bois* (1993), 459.

25. Ibid., 461.

26. W. E. B. Du Bois, *Dark Princess: A Romance* (1928; reprint, with an introduction by Claudia Tate, Jackson: University Press of Mississippi, 1995), 310–11. Claudia Tate's comment (ibid., xx–xxi) that *Dark Princess* could be seen as a consolidation of the opening "Credo" of *Darkwater* and the 1915 pageant deepens the textual connections and extends the temporal horizons of the context that I want to construct.

27. W. E. B. Du Bois, "The Drama among Black Folk," *The Crisis*, August 1916, 169–73, 171 (hereafter "DBF," with page numbers given in the text).

28. The frequently anthologized "Drama among Black Folk" incorporates passages from

"The Star of Ethiopia," and, reflecting yet another set of autobiographical and dramatic inter-textualities, Levering Lewis comments that *A Pageant in Seven Decades* is the "skeleton" for *Dusk of Dawn*, with *The Souls of Black Folk* and *Darkwater* "the flesh" (David Levering Lewis, *W. E. B. Du Bois: The Fight for Equality and the American Century, 1919–1963* [New York: Holt, 2000], 472).

29. *The Selected Writings of John Edward Bruce: Militant Black Journalist*, ed. Peter Gilbert (New York: Arno/New York Times, 1971), 177 ("Race is the key to History"), 132 ("chair of Negro history"), 6 (Schomburg), 132 ("thinking black"), 169 ("Socialist Orators"). "The Garvey movement made a more successful appeal to the multitudes than the Pan-African idea advanced by Dr. Du Bois," wrote Woodson and Wesley (Carter G. Woodson and Charles H. Wesley, *The Negro in Our History*, 10th ed. [Washington, D.C.: Associated Publishers, 1962], 550–51).

30. Levering Lewis, *W. E. B. Du Bois* (1993), 379.

31. On Du Bois's encyclopedia project, see ibid., 379–80.

32. Cedric J. Robinson, *Black Marxism: The Making of the Black Radical Tradition* (London: Zed, 1983), 273, 271. On the "varieties of black historicism," see Moses, *Afrotopia*, 18–43.

33. See David W. Blight, "W. E. B. Du Bois and the Struggle for American Historical Memory," in *History and Memory in African-American Culture*, ed. Geneviève Fabre and Robert O'Meally (New York: Oxford University Press, 1994), 45–71.

34. For one of the most extensive recent treatments of Du Bois's philosophy and methodology of history, see Zamir, *Dark Voices*, 68–109.

35. On Du Bois's move away from an early faith in empirical social science, see Rampersad, *The Art and Imagination of Du Bois*, 170–72; and Liss, "Diasporic Identities."

36. See Du Bois, "Negro Art and Literature," 318.

37. Levering Lewis argues that, for Du Bois, "sociology was history abstracted" (*W. E. B. Du Bois* [1993], 203). On the "interdependence" of socioeconomic phenomena, an interdependence that is redefined by Du Bois's "historicized account," see Zamir, *Dark Voices*, 90. For the recent publication, for the first time, of "Sociology Hesitant," accompanied by an excellent set of essays, see *Sociology Hesitant: Thinking with W. E. B. Du Bois*, ed. Ronald Judy, a special issue of *Boundary 2*, vol. 3 (fall 2000).

38. On *Black Reconstruction in America* and the problem of objectivity in science, see Aptheker, "The Historian," 255–57.

39. Moses, *The Golden Age of Black Nationalism*, 135.

40. Du Bois, preface to Aptheker, ed., *Documentary History*, vii. On the "car-window sociologists" of *The Souls of Black Folk*, see Zamir, *Dark Voices*, 102–3.

41. Yet Wilson Moses counters that intellectual Pan-Africanism owes more to biblical traditions than to Egyptology or Freemasonry (*Afrotopia*, 16).

42. See Hobsbawn, *Primitive Rebels*, 163–65.

43. See Johnson, *The Masters Revealed*, 4–5, 81–83; Campbell, *Ancient Wisdom Revived*, 13; Kerr and Crow, eds., *The Occult in America*, esp. 1–9; Ellwood, "The American Theosophical Synthesis."

44. See Mary Farrell Bednarowski, "Women in Occult America," in Kerr and Crow, eds., *The Occult in America*, 177–95.

45. On *The Bostonians*, see Kerr, *Mediums, Spirit-Rappers, and Roaring Radicals*.

46. On the racist uses of occultism, see Goodrick-Clarke, *The Occult Roots of Nazism*; and Noll, *The Jung Cult*, 58–69, 75–86. On Blavatsky's politics, see Washington, *Madame Blavatsky's Baboon*, 165. On the history of the swastika, see Malcolm Quinn, *The Swastika: Con-*

structing the Symbol (London: Routledge, 1994). On the racial politics, broadly construed, of a variety of occult movements, see Gilroy, *Against Race*, 138–76, 207–37.

47. For the terms *stepladder radical* and *street historian*, I am indebted to Ralph Crowder.

48. Howe, *Afrocentrism*, 66–69, 122–24; Moses, *Afrotopia*, 217.

49. On Du Bois's "penchant for dramatic form," see Sundquist, ed., *Du Bois Reader*, 303–4. On his "fabulous dramaturgy," see Levering Lewis, *W. E. B. Du Bois* (1993), 461. In addition to the historical pageants and stage plays produced by black and leftist political activists, the uses of political pageantry would include the chief forms of Masonic symbolic activity (the traditions of masking, costuming, and symbolic regalia, the initiation rites, and parades). See Clawson, *Constructing Brotherhood*, 42–45, 228–31.

50. Claude McKay, *Harlem: Negro Metropolis* (New York: E. P. Dutton, 1940), 155.

51. For example, Hill, "Making Noise."

52. See, e.g., Levering Lewis, *W. E. B. Du Bois* (2000), 50–75; Rampersad, *The Art and Imagination of Du Bois*, 148–49.

53. On the revolutionary and Enlightenment ideals of the Masons, see Hobsbawm, *Primitive Rebels*, 162–67; and Jenkins, *Mystics and Messiahs*, 78–82. On the reformist tradition, see Clawson, *Constructing Brotherhood*, 113–14.

54. On black fraternalism and race pride, see St. Clair Drake and Horace Cayton, *Black Metropolis*, 2 vols. (New York: Harcourt Brace, 1962), 669. On black fraternalism as a middle-class phenomenon, see William A. Muraskin, *Middle-Class Blacks in a White Society: Prince Hall Freemasonry in America* (Berkeley: University of California Press, 1975), 133–34, 237–50; and also Loretta J. Williams, *Black Freemasonry and Middle-Class Realities* (Columbia: University of Missouri Press, 1980), 38–46, 83–85.

55. W. E. B. Du Bois, *The Philadelphia Negro* (1899; reprint, with an introduction by Herbert Aptheker, Millwood, N.Y.: Kraus-Thomson, 1973), 222–24, 33–34 (hereafter *PN*, with page numbers given in the text). On concerns over black fraternities and secret societies, see Williams, *Black Freemasonry*, 84–86.

56. On these various positions, see Muraskin, *Middle-Class Blacks in a White Society;* and Williams, *Black Freemasonry.* On fraternalism and cultural contradiction, see Carnes, *Secret Ritual and Manhood.*

57. Clawson, *Constructing Brotherhood*, 14, 228, 231–38.

58. Wallace, "'Are We Men?'" Summarizing the various positions on fraternalism, Clawson argues for the broad, exclusionary tendencies of modern American Masonry but notes that evidence from earlier periods suggests a "much greater degree of openness to cultural difference." Later, however, fraternal groups, including the Masons and the Odd Fellows, were "strongholds of nativist sentiment," with Masonic lodges serving as Klan recruiting grounds in the 1920s (*Constructing Brotherhood*, 130). Yet historians have also traced the wider influence of Masonry and fraternal ritual on a variety of progressive political causes, especially American working-class and labor movements (see, e.g., Hobsbawm, *Primitive Rebels*, 153, 157; Clawson, *Constructing Brotherhood*, 136–44).

59. Gilroy, *Against Race*, 221–25.

60. Howe, *Afrocentrism*, 66.

61. Charles Wesley, *Prince Hall: Life and Legacy* (Washington, D.C.: United Supreme Council Southern Jurisdiction, Prince Hall Affiliation; Philadelphia: Afro-American Historical and Cultural Museum, 1977), 180.

62. See Mrs. S. Joe Brown, *The History of the Order of the Eastern Star among Colored People* (1925; reprint, New York: G. K. Hall, 1997), xvi, xxi. On the overall contribution of the black women's club movement, see Carby, *Reconstructing Womanhood.*

63. Carnes, *Secret Ritual and Manhood*, 107–27.

64. To the sociologist William A. Muraskin and the literary critic Maurice Wallace, the Masonic connection rates literally just a footnote to the Du Bois scene. Muraskin cites a 1947 article of Du Bois's, "The Winds of Time," in which Du Bois praises Black Freemasonry as an example of a viable, separate black organization, adding that Du Bois had been made a Mason in 1910, "but it is unlikely that this affected his judgment 37 years later" (*Middle-Class Blacks in a White Society*, 56 n. 42). Wallace lists Du Bois among other prominent Masons ("'Are We Men?'" 419 n. 1). Stephen Howe traces the Masonic sources of Afrocentric writing, including Du Bois's *The Negro*, and comments that, although there is no evidence one way or the other for Du Bois's membership in the organization, it seems a "reasonable presumption" that he and other Niagara luminaries like William Monroe Trotter were members at some time (*Afrocentrism*, 66–72).

65. Wesley, *Prince Hall: Life and Legacy*, 186–87. On the "Credo" and its place in black popular culture, see also Marable, *Du Bois*, 67.

66. August Meier and Elliot Rudwick, *Black History and the Historical Profession, 1915–1980* (Urbana: University of Illinois Press, 1986), 3.

67. McKay, *Harlem*, 140–41.

68. Schomburg quoted in Elinor Des Verney Sinnette, *Arthur Alfonso Schomburg, Black Bibliophile and Collector: A Biography* (Detroit: Wayne State University Press, 1989), 62.

69. Du Bois and John E. Bruce are rarely discussed together, although the Du Bois–Garvey connection has been explored (see Moses, *Afrotopia;* and Zamir, *Dark Voices*).

70. Piatigorsky, *Who's Afraid of Freemasons?* xiii–xiv, 13–14, 198–200.

71. Wesley, *Prince Hall: Life and Legacy*, 181.

72. The color-line aphorism originated in Du Bois's "Address to the Nations of the World," 125.

73. Levering Lewis, *W. E. B. Du Bois* (1993), 278. For Levering Lewis's comments on the "rather offhand passage" ("excessively modest," he notes, quoting Aptheker) in which Du Bois accounts for the genesis of *The Souls of Black Folk*, see Levering Lewis, *W. E. B. Du Bois* (1993), 277–78. Du Bois's revisions of the essays in *The Souls of Black Folk* have been studied by a number of scholars (see, e.g., Herbert Aptheker, introduction to *The Souls of Black Folk*, by W. E. B. Du Bois [Millwood, N.Y.: Kraus-Thomson, 1973], 5–45; Robert B. Stepto, *From Behind the Veil: A Study of Afro-American Narrative* [Urbana: University of Illinois Press, 1979], 52–91).

74. "The African Roots of War" was first published in the *Atlantic Monthly* (May 1915, 707–14) before Du Bois incorporated it into *Darkwater* under the title of "The Hands of Ethiopia." Thomas Holt has discussed at some length Du Bois's various uses and revisions of his most "axiomatic" text, the passage on double consciousness, first formulated and published in "Strivings of the Negro People" (*Atlantic Monthly*, August 1897, 194–98), and the reappearing in "Of Our Spiritual Strivings," the lead essay of *The Souls of Black Folk* (see Holt, "The Political Uses of Alienation," 301–6).

75. Here, in another instance of self-citation, Du Bois quotes in *Dusk of Dawn* the Atlanta University "Studies of the Negro Problems" series statement of aims in order to bring forth his own frustrated ambition, the prophetic not-to-be that haunted the project from its inception. "But I was not thinking of mere conferences," Du Bois writes in the autobiographical now. "I was thinking of a comprehensive plan for studying a human group and if I could have carried it out as completely as I conceived it, the American Negro would have contributed to the development of social science in this country an unforgettable body of work" (*DD*, 63–64). The subjunctive

tense of this statement, so often quoted out of context, is critical to its mood of the might-have-been, a lament that, paradoxically, brings out the latent force of the annual statement of aims, written in fairly dry, analytic prose (entirely quotations from the reports themselves), that follows.

76. David Levering Lewis says that "The Study of the Negro Problems" was itself a "replay" of Du Bois's 1891 American Historical Association address, delivered again in November 1897, in a telling change of venue, before the American Academy of Political and Social Science (see n. 1, chap. 1, above). The 1891 speech was "precedent-breaking, well-received, and widely commented upon" (Levering Lewis, *W. E. B. Du Bois* [1993], 193).

77. Following Du Bois's lead, scholars cite the same often-quoted passages that show his early belief in sociology as "a science of human action," but, in so doing, they read these passages in isolation rather than in the original context. See, e.g., Aptheker, "The Historian," 254–55; Liss, "Diasporic Identities"; Reed, *Du Bois and American Political Thought*. This is not the best way to track the changing uses and meanings of the citations as they are incorporated over time into different textual and disciplinary modes. Zamir is the exception, having produced a study that "tests the autobiographical recollections against the early writings themselves" (*Dark Voices*, 11). Zamir mentions in a note that Du Bois "reworked" certain early sociological passages for *Dusk of Dawn* (*Dark Voices*, 238 n. 3).

78. Many others, of course, have corroborated Du Bois on the enduring place of *The Philadelphia Negro* in the history of American sociology. In *An American Dilemma* (1944), Gunnar Myrdal described it as a "model of what a study of a Negro community should be" (quoted in Green and Driver, eds., *W. E. B. Du Bois on Sociology,* 113). See also James E. Blackwell and Morris Janowitz, eds., *Black Sociologists: Historical and Contemporary Perspectives* (Chicago: University of Chicago Press, 1974); Reed, *Du Bois and American Political Thought;* Dan S. Green and Edwin D. Driver, introduction to Green and Driver, eds., *W. E. B. Du Bois on Sociology,* 1–48.

79. Levering Lewis, *W. E. B. Du Bois* (1993), 202, 210, 189. See Levering Lewis's thorough discussion of the genesis, methodology, and reception of the Philadelphia study (ibid., 179–210). He comments specifically on the "vivid narrative power" of *The Philadelphia Negro,* providing evidence of a review to that effect (ibid., 205).

80. Holt sees the fall 1897 address as providing "the methodological template"—"at once empirical, comparative, and historical"—for the Philadelphia study while reading the 1897 "The Conservation of Races" as "its conceptual and political complement." See Thomas C. Holt, "W. E. B. Du Bois's Archeology of Race: Re-Reading 'The Conservation of Races,'" in *W. E. B. Du Bois, Race, and the City: The Philadelphia Negro and Its Legacy,* ed. Michael B. Katz and Thomas J. Sugrue (Philadelphia: University of Pennsylvania Press, 2000), 60–76, 63.

81. The reworking of earlier essays for inclusion in *The Souls of Black Folk* proceeded in a similar fashion, new material being added and, as Levering Lewis notes, "themes heightened by new endings" (*W. E. B. Du Bois* [1993], 278).

82. Levering Lewis, *W. E. B. Du Bois* (1993), 206.

83. Aptheker, introduction to *The Souls of Black Folk*, 22.

84. On the submerged presence in the autobiographical text of the contradiction in the thesis statements of *The Philadelphia Negro,* see Zamir, *Dark Voices,* 100–101.

85. Levering Lewis, *W. E. B. Du Bois* (1993), 203.

86. On these points, see generally *PN,* 221–34, 422–23.

87. Paul Jefferson, "Working Notes on the Prehistory of Black Sociology: The Tuskegee Negro Conference," *Knowledge and Society: Studies in the Sociology of Culture Past and Present* 6 (1986): 119–51, 122–23, 140–41.

88. The position that Du Bois takes in *Dusk of Dawn* develops—echoes and anchors—other, earlier statements that he made during the 1930s in *Black Folk Then and Now* and *Black Reconstruction in America*.

89. Sundquist, ed., *Du Bois Reader*, 481. For a detailed account of the provenance of the essays in *Darkwater*, see Herbert Aptheker, introduction to Du Bois, *Darkwater*, 11–12; Levering Lewis, *W. E. B. Du Bois* (2000), 11–23. On the revisions of previously published texts and their incorporation in the combined lyric and analytic sections of *Darkwater*, see Sundquist, *To Wake the Nations*, 580–90. Sundquist's extended reading provides by far the best critical account of *Darkwater* that we have and, throughout, informs my own.

90. Sundquist, *W. E. B. Du Bois*, 580–81.

91. William Matthew Flinders-Petrie, the author of the six-volume *History of Egypt* (London: Methuen, 1894–1905), was among those with whom Du Bois originally wanted to collaborate on the idea of an *Encyclopedia Africana* (see Du Bois, "A Portrait of Carter G. Woodson," 281).

92. Sundquist, *To Wake the Nations*, 559. On "Ethiopia as an uncolonized territory of the spirit," see ibid.

93. Du Bois, *The Suppression of the African Slave-Trade to the United States of America, 1638–1870* (1896), in Du Bois, *Writings*, ed. Nathan Huggins (New York: Library of America, 1986), 196–97.

94. On the "monumental history" of dynastic Egypt, see Moses, *Afrotopia*, 6. Robinson (*Black Marxism*, 272), Sundquist (*To Wake the Nations*, 506–7), Moses (*Afrotopia*, 47–48), Levering Lewis (*W. E. B. Du Bois* [1993], 280), and Howe (*Afrocentrism*, 123–24) all point out the contradictory lure of Egypt.

95. Moses, *Afrotopia*, 7, 15–16.

96. Howe, *Afrocentrism*, 66–67. Another measure of the uses of Egypt that derive from its enigmatic qualities is the way in which the same "proof"—of, e.g., the race of the ancient Egyptians—requires different assumptions and produces different conclusions, functioning in the autobiographies both as social-scientific argument and as lyrical outburst, depending on the textual context.

97. These contradictions have been most clearly articulated by Hazel Carby (*Race Men* [Cambridge, Mass.: Harvard University Press, 1998], 9–41), who sees Du Bois as a conflicted "race man"; Joy James (*Transcending the Talented Tenth: Black Leaders and American Intellectuals* [New York: Routledge, 1997], 35–37), who identifies his position as "profeminist"; and Claudia Tate (*Domestic Allegories*, 131–32), who focuses on his view of domesticity. Nellie McKay argues that Du Bois's four autobiographical texts demonstrate how central black women have been to the development of his intellectual thought (see her "W. E. B. Du Bois: The Black Women in His Writings—Selected Fictional and Autobiographical Portraits," in *Critical Essays on W. E. B. Du Bois*, ed. William L. Andrews [Boston: G. K. Hall, 1985], 230–52, 230–31, and "The Souls of Black Women Folk in the Writings of W. E. B. Du Bois," in *Reading Black, Reading Feminist: A Critical Anthology*, ed. Henry Louis Gates Jr. [New York: Meridian, 1990], 227–43). For an excellent overview of feminist work on Du Bois, see Farah Jasmine Griffin, "Black Feminists and Du Bois: Respectability, Protection, and Beyond," *Annals of the American Academy of Political and Social Science* 568 (March 2000): 28–40.

98. Sundquist, *To Wake the Nations*, 584.

99. Ibid.

100. James, *Transcending the Talented Tenth*, 37.

101. "World War and the Color Line," *The Crisis*, November 1914, 28–30, 28.

102. For the best, most detailed and extensive account of the strategy by which Du Bois revised these pieces and worked them into the fabric of *Darkwater*, see Sundquist, *To Wake the Nations*, 582–84. For general comments on the changes in the various versions of these texts, see Levering Lewis, *W. E. B. Du Bois* (2000), 11–19; and Moses, *The Golden Age of Black Nationalism*, 277 n. 7 (who notes that "The Riddle of the Sphinx" appeared with some "interesting alterations").

103. Wesley, *Prince Hall: Life and Legacy*, 186.

104. Tate, introduction to Du Bois, *Dark Princess*, xx–xxi.

105. Sundquist, *To Wake the Nations*, 581.

106. *Demand* is Du Bois's term (see *D*, 513). The phrase *Africa for Africans* is Edward Blyden's (in "Africa for the African" [1872], in *Origins of West African Nationalism*, ed. Henry S. Wilson [London: Macmillan, 1969], 231–38), possibly derived from Martin Delany's initial use (in *Blake; or, The Huts of America* [1861–62; reprint, Boston: Beacon, 1970]), and popularized by such Pan-Africanists as J. E. Casely Hayford (*Ethiopia Unbound: Studies in Race Emancipation* [1911; reprint, London: Frank Cass, 1969]). For more detail on the genealogy of Blyden's phrase, see Sundquist, *To Wake the Nations*, 557–58.

107. W. E. B. Du Bois, "The African Roots of War" (1915), in *W. E. B. Du Bois: A Reader*, ed. David Levering Lewis (New York: Henry Holt, 1995), 642–51, 649–50.

108. Ibid., 642–43. For the Latin line that begins both essays, "Semper novi quid ex Africa," see ibid., 642; and *D*, 511. For the concluding line, see *N*, 242.

109. Sundquist, *To Wake the Nations*, 582.

110. W. E. B. Du Bois, "The Burden of Black Women," in Levering Lewis, ed., *Du Bois: A Reader*, 291–93, 291.

111. Sundquist, *To Wake the Nations*, 584.

112. Levering Lewis, *W. E. B. Du Bois* (1993), 460.

113. *The Christmas Crisis: Pageant Number*, December 1915, 94.

114. See Clawson, *Constructing Brotherhood*, 192–99; William H. Grimshaw, *Official History of Freemasonry among the Colored People in North America* (1903; reprint, New York: Negro Universities Press, 1969), 359–60; *Order of the Eastern Star: An Instructive Manual on the Organization of Chapters of the Order with Ritual and Ceremonies* (Chicago: Ezra A. Cook, 1923); Mrs. Brown, *History of the Order of the Eastern Star*.

115. On synthesis, see Posnock, *Color and Culture*, 411 (quoting Harold Cruse).

EPILOGUE

1. Peter Osborne, *The Politics of Time: Modernity and Avant-Garde* (London: Verso, 1995); Gilroy, *Against Race*, 334–39. On theories of temporality, especially philosophical and historical approaches to the problem of time, see Johannes Fabian, *Time and the Other: How Anthropology Makes Its Object* (New York: Columbia University Press, 1983); Reinhart Koselleck, *Futures Past: On the Semantics of Historical Time*, trans. Keith Tribe (Cambridge, Mass.: MIT Press, 1985).

2. Du Bois, "The Conservation of Races," 38.

3. Benjamin, "Theses on the Philosophy of History," 255.

4. Frantz Fanon, "On National Culture," in *The Wretched of the Earth*, trans. Constance Farrington, with a preface by Jean-Paul Sartre (New York: Grove, 1963), 206–48, 227.

5. For Bhabha's reading of Fanon's "occult instability," see his "DissemiNation," 302–4.

6. Fanon, "On National Culture," 227.

7. Benjamin, "Theses on the Philosophy of History," 257.

8. Gilroy, *The Black Atlantic*, 198.

9. Bhabha, "DissemiNation," 304.

10. Benjamin, "Theses on the Philosophy of History," 261, 263.

11. Benedict Anderson, *Imagined Communities: Reflections on the Origin and Spread of Nationalism* (London: Verso, 1983; rev. ed., London: Verso, 1991), 24.

12. Benjamin, "Theses on the Philosophy of History," 255.

13. Ibid., 255, 263.

14. Ibid., 261, 254.

15. Ibid., 263.

16. On the extensive hermeneutic tradition associated with Ethiopianism, see Theophus H. Smith, *Conjuring Culture: Biblical Formations of Black America* (New York: Oxford University Press, 1994).

INDEX

Abel, Elizabeth, 214n20
Abrahams, Edward, 212n62
activism, political, 153, 160–63, 165, 167, 169, 171
Addams, Jane, 179
Afrocentrism, 151, 211n55
Agassiz, Louis, 55
alchemy, 8
allegory, 37, 81
American Revolution, 80–81, 83, 85–86, 89, 102
ancient Egyptians, debate over race of, 7, 26
Anderson, Benedict, 203
Anderson, Eric, 221n37, 224n75
Andrews, William L., 233n97
anthropology, 55
Anti-Imperialist League, 100
anti-Semitism, 13–14, 46, 118, 140; and race slavery, 143; and racism, 117
Appiah, Kwame Anthony, 51, 209n20, 216n47, 219n2, 227n5
Aptheker, Herbert, 148, 165, 181, 207n4, 208n9, 227n7, 229n38, 230n55, 231n73, 232n77, 233n89
archaeology, 32, 35, 47–48, 56, 69
Arendt, Hannah, 214n13
art, and politics, 200
Association for the Study of Negro Life and History, 167

Baker, Houston, 45, 49, 216n43
Baldwin, Mark, 63

Ballou, Robert O., 217nn60, 62
Barnum, P. T., 55–56
Beard, Dan, 122, 163
beauty, Western ideologies of, 51–52
Bednarowski, Mary Farrell, 229n44
Benjamin, Walter, 40–41, 43–44, 71, 201–5
Berg, Rick, 211n43
Berger, Sydney E., 225n12
Bernal, Martin, 52
Bernheim, Hippolyte, 58
Berzon, Judith, 207n7
Besant, Annie, 153, 166, 215n28
Bhabha, Homi K., 24, 202–3, 211n54
Binet, Alfred, 58, 61, 63
birthmark, and identity, 65, 217n61
Birth of a Nation school. *See* Dunning school of Southern history
black history (African American history, pan-African history, Negro history), 14, 24, 30, 148–50, 152–53, 155–56, 159–60, 164, 167–68, 175, 198; popular, 156, 160, 167–68, 175
black inferiority, 56–57, 60, 68
black-Jewish connection, 5, 13–14, 118, 142–44, 146
black matriarchy thesis, 11
black supremacy, 128–29
black vote/black voters, 78–80, 83–84, 87–88
blacks in the military, 101
Blackwell, James E., 232n78